A Brief History of Christian Music

To Lucy

A Brief History of Christian Music

From Biblical Times to the Present

Andrew Wilson-Dickson

A LION BOOK

Copyright © 1992 Andrew Wilson-Dickson
This edition copyright © 1997 Lion Publishing

The author asserts the moral right
to be identified as the author of this work

Published by
Lion Publishing plc
Sandy Lane West, Oxford, England
ISBN 0 7459 3773 X
First edition (illustrated) 1992
10 9 8 7 6 5 4 3 2 1 0

A catalogue record for this book is available
from the British Library

Typeset in 11/12 Lapidary 333
Printed and bound in Great Britain by
Caledonian International Book Manufacturing Ltd, Glasgow

Contents

Preface

Some of my earliest memories are of church music. As a family we used to attend the local country church at Wotton near Dorking, where at the age of six I was put in the choir, intrigued but mystified by the sounds and sights around me. My schooling then fostered in me a strong identity with the music of the Church of England, though after countless sermons I failed to understand its relevance.

At Cambridge, however, I was challenged spiritually, partly through the love and concern of Simon Barrington-Ward, then Chaplain of Magdalene College and now Bishop of Coventry. Later on, at York, I began to explore the musical implications of my fledgling faith. During that time I moved back and forth from the splendour and formality of services at York Minster to the passionate emotional commitment of David Watson's church, then at St Cuthbert's, Peasholme Green.

Since then my composer's inquisitive ear has led me to search for music which can be an expression of faith and joy for a Christian community, using all the skills available to them. Of necessity, this has meant crossing musical barriers set up by class and by denomination. This book continues that process in another dimension. Of necessity, therefore, it deals as much as possible with music habitually employed in Christian worship. I have used 'Christian music' as a shorthand for this restrictive concept, without any further implications concerning spirituality or superiority. Inevitably the field is not always clearly fenced off, but I hope the reader will understand that there must be boundaries in so vast a topic. Nonetheless, the absent subjects will be noted: where is the Christian music of Scandinavia, the rich Christian folk traditions of Caucasian Georgia, or of Corsica? And what about the music of India and the Far East? Perhaps a future edition will embrace these and other areas too.

In writing both the first edition (1992) and the present book, the contents have been greatly enriched by the generous assistance of many people: in the United Kingdom, Rifka Kashtan, Anthony Papyiannis, Christine Pullen, Sue Glover, David Fanshawe (in particular for the musical example in chapter 39), Frances Case, Robert Spencer, the students of West Hill College in Birmingham, Dr John Corrie, Pearl Bishop, and Bob and Tina Gardiner. The libraries of the Welsh College of Music and Drama and the University of Wales, Cardiff, have provided efficient and essential services. Many others across the world have been quick to respond to my appeals for help, often by Internet: in New Zealand, John Wells, Alison Stewart, Brian Carrell; in Australia, June Nixon, Robert Boughen, Roger Brown, Dr Geoffrey Cox; in the Americas, Prof. Ruth Steiner and Joseph P. Braisted. I extend my thanks also to the publishers, particularly to Robin Keeley, Philip Law, Angela Handley and Nick Rous who have dealt with the vagaries of a musical mind with tolerance and compassion. Finally, I extend deep gratitude to Lucy my wife, who has read every word with patience and advised me with wisdom, generously creating the space to allow me to finish an unfinishable subject.

Expanding the original book has challenged me again with a glimpse of the fecundity of imagination with which humanity has responded to the creator God. Not only may that richness be encouraging, but also may a greater understanding of the diversity of worship help Christians to become more respectful and tolerant of each other. Best of all, may we continue to rejoice in the endless variety of ways that Christians have chosen to worship, down the ages and across the world.

Andrew Wilson-Dickson
June 1997

Introduction –
The Power of Music

> Now the Spirit of the Lord had left Saul and an evil spirit from God
> filled him with terror. Saul's servants said to him, 'Look, an evil spirit
> of God is the cause of your terror. Let our lord give the order, and
> your servants who wait on you will look for a skilled harpist; when the
> evil spirit of God troubles you, the harpist will play and you will
> recover.' Saul said to his servants, 'Find me a man who plays well and
> bring him to me.' One of the soldiers then spoke up… And so David
> came to Saul and entered his service… And whenever the spirit from
> God troubled Saul, David took the harp and played; then Saul grew
> calm, and recovered, and the evil spirit left him.[1]

This biblical narrative makes a dramatic claim. It suggests that music has a
power to penetrate the mind where other forces fail, breaking down barriers
directly and immediately. The mysterious nature of this process and its
potency have never ceased to intrigue philosophers and creative artists.

That music can release prisoners of evil and bring them out into the light
of sanity has resonances with the myth of Orpheus, the Greek god whose
playing of the lyre could tame even the inhabitants of the underworld. Such
powers foreshadow in legend those of Christ, who has been similarly
depicted as a musician, particularly in the early days of Christianity. Legends
from almost every culture and age have stories of the powers that music can
'raise or quell'. Even as late as 1621, Robert Burton in his book *The Anatomy
of Melancholy* was prepared to take on trust ancient and picturesque stories
about the effects of music:

> In a word, [music] is so powerful a thing that it ravisheth the soul, the
> queen of the senses, by sweet pleasure… and corporeal tunes pacify
> our incorporeal soul… And 'tis not only men that are affected…
> Fish… as common experience evinceth, are much affected with
> music. All singing birds are much pleased with it, especially
> nightingales… and bees among the rest, though they be flying away,
> when they hear any tingling sound, will tarry behind. Harts, hinds,

> horses, dogs, bears are exceedingly delighted with it… and in Lydia in the midst of a lake there be certain floating islands (if ye will believe it) that after music will dance.[2]

This delightful vision recalls picturesque images in the biblical psalms: 'Let the rivers clap their hands, and the mountains shout for joy together.'[3]

Just as potent are the myths that propose the sound of singing as an agent for creation. These are quite widespread, from the American Indians to the Australian Aborigines:

> There was only water, and over it a fog. On the water was foam. The foam moved round and round continually, and from it came a voice. After a time there issued from the foam a person in human form. He had wing-feathers of the eagle on his head. This was Taikó-mol. He floated on the water and sang.[4]

C.S. Lewis elided the magic power of music with the biblical creation stories in his fables about the land of Narnia:

> The Lion was pacing to and fro about that empty land and singing his new song. It was softer and more lilting than the song by which he had called up the star and the sun; a gentle, rippling music. And as he walked and sang the valley grew green with grass. It spread out from the Lion like a pool. It ran up the sides of the little hills like a wave.[5]

And in another wonderful gloss on the first chapter of John, the medieval mystic, Hildegard of Bingen (1098–1179), conjured up the same creation scene in terms barely removed from the musical:

> The Word sounded and brought all creatures into being. In this way the Word and God are one. As the Word sounded, he called to himself all of creation which had been predestined and established in eternity. His resonance awakened everything to life…[6]

In all these examples the natural world – minerals, flora and fauna – is shown to be sensitive to music. While there is sometimes unexpected truth in such folklore, Hildegard (among many others) wrote from her direct experience of music and its power to act on sentient humanity.

Recognition of music's Orphean powers is rare in the present rationalism of Western culture. Here music is thought of as one of 'the arts' and thus relegated to areas of life regarded (like religion) as decorative, perhaps enhancing, but inessential. But in many non-Western societies, a different perspective puts an innate sense of the supernatural at the centre of life, together with its expression in music, dance, painting and sculpture. Eastern cultures, largely untouched by Western Christianity, have always thought this way. In Bali, for instance, there is no word for 'art', not because there is no music, theatre or sculpture (on the contrary, their traditions are among the richest in the world) but because these creative activities are inseparable from life. To such peoples, music is known to have a unique control over the senses, and full advantage is taken of the fact.

Slowly, attitudes are changing in the West. Psychologists and psychiatrists, bound as they are by the scientific requirements of objective observation and deduction, are becoming more willing to acknowledge that religious awareness and artistic endeavour may be essential to mental well-being.

The neurologist Oliver Sacks is well aware of the ability of music to restore lucidity to those who have lost it or have never known it:

> The power of music, narrative and drama is one of the greatest practical and theoretical importance... We see how the retarded, unable to perform fairly simple tasks involving perhaps four or five movements or procedures in sequence, can do these perfectly if they work to music... The same may be seen, very dramatically, in patients with severe frontal lobe damage and apraxia – an inability to *do* things, to retain the simplest motor sequences and programmes, even to walk, despite perfectly preserved intelligence in other ways. This procedural defect, or motor idiocy... which completely defeats any ordinary system of rehabilitative instruction, vanishes at once if music is the instructor...
>
> What we see, fundamentally, is the power of music to organise – and to do this efficaciously (as well as joyfully!), when abstract or schematic forms of organisations fail... Thus music, or any other form of narrative, is essential when working with the retarded or apraxic...[7]

Sacks provides an example of this restorative power of music through one of his patients, Rebecca, who on one of her consultations summed up the way music worked for her: 'I'm like a sort of living carpet. I need a pattern, a design, like you have on that carpet. I come apart, I unravel, unless there's a design.'[8]

Significantly, one of Rebecca's patterns for life was that of worship:

she loved the lighting of the Shabbath candles, the benisons and orisons which thread the Jewish day; she loved going to the synagogue, where she too was loved (and seen as a child of God, a sort of innocent, a holy fool); and she fully understood the liturgy, the chants, the prayers, rites and symbols... All this was possible for her, accessible to her, loved by her, despite gross perceptual and spatio-temporal problems.[9]

That the West is beginning to rediscover the healing potency of music is indicated by the discipline of music therapy, established only over the past forty years and now part of the health-care facilities of many countries. In a phrase that would also summarise perfectly the harp-playing skills of David in the Old Testament, the modern therapist 'must be a highly skilled musician capable of musical creativity with clinically directed aims'.[10] The areas of modern medicine in which music has been recognised as beneficial are strikingly wide-ranging: in surgery, neo-natal intensive care, pediatric medical care, pain reduction and stress management.[11]

Sacks points out the similarity of the benefits offered by worship and music; in Rebecca's case both provided the design and order that she so clearly needed for her life. These links between worship and music are deep-seated, for they both spring from a God-implanted desire to search for truth and order. Music is a manifestation of that search in the mental and physical realms, while worship is its expression in the cosmic. What is more, God has ordered his creation in such a way that the unfolding of its truths is profoundly satisfying, both mentally and emotionally. As the Westminster Confession puts it: 'Man's chief and highest end is to glorify God, and fully to enjoy him for ever.' Thus worship (literally 'worth-ship') is a fundamental human activity. It is, at best, the acknowledgment and celebration of God's utter perfection. Enjoyment of God begins with the privilege of discovering him. God has revealed himself in the way that humankind can best understand: through his son Jesus. But there is still much to be learnt about him through human creativity, which is at its most truthful when it reflects God's own creative nature. Paul, in his letter to the church at Rome, was sure that the evidence of that creativity was all around him: 'Ever since the creation of the world his [God's] invisible nature, namely, his eternal power and deity, has been clearly perceived in the things he has made.'[12]

Music, like other arts, is itself a response to the pattern and order of

God's creation. The composer Vaughan Williams was therefore able to observe that 'music is the reaching out towards the utmost realities by means of ordered sound.'[13]

Music's power is diverse: it may merely entertain, but it can also excite, persuade, move and cure. It also acts upon its hearers in a number of ways: some react to it simply on an instinctive level, some search it for clues about their very existence, others listen for its messages about human behaviour. For music to satisfy three such differing expectations, it must be a versatile art. The romantic notion that it is a universal language accepted and understood by all is far too simple. On the contrary, music has often been the subject of fierce debate and has excited dissension and strife – especially among Christians. Because of this, a brief exploration of those three ways in which music can act on its hearers is highly relevant. They may be placed under three headings: *ecstasy*, *symbol* and *rhetoric*.

The ecstatic dimension of music

Reaction to music can be immediate, even instinctive. Most people experience a compulsive physical response to the sensation of a regular pulse. The natural world (let alone the industrial) is full of noises that repeat – even the simple acts of walking or running produce them. Synchronising the mind and body with the beat that they produce can be pleasurable. Perhaps this pleasure is linked prenatally to the sound of the mother's heartbeat and its associations with security. Whatever the reason, it is then but a small step to re-create the sensation for enjoyment, perhaps by clicking sticks or bones together, or by hitting a drum.

Ecstasy may seem far too strong a word for subliminal reactions that merely set feet tapping and hands clapping rhythmically during a song. But if the beat becomes insistent and compelling then the state induced may rightly be called ecstasy, since the word means 'put out of one's senses'. Some music can overtake the mind until it is oblivious to all else:

the rhythm literally forces us into physical movement. Our magical impulses stir once again into wakefulness, and indeed we sometimes enter a kind of trance-state that is completely foreign to our normal consciousness.[14]

Trances are deliberately induced in some religions, often by means of rhythm and its physical expression. The primal forces summoned up by the music of ecstasy clearly have great strength.

The symbolic dimension

In direct contrast to the ability of music to possess or control is its capacity to act as a signpost for a concept lying outside or beyond it. The most potent symbol was expressed by early Christian writers, who imagined that integrated patterns of music (and of other arts, too) were part of a great symphony of order, initiated and sustained by God, the 'greatest of all composers, who has composed the universe of universes'.[15]

In the second century after Christ, Clement of Alexandria wrote that God's creative song:

> ordered the universe concordantly and tuned the discord of the elements in an harmonious arrangement, so that the entire cosmos might become through its agency a consonance.[16]

So the music composed and played by human beings became a symbol for the infinitely grander patterns and synchronies of God's creation. Accepting that music possesses a mystical dimension has important consequences for Christians. In particular, it allows music to be understood in terms of beauty, for, according to St Thomas Aquinas, 'beauty is the splendour of order'.[17]

This in turn permits music to be judged true or false according to the accuracy with which it reflects the nature of God's creation. For some artists, like the poet Ezra Pound, this provides a yardstick for the assessment of good and bad art:

> Bad art is inaccurate art. It is art that makes false reports... If an artist falsifies his report as to the nature of... god... of good and evil... of the force with which he believes or disbelieves this, that or the other... if the artist falsifies his reports on these matters... then that artist lies. By good art I mean art that bears true witness, I mean art that is most precise...[18]

Here, in music's attempt to address fundamental issues, is a further link with worship. It is hardly surprising that one is to be found at the service of the other in almost every religion in the world.

Rhetoric – the music of feeling

Music's third ability is to arouse emotion. Like ecstatic music, this expressive quality springs from deep wells in human consciousness. Consider, for example, the fact that children are able to express their feelings by sounds, some of which could be called melodic, long before they learn to speak. Some linguists have offered this as evidence that vocal music came before language in the developing skills of humanity.

Even when language has been established, melody can be a more potent means of conveying feeling, a fact most remarkably demonstrated in the realm of Christian music.

In the North American states of Georgia and South Carolina, eighteenth-century traditions of life and worship are still preserved. In the intense spiritual atmosphere of remote and isolated Baptist congregations, the high point of the service is the sermon, which the preacher delivers on an upward curve of emotion. His voice begins in relaxed and natural tones, but as the intensity of the message gathers force the pitch of his voice rises and falls through a widening range, individual notes emerging ever more clearly until he has made the transition to impassioned singing. At this point the congregation are drawn in and begin to sing with the preacher.[19]

As the great nineteenth-century man of letters, Thomas Carlyle, noted:

> All passionate language does of itself become musical – with a finer music than mere accent; the speech of a man even in zealous anger becomes a chant, a song.[20]

The art of persuasion by speech was highly developed in the age of classical antiquity. The ancient Greek system of education in the skill of language, the *trivium*, was three-way, consisting of *grammar*, *dialectic* and *rhetoric*. Rhetoric was not at all the dismissive term it is today, but a highly organised armoury of techniques by which an orator might win over his audience.

Western musicians have long believed that their art, too, has rhetorical powers. For centuries they have exploited the classical techniques of rhetoric in order to make their music emotionally persuasive. The history of Western classical music is the evidence of their success, and, while there are exceptions,[21] music which strives to arouse feelings has remained the dominant force in Western classical and popular music.

The Western classical tradition

From a broad perspective, this tradition of rhetorical music is relatively short-lived and geographically confined, but Westerners have tended to imagine that it is the only framework for organising music purposefully and truthfully. This assumption is one explanation of the West's dismissal of the music of other cultures as barbaric or outlandish. A history of 'modern' music published in 1875 typifies this view:

> The history of music is altogether European. Not that the orientals have, or have had, no music of their own... but that... their music has no charm, nor indeed meaning, for us... The modern European system is nearer the truth than any other.[22]

Nowadays such an attitude would be deplored, but its consequences still linger on, especially in areas of Christian music cloistered by tradition. A perspective limited to the view from one particular culture can lead to misunderstandings: an audience or congregation attuned to rhetoric may be left cold by music which is primarily symbolic, and be horrified, even revolted, by the music of ecstasy.

In Christian circles, such misunderstandings can be compounded by denominational tunnel vision. Christian music today springs from an extraordinary diversity of traditions: it may be ecstatic, symbolic or rhetorical depending on its origins. Each strand of Christianity has its musical signature. Hugo Cole, the critic and composer, noted the relationship of

> the musics of the various faiths, denominations and congregations to the faiths themselves... The connection is very close, and expresses itself unambiguously to one alert to musical tones of voice.[23]

It is fatally easy to perceive these distinct tones of voice merely as signposts signifying potentially threatening differences. But God's view of this diversity, according to the Bible, is inclusive. Twice the New Testament book of Revelation stresses that representatives of 'every race, language and nation' will be privileged to worship at the great and final gathering before the throne of God.[24] In the searching light of this apocalyptic vision it is evident that God not only accepts but rejoices in the varieties of race, culture and language of the people that have committed themselves to him.

God's kingdom can only continue to be built among humanity as this process of mutual acceptance goes forward. It is the intention of this book not only to point out the varieties of human experience embodied in Christian music but also to enjoy its richness and diversity. My hope is to encourage readers, not only in a better understanding of their own Christian heritage, but also in the discovery of a deeper sympathy with Christians of other cultures and with their unique styles of worship.

Notes

1. 1 Samuel 16:14–23.

2. R. Burton, *The Anatomy of Melancholy*, edited by R. Jackson, London, 1972, vol. 2, p. 117; compare with Psalm 29:6, 96:11–12, 98:7–8, 114:4.

3. Psalm 98:8.

4. Yuki (American Indian) creation myth, in M. Weigle, *Creation and Procreation*, Philadelphia, 1984, p. 181.

5. C.S. Lewis, *The Magician's Nephew*, London, 1980, p. 97.

6. Hildegard, *Liber divinorum operum* 4, 67, quoted in F. Bowie and O. Davies, *Hildegard of Bingen*, London, 1990, p. 27.

7. O. Sacks, *The Man Who Mistook His Wife for a Hat*, London, 1985, p. 176.

8. O. Sacks, p. 173.

9. O. Sacks, p. 170.

10. From the British Society for Music Therapy's information booklet, East Barnet, p. 11.

11. See M. Heal and T. Wigram, *Music Therapy in Health and Education*, London, 1993, chapter 15.

12. Romans 1:20.

13. R. Vaughan Williams, *National Music and Other Essays*, Oxford, 2nd edition, 1987, p. 206.

14. P.M. Hamel, *Through Music to the Self*, Tisbury, Wilts, 1978, p. 89.

15. Words of the composer Karlheinz Stockhausen and recorded in R. Dufallo, *Trackings*, Oxford, 1989, p. 213.

16. Clement of Alexandria (about AD150–215), Protrepticus 1:1–3, quoted in J. McKinnon, *Music in Early Christian Literature*, Cambridge, 1987, p. 30.

17. See A. Storr, *The Dynamics of Creation*, London, 1972, p. 100.

18. T.S. Eliot, *The Literary Essays of Ezra Pound*, London, 1960, pp. 43 and 45.

19. This style of preaching is recorded on *The Gospel Ship*, New World Records, New York, no. NW294.

20. Quoted in Bruce Chatwin, *The Songlines*, London, 1987, p. 302. Bruce Chatwin includes other similar observations well worth reading.

21. The subject is explored in A. Storr, *Music and the Mind*, London, 1992, p. 66 and following.

22. J. Hullah, *The History of Modern Music*, London, 1875, pp. 5 and 7.

23. H. Cole, *The Changing Face of Music*, Oxford, 1978, p. 92.

24. Revelation 5:9 and 7:9.

PART 1

The Birth of Christian Music

From Old Testament times to AD1400

Chapter 1

Music in the Old Testament

Christianity began in the midst of Jewish society. Its sensational message of salvation was first proclaimed there by a Jew whose family history linked him to King David, the greatest hero of Israel's history. Early Christian converts respected Jewish customs and continued to live and worship in the community of their families and forbears. The roots of their new faith were embedded in ancient practice, and they referred constantly in their writings to the Hebrew scriptures whose prophecies they believed were fulfilled in the coming of Jesus, the Messiah. The place that music occupied in Jewish life thus forms an important backdrop to this study, the continuity in liturgical music from Judaism to Christianity being one of the vital spans in the bridge that links the two faiths.

The biblical Old Testament is a wonderfully detailed documentary of a people's mythology, history and philosophy. But it is primarily a collection of sacred writings and was never intended to chronicle every facet of Jewish life. The incompleteness of the picture it paints is sometimes tantalising. There are, on the one hand, passages of fine detail where Bible characters come to life, fully rounded, recognisable in their humanity. But in other places the writers fall silent: they fail to tell us what to them was obvious, for they could not be expected to predict the requirements of a readership 3,000 years on. As a source of information about music in Jewish society the Old Testament is characteristic: occasional vivid detail between frustrating gaps which may never be filled. Music is one of the areas where the Bible does not readily yield its secrets.

The Old Testament covers a long period – some 2,000 years – and during this time Hebrew culture changed greatly. Its earliest history is nomadic and tribal, a dramatic contrast with the high civilisation that had developed by the time Solomon's temple was built (in about 900BC). The musical details of the Old Testament books become gradually more plentiful over the two millennia.

The earliest music

Early references to music in the Bible are indirect, such as the following snatch of song recorded in the book of Numbers. 'Israel', that is, God's people, were journeying to the land promised to them. Then it was that Israel sang this song:

> … Sing out for the well
> that was sunk by the princes
> and dug by the leaders of the people
> with the sceptre, with their staves.[1]

This song refers to a particular situation but probably became a time-honoured ritual at a tribe's approach to a watering-place. There is, however, no clue to how the music sounded.

The study of musical cultures across the world suggests that remote and isolated settlements may preserve musical traditions intact for millennia. It is no surprise, then, to find that the Bedouin Arabs of today share aspects of their music with the nomadic Jews of the Old Testament. Bertram Thomas, an inveterate traveller of the Middle East, recorded the final morning of a long desert journey across southern Arabia with the Bedouins earlier this century:

> We were arriving. The Bedawin moved at a sharp pace, chanting the water chants. Our thirsty camels pricked up their ears with eager knowingness. The last sandhill was left behind. After the next undulation we saw in the dip of the stony plain before us Na'aija, where we had planned a final watering, and beyond it the towers of Doha silhouetted against the waters of the Persian Gulf.[2]

The characteristic Bedouin 'shouts' – set formulae identifying a particular tribe – are probably paralleled in biblical phrases such as 'a hand upon the banner of the Lord'.[3] The ark of the covenant almost certainly began and ended its journeys with musical shouts of this kind, recorded in the book of Numbers:

> And as the ark set out, Moses would say,
> 'Arise, Yahweh, may your enemies be scattered
> and those who hate you
> run for their lives before you!'

And as it came to rest, he would say,
'Come back, Yahweh,
to the thronging hosts of Israel.'[4]

One or two early songs are more vividly drawn, particularly the Song of Miriam in Exodus. It is particularly interesting that here the song is led by a woman:

Miriam the prophetess, Aaron's sister, took up a timbrel, and all the women followed her with timbrels, dancing. And Miriam led them in the refrain:

'Sing of Yahweh: he has covered himself in glory,
horse and rider he has thrown into the sea.'[5]

The impression is of a wild, vigorous and noisy music, inseparable from physical movement. The short lines and simple text indicate plenty of repetition, perhaps simple stepwise melodies constantly returning to a few central pitches. Together with an infectious beat, it probably led to the ecstatic state which such music can readily induce.

Singing has been, and still is, accompanied by instruments in the folk-music of the Near East. The Hebrew names for two families of stringed instruments mentioned in the books of Chronicles and Kings make the connection: *kle shir* (translated as 'lyre') means 'the tools of singing' and *lsharim* (translated as 'harp') means 'for the singers'. What are nowadays called lyre and harp are among a number of instruments mentioned extensively in books concerned with the settlement of the Jews in the Holy Land.

In common with many cultures today except those of the developed world, music seemed to have a place in almost every activity and at almost every event in ancient Jewish life. Songs of war, in victory and in defeat, are recorded in several places in the Bible. One of the most striking is the song of the women who greeted David after his conquest of the Philistines, recorded in the first book of Samuel:

[They] came out to meet King Saul from all the towns of Israel, singing and dancing to the sound of tambourine and lyre and cries of joy; and as they danced the women sang [the word used here is *anah*, 'to answer' or 'to respond']:

'Saul has killed his thousands,
and David his tens of thousands.'[6]

The constant repetition of this refrain must have taken the singers on an upward curve of ecstatic joy, though at the same time feeding Saul's cancerous jealousy. David's later triumphs were the scene of even wilder rejoicing as he led the ark to Jerusalem:

> David and all the House of Israel danced before Yahweh with all their might, singing to the accompaniment of lyres, harps, tambourines, sistrums and cymbals.[7]

The variety of instruments, with percussion and dance, was evidently a potent mixture; the traditions of many oriental cultures suggest that they would have utilised the simplest and most direct music. Such release and catharsis demands that the partakers are wholly at one with what is being celebrated, abandoning themselves willingly. Once again the women seem to have been fully involved in the celebrations.

The result was striking. David's emotional demonstration of commitment highlighted division and dissent. Michal, David's wife, whose relationship with him must have become an uneasy one by this time, found such histrionics distasteful; she 'despised him in her heart' and later rebuked and scorned him.

Temple music

Up to this point, the music described has not been the property of the professional musician, but of people in general – the 'House of Israel'. But in a second description of the arrival of the ark of the covenant in Jerusalem[8] there is the earliest reference to the formation of a trained and official body of musicians to lead worship (hereditarily the privilege of the House of Levi). All manner of musical instruments are mentioned, together with the text of a song of thanksgiving more extensive than any recorded hitherto.[9]

After the building of the temple of Solomon (about 900BC), the liturgy becomes sumptuous and spectacular. The Bible describes the opening ceremonies and the part that music played in them in some detail:

> The entire body of levitical cantors, Asaph, Heman and Jeduthun with their sons and brothers, was stationed to the east of the altar, robed in fine linen and playing cymbals, harps and lyres. A hundred and twenty

priests accompanied them on the trumpet. All those who played the trumpet, or who sang, united in giving praise and glory to Yahweh. Lifting their voices to the sound of the trumpet and cymbal and instruments of music, they gave praise to Yahweh, 'for he is good, for his love is everlasting'.[10]

Such ceremonial splendour was by no means unique in the ancient world. There are detailed descriptions from Egypt and Sumeria of temple-worship earlier than 2000BC. Babylon, too, had a similar and long-established tradition, with guilds of singers, players and artists of all kinds forming part of a 'learned community, a kind of college, which studied and edited the official liturgical literature'.[11]

The temple at Jerusalem had a chequered history. It was destroyed in 586BC, rebuilt from 520BC and further desecrated in 168BC when Antiochus used it to house a heathen altar. Through all this the traditions of temple worship were preserved, some graphic accounts of them being recorded during the latter period, particularly in sources outside the canonical books of the Old Testament.

The apocryphal book Ecclesiasticus (about 200BC) contains a vivid description of the service for the Day of Atonement[12] which is paralleled in the Talmud. This latter collection of Jewish teaching also contains this description of the final part of the daily services of offering:

> They gave him the wine for the drink-offering, and the Prefect stood by each horn of the altar with a towel in his hand, and two priests stood at the table of the fat pieces with two silver trumpets in their hands. They blew a prolonged, a quavering (?) and a prolonged blast. Then they came and stood by Ben Arza, the one on his right and the other on his left. When he stooped and poured out the drink-offering the Prefect waved the towel and Ben Arza clashed the cymbals and the Levites broke forth into singing. When they reached a break in the singing they blew upon the trumpet and at every blowing of the trumpet a prostration. This was the rite of the Daily Whole-offering... This was the singing which the Levites used to sing in the temple.[13]

This source also mentions that the choir had at least twelve singers, all men, with supplementary boys 'to add sweetness', and that the instruments consisted of nine or more lyres (*kinnor*), kithara (*nebel* – though usually translated as 'harps' or 'lyres'), between two and twelve cane pipes (*halil*) and cymbals (*mezaltaim*). The pipes (often called 'flutes' in translation) were in reality twin-bodied reed instruments, very like the *auloi* depicted in Greek iconography. They were played at certain times of year – at Passover and during the eight days of the Feast of Tabernacles.[14]

From the same period, the Roman *Letter of Aristeas* gives a vivid eye-witness account of temple sacrifice, of which this is only a short extract:

> [During the sacrificial service] the deepest silence prevails, so that one would suppose that there was not a single person in the place, although the ministers in attendance number some 700, not to mention the large multitude of those who await their sacrifices to be offered; everything is performed with reverence and in a manner worthy of the Divine Majesty.[15]

The Dead Sea Scrolls of the Essenes (a Jewish sect) were discovered at Qumran in 1947, but have not yet been dated with certainty. Whether or not they are contemporary with biblical writings, they write about music and instruments in very similar terms:

> …I raised a bitter lament
> and made a doleful moan and groan
> and plied my harp [*kinnor*] in mournful dirge…
> But suddenly I perceived
> that there was no more affliction
> to rack me with pain.
> Then did I ply my harp
> with music of salvation,
> and my lyre [*nebel*] to the tune of joy;
> yea, I plied the pipe [*halil*]…
> in ceaseless praise.[16]

The psalms in temple worship

Though they were not the only texts sung in the temple, the biblical psalms, *tehillim* in Hebrew, occupied a central place in its liturgy and numerous references give some insight into how they sounded. The Talmud gives a list of psalms appropriate for each day of the week:[17]

On the first day:	Psalm 24
On the second day:	Psalm 48
On the third day:	Psalm 82
On the fourth day:	Psalm 94
On the fifth day:	Psalm 81
On the sixth day:	Psalm 93
On the Sabbath:	Psalm 92

The book of all 150 psalms was compiled over a long period, its present form being established well after the exile and the rebuilding of the temple. Some of the titles, such as 'a psalm of Asaph' or 'of the sons of Korah', indicate the repertoire of a particular hereditary guild of musicians; others indicate the occasions on which the psalms were used, still others giving the name of the melodic formula used to accompany them (similar to Indian *ràgs* or Arabic *maqamât* which also bear evocative names).

Both the Talmud and many of the psalm-headings show that the Levites sang accompanied, often by plucked stringed instruments. The musical structure was governed by the liturgical sections into which psalms were divided ('... when they reached a break in the singing they blew upon the trumpet').[18] These breaks are sometimes indicated by the word *Selah,* often translated as 'pause'.

The precise musical setting of the psalms will always be a matter for speculation, but the structure of the verses offers some clues. Firstly, the familiar parallelism of the Hebrew poetry readily suggests musical equivalents:

> I am up before dawn to call for help,
> I put my hope in your word.
> I lie awake throughout the night,
> to meditate on your promise.[19]

A number of musical responses to the poetic structure developed in Jewish worship. The word *anah*, meaning 'to respond', is important here. It was used in describing the music at David's victory celebrations and is still found today in connection with Jewish antiphonal singing.

The Talmud elaborates considerably on the concept of 'response'. It describes a number of possibilities: for instance, how a soloist may sing the entire melody of a verse, the other singers answering with a repeat of the same first half-verse; or how the soloist and singers may take alternating half-verses; or perhaps all may sing a refrain after each verse;[20] finally, for teaching purposes, the soloist's half-verses might be repeated by the rest. But in few of these schemes does there appear to be room for participation by the people; the temple choir, it seems, sang on their behalf.

Hebrew poetry does not rhyme, nor does it have a consistent metre like a modern hymn-tune or classical poetry. It has pronounced weak and strong stresses, but their number is free. (A number of modern translations, such as the *Jerusalem Bible*, attempt to convey something of these qualities.) The musical rhythm was therefore probably dictated by the text and not confined to a steady beat, while the melodic scheme would have to be able to accommodate irregular verse-lengths.

The names of tunes which head some of the psalms probably consisted of a pair of short melodic ideas, one for the first half-verse and one for the second, not unlike Gregorian chant. Harmonisation would have been most unlikely, but drones of unisons, fourths and fifths have been suggested.[21]

Even in translation, the nature of the psalms have produced remarkably consistent patterns of musical setting over a period of nearly 3,000 years. Plainsong, Anglican chant, or the more recent settings of Joseph Gelineau all echo the patterns of the original Hebrew. In spite of what one writer has called the 'rash and apparently uncontrollable innovations' in modern psalm-singing,[22] this suggests that the structure and beauty of the Hebrew psalms are too strong to be neglected by musicians and will continue to enrich both Jewish and Christian music.

Worship – impulsive or formal?

The function of music in worship changed in the thousand years or so from the time when David danced in triumph before the ark of the covenant to the time of Christ, in response to changes in society.

The early descriptions are often of music being created impulsively, as a response to events (such as David's triumphs) and enabling the release of emotions among a people willing to express them openly. Such scenes of abandon are recalled nowadays in the practices of a number of Christian communities around the world – above all in the music of the Ethiopian Orthodox Church which maintains remarkable links with the distant past.

Music therapists today are quite certain that, under the right conditions, such open expression of feeling is beneficial and healthy:

> Music therapy permits what the analyst discourages: the acting out of the emotions. But with music this is done with some control through the guilt-free medium of non-verbal sound.[23]

In this respect music therapy is still out of step with the received wisdom of Western society, for many Europeans fear and discourage the expression of deeply-felt emotion. The problem of coping with grief provides a very clear example.

Western funerals are designed to keep expressions of anguish and sorrow out of sight; grief publicly expressed is an embarrassment, even when it would seem to be justified and understandable. In other parts of the world relatives and friends of departed loved ones demonstrate their feelings freely and physically, rocking their bodies, wringing their hands, weeping and wailing. Their singing is a highly emotional outpouring from depths of feeling.

It is this elemental side of music which is at work in many scenes in the history of ancient Israel; it accompanies (or makes possible) the expression of strong emotion, which in turn is often the cause of dramatic events such as the collapse of the walls of Jericho[24] or a prophecy.[25]

Yet, echoing the dissent of Michal at David's dance before the ark, there have been countless objections from Christians when music has been given the freedom to wield this power. In the Old Testament there is a gradual move away from this ecstatic dimension to liturgical music of a more contemplative kind, formal, symbolic and ritualised. The change, in keeping with the style of worship to which it belonged, coincided with the move from open-air ceremonies to a liturgy celebrated in the cavernous acoustics of a large building.

Worship in the temple must have been thrilling and colourful to eye and ear, but in its latter days the music became part of a ritual which seems to have left little room for spontaneity. Instead, it acted more as symbol. Trumpets, for example, represented God's power, authority and majesty, while the cantillation of scripture was a potent reminder of the sanctity of the scriptures, setting the word of God apart from the unsanctified conversations of daily life. This won the chant a central place in Hebrew worship.

While the startling power of ecstatic music may be sacrified in their favour, musical symbols are nonetheless valuable tools in the search for truth, above all in their ability to summarise or to enclose a complex thought in one simple and striking image.[26] These two abilities of music, to possess and to symbolise, have profoundly affected the quality and nature of Christian worship whenever music makes an appearance. Unhappily, those convinced of the efficacy of one have tended vigorously to deny the value of the other, and the divisions thereby created have been deep and damaging.

Notes

1. Numbers 21:17–18.

2. B. Thomas, *Arabia Felix*, London, 1932, p. 298.

3. Exodus 17:16.

4. Numbers 10:35–36.

5. Exodus 15:20–21.

6. 1 Samuel 18:6–7.

7. 2 Samuel 6:5–6, *New Jerusalem Bible*, London, 1985.

8. 1 Chronicles 15.

9. 1 Chronicles 16:8–36.

10. 2 Chronicles 5:12–13.

11. S. Langdon, *Babylonian Liturgies*, Paris, 1913, p. xii.

12. Ecclesiasticus 50:1–21.

13. Tamid VII:3.

14. Talmudian tractate Arakin II:3.

15. Quoted in W.O.E. Oesterley, *The Jews and Judaism During the Greek Period*, London, 1941, p. 205.

16. Psalm 18 of the Dead Sea Scrolls, quoted in A. Sendrey, *Music in Ancient Israel*, London, 1969, p. 193. See also Isaiah 16:11.

17. Tamid VII:4.

18. Tamid VII:3.

19. Psalm 119:147–48.

20. Psalm 136, Deuteronomy 27:16–26.

21. C. Sachs, *The Rise of Music in the Ancient World*, New York, 1944, p. 98; Sendrey, pp. 438–40.

22. Foreword to the Proceedings of the 5th International Church Music Congress, 1966; quoted in J. Overath, *Sacred Music and Liturgy Reform After Vatican II*, Rome, 1969.

23. M. Priestley, *Music Therapy in Action*, London, 1975, p. 19.

24. Joshua 6:1–20.

25. 2 Kings 3:15.

26. The nature of music and its capacity to symbolise and thereby to 'increase our grasp and mastery of reality' is discussed in chapter 11 of A. Storr, *The Dynamics of Creation*, London, 1972. See particularly p. 144.

Chapter 2

From Synagogue to Early Christian Church

The Bible provides ample evidence of the gradual development of synagogue worship, with its origins in the period of Babylonian captivity known as the Exile. But although the distinction between synagogue (the institution) and synagogue (a building) is an important one, the word itself simply means 'place of assembly'.

The book of Nehemiah, which marks the beginning of the Jews' return from exile in the early sixth century BC, gives a moving and vivid account of such an assembly, where, in the open air, 'Ezra the scribe stood on a wooden pulpit which they had made for the purpose' to read from the Book of the Law.[1] Meetings for civil matters, for worship and particularly for religious instruction became commonplace, the New Testament providing plenty of examples of the latter.[2] The earliest buildings in which such meetings were held date from the middle of the third century BC, the time of the dispersed Jews in Egypt. The style of worship in synagogues was based on the practices of the temple, though moderated by omitting the sacrificial acts and rituals (these were replaced in the synagogue by prayers or readings referring to sacrifice, there being no altar).

A Levite, Joshua ben Chananiah, writing shortly after the time of Christ, noted that 'the [temple] choristers used to go in a body to the synagogue from the orchestra by the altar, and so participated in both services.'[3] He was writing at a time of tension between temple and synagogue, which serves to highlight the difference between the two institutions. In *The Sacred Bridge,* Werner notes that

The temple had developed a type of liturgy which, with its hierarchy, its sacrificial cult, and its rigid organisation, engendered a sharp distinction between the officers of the ritual and the community of the faithful, the latter being almost passive bystanders.[4]

Synagogue worship, on the other hand, was organised and conducted by lay people and not by a hereditary priesthood. Services consisted of readings from the Law and from the Prophets, of psalmody, teaching, prayer and final blessing.

The psalms, prayers and readings would be cantillated, that is, recited in a heightened speech resembling simple song. Its basis was the chanting of the text on a single note, but with simple melodic alterations to indicate the grammatical structure. The Christian liturgy of the East still uses the technique extensively – scholars of Byzantine music call it *ekphonesis* (exclamation).[5] The principles behind cantillation are elaborated in chapter 4. Synagogue music needed the skilled leadership of a cantor, whose sole responsibility it became in later times.

Music in the early christian church

Momentous as its appearance was, Christianity did not require an entirely new set of principles to guide its worship. On the contrary, connections between Jewish and early Christian worship are well documented and new links are still being discovered. Even the temple worship is relevant here, not so much as a direct influence – Jesus and his disciples were generally antagonistic to what went on there,[6] but through the synagogue, which had adapted the ceremony of the temple to its own use. These links may provide one of the reasons for the relative scarcity of musical reference in the New Testament, for there would be no need to record the detail of long-established practice. Because Christians saw their faith as a completion of Judaism, they were able to continue to use many parts of Jewish liturgy, but to see them in a new light.[7]

The traditions of the synagogue continued to be absorbed into Christian worship for some time, in spite of the persecutions of AD44 and the Council of Jerusalem, which in AD49 ruled that pagan converts to Christianity need not keep the Law of Moses.[8] Cantors, trained to lead the singing in the synagogue and then converted to the Christian faith, continued to put their skills to use in their new church.

A sacred bridge?

Not only did the early Christians speak Aramaic – the language of Jesus himself – as did their fellow Jews in Palestine, but they shared with them a similar 'church year'. The Jewish New Year begins in the autumn, which is when the earliest Christians celebrated the birth of Christ[9] – Christmas has only been celebrated on 25 December since the fourth century. The Christian Easter Eve coincided exactly with the time of Passover, a fact fundamental to an understanding of the significance of the Eucharist. Both church and synagogue had (and still have) in common: the idea of baptism, the 'Liturgy of the Word' (which for the Christian is the first part of the Eucharist, consisting of readings, the singing of psalms and hymns, teaching and prayers), fasting and the encouragement to develop a personal life of prayer. Furthermore, the scriptural content of synagogue and early Christian worship has been shown to correspond in some remarkable ways.[10]

These points of comparison are well documented, but to match the *music* of the early church to that of the synagogue is more difficult. Neither Jews nor Christians are known to have noted down any of the music they used for worship until at least the sixth- or seventh-century AD. The best and perhaps only means of investigation is indirect – by comparing the oldest written musical sources of the Christian church with the present-day singing of those Jewish communities which have preserved their traditions over two millennia.

The highly orthodox Yemenite Jews (culturally isolated to a unique degree until recently) form one society whose music shows some remarkable correspondences with the earliest known Christian sources. Example 1 compares two chant formulae for the Lamentation of Jeremiah

La - me - na - tze - ach al ha - gi - ttit   mi - ze - mor le - a   ssaf.

Je - ru - sa - lem, Je - ru - sa - lem, con - ver - te - re ad Do - mi - num De - um tu - um.

EXAMPLE 1

from two entirely different sources. The upper one was transcribed in the late nineteenth century from Yemenite singing and may represent a pre-Christian tradition; the lower is medieval Gregorian chant. While some of the conclusions of Eric Werner's book *The Sacred Bridge* (from which the example comes) are now being questioned, it is still essential reading for those exploring the musical relationships of Judaism and Christianity.

'Psalms, hymns and spiritual songs'

One of the most striking but tantalising references to music in the New Testament occurs in two letters of Paul, to the Colossians (3:16) and to the Ephesians both of which date from around AD61–63. Paul exhorts his readers to

> be filled with the Spirit. Sing the words and tunes of the psalms and hymns when you are together, and go on singing and chanting to the Lord in your hearts…[11]

The Greek terms that Paul used here were ψαλμος (psalm) from the verb ψαλλω (to 'move by a touch'). Might this be a reference to the *kinnor* and *nebel*, the plucked instruments of temple worship? υμνος (hymn) from the verb υμνεω (to 'sing praise') occurs also in Matthew 26:30, Mark 14:26 and Acts 16:25. In the latter, it is the word used for Paul's singing in prison and thus suggests unaccompanied voices. ωδη is a simple word for 'song', but since its English equivalent (ode) has since acquired other resonances, ωδη is now translated in a variety of ways: 'inspired song', 'spiritual song', 'sacred song' as well as simply 'song'. The word is also used in Revelation 5:9, 14:3, and 15:3.

How these terms should be distinguished from each other, or even whether distinction is helpful, is a matter for speculation. One possible difference between 'psalms' and 'hymns' may have to do with language – the former signifying Hebrew, the traditional language of worship, and the latter Greek or Aramaic. This might be complemented by a change of musical style, but without any written evidence, there may never be certainties here.

The continued specific and modern use of these terms makes an understanding of their origins doubly difficult. For instance, an early definition of 'hymn' from Augustine of Hippo (354–430) is very broad, ignoring the characteristics of most of today's hymnology:

A hymn is a song containing praise of God. If you praise God, but without song, you do not have a hymn. If you praise anything, which does not pertain to the glory of God, even if you sing it, you do not have a hymn. Hence, a hymn contains the three elements: *song* and *praise* of *God*.[12]

The words of some early hymns are recorded in the New Testament, a number of them in the book of Revelation,[13] such as this fragment:

And I seemed to hear the voices of a huge crowd, like the sound of the ocean or the great roar of thunder, answering, 'Alleluia! The reign of the Lord our God the Almighty has begun; let us be glad and joyful and give praise to God, because this is the time for the marriage of the Lamb...'[14]

The acclamation 'Alleluia' suggests a refrain, following traditional practice in Jewish psalmody. The Gospel of Luke includes some songs which were perhaps already established in the worship of the early church by the time he recorded them. They are the song of Mary (the Latin version begins *Magnificat*), the song of Zechariah (*Benedictus*) and the song of Simeon (*Nunc Dimittis*).[15] By translating these songs back from the Greek of the Gospels to the original Aramaic, the characteristic rhythms and structure of Hebrew psalms are revealed, suggesting that they were chanted in the same way. The words of other early Christian hymns are quoted by Peter and Paul in their letters.[16]

Beyond these glimpses of the earliest Christian worship in the first century, other evidence in the New Testament is circumstantial. The author of the book of Revelation, for instance, seems to base his visions of worship in the heavenly Jerusalem in chapters 4 and 5 on the words of the Sanctus ('Holy, holy, holy'), still used today in the Eucharist. A similar text must therefore have been part of Christian worship in his own day.

Some early Christian writing not accepted into the canon of the New Testament still gives corroborative evidence of liturgical practice in the first two centuries AD. The apocryphal book, the Acts of John, contains a remarkable early hymn with references to music and even to dance:

Before his arrest... [Jesus] gathered us all together and said: 'Before I am given over to them, let us sing a hymn to the Father...' So he bade us form a circle, as it were, holding each other's hands, and taking his place in the middle he said: 'Answer Amen to me.' Then he began to hymn and to say: 'Glory be to thee, Father.' And we, forming a circle, responded 'Amen' to him.

'Glory be to thee, Word,
Glory be to thee, Grace.' 'Amen.'
'Glory be to thee, Spirit...' [etc.]
'Grace dances; I would play on the aulos [pipes];
Dance, all of you.' 'Amen.'
'I wish to mourn;
Beat your breasts, all of you.' 'Amen.'
'The one octad sings with us.' 'Amen.'
'The twelfth number dances above.' 'Amen.'...
'Who dances not, knows not what happens.' 'Amen.'[17]

This extraordinary hymn, known now through its musical setting by Gustav Holst, points to some significant and turbulent developments of Christianity from the second century onwards. First of all, heresies became a problem: this hymn was written by Gnostic Christians who favoured spiritual knowledge gained as much from the ancient wisdom of astrology and cosmology as by faith in God's supernatural power. Such heresies were the subject of many meetings, such as the Council of Nicaea in 325, where church leaders strove to define Christian doctrine as the spreading faith became influenced by many cultures. The hymn also betrays a widening gap between Judaism and Christianity. The references to piping and mourning can be understood in the light of the saying recalled by Jesus:

We played the pipes for you,
and you wouldn't dance;
we sang dirges,
and you wouldn't be mourners.[18]

The mystical references to numbers are typical of the Gnostics, recalling Greek philosophies of the time and foreshadowing a view of creation which became fundamental to Christian musicians and thinkers of the Middle Ages.

The spread of Christianity

First, then, those of the sect were arrested who confessed; next, on their disclosures, vast numbers were convicted... And ridicule accompanied their end: they were covered with wild beasts' skins and torn to death by dogs; or they were fastened on crosses, and, when daylight failed, were burned to serve as torches by night. Nero had offered his gardens for the spectacle.[19]

Thus wrote Tacitus, the Roman imperial historian and vehement Christian-hater, recording events of Nero's reign from AD54–68. The story was to be repeated again and again, with horrific variations, over the next two centuries.

Why were the Christians such a menace? They were reputedly not criminals but pacifists, honest and trustworthy, as some contemporaries such as Pliny had recorded. But they bore the marks of conspiracy: followers of a man executed for treason and obstinately refusing to acknowledge or sacrifice to the gods by which Roman civilisation swore and which gave the emperor his divinity. In short, they were members of an illegal society which had to be stamped out.

Apart from the physical threat of torture and death, Christians also faced the spiritual threat of heresy. As the faith spread rapidly to nations outside Palestine – to Greece, to Gaul, to Egypt, to Syria and Rome – the resident philosophies and religious beliefs of these nations had their effect.

The great diversity of doctrine that could be called 'Christian' caused deep concern to the leaders of the early church. The Gnostics, for instance, were not Christians by the standards of most of today's denominations, and the urgent need for conformity was already being voiced by the end of the first century.

Clement of Rome recommended in his *Letter to the Corinthians* (written about AD95) that the laity should obey the clergy, even on pain of death, shifting the balance of power very much in favour of the ecclesiastical leadership. Later, Bishop Irenaeus (about AD130–200) insisted that salvation was only possible through the one church, and that outside it 'there can be no salvation'. By about AD200, Christian leaders were working urgently to create and to strengthen a catholic, that is, a universal, church.

Their efforts were assisted by the unstable political circumstances in which Christians had to live:

Pressed by their common danger, members of scattered Christian groups throughout the world increasingly exchanged letters and travelled from one church to another. Accounts of the martyrs, often taken from records of their trials and from eyewitnesses, circulated among the churches in Asia, Africa, Rome, Greece, Gaul and Egypt. By such communication, members of the diversified earlier churches became aware of regional differences as obstacles to their claim to participate in one catholic church.[20]

Far from scattering and confusing the early church, persecution and heresy worked to strengthen it. The early church fathers strove to define the faith in order to excommunicate heretics (later on they were to use more brutal methods) by establishing agreements on forms of worship, selecting and canonising the writings of the New Testament and by proposing a creed which all Christians could confess.

Musically, too, persecution had its effect. Christians assiduously distanced themselves from the immoral aspects of the societies that persecuted them, above all from the Roman. Thus Pliny the Younger, Roman governor of Bithynia and Pontus notes, as an unbeliever, the sobriety and morality of Christian life. He was writing to the emperor, Trajan, for guidance on the attitude he should take to Christians:

> They affirmed, however, that this was the extent of their fault or error, that they were wont to assemble on a set day before dawn and to sing a hymn among themselves to the Christ, as to a god, and that they pledged themselves by vow not to some crime, but that they would commit neither fraud, nor theft, nor adultery, nor betray their word, nor deny a trust when summoned; after which it was their custom to separate and to come together again to take food – ordinary and harmless food, however.[21]

Given the context of debauchery in which dancing and instrumental music often occurred in Roman society, such activities were shunned in Christian circles. For example, this commentary on Isaiah dating from the fourth century clearly associates lyre-playing with prostitution:

> You place a lyre ornamented with gold and ivory upon a high pedestal as if it were a... devilish idol, and some miserable woman, rather than being taught to place her hands upon a spindle, is taught by you... to stretch them out on the lyre. Perhaps you pay her wages or perhaps you turn her over to some female pimp, who, exhausting the licentious potential of her own body, presides over young women as the teacher of similar deeds.[22]

There are many similar examples in contemporary writing. This vitriolic attack on both instrumental music and dancing dates from the fourth century:

in blowing on the *tibia* [pipes] they puff out their cheeks… they lead obscene songs… they raise a great din with the clapping of *scabella* [a type of foot percussion]; under the influence of which a multitude of other lascivious souls abandon themselves to bizarre movements of the body, dancing and singing… ultimately raising their buttocks and hips to sway with the rippling motion of their loins.[23]

Evidently the style of singing in worship was absolutely distinct from the night-club atmosphere described here.

Christianity – a state religion

It was the emperor Constantine (about AD274–337) who brought about a fundamental change in the political status of Christians. A legend tells that, before joining battle with Maxentius for the leadership of the Roman empire, Constantine saw a cross blazing in the sky inscribed with the words *in hoc signo vinces* – 'in this sign you will conquer'. Constantine took his subsequent resounding victory to be a sure sign of God's favour and his conversion to the Christian faith reversed the fortunes of Christendom at a stroke. Through the Edict of Milan in 313 he not only granted Christians freedom of worship throughout the empire, but also put many in positions of public authority and allowed the church to own property.

In 328 Constantine created a great new city in the East bearing his name – Constantinople. It was to become a bastion of Christian culture and learning, a formidable rival to the other Christian patriarchies around the Mediterranean – Antioch, Jerusalem, Alexandria and Rome. Worship in these centres was conducted in splendid new buildings and with great ceremony, in keeping with Christianity's new image as a state religion. What is more, Christians in different countries began to worship in different languages, rather than in the Greek which had become the common language of earlier times. A number of different liturgical traditions arose, defined by geographical area and sometimes by the language adopted. The Western churches (within such areas as Spain, the Celtic countries and Gaul) adopted Latin for worship, Eastern countries tending to use the vernacular – Arabic in Syria, Greek in Byzantia, Coptic in Egypt. The effects of these ancient languages on Christian worship is still evident, as a number of the traditions laid down at this period are alive to this day. The story of these Eastern traditions is continued in Part 5.

Notes

1. Nehemiah 8, 2 Chronicles 7:7–9.

2. Acts 18:4.

3. E. Werner, *The Sacred Bridge*, London, 1959, pp. 24–25; A. Sendrey, *Music in Ancient Israel*, London, 1969, p. 181.

4. Werner, p. 25.

5. *Ekphonesis* was a method of chanting continued in the Byzantine Church. See chapter 28.

6. Matthew 21:12.

7. See Acts 24:14–16, 26:4–8.

8. Described in Acts 15.

9. Werner, p. 79.

10. Werner, pp. 83–94, 156–158.

11. Ephesians 5:19.

12. Augustine, *Ennarrationes in psalmos* 72:1; quoted in J. McKinnon, *Music in Early Christian Literature*, Cambridge, 1987, p. 158.

13. Revelation 5:9–10, 19:1.

14. Revelation 19:6–9.

15. Luke 1:46–55, 67–79, Luke 2:29–32.

16. 1 Peter 1:3–5, 1 Timothy 3:16, Philippians 2:6–11.

17. Acts of John 94–97, quoted in McKinnon, p. 25.

18. Matthew 11:17.

19. E. Pagels, *The Gnostic Gospels*, London, 1980, p. 76.

20. Pagels, p. 99.

21. Quoted in J. McKinnon, p. 27. The significance of this passage and of Philippians 2:5–11 to an understanding of early Christian hymns and their place in worship is discussed in R.P. Martin, *Worship in the Early Church*, London, 1964.

22. Pseudo-Basil, *Commentary on Isaiah* 5:158, quoted in J. McKinnon, p. 70. The passage being commented on is Isaiah 5:11–12.

23. Arnobius (d. about AD330), *Adversus nationes* 2:42, quoted in McKinnon, p. 49.

Chapter 3

The Western Middle Ages

The terms 'Middle Ages' and 'medieval' were coined in the fifteenth century by European thinkers – artists and musicians among them – who turned their attention with renewed intensity to the world of classical antiquity as a model for their own age.

The bridge between their new classical age and the original one was the *medium aevum,* the 'middle age', whose beginning is usually reckoned from the fall of imperial Rome and the time of Pope Leo the Great. Though the Renaissance represented an important turning-point in European thought, the medieval culture it gradually replaced had itself been influenced by certain classical writers and their philosophy, with important consequences for Christian music.

During the fifth century the church hierarchy increased its power yet further. Pope Leo the Great (Leo I, 440–61), showed himself to be an impressive diplomat, negotiating the retreat across Europe of Attila the Hun in 452 and later dissuading the conquering Ostrogoths from pillaging Rome. So it was by default that the church authorities found themselves taking up the reins of international politics as Roman imperial power collapsed around them.

Gregory the Great

A number of popes built on this power-base, none more impressively than Gregory the Great, who was born in about 540 and pope from 589 to 604. Gregory was a highly intelligent man, with considerable leadership ability. With immense energy, he set about re-establishing Roman authority, both civil and ecclesiastical. He worked in international and local politics, rebuilding the fabric of the city (the aqueducts, for instance). He developed a welfare system of charities and hospitals, revising and tightening a tax system to pay for the administration of the city and its surroundings – all of which was put into effect by the clergy. Law and the penal code were redrawn in detail under his supervision.

Yet he also preached and wrote voluminously concerning faith and doctrine, aware of the need for a clear and unequivocal voice in Christian matters. Pope Gregory's double success in law and faith was of prime importance for the missionaries sent to the remoter corners of Europe. They needed to be able both to present an authoritative gospel and to offer an efficient network of administration to the barbarian kings. In 597, for instance, Gregory's mission to England landed in Kent and within twenty years not only was the Kentish king converted to Christianity, but he had also accepted a workable legal system along with it.

As part of the process of increasing the authority of the Church of Rome, Gregory strongly encouraged conformity in styles of worship. The differing Latin liturgies (Mozarabic, Gallican, Ambrosian, Celtic) were gradually absorbed into the Roman, with an inevitable effect on the melodies that characterised them.

Music was still not being written down, so it is difficult to tell what those changes were, but by the time music was widely notated (around the tenth century) there was near universal agreement on the shape of worship – the church year was established in fine detail, along with its liturgical structure and its music. One or two centres held out against change and, as a result of past dispensations, the Mozarabic liturgy can still be heard today in the Spanish cathedral of Toledo,[1] as can the Ambrosian in the northern Italian cathedral of Milan.

But Pope Gregory, a great diplomat, administrator and theologian, would probably be surprised to know that he is most widely remembered for the changes to the music for the Roman liturgy which took place during his papacy. This enduring attribution is the result of the apocryphal musical deeds that medieval scholars later invented for him. A common pictorial theme shows Gregory copying down music from a dove (the Holy Spirit) at his ear. It is this long-standing tradition which gives the name *Gregorian* chant to a collection of Christian music of extraordinary richness.

Notes

1. In the *motu proprio* of 1571, Pope Pius V wrote, 'let [chants] be sung in the Spanish kingdoms according to the form of the Church of Toledo which has been handed down from a most ancient time.' See R.F. Hayburn, *Papal Legislation on Sacred Music*, Collegeville, Minnesota, 1979, p. 35.

Chapter 4

The Monastic Tradition

For some believers the new opulence of Christianity's status as an imperial religion was inappropriate, even repugnant. Antony (about AD251–356) is believed to have been the first to propose extreme asceticism as an essential foundation for Christian living. The means of this deprivation were prayer, fasting, celibacy and isolated contemplation in the most inhospitable place on earth – the Egyptian desert. Antony's example was followed by many others who established communities all over Europe and the Middle East in pursuance of lives lived wholly in the service of God.

Not all Christians shared this drastic view of the life of faith. A Spanish nun, Egeria, who made a pilgrimage to Jerusalem at the beginning of the fifth century, offered a more familiar picture of Christian life through her record of the journey. The account is a rare and fascinating one. Egeria describes Sunday morning worship in Jerusalem, perhaps on Easter Day, in considerable detail. First of all she observes the large crowd collecting in front of the church doors – they arrived early to be sure of getting in (she calls this a vigil):

> Before cockcrow the whole crowd collects, as many as the place will hold. For, as they are afraid that they may not be there at cockcrow, they come beforehand and sit there. And hymns and antiphons are sung; and after each hymn or antiphon a prayer is offered. For the priests and deacons are always there for vigils, on account of the crowd...

She then describes the service of Matins, the first of the day:

> But when the first cock has crowed, the bishop descends and enters... All the doors are opened and the whole crowd streams into the sanctuary. Here innumerable lights are shining; and when the people have entered, one of the priests recites a psalm, and they all respond; then prayer is offered.

Two more psalms and prayers follow, then:

> censers are brought into the sanctuary, so that the whole basilica is
> filled with odours. Then where the bishop stands inside the rails, he
> takes the Gospel and advances to the door and himself reads of the
> Lord's resurrection.
>
> And when he has begun to read this, there is such a moaning and
> groaning of all the people, and such weeping… for that the Lord
> endured such grievous things for us. Then the Gospel having been
> read, the bishop comes forth and is led to the Cross with hymns, and
> all the people with him. There again one psalm is recited and prayer
> offered. Again he blesses the faithful, and the dismissal is given.
>
> As the bishop comes forth they all approach to kiss his hand; and
> presently the bishop betakes himself to his own house. From that
> hour all the monks return to the sanctuary and psalms and antiphons
> are sung till daylight…
>
> If any of the laity, either men or women, wish it, they stay there till
> it is light; but if they do not wish to do so, they return to their houses
> and go to sleep again.

At dawn Egeria moves to the Great Church of Constantine, built on
Golgotha, where first of all she hears many sermons from a number of
priests during a service lasting till about ten in the morning. After this:

> the monks escort the bishop with hymns from the Great Church to
> the sanctuary. And when the bishop arrives with hymns, all the doors
> of the sanctuary basilica are opened; and all the people enter (that is,
> the faithful; for the catechumens [converts under instruction but not
> yet baptised] enter not).

Then the baptised Christians all take Communion together. Finally she adds:

> Among all these details this is very plain, that psalms or antiphons are
> always sung; those at night, those in the morning, and those through
> the day, whether at the sixth hour [midday] or ninth hour [mid-
> afternoon] or vespers [early evening], being always suitable and
> intelligible as pertaining to the matter at hand.[1]

These final comments suggest that the traditional daily round of services
(*Opus Dei*, the work of God, the Daily or Divine Office) was already
established by the fifth century and a comparison of Egeria's experience

with the fuller details of the liturgy to follow will show some interesting common ground.

Egeria stresses the importance of music, particularly the thread of psalm-singing which runs through all she describes. There are plenty of opportunities for the congregation to participate in the music: 'everyone responds' in the psalms. This suggests one of the traditional Jewish practices, that of cantor and congregation singing alternate verses. The reference to hymns here may mean a distinct type of music somewhat different from psalms – such as the hymns of Ambrose of Milan. An antiphon is a short sentence in song, which grew further in its importance for medieval psalm-singing.

In Egeria's time the two parts of the Eucharist – the Liturgy of the Word and the Communion – were geographically separated by being held in different buildings (the Christians returned to the basilica for the Communion where they had earlier heard Matins) and only baptised Christians were permitted to attend the latter. These two sections of the service are still identifiable in many denominations today, though the banishment of *catachumens* from Communion was abandoned during the sixth century. The liturgy was clearly ceremonial, but this did not preclude emotional involvement on the people's part, particularly at the reading of the Gospel. The women, too, seem to have been given equal rights among the congregation, a state of affairs which was to change in harsher times to come.

Egeria's diary also reveals early links between the liturgy of the common people and that of monastic life. It was often monks, after all, who conducted worship in many Roman basilicas, and their practice provided the design for worship in church and abbey alike.

The Rule of Benedict

One of the early Christians most influential in shaping monastic tradition was Benedict of Nursia (c. 480–530), the abbot and founder of the monasteries of Subiaco and Monte Cassino in Italy. He proposed a Rule for his Order, a 'school of the Lord's service, in which we hope to order nothing harsh or rigorous'. The Rule divided the day into six hours of prayer, five of manual work and four of the study of Scripture.

Many other fraternities came into existence later, but the example of Benedict was the most important. Even the worship of the Protestant Church has inherited parts of his Rule, such as the addition of a doxology (the 'gloria') to the ending of psalms.

The Rule's six hours of prayer are divided up into a daily round of services, consisting of the Mass (the Lord's Supper or Eucharist) and the Divine Office:

Matins ('morning')	before daybreak
Lauds ('praises')	at dawn
Prime (at the first hour)	6 a.m.
Terce (third hour)	9 a.m.
Sext (sixth hour)	midday
None (ninth hour)	3 p.m.
Vespers ('evening')	about 6 p.m.
Compline ('completion')	end of the day

These services are linked together by their common basis in the biblical psalms, in such a way that the whole cycle of 150 psalms is sung every week. The Lesser Hours (that is, Prime, Terce, Sext and None) are simple and unadorned, lasting perhaps twenty minutes each. They all have a similar pattern and begin with a greeting, probably sung, such as

Priest: *Dominus vobiscum* [The Lord be with you]
Congregation: *Et cum spiritu tuo* [And with your spirit].

After this, a hymn is sung, followed by three psalms. A passage from scripture is then chanted by a reader, followed by a short response from everyone. A brief dismissal concludes the worship.

Cantillation

The Lesser Hours contain some of the most straightforward types of chant, based on a relationship between words and music of great simplicity. A great deal of the chant has its origin in cantillation, the heightened speech used in synagogue worship. At its simplest, it translates into musical shapes the natural rise and fall of the voice when reading. Evidently the degree of inflexion was sometimes a matter of taste, for Augustine complained rather disparagingly that Athanasius 'used to oblige the readers to recite the psalms with such slight modulation of the voice that they seemed to be speaking rather than chanting'.[2]

The modulation of the speaking voice is of fundamental importance to Gregorian chant. In prayers or readings, for instance, the cantor or priest will chant on one note, which he may alter to make a very simple and brief melodic inflexion at points of punctuation.

In many languages a question is conveyed by raising the pitch of the voice at the end of a sentence, and this becomes part of the grammar of Gregorian chant. A full stop is conveyed by a fall in the voice, and likewise a comma. There are many different formulae, but all aim to make the chant respond to the grammar of the text. Worship in the early Middle Ages did not permit instrumental accompaniment, so the voice was entirely unaccompanied.

The chanting of psalms follows this principle. The Hebrew verses of the psalms are planned in complementary halves, so the music of the chant follows this fundamental grammatical outline. Each verse is sung to a reciting note called the tenor (from the Latin *tenere,* 'to hold'). The half-way point of the verse is marked by a simple melodic bend called the mediant (meaning 'half-way') and the end is marked by a slightly more elaborate melodic shape called the termination. Example 2 shows the first two verses of Psalm 133 set to the eighth psalm-tone, whose final (last note) and tenor

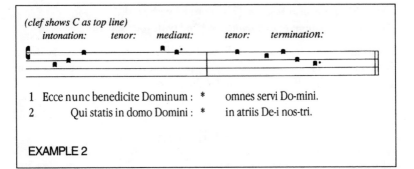

(clef shows C as top line)
   intonation: tenor: mediant: tenor: termination:

1   Ecce nunc benedicite Dominum :   *   omnes servi Do-mini.
2   Qui statis in domo Domini :   *   in atriis De-i nos-tri.

EXAMPLE 2

correspond to mode 8 on the modes chart (Example 3). The first half-verse was sung by the cantor, the rest taken by alternate sides of the choir, verse by verse. (The notation used here, sometimes called Gothic or 'square', was commonplace in the thirteenth century and is still used in modern chant-books. It is the ancestor of modern Western notation and can be read quite easily by those with a little musical training.)

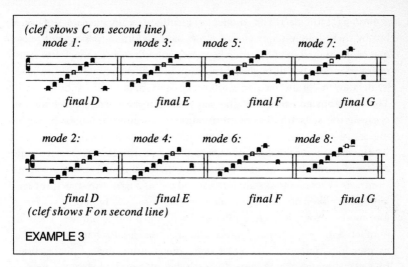

(clef shows C on second line)
mode 1:   mode 3:   mode 5:   mode 7:

final D   final E   final F   final G

mode 2:   mode 4:   mode 6:   mode 8:

final D   final E   final F   final G
(clef shows F on second line)

EXAMPLE 3

These principles and patterns hold good for any psalm-verse, whether the words are describing 'war arrows hardened over red-hot charcoal' or 'I call to the Lord and he answers me'. In short, the music does not attempt to describe the meaning of the text, but rather adorns or clothes the words in song. The rising scale at the very beginning of the psalm (called the intonation and sung by the cantor or priest alone) assists the main body of singers to tune in to the musical scale being used. The cantor's task is to select a vocal range comfortable for the congregation.

Modes

Each psalm was chanted to psalm-tones, melodic formulae corresponding to differing scale-systems. A comparison of these scale-systems, or 'modes' with the more recent harmonic practice used in most Christian music today reveals the distance musical priorities have moved in more than a thousand years.

Most popular Western music today uses two modes, major and minor. Like all modes, they are defined by the characteristic intervals that form them. The major mode – what is now called the major scale – starts with two intervals of a tone (in C major, C to D, then D to E) but the distinct quality of the minor mode is created by the second interval only being a semitone (D to E flat). Thus modes are identified not by the names of notes, but by their unique sequences of intervals. In addition, passages of music may be presented in contrasting keys, not only through a change from, say, major to minor, but through transposition to a different pitch level. A piece by Beethoven, for instance, may follow a passage in the key of C by one in E. The collisions and tensions that can result are one of the chief ways of creating the sensation of evolution and story telling in longer pieces of music.

The musical sensitivities and expectations of a medieval cleric were quite different from those of musicians using the major/minor scale system. Contrasts generated to sustain interest and to build narrative structures on a large scale played no part in his thinking. His music was built on a system of four modes – four different arrangements of tones and semitones. These he numbered in Greek: *protus, deuterus, tritus* and *tetrardus*. Each mode existed in two versions, authentic and plagal, depending on the range of pitches used. In a plagal mode, a melody will use pitches above and below the *final* or finishing note in roughly equal measure, but the authentic modes place the final at or near the bottom of the melodic range. So the total number of modes (counting four types each coming in two versions) was eight. Example 3 lists the eight modes as ascending scales illustrating the approximate range of melodies in that particular mode. The finals are the key-notes on which the tunes finish and the white notes are the tenors used for recitation.

The simple principles of cantillation allowed verbal punctuation and sentence construction to be embedded in singing. In this way the chant provided some simple clues about the structure of the text. Example 4 shows a formula for the cantillation of the Gospel which highlights the grammatical structure.

As in many other tones, melodic shapes are assigned to commas, pauses, question-marks and full-stops, mimicking spoken inflexions at these points. Composing in modes extended the expressive possibilities of chant, for by writing in a certain mode, a composer could draw on certain melodic turns of phrase that he knew others had used before him. In time, particular figures became common currency for that mode, giving the modes distinct characters often described in emotive terms:

The composer... must therefore consider how he may adapt his own chant to a pre-arranged mode, for just as men do not all delight in the

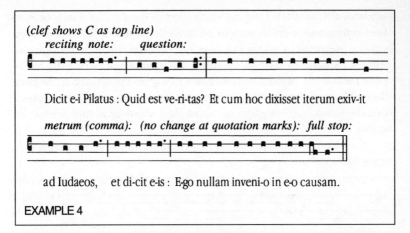

(*clef shows C as top line*)
reciting note: *question:*

Dicit e-i Pilatus : Quid est ve-ri-tas? Et cum hoc dixisset iterum exiv-it

metrum (comma): *(no change at quotation marks):* *full stop:*

ad Iudaeos,   et di-cit e-is : E-go nullam inveni-o in e-o causam.

EXAMPLE 4

same dish but some in sweet things, some in bitter... so it delights some to hear the fastidious and courtly wanderings of the first mode, others the falling and dark profundities of the second. Some are more fortified by the austere and haughty dancing of the third; the sound of the fourth attracts some as if in a caressing and flattering way. Others are soothed by the delightfulness of the saucy fifth; others are moved by the voice of the sixth as if by a sweet lover's plea or by the song of the nightingale. To others, the extrovert leaps of the seventh seem delightful; others willingly attend the seriousness of the eighth.[3]

This description – quite common in the Middle Ages – comes from *Summa Musice*, a singing manual for choir-boys dating from about 1200. To modern ears, chant may well sound much the same no matter which mode is being used. This is not necessarily an indication that the author of *Summa Musice* was on a flight of fancy, but that his thorough immersion in modal chant gave him sensations that are now denied us. More importantly, it shows that medieval musicians were aware of and interested in music's rhetorical powers.

Antiphon

The antiphon was a particular feature of medieval psalm-singing. A number of psalms have a short refrain placed between each verse; Psalm 136 ('his love endures for ever') is an example, as are the 'Hallel' psalms which are punctuated by shouts of *Hallelujah* ('praise the Lord'). Thousands of such short refrains were freely composed in medieval times, to be interlaced between psalm-verses in order to make a spiritual comment or to emphasise a theme of worship. The words might be drawn from one of the psalm verses themselves, or from another passage of scripture. Whatever the case, since the refrain alternated with the psalm verses, it was called an antiphon, from the Greek 'sounding against'. Example 5 shows an antiphon for Palm Sunday, freely composed to a text closely based on Matthew 21:8 and 9. It is typical of Christian chant that its word-setting should be contemplative rather than dramatic.

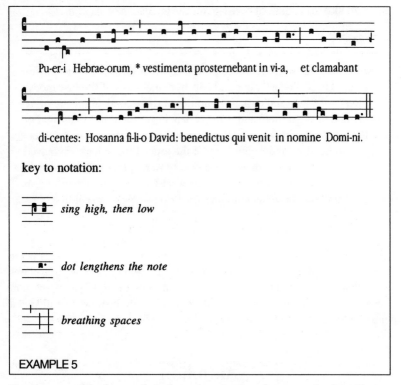

Pu-er-i Hebrae-orum, * vestimenta prosternebant in vi-a,   et clamabant

di-centes: Hosanna fi-li-o David: benedictus qui venit in nomine Domi-ni.

key to notation:

sing high, then low

dot lengthens the note

breathing spaces

EXAMPLE 5

To sing even this short refrain between every psalm-verse (and in Matins there are nine psalms to be sung) would extend worship beyond human endurance, so the convention was established that, in most cases, the antiphon was only sung at the beginning and end.

Hymns

Another type of music in the Divine Office is the hymn. In New Testament times and even up to the fifth century, Augustine's definition of hymn held good, that it was simply a 'song in praise of God'. Gradually a new type of liturgical song became popular. It was different from other types of chant in that it did not use the words of scripture (though it might have been closely based on them) but was freely composed in words and music.

The use of this type of hymn began with Eastern Christians and became an important part of the Byzantine liturgy. It was Ambrose (Bishop of Milan from 374) who encouraged their use in the Western church. Augustine records in his autobiographical *Confessions*:

> the church at Milan had begun to seek comfort and spiritual strength in the practice of singing of hymns, in which the faithful fervently united with heart and voice... Ever since then the custom has been retained, and the example of Milan has been followed in many other places, in fact in almost every church throughout the world.[4]

Ambrose himself wrote a number of hymns and was not unaware of his talent:

> They also say that the people are led astray by the charms of my hymns. Certainly; I do not deny it. This is a mighty charm, more powerful than any other. For what avails more than the confession of the Trinity, which is proclaimed daily in the mouth of all the people?[5]

Frequent disagreements between Ambrose and the secular powers allowed him to prove the point. In 386 the emperor's mother Justina attempted to force him to hand over a church building for the use of liberal Christians (unable to accept the doctrines of the Council of Nicaea) but Ambrose refused. He demonstrated his resolution by organising a congregational sit-in during which his hymns kept morale high. The secular powers eventually capitulated.

Many hymns have been attributed to Ambrose, but four hymns reckoned to be authentically his are *Aeterne rerum conditor, Deus Creator omnium, Iam surgit hora tertia* and *Veni redemptor gentium*.

These hymns are composed in metrical stanzas, quite unlike biblical poetry, and it may be interesting for modern hymn-writers to note that Ambrose does not feel obliged to provide rhyme.

Example 6 shows what may be the most famous early Western Christian hymn, *Veni Creator Spiritus*, the words of which date from at least as far back as the eleventh century. An early source (from a monk of St Gall in about 1220) ascribed the words to the emperor, Charlemagne (747–814), but like so many medieval claims, this is more likely to be legend than fact. The English translation is by J.M. Neale (1818–66), a hymnodist and a fine translator of Latin hymns into English.

O lux be-a-ta Tri-ni-tas, Et prin-ci-pa-lis u-ni-tas;

Jam sol re-ce-dit ig-ne-us: In-fun-de lu-men cor-di-bus.

EXAMPLE 6

Notes

1. Quoted in P. Weiss and R. Taruskin, *Music in the Western World*, London, 1984, pp. 21–23, and (in another more extensive translation) J. McKinnon, *Music in Early Christian Literature*, Cambridge, 1987, p. 113.

2. Augustine, *Confessions*, Book 10, xxxiii (50).

3. Christopher Page, *Summa Musice*, Cambridge, 1991, p. 118.

4. Augustine, *Confessions*, Book 9, vii (15).

5. McKinnon, p. 132.

Chapter 5

Music of the Spheres – the Medieval World-View

At the foundations of Gregorian chant lay two simple concepts: the heightened speech of cantillation and the free composition of songs setting scripture or sacred poetry. By a process of glacier-like evolution, these fundamental principles came to be housed in a highly adorned liturgy, itself part of a church year which prescribed every aspect of worship down to the minutest details. The immeasurably increased solemnity of the worship of the Middle Ages was a product of both temporal and spiritual forces. Not only did the church wish its sacrifices of praise to reflect the majesty and glory of the God whose ambassador it was, but it also needed a ritual of splendour to suit its status as a powerful political force.

The medieval Christians' understanding of the world is a further dynamic in this evolution towards complexity. To see God in all things was their first and fundamental principle. Paul's letter to the Romans says:

> Ever since God created the world his everlasting power and deity... have been there for the mind to see in the things he has made.[1]

The people of the Middle Ages were certain of God's existence and of supernatural powers at work around them: it was truly an 'age of faith'. The church cited the Bible as the final written authority for all points of doctrine, but the nature and diversity of God's creation was also minutely scrutinised, for it was believed that its every detail bore a message for humanity.

Hidden messages

One of the most charming examples of this can be found in bestiaries. A medieval bestiary is a kind of natural history book, a compilation by a monastic scribe of everything there was to be known about the animal kingdom. They are fascinating documents, with the most entertaining illustrations, for a Yorkshire monk was unlikely to have seen, for example, an elephant, and his second- or third-hand sources of information left much to his imagination. Without the opportunity to travel the author had no sure way of telling what was fable and what was fact. Thus the bestiaries unwittingly mix real animals (many like horse and dog being accurately and lovingly described) with mythical creatures like the phoenix, the manticore or the basilisk. All are treated with equal respect.

But the real purpose of the book is to bring out the meaning that lies behind creation. What, for instance, has God to teach us through the basilisk?

> The Basilisk... is the king of serpents. People who see it run for their lives, because it can kill them merely by its smell. Even if it looks at a man, it destroys him. Nevertheless, Basilisks are conquered by weasels... God never makes anything without a remedy.[2]

Thus every phenomenon of nature, whether real or imagined, was a sermon on the nature of God, once the church had unlocked the door to its meaning.

Numerology

While the authors of the bestiaries rejoiced in the wonder of living things and their lessons for humanity, the most powerful sermon of all lay in the numbers and proportions that ordered the natural world. The medieval preoccupation with number amounted to an obsession. Biblical commentators were so concerned with the hidden meaning of number that they might neglect a straightforward message. For example, a verse from Psalm 33 invites everyone to: 'Give thanks to the Lord on the harp; with the ten-stringed psaltery chant his praises.' The difficulty the church authorities had with the literal use of musical instruments for praise (see chapter 2) led a third-century writer to an allegorical interpretation:

> The musical instruments of the Old Testament are not unsuitable for us if understood spiritually... The harp is the active soul; the psaltery

is pure mind. The ten strings can be taken as ten nerves, for a nerve is a string. Therefore, the psaltery is taken to be a body having five senses and five faculties...[3]

The significance of number led the church to construct great edifices of learning around the significance of the Holy Trinity, the twelve apostles, the twenty-four elders of the book of Revelation, the proportions of the ark[4] or the number of the beast.[5]

The idea of a universe synchronised in every detail by numbers and their proportions is classical and pagan, but through the works of Pythagoras and Plato[6] it was readily accepted by Christians. By marrying a study of astronomy with biblical references to heaven, the picture emerged of a universe created and sustained by God, whose planets created a cosmic music through their harmonious movement. Like the Greeks before them, Christians understood astronomy and music to be inextricably bound together by their common basis in number. As the Roman philosopher Boethius wrote in the sixth century:

> There are three types of music. The first type is the music of the universe (*musica mundana*), the second, that of the human being (*musica humana*), and the third type is that which is created by certain instruments (*musica instrumentis constituta*) such as the *kithara*, or *tibia* or other instruments which produce melodies.
>
> Now the first type, that is the music of the universe, is best observed in those things which one perceives in heaven itself, or in the structure of the elements, or in the diversity of the seasons. How could it possibly be that such a swift heavenly machine should move silently in its course?... it is impossible that such a fast motion should produce absolutely no sound, especially since the orbits of the stars are joined by such a harmony that nothing so perfectly structured can be imagined... Thus there must be some fixed order of musical modulation in this celestial motion.[7]

Thus even the humble *musica instrumentalis constituta* was linked through the music of the human soul ultimately to the music of the spheres, for all three were part of the same divinely controlled system. Humanity had therefore to strive to make music which synchronised with this harmoniously vibrating universe and which would thereby form a worthy part of God's great symphony of proportions.

The treatise *Summa Musice* is typical of its time (about 1200) in fitting the four types of mode into the greater cosmological picture:

> The Ancients of music divided the modes into four, namely into the *Protus, Deuterus, Tritus* and *Tetrardus*, that is to say first, second, third and fourth, but one may ask what reasoning led them to make this fourfold division. To which it may be replied... that music is founded upon a supreme and benign harmony of sounds. It is rationally organised therefore according to the number and proportion of things which are known to possess concord... that it to say the Elements [which] form the Macrocosm, that is to say the Greater World.
>
> Fire is hot in the highest degree, Air moist, Earth dry and Water cold. Drawing the rationale of their number from this, the first preceptors divided the modes into four. The same fourfold division... is found in the Microcosm, that is to say the Lesser World which is Man. He is constituted from four Humours, namely Choler, Blood, Phlegm and Melancholy.[8]

This all-embracing medieval vision gradually blurred and faded as faith in scientific discovery replaced belief in the unknown and unseen. One of the last representations of the medieval (and ultimately Pythagorean) view of the cosmos, was published by Athanasius Kircher in 1650.[9]

In our own age, scientific observation on the greatest and smallest scales (astro- and sub-atomic physics) show that the cosmos has indeed a harmoniousness, but of a complexity far beyond the imaginations of medieval astronomers and philosophers. At the same time, some recent discoveries might not surprise them so much. The sun's turbulent surface has excited much interest, as it appears to be harmoniously synchronised by sound vibrations deep in the sun's interior. Its study has created a new discipline, helioseismology, dedicated in only a slightly new sense to studying the 'harmony of the spheres'.

Notes

1. Romans 1:20.

2. T.H. White, *The Book of Beasts*, London, 1969, p. 168.

3. Pseudo-Origen, *Selecta in psalmos* 32:2–3, quoted in J. McKinnon, *Music in Early Christian Literature*, Cambridge, 1987, p. 38.

4. Genesis 6:15.

5. Revelation 13:18. The books of Daniel and Revelation are closely linked and rich in number symbolism.

6. The only book of Platonic dialogue known to the Middle Ages was *Timaeus*; quoted in P. Weiss and R. Taruskin, *Music in the Western World*, London, 1984, p. 9.

7. Quoted in Weiss and Taruskin, p. 33. Boethius (about AD480–524) was a Roman philosopher and a Christian whose writings on music formed the basis of the philosophy of music for hundreds of years.

8. C. Page, *Summa Musice,* Cambridge, 1991, p. 92.

9. A. Kircher, *Musurgid Universalis*, Rome, 1650; see J. Godwin, *Athanasius Kircher*, London, 1979, p. 21.

Chapter 6

Music for the Liturgy

The services in which liturgical elaboration was most evident were Mass and its two preparatory vigils, Vespers and Matins.

Vespers

Vespers begins with a versicle and response from verse 1 of Psalm 70, and continues with five psalms, each with its own antiphon. A reading is then followed by a hymn, which in turn leads to the high point of the service, the singing of the *Magnificat*, the song of Mary. Like the psalms, the *Magnificat* begins and ends with an antiphon (a so-called Marian antiphon). The importance of the occasion – especially on solemn feasts in the church year – is symbolised by the more involved melodies.

Vespers continues with responsive prayers, and the service finishes with the closing versicles and responses. Such elaborate music, particularly its melismas (several notes to one syllable) effectively excluded a lay congregation from singing, making it the property of the trained choirs of monasteries, cathedrals and college chapels.

Matins

Matins, if anything more ornate than Vespers, is built round the singing of nine psalms. These psalms are grouped in three 'Nocturns' (night-watches) and alternate with readings which in turn are followed by elaborate responsories.

These responsories illustrate another step in the elaboration of the chant. As their name suggests, they are intended as a response of praise and adoration to the scripture which has just been read. Many consist of an antiphon (the freely-composed refrain), a psalm-verse, and a repetition of the antiphon. The whole is so decorated that the original long reciting note or 'tenor' is almost submerged in the surrounding invention (see Example 7). The ninth and final reading is followed by the singing of the canticle *Te Deum Laudamus*.

Mass

The celebration of the Eucharist is, of course, at the centre of Christian worship. There is clear evidence in the New Testament that Jesus' disciples took seriously his command to 'do this as a memorial of me', recorded in Luke's Gospel, and there are many later references to the holding of Eucharistic feasts. Its importance is not simply a remembrance of the person of Jesus, but a celebration of what, after the first Eucharist (the Last Supper), became his sacrifice once-and-for-all and on behalf of everyone. As Paul wrote in his first letter to the Corinthians:

As often as you eat this bread and drink this cup, you proclaim the Lord's death until he comes.[1]

The depth of meaning of the eucharistic feast encouraged Christians to celebrate it with particular solemnity even in the early days of the church. As a result, special musical traditions have accompanied it from the earliest times. By the eleventh century Mass was often celebrated with sufficient ceremony to justify it being termed ritual theatre. Its many striking visual symbols went hand-in-hand with elaborate music.[2]

The celebration of the Lord's Supper or Eucharistic Feast was known in the first few centuries of Christianity as *dominicum*, meaning 'the Lord's'. It is not understood why this name should have been replaced by 'Mass' sometime after the fifth century. The word 'mass' is a reference to the last words of the service: *Ite, missa est*, literally 'Go, it is the dismissal'. 'Mass' is an anglicisation of *missa*. Eastern Orthodox Christians call the service 'Divine Liturgy'.

Within its basic shape, the relative solemnity of Mass varied according to the place and circumstances of its celebration. At Easter, Christmas or Pentecost, for instance, the ceremony and its music would be especially elaborate. Dispensations allowed local variations in liturgical detail, such as the distinctive Sarum Use, established at Salisbury with the building of the cathedral in the early thirteenth century and which became widely used in England up to the Reformation. There were also dramatic differences in the human and financial resources available from place to place, but the structure of the service would remain essentially the same, whether celebrated in a village church, Cluny Abbey in France or Salisbury Cathedral in England.[3]

The eleventh-century Mass

This plan outlines a Mass as it might have been celebrated in a well-endowed church in the eleventh century. The **Ordinary** of the Mass (indicated here with bold text) is the term given to the texts that never change; the *Proper* texts (in italic) are those which vary with the church's calendar.

The liturgy of the word:

Introit
Antiphon, psalm-verse and repeat of antiphon
Sung by the choir as the priest and ministers process to the altar

Kyrie
Often a threefold repetition of 'Lord, have mercy' and 'Christ, have mercy'
Everyone sings

Prayers
The priest offers prayers of confession and forgiveness

Gloria
Free composition
A song of thanks and praise (see Luke 2:14)

Versicle and response
'The Lord be with you' – 'And also with you'
Exchanged between priest and congregation

Collects
Cantillation
Prayers for the day

Epistle
Cantillation
New Testament reading

Gradual
Antiphon, psalm-verse, antiphon
Highly elaborate music for the choir

Alleluia
'Alleluia', psalm-verse, 'Alleluia'
For the choir

Sequence
Free composition
For the choir

Gospel
Cantillation
The service book is carried to the rood-loft with great ceremony

Credo
Free composition
A statement of faith for all to say or sing.

Eucharistic Feast:

Offertorium
Antiphon only
For the choir

Prayers
Including *Sursum corda* – 'Lift up your hearts' – and the Proper
Preface for the day
Preparation for the Communion

Sanctus and **Benedictus**
Free composition. The Sanctus is repeated after the Benedictus
Everyone sings

The Canon of the Mass
Consecration of the bread and wine

Pater Noster – The Lord's Prayer
Free composition
Recitation by the priest

Agnus Dei
Free composition in three parts, each beginning *Agnus Dei* –
'Lamb of God'
Everyone sings

The Communion
The bread and wine are received with great ceremony

Communion
Antiphon only
For the choir

Versicle and response

Postcommunion
Cantillation

Ite, Missa Est
Versicle of dismissal to which everyone responds *Deo gratias* –
'thanks be to God'.

The two parts of the Mass, the Liturgy of the Word and the Eucharistic Feast, were two separate services in the time of Egeria. Though they were merged in the later Middle Ages, their distinct characters can still be sensed in eucharistic celebrations today, one being a preparation for the other.

The unchanging texts of the Mass *Ordinary* are familiar for listeners to classical music, as many composers of the last 600 years have used them for their Mass settings. In the first few hundred years of Christianity, however, these were the words intended for the whole assembly to utter with the help of simple chants. The *Proper* texts, those appropriate for a particular occasion, were then more appropriately sung by members of the choir (the *schola cantorum*) or perhaps by a small group of expert cantors. The musical creativity of the *schola* gradually changed the *Proper* into a complex art-music, its unique elaboration by polyphony laying the foundations for the future development of Western music.

By the eleventh century, however, a further distinction was made between the community in the choir-stalls and the celebrants in the sanctuary. Masses were thought of as essentially 'private' to the celebrants, who enacted a number of ceremonies and recited prayers sometimes out of the sight and hearing of everyone else. Furthermore, the common people in the nave (west of the choir-screen) would only be onlookers. Divine Liturgy in the Greek Orthodox tradition today is similarly 'layered'; at several points the priest prays or enacts ritual behind the *ikonostasis* while the cantor maintains the continuity of the chant.

Example 7 illustrates the degree of complexity that chant had reached by this period. *Immolabit haedum* is a responsory for Matins at the feast of Corpus Christi and consists of a central verse flanked by an antiphon. The psalm-tone for the verse has been highly decorated, but its original structure can still be perceived – the tenor is marked by x's.

EXAMPLE 7

Notes

1. 1 Corinthians 11:26.

2. See for instance G. Every, *The Mass*, Dublin, 1978.

3. The Sarum Use and the distinctions between monastic and secular liturgy are explained in detail in J. Harper, *The Forms and Orders of Western Liturgy*, 1991.

Chapter 7

From the Ear
to the Page

Over a period of nearly a thousand years, Christian music was sung and passed on to the following generation entirely by memory, an extraordinary feat by any standards. Isidore of Seville (about 560–636) wrote a definition of music which included the statement: 'Unless sounds are held in the memory by man they perish, because they cannot be written down.'[1]

At a time when books were rare and when only a small proportion of the population could read, the memorising of vast amounts of scripture was necessary and commonplace.[2] Occasionally today people with highly trained memories can still demonstrate these mental skills, usually as no more than a party trick, of little use in an age of calculators and digital data storage. However, worshipping Christians of all ages have found that the combination of words and music is of immense help in committing the Word of God to memory and to the mind.

The Alleluia and the Sequence

The cantors' capacity for the retention and recall of the chant was eventually stretched beyond its limits. Significantly enough, the breakdown occurred in the one area where words were not available to assist the memory – in the final syllable of the Alleluia.

One of the gifts of the Spirit mentioned by Paul in his letters to the churches is the gift of 'tongues'.[3] This gift has been exercised and enjoyed down the ages as a free expression of praise. Sometimes the gift of tongues extends to song, perhaps to an unknown language, perhaps to a simple word like 'Alleluia', or uses no words at all. The Alleluia of the Proper may be evidence of this gift having been used during Mass.

The Alleluia is a psalm-verse with an antiphon set to the word 'alleluia'. Where its origin could lie in a spontaneous musical expression of praise in an outpouring of the power of God's Spirit, at a later stage the music became more formalised. Whatever their origin, Alleluias became characterised by their remarkable musical extension of the final syllable. Example 8 is an Alleluia for Easter Sunday, the final syllable being sung to a 45-note melisma (a passage of several notes on one syllable).

the jubilus, 'rejoicing'

Al- le- lu- ia..

EXAMPLE 8

By this time music was no longer the humble servant of the words as in the simple chants of the Lesser Hours, but an expression of praise in an abstract medium without the aid of text. Not for nothing did Augustine refer to this unique type of chant as *jubilus* – 'rejoicing':

> One who rejoices (*jubilat*) does not speak words, but it is rather a sort of sound of joy without words, since it is the voice of a soul poured out in joy and expressing, as best it can, the feeling, though not grasping the sense... Filled with too much joy, he cannot explain in words what it is in which he delights... and whom does jubilation benefit but the ineffable God?[4]

Such spontaneous musical praise did not make special demands on the memory, but the traditional melodies with long melismas caused serious difficulties.

A characteristic solution was described by Notker Balbulus ('the stammerer', c. 840–912), a monk at the monastery of St Gall in Switzerland:

> When I was still young, and very long melodies *(longissimae melodiae)* – repeatedly entrusted to memory – escaped from my poor little head, I began to reason with myself how I could bind them fast.[5]

He related how a monk from Jumièges near Rouen sought sanctuary with him as his own monastery had been sacked by the Normans (in 862). The

French monk had brought with him some verses which he had set to the textless *jubilus* of the Alleluia. Realising that the additional text was the solution to his memory problem, Balbulus then set about composing his own improved texts. Now he had words which, when put to the former melismas, 'bound them fast' in his memory. The story is undoubtedly over-simplified, for the music that Notker and others left does not relate in such a straightforward way to Alleluia melodies. Although Notker called his new pieces 'hymns' (under the title *Liber hymnorum*) other sources call such compositions *sequentiae*, as they were indeed sung on solemn occasions following the Alleluia. Furthermore, early manuscripts begin with an opening musical flourish on the word 'Alleluia'. At some point it seems, lively artistic imagination turned textless chant into a new musical genre.

Separated from their origins, sequences became immensely popular from the eleventh to the thirteenth centuries as vehicles for long and complex meditative song. An alternative name for them was 'prosa' for the early texts were indeed prose, but later on, rhymed texts became popular. Some of the most beautiful and unusual were written by the abbess, Hildegard of Bingen (1098–1179); indeed, her life and music has created considerable interest recently and her music can be heard on several recordings. Hildegard is intriguing not only because her life is well-documented, giving an unusually clear view of a woman's life in a male-dominated society, but because her expressions of faith took such a variety of forms: through pictures, visions, letters, a medical treatise, poems and music. Her earliest visionary work was *Scivias* ('Know the ways'), the last section of which is called *Ordo Virtutum*, a 'play of virtues' or morality play. This she later set to music in a remarkable fashion, the modes and contours of the melodies rhetorically depicting the personalities that sing them.

Hildegard's seven sequences are among her best-known work, brought together in a collection called *Symphonia armonie celestium revelationum* – 77 poems, all set to music. The texts are visionary and the melodies that accompany them strikingly original. She did not hesitate to break musical conventions of the time in order to express, through an unusual rhetoric, the intensity of her message, as Example 9 (the opening of the sequence *O ignis spiritus*) illustrates.

It was not until the reforms of the Council of Trent in 1562 that the large numbers of sequences permitted in medieval liturgy were reduced. In the Gregorian chant-books of the Roman Catholic Church today only a handful are listed of the thousands once sung.

O ig-nis spi-ri-tus pa-ra-cli-ti, vi-ta vi-te om-nis cre-a-tu-re,

sanc- tus es vi-vi-fi-can-do for-mas.

EXAMPLE 9

Troping

The term used for the addition of music or text (or both) to an already
existing vocal piece is 'troping'. Apart from the obvious possibilities of
adding melodic embellishments to a chant such as melismas, troping was
one of the most favoured ways of adorning Christian music and of
heightening its solemnity. As an example, the words *Christe Eleison* ('Christ,
have mercy') on a solemn occasion might become: *Christe, rex unice, Patris
almi Nate co-aeterne, eleison* ('Christ, the only king, eternally begotten of the
beloved Father, have mercy').[6]

At the great feasts of Easter and Christmas, a liturgical drama might be
placed as a prelude to Mass before the Introit, troping, or adding to, the
Mass itself. The *Quem Quaeritis* ('whom do you seek') dialogue, for instance,
could either be a re-enactment of the Easter morning scene with Mary at
the tomb of Jesus, or of the (non-scriptural!) visit of three midwives to the
crib of Jesus on Christmas night, according to the season.

Drama is possibly a misleading term for tropes of this kind. Although the
stories featured both male and female characters, liturgical circumstances
did not usually permit the sexes to mix. Furthermore, the participants
usually wore ecclesiastical vestments rather than costume. The impression is
of a dignified and restrained re-enactment. On the other hand, detailed
rubrics often give a compelling picture of a character's feelings through
gesture. In the Fleury *Slaughter of the Innocents*, for instance, a mother,
Rachel, laments the death of her children:

> Then Rachel is led in and the two women console her; and standing over her children she weeps, sometimes falling down, singing: alas...[7]

The Play of Daniel from Beauvais Cathedral is particularly vivid. It tells at length and with stirring music the main strands of the story of Daniel: his interpretation for King Belshazzar of the writing on the wall, his refusal to worship King Darius, his brush with the lions and the ultimate fate of Darius' followers. The directions at this latter point suggest a serious challenge for the staging: 'They being cast into the pit will be instantly devoured by the lions...' Exceptionally, there seems to be evidence of instrumental players:

> King Darius will immediately appear with his nobles, and the harp-players will go in front of him, while the nobles sing...

and individuals are required to convey passion: 'Then the King descending from the throne, will come to the pit, saying tearfully:', or 'The King will be amazed and cry out.'[8]

Drama abounds here, suggesting that the context of the Play of Daniel was perhaps not a liturgical one, and that the process of troping has brought into existence an independent art-form. Certainly the style of performance had moved from the symbolic firmly into the realm of the rhetorical and dramatic.[9]

Notation

There is ample evidence from this period onwards of the use of boys in the cathedral choirs of medieval Europe. The assertion in Psalm 8 that the Lord's majesty was recounted by children and sucklings [*lactentium*] was an important justification for the foundation of choir-schools whose education set their inmates on the road to a career in the church. The thoroughness of this training allowed the boys to take responsibility for complex chant – some of which began to demand a reliable method of notation. Guido D'Arezzo (c. 995–1050), an Italian monk, did much to develop a miraculous new facility which allowed the choristers in his charge to sing new chants without having heard them first, in other words, to sight-read. He wrote to a friend:

> Pope John [XIX, 1024–33], who governs the Roman Church, heard of our song-school's reputation. He heard in particular of how, by

means of our antiphoners [books of antiphons] boys could learn songs they had never heard. He was greatly astonished, and sent three messengers to bring me to him... The Pope was most glad to see me... and asked a great many questions. He turned over the pages of the antiphoner as if it were some great prodigy... He did not move from the place where he sat... until he had learned to sing one versicle that he had never heard. What more is there to say? I had to leave Rome soon – the summer fevers in those wet and swampy places were death to me. We agreed, however, that when the winter returned I would return with it, to explain our work to the Pope... and to his clergy.[10]

Other methods of writing down music had been used for at least a century before this, but by signs placed above the words, they could only serve as a reminder of what the singer already knew. Guido, however, put the signs (the neumes) on parallel lines representing certain notes of the mode, the signs then standing for actual notes. Sometimes for additional help the lines were colour-coded; yellow or green for the note C, red for F.

There was no indication of the relative duration of the notes (there are therefore widely differing schools of thought on the performance of the chant), but even so, the basis of modern notation had been laid down.

Guido also invented the first solmisation method (a sol-fa system) to help his choirboys to distinguish the tones and semitones of which the modes are constructed. One key to his method was a hymn in praise of St John, *Ut queant laxis*, which by good fortune began each line on a new note of an ascending scale. The syllables sung at the beginnings of the lines could be separated from the hymn and made to represent each note of the scale, as Example 10 makes clear.

UT que-ant la-xis   RE-so-na-re fi-bris   MI-ra ge-sto-rum   FA-mu-li tu-o-rum

SOL-ve pol-lu-ti   LA-bi-i re-a-tum,   Sanc-te Jo-an-nes.

EXAMPLE 10

The importance of the development of notation cannot be stressed too strongly, for it allowed new types of music to be created which would have been quite out of the reach of traditions where music was passed on by ear. Up to this time, Christian music was, like a folk tradition, bound to change as it was passed on and interpreted afresh by a new generation. But music written down was music fixed, locked, as it were, into a certain shape. Finally, the composer could put his name to the manuscript and become associated with it even long after his death.

Until notation arrived, only a few composers of Christian music were known, but very gradually from that time on, more individuals were to become identified with their music and today, 900 years later, they are extolled as 'artists', as spokespeople for their culture, expecting recognition and dues from society. The process of this change was slow, but it gradually created in the West a unique musical tradition. It brought rich blessings to Christian worship and later created the art-form now called 'classical music', but at the same time it has been controversial and divisive.

A few people have realised that the invention of musical notation brings curses as well as blessings. For example, composers over the centuries have become more and more precise in their requirements, first finding ways to indicate the length of notes, then specifying their medium (voice or various instruments), then their loudness and speed of execution, and most recently the phrasing and articulation. But performers have in turn been given less and less room to be creative and to make their own decisions in these areas. Similarly, Balbulus' addition of words to the *jubilus* in the Alleluia allowed him to regain control of his memory, but only at the expense of altering the very nature of the *jubilus* itself.

Thus for every gain, which the present post-industrial society usually regards as an 'improvement', there is usually a loss. What Socrates was once reported to have said about the invention of the alphabet might equally well apply to the adoption of musical notation:

> This discovery... will create forgetfulness in the learner's souls, because they will not use their memories; they will trust to the external written characters and not remember of themselves. The specific which you have discovered is an aid not to memory but to recollection, and gives... only the semblance of truth; they will hear much and learn nothing; they will appear to know much and will generally know nothing; they will be tiresome company, for they will seem wise without being wise.[11]

Notes

1. Quoted in P. Weiss and R. Taruskin, *Music in the Western World*, London, 1984, p. 41.

2. The highly effective techniques used in early Christian times to marshall the brain's huge potential for memorisation are described in F. Yates, *The Art of Memory*, Harmondsworth, 1969.

3. 1 Corinthians 12:10.

4. Augustine, *Ennarrationes in Psalmos* 32 and 99, quoted in J. McKinnon, *Music in Early Christian Literature*, Cambridge, 1987, pp. 157 and 158.

5. Quoted in Weiss and Taruskin, p. 46.

6. From a troped Kyrie from Salisbury Cathedral, and quoted in W.T. Marrocco and N. Sandon, *Medieval Music*, Oxford, 1977, p. 29.

7. See W. Smoldon, *The Music of the Medieval Church Dramas*, Oxford, 1980, p. 217.

8. Quotations in translation from W.L. Smoldon and D. Wulstan, editors, *The Play of Daniel*, Plainsong and Medieval Music Society, 1976.

9. See J.E. Stevens, *Words and Music in the Middle Ages*, Cambridge, 1986, chapter 9.

10. Quoted more fully in Weiss and Taruskin, p. 51.

11. Quoted in H. Cole, *Sounds and Signs*, Oxford, 1974, p. 149.

Chapter 8

From Gregorian Chant to Polyphony

For the first eight hundred years of Christian worship the musical vehicle for the liturgy was melody. It might take the form of a cantillated prayer of extreme simplicity or of an ornate Gradual for a solemn occasion. But whatever its complexity, monody – the single line of melody untainted by any accompaniment – was the most perfect and satisfying symbol for the unity of Christian believers. It was the advent of notation that allowed polyphony – many melodies together – to develop, in directions that have since made Western music unique.

When buildings are constructed on land that is plentiful, the area they occupy is not a critical factor in their design, and conurbations can be made up of low-storey houses spreading outwards from a centre. But as soon as space becomes restricted, then the cost of land rises and economics dictate that buildings must become taller if housing expansion is to continue. So it was with Gregorian chant. The limits of human endurance meant that solemn chant had developed to its greatest practical length. But a continuing desire for its adornment on special occasions led musicians to consider embellishing the chant in another way altogether: by singing different melodies simultaneously.

The first steps towards a new concept of singing, known as *organum*, came mostly from France. For a long time France had favoured a special quality of ceremony in worship. The choir at the Abbey of St Martial at Limoges, for instance, gradually took to singing certain items of the Mass by splitting the choir into parts, one group singing the original chant and others singing four or five or eight notes below. This provided a simple method of introducing a further degree of decoration into the chant, but one which nonetheless needed no writing down.

Other possibilities were explored too, especially those which allowed the two parts to become more independent. This freer type of *organum* required one part to sing the original chant and a second line to supply a more florid part against it. One of the most valuable collections of these two-part pieces, the Winchester Troper, was compiled during the tenth and eleventh centuries at Winchester Cathedral in southern England. This precious manuscript exemplifies the different sorts of troping (interpolations and additions to the chant) as well as the two-part 'florid' *organum*.

The beginnings of polyphony

The great Cathedral of Notre Dame is perhaps the best known of all Gothic buildings. Considering its immense size and complexity, it was built with considerable speed between 1163 and 1250, the bulk of it being complete by 1200. The creation of such a magnificent structure is evidence that France was beginning to enjoy a period of stability and affluence, a country in whose towns culture and learning could flourish as never before. During the building of the new cathedral, composers working at its music school were notating a type of *organum* more lavishly decorated than anything yet heard.

An anonymous treatise reveals the names of two famous composers from Notre Dame at this period, both canons at the cathedral:

> Léonin was the best composer of *organum*. He wrote the *Great Book of Organum*, for Mass and Office, to augment the Divine Service. This book was used until the time of the great Perotin, who shortened it and rewrote many sections in a better way... with the most ample embellishments of harmonic art.[1]

This once again draws attention to the continuing delight of Christians in elaborating the liturgy, and luckily the Great Book itself survives. Corroborative evidence shows that the florid *vox organalis* added to the chant was sometimes improvised from a number of stock musical phrases. Certainly the special expertise of the musicians was rewarded accordingly:

> And to each clerk of the choir who will attend Mass, two deniers, and to the four clerks who will sing the Alleluia in *organum*, six deniers...[2]

As in the music of the Winchester Troper, Léonin's pieces (compiled between about 1150 and 1170) supplied an extra vocal line. This was added to sections of chants which in themselves were already decorative – such as Graduals or Alleluias at Mass or Responsorial chants at Matins.

The extra line that Léonin added (called the *duplum* or second part) needed considerable singing skill. It had to be sung quite fast, not least because as many as forty notes of the *duplum* fitted to just one of the original chant. As a result, some parts of the chant became greatly stretched out, with its singers spending perhaps twenty seconds or half a minute on a single note. The words, of course, progressed even more slowly. No wonder then that Perotin, Léonin's successor, shortened parts of these compositions. At the same time he enriched the harmony still further by adding new voice-parts: a *triplum* (third part) and sometimes even a *quadruplum* (fourth part). The independence of the vocal lines can now properly be called polyphony.

Another feature of this remarkable music was the presence of a regular pulse in triple time. The 'perfection' of the number three was inherent in the medieval world-view. As the theorist Jean de Muris wrote in 1319:

> That all perfection lies in the ternary number is clear from a hundred comparisons. In God, who is perfection itself, there is singleness in substance, but threeness in persons; He is three in one and one in three. Moreover: [there are]... in individuals generation, corruption and substance; in finite time-spans beginning, middle and end; in every curable disease onset, crisis and decline. Three is the first odd number and the first prime number. It is not two lines but three that can enclose a surface. The triangle is the first regular polygon...[3]

Not only does a triple metre demand that notes should relate to each other in their length (some being twice or three times the duration of others) but the very complexity of the Notre Dame organum necessitated a system for indicating the resulting rhythms as well as the pitches, in order that voices could remain synchronised.[4] This was achieved by a method extended, typically enough, from Ancient Greek practice. Rhythms were adapted from those of Greek or Latin poetry, which are made up of groupings of simple patterns called 'feet'. The six patterns (called modes, signifying 'ways' or 'manners') used by earlier polyphonic composers are shown in the table on the following page.

The rhythmic feet were signified by the systematic grouping or bunching-up of notes in neumes. When later composers wished to break free from these simple rhythms, further symbols and rules had to be created, resulting in an evolving and complex system of notation.

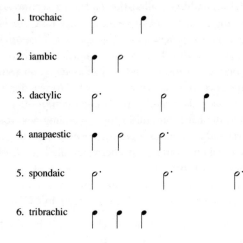

The startling effect of the choir suddenly changing from the lone and sinuous melody of the chant to three- or even four-part music did not please everyone. There are records of an increasing number of complaints from churchmen of this elaborate music. John of Salisbury, a contemporary of Perotin, wrote a particularly vitriolic criticism:

> Music sullies the Divine Service, for in the very sight of God, in the sacred recesses of the sanctuary itself, the singers attempt, with the lewdness of a lascivious singing voice and a singularly foppish manner, to feminise all their spellbound little followers with the girlish way they render the notes and end the phrases. Could you hear the effete emotings of their before-singing and their after-singing, their in-between singing and their ill-advised singing, you would think it an ensemble of sirens, not of men… Indeed when such practices go too far, they can more easily occasion titillation between the legs than a sense of devotion in the brain.[5]

But such criticism cannot have represented the majority in the liturgical corridors of power, as the practice quickly spread to a number of monasteries and cathedral churches across Europe.

The motet

Where the original plainsong melody used a *melisma* – a number of notes sung to one syllable – the composers of Notre Dame felt it appropriate in their *organum* settings to make the chant move along faster and in rhythm. Strange though it may seem, they took to writing these sections (called *clausulae*) separately from the main piece, so that one could be substituted for another, like engine spare parts.

Before long, these sections were soon being performed as separate pieces in their own right. What is more, composers started to add completely new sets of words to the upper parts (yet another example of troping), creating what they called a 'motet', that is, a piece with words to the added lines (from the French *mot*, meaning 'word').

The result is the most sophisticated musical form known to the Middle Ages, a piece in two, three or even four parts, whose foundation (the so-called *tenor*) is a fragment of chant, snipped out, as it were, from the middle of a traditional melody. The tenor had a regular pulse imposed on it, while around it were added between one and three freely-composed voice-parts with new texts. By this means it was perfectly possible for up to four different sets of words to be sung together. Example 11 gives the opening of a three-part motet found in both the Montpellier and Bamberg codices, important manuscripts from the late thirteenth century. The rhythm is mostly trochaic.

Motet technique was developed in a number of ways in the thirteenth century, which were not by any means always pleasing to the church. Such pieces became popular for secular ceremonies (at banquets for instance) and popular tunes would be incorporated in them. Some of these found their way back into church motets, and Pope John XXII in 1323 was compelled to issue a Papal bull, in which he made some very significant complaints:

Certain disciples of the new school... prefer to devise new methods of their own rather than to sing in the old way. Therefore the music of the Divine Office is disturbed with these notes of quick duration. Moreover, they... deprave it with discants and sometimes pad out the music with upper parts made out of profane songs. The result is that they often seem to be losing sight of the fundamental sources of our melodies in the Antiphoner and Gradual... The consequence of all this is that devotion, the true aim of all worship, is neglected, and wantonness, which ought to be shunned, increases. We hasten to forbid these methods...[6]

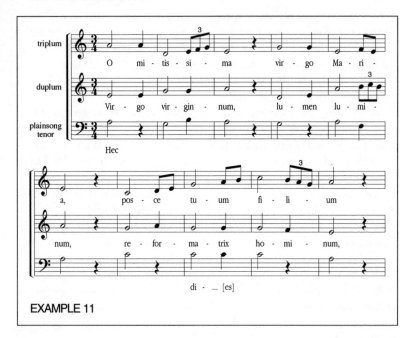

EXAMPLE 11

The conductus

Not all medieval part-music had the complex structure of the motet, for the church initiated another type of polyphony in its continuing pursuit of the 'embellishment of harmonic art'. During the twelfth century it became customary in services of solemnity to lead the lesson-reader to the lectern with a short song called a *conductus* (from the Latin *conducere*, to lead). The *conductus* of Example 12 dates from the mid-twelfth century. The words of the last verse read: 'Clean and pure therefore let this gathering be that hears and perceives what the lesson says.'

Once again, more complex and lengthy chants of this processional type developed as musicians delighted in the addition of as many as three extra parts against the original. The result was a piece of music newly composed in

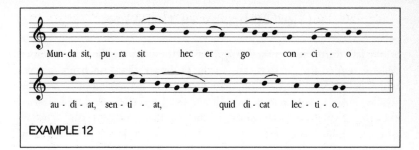

Mun-da sit, pu-ra sit   hec er - go   con-ci - o

au-di-at, sen-ti-at,   quid di-cat   lec-ti-o.

EXAMPLE 12

all parts (not usually based on traditional chant or other tunes) and with all voices singing the same text.

Franco of Cologne, a composer and theorist of the later thirteenth century, described how such pieces were written:

> He who wants to write a *conductus* should first invent as beautiful a melody as he can, then using it as a *tenor* is used in writing discant [in other words, writing another melody against it, the *tenor* being the original 'beautiful melody']. He who wishes to construct a third part [*triplum*] ought to have the other two in mind, so that when the *triplum* is discordant with the *tenor*, it will not be discordant with the discant, and vice versa.[7]

This method of composition is very different from classical music of the last few hundred years. If a choir sings a four-part hymn or anthem, for instance, all voices fill in a particular harmony. If one is missing, or breaks down, the effect on the composer's intentions is probably fatal. But in medieval times polyphonic music was perceived as a number of layers. The composing process began with the *tenor*, then the *discant* or *duplum*, then the *triplum*, then the *quadruplum* – as many layers as circumstances required. A composer (like Perotin) would feel quite at liberty to add another layer to pre-existing music, or to perform a piece with one of the upper layers missing. Such methods would produce truly appalling results if applied to classical music, but make good sense in the field of Western popular music today. In jazz especially, the 'tenor', in the form of the harmonic skeleton of popular song 'standards', is common property, to be surrounded by other musical lines depending on the occasion.

Like the motets, medieval songs in *conductus* style became fashionable outside the church as well as within it and courtly musicians used the idiom to create part-songs about the Crusades, about politics and about love.

The Ordinary of the Mass

In the late thirteenth century, polyphonic settings during the celebration of Mass extended for the first time to the Ordinary, those unchanging texts which had at one time been opportunities for the expression of faith of the whole Christian community. In well-endowed cathedrals and monasteries the Ordinary texts were left more and more to the choir, who sang on behalf of those present (and perhaps even of those absent). It is a poignant irony that much of the outstanding Christian music of the Middle Ages, and the superb cathedrals that echoed to it, can be understood as monuments to the vaingloriousness of the church during this period.

Rich church: poor people

The evolution of chant into a complex art-form continues to fascinate musicians, not just on account of the music's inherent beauties but also because it lays the foundations for Western art-music. But this same evolution put most Christian music far beyond the grasp of the common people of its time. Their own musical expression of faith was only to be heard outside the walls of church and cathedral. Feast-days, for instance, gave opportunities for great processions accompanied by rough-hewn music, such as the immensely popular *laude spirituale* (spiritual praises) of the later Middle Ages. Such colourful events have their close parallels in Italy, Spain and South America today.

Folk-music like the *laude* was the chief Christian expression of a people barely able to find the basic necessities of life. The masses also desperately lacked education and spiritual guidance to rescue them from a faith riddled with superstition. In these fundamental needs of body and soul they were largely disregarded by the church.

Even provisions to educate the local parish priest were almost non-existent. Complaints were heard from all quarters: the Bishop of Angers wrote in 1222 that his priests included:

> innumerable contemptible persons of abject life, utterly unworthy in learning and morals... from whose execrable lives and pernicious ignorance infinite scandals arise. The church sacraments are despised

by the laity, and in many districts the lay-folk hold the priests as vile and... despicable.[8]

But the church hierarchy was sufficiently élitist for the bishops themselves to be far above contradiction. The institution's enormous wealth was confined to a minority of powerful prelates, who were not ashamed to make their position in society clear by parading their affluence in public. Bishops travelled with mounted retinues of dozens. A maximum of such facilities was laid down by Walter, Archbishop of Canterbury in the mid-thirteenth century: an archbishop could have no more than fifty men and horses; bishops thirty; archdeacons seven, and no hounds or hawks. His edict was not adhered to.[9]

The church began to establish the tradition that forgiveness of sins could be bought. Friars would be permitted to sell 'indulgences' so that those who could afford them were given the reassurance that their journey to heaven would be made easier.

The Benedictine order became a travesty of its origins. Benedict's Rule of silence, of work on the land, of humble devotion with the minimum of material support was left far behind, far enough for the Cistercian order to be founded at the end of the eleventh century to re-establish these principles.

In 1338 there were ninety monks in the Benedictine monastery of Mont St Michel in Normandy. Of the monastic income of £9,000 a year, £1,700 was spent on food, £500 on clothing, £460 on repairs, £500 on taxes, £300 on lawsuits, £120 on fuel and £2,200 on wine.[10]

Worship in the great cathedrals and abbeys took place in the choir, a church within a church, sealed off by screens from the greater building. Ordinary people were generally only allowed into the nave, which was often used for trade, like an indoor market. The townsfolk had no place in the spiritual life of these great buildings, except that the acquisition of money lay behind many of the services held there. For those who were rich enough, a fee would pay for a commemorative Mass for a departed loved one or for a Mass for the benefit of one's own soul.

The life of Guillaume de Machaut illustrates well the blend of secular and sacred that was common in this period. Born in about 1300, after taking holy orders – joining the clergy – he was made a canon of Rheims and of St Quentin, attached to the cathedral. He had also, from 1323, been secretary to John of Luxembourg, King of Bohemia, who had taken him on his military campaigns all over Europe before Machaut became canon. King John was killed at Crecy in 1346 and from that time Machaut was patronised by the kings of France, Cyprus and Normandy, his fame as a poet and musician spreading throughout the European courts.

In spite of his holy orders and with a few notable exceptions, his creative energies were devoted to writing long, elegant and sophisticated love-poems, some of which he set to music. Some of the love-lyrics he wrote in his sixties were inspired by his relationship with a nineteen-year-old girl. The poetry of this 'jolly and worldly ecclesiastic' was known and admired by a younger contemporary of his, Geoffrey Chaucer (1340–1400).

Apart from some motets with sacred texts, Machaut's outstanding music for the church was his *Messe de Notre Dame,* a comprehensive setting of the Ordinary of the Mass for four voices. Settings of the Ordinary already existed by this time, but they seem to be compilations of pieces from various sources and not always complete. His setting is ornate and written with extreme care and great creative energy – it was probably created for some special occasion. Up to the eighteenth century, a commemorative brass could be found in Rheims cathedral, which well illustrates common practice:

> Guillaume de Machaut and his brother Jean
> Are joined in this harmonious place as cup to mouth.
> Their memorial is, according their wish,
> That the prayer for the dead, on every Saturday,
> For their souls and those of their friends,
> May be said by a priest about to celebrate faithfully,
> At the altar by the
> Roella, a mass which is to be sung…
> We have set aside money…
> For payment for the said mass and in order to nourish,
> By that means, those present and diligently attending.
> These brothers may the Lord save, who takes all sin away.[11]

It is possible that Guillaume intended his own music to be sung at the Saturday masses he founded, at least on occasion.

Machaut's Mass is the first known setting of the type that countless composers have written since, consisting of a *Kyrie, Gloria, Credo, Sanctus, Agnus Dei* and a final *Ite, Missa Est.* Machaut uses the composing techniques of both motet and conductus, moving from music of intellectual sophistication and artistry (such as the *Amen* to the *Credo*) to a simpler style that suggests that he may have taken some heed of Pope John XXII's Bull of a few years earlier. As a monument to the Middle Ages' expression of spiritual truth, it is outstanding.

Notes

1. Anonymous IV, quoted in the *Pelican History of Music*, vol. 1, London, 1982, p. 224.

2. Quoted in C. Wright, *Music and Ceremony at Notre Dame of Paris, 500–1550*, Cambridge, 1989, p. 339.

3. Quoted in P. Weiss and R. Taruskin, *Music in the Western World*, London, 1984, p. 69.

4. The complexities of modal rhythmic notation are described in W. Apel, *The Notation of Polyphonic Music*, Cambridge, Mass., 5th edition, 1961.

5. Quoted in Weiss and Taruskin, p. 62.

6. Quoted in Weiss and Taruskin, p. 71.

7. Franco of Cologne, *Ars Mensurabilis Musicae*, chapter 11. Further extracts from this important treatise can be found in O. Strunk, *Source Readings in Music History*, New York, 1996, pp. 139–59.

8. P.B. Johnson, *A History of Christianity*, London, 1976, p. 228.

9. Johnson, p. 213.

10. Johnson, p. 238.

11. Quoted in D. Leech-Wilkinson, *Machaut's Mass*, Oxford, 1990, pp. 7–13.

Chapter 9

Wycliffe's Challenge to the Church

Behind the Christian music of the Middle Ages lie spiritual and musical developments in sharp contrast. The musical changes were creative, stimulating and positive, but they occurred alongside a depressing spiritual decline.

On the one hand, elaboration of the liturgy led Christian music to a unique exploration of the rich and exciting world of polyphony, culminating in the splendour of Machaut's Mass. The contrasting spiritual deterioration on the other hand was brought into sharpest focus by Machaut's contemporary, John Wycliffe, an Oxford scholar and theologian who offered the most vigorous challenge to the abuses of the Roman Church.

Considering the breadth of Wycliffe's criticism, it seems surprising that he died in his own parish of Lutterworth in Leicestershire with his head still on his shoulders (in 1384). He condemned at every opportunity the church's temporal riches, which he saw as an effective stumbling-block to any return to Christ-like humility. He continually pointed out that the Gospels provided no justification for the church's pride and materialism and that it was the duty of the secular powers to take ecclesiastical reform into their own hands.

He condemned the sale of indulgences, scorned the doctrine of transubstantiation (by which the church taught that at the Eucharist the real nature or 'substance' of the bread and wine changed into Christ's body and blood, though their outward appearance remained the same) and held that the doctrine of papal supremacy was to be doubted. The pope's position on the latter point was already undermined by the presence, for most of that century, of two rival popes, at Rome and Avignon.

Above all, Wycliffe believed that everyone had a right to read and hear the Bible in his or her native tongue and he duly translated the Bible into English for the purpose. From Wycliffe's few words about Christian music, it is clear that he thought of its elaborate traditions as divisive and vainglorious:

> In the old days, men sang songs of mourning when they were in prison, in order to teach the Gospel, to put away idleness, and to be occupied in a useful way for the time. But those songs and ours do not agree, for ours invite jollity and pride, and theirs lead to mourning and to dwelling longer on God's Law. A short time later vain tricks began to be employed – *discant, contre* notes, *organum* and *hoquetus*[1] …which stimulate vain men more to dancing than to mourning… When there are forty or fifty in a choir [sic!], three or four proud and lecherous rascals perform the most devout service with flourishes so that no-one can hear the words, and all the others are dumb and watch them like fools.[2]

With his observation that the music is too complex for the words to be heard, Wycliffe strikes at the heart of the musical dilemma, a problem which he saw as part of the wider issue of the travesty of the Christian gospel. For the first time the questions which re-echo down to the present day are firmly raised: Can art-music have a place in Christian music? Is ornate choral music inherently unhelpful to Christian worship, or did Wycliffe only condemn it through its association with a distorted gospel? Can high-art music enhance the church's offering of praise to God, or must music always remain the servant of the ordinary worshipper? Within 150 years, the Western church was to be split to its foundations over these issues.

Notes

1. *Hoquetus* was the practice of sharing out short phrases or single notes of melody between two players or singers. The word is related to 'hiccup'.

2. J. Wycliffe, pamphlet, 'Of feyned contemplative lif, of songe, and worldly bisynesse of Prestis, etc.', in F.D. Matthew, *The English Works of Wyclif hitherto unprinted*, Early English Text Society, Vol. 74, 1902.

PART 2

Renaissance and Reformation

1400–1600

Chapter 10

Luther and the Reformation

In fifteenth-century Italy scholars and educated people were increasingly fascinated by the ancient civilisations of Greece and Rome. More ancient manuscripts of literature and philosophy of the 'classical' era were discovered, translated and circulated, such as the important first-century treatise on rhetoric by Quintilian: *Institutio Oratoria*. An awareness grew that before the invasions of the Goths in the fifth century, Rome had been the centre of a civilisation unparalleled in the world. By comparison, the art and culture of medieval Italy was seen to be undistinguished; the cultural centres of Italy should be restored to their former glory.

Artists, sculptors and architects developed an increasing respect for the achievements of the classical age, whose work was still to be seen all around them. The perfection of the human form in Greek sculpture, for instance, demonstrated an impressive knowledge of anatomy which artists were determined to rediscover. Architects not only made detailed mathematical studies of classical buildings, but became fascinated by the theory and philosophy behind their design. The ancient Roman architect Vitruvius, for instance, had proposed that the proportions of the human frame should act as the basis of proportioning buildings, an idea seized upon by Renaissance architects. Painters sought ways of becoming more persuasive in their biblical story telling, abandoning the two-dimensional and symbolic style of the Middle Ages for a new realism, and conveying as compellingly as possible the human drama of the scene and the movements and emotions of the characters. A true understanding of perspective became a vital technique.

In short, humankind – the body, the mind and the soul – became the centre of enquiry. This was not yet an arrogant humanism usurping God's 'everlasting power and deity', but an awareness that human beings were the prime evidence of God's creativity, even his greatest creation. As Psalm 8 puts it:

You have made him little less than a god,
you have crowned him with glory and splendour,
made him lord over the works of your hands,
set all things under his feet.

Unlike painting, sculpture and architecture, changes in musical outlook were not as obvious or as rapidly adopted. Perhaps it was because musicians were unable to enjoy firsthand experience of the music of the ancient Greeks. Commentaries and theoretical treatises were their only contact with the music of the classical world. Nonetheless, medieval principles of composition gradually changed and polyphonic music became more integrated. Layers of parts could not be added or subtracted at will. Very gradually, too, a sense of harmonic progression developed which was the means for music to become a persuasive and rhetorical art, influencing the emotions as much as the mind.

This shift in perspective is summarised in the word 'Renaissance' – rebirth – and it had profound implications for everyone, not merely for theologians and scholars, for alongside it began a Christian Reformation affecting the whole of Europe. By the beginning of the sixteenth century the church, its music and liturgy, was on the brink of profound transformation.

The seeds of dissent

Wycliffe's bitter complaints were followed by others after his death in 1384. But the church was still powerful enough to exercise an effective control over doctrine and forms of worship. There were regional differences of style and emphasis, but they were more like differing dialects than distinct languages. All in all, there was a megalithic unity to Western Christendom which was to remain intact for some time to come.

A reformation in Bohemia (now part of the Czech Republic) led by Jan Hus (c. 1369–1415) and directly inspired by Wycliffe's writings was crushed by the execution of Hus himself. Nevertheless, there is evidence of the Lollards, an English Wycliffian sect, throughout the fifteenth century. Meanwhile, the renaissance of classical learning enabled Christians such as Desiderius Erasmus (c. 1466–1535) to produce new and authoritative translations into English of early Christian writings, particularly the New Testament. These and other reforming movements throughout the fifteenth century increased the number of intellectuals among the secular authorities, eager and ready for reform.

Rebellion by the peasantry, on the other hand, was not the way forward. The violence with which both the English Peasants' Revolt (1381) and the German Peasants' March were crushed proved that both church and secular authorities were united against them. Reform of the church had to come from within.

The dissension which had been simmering for so long finally erupted with the Reformation of the early sixteenth century in which the Christian faith was split into a number of strands. In spite of some genuine desire to maintain unity, Christianity suffered its second fundamental schism, this time into several fragments, as opposed to the earlier division into the two great strands of East and West (see chapter 27).

Martin Luther

Luther, an Augustinian monk of Wittenburg, had the dogged determination and the conviction to challenge the Roman Church head on. His attack initially took the form of the famous ninety-five theses, which he posted on the door of the church at Wittenburg Castle on 31 October 1517. This might have been of merely local interest had it not been for the invention of printing. Printed pamphlets allowed news to spread with lightning speed. By this means Luther's public protest had travelled the whole of Europe within a month and found widespread support. He followed up his theses with the printing and distribution of hundreds of tracts over the next three years.

He was protected from being burned as a heretic by Frederick the Wise, founder of the university at which Luther was professor of theology, but in 1521 the emperor, Charles V, summoned him to justify himself. In a letter Luther described the proceedings succinctly:

> All they said was: 'Are these books yours?' 'Yes.' 'Will you recant?' 'No.' 'Then get out.'[1]

After the excommunication which followed, Luther was given further protection by Frederick and took the opportunity to write more pamphlets, to begin a German translation of the New Testament (a task for which he was well qualified) and to consider new forms of worship. An increasing number of German states were prepared to allow their churches to adopt his reforms and the movement was expanding rapidly.

Luther's challenges to the church included all those of Wycliffe – the moral need for the church to put its own house in order, the right of every person to read the Bible for themselves, the condemnation of the sale of indulgences – but hinged on one vital point. His reading of the apostle Paul and of Augustine of Hippo, and above all, his own personal experience, convinced him utterly that no one could earn righteousness in God's sight; faith in Christ and repentance were the only route. Therefore indulgences, pilgrimages, monastic orders, as ways of buying or earning one's way into God's favour, were utterly unacceptable, spurious inventions of the church to line its coffers.

Such a message earned him support from the secular powers, for it would inevitably lead to a transfer of wealth from church to state. But Luther's desire for change was not motivated by politics but by sincere Christian conviction and the consequence of a balanced spiritual and family life.

Luther's experience as an Augustinian monk had taught him the value of a devotional life of prayer and also gave him a deep love of music. Not only was he profoundly familiar with the traditional Gregorian chant but his training as a singer and lutenist enabled him to compose adequately in the polyphonic style of the times. In common with the ancient Greeks, he knew the power of music, for good and ill:

> Next to the Word of God, music deserves the highest praise. She is a mistress and governess of those human emotions… which control men or more often overwhelm them… Whether you wish to comfort the sad, to subdue frivolity, to encourage the despairing, to humble the proud, to calm the passionate, or to appease those full of hate… what more effective means than music could you find?[2]

Here he appears to be stressing less the symbolic aspect of music, characteristic of the Middle Ages, and more the human aspects of the art and its effects, good and bad, on the emotions. In this respect Luther was a product of the Renaissance.

Luther's fundamental desire that Christians should worship God in sincerity and with understanding did not mean that he wished to abandon the Latin Mass. On the contrary, he suggested a double solution to the problem of congregational involvement, through the Formula Missae of 1523 and the German Mass of 1526.

The Latin Mass, he suggested, should be for the use of cathedrals and abbeys where such solemnity was appropriate and where the majority of the participants understood the language. The German Mass, on the other hand, was for the benefit of the local parish church, where songs, readings and prayers should be in a language that everyone could understand. In practice and after some years of experiment, many services were conducted in a mixture of both languages, with musical settings in one or the other, even alternating verses of hymns in Latin and German. Scripture readings might be in one tongue and repeated immediately in the other.

The more formal type of Lutheran Mass was not at all unlike the Roman Mass in the outline given in chapter 6. Its musical basis was still that of chant. Luther suggested that polyphonic music could adorn certain parts of the liturgy as well as much of the ceremonial, including the vestments, the candles, even the elevation of the host (showing the bread and wine to the people just before Communion). But there was a vital difference: this was a corporate act, shared by the congregation. No Christians were barred from entering, and both bread and wine were offered to everyone. Luther emphasised congregational participation in the music, too. He suggested including German songs at certain points. He also encouraged the use of the Daily Office – particularly the Greater Hours of Vespers, Compline and Matins – and that all 150 psalms be 'preserved in the ears of the church'.[3]

Reacting against centuries of tradition, Luther did not insist that a rigid liturgical rule had to be followed: 'It is not necessary... that ceremonies, instituted by men, should be observed uniformly in all places.'[4] He was anxious and insistent that his ideas should not become sectarian; his desire was for reform, not schism. Unfortunately, as a study of J.S. Bach will show, this lack of firm edicts allowed the Lutheran movement later to lose its clear sense of direction.

Luther's musical ideas were most striking in the *Deutsche Messe*, which includes musical examples of the kind of German singing he hoped to encourage. Once more his starting-point was the church's long-standing musical traditions. He and his helpers set about translating the Latin texts into German while carefully and sensitively remoulding the tunes so that they could fit the different stress-patterns of the German language. Usually this meant simplifying the chant and making it more direct and strong. Latin hymns in the Ambrosian style were the easiest to transform, but chants for the Ordinary of the Mass were adapted to German, the greater flexibility of chant and Latin text making the task rather more involved.

Luther also used simple melodies familiar to ordinary people – Latin or German devotional songs, school songs, children's songs, folk-songs or carols. A number of these melodies have since spread widely through the Christian world – *Resonet in Laudibus (Joseph lieber, Joseph mein), Quem Pastores Laudavere* and *In Dulci Jubilo* are three examples. Words were sometimes slightly altered (as in the latter, to remove an unacceptable emphasis on the Virgin Mary) or completely rewritten. For example the tune to the love-song *Innsbruck ich muss dich lassen* – 'Innsbruck I must leave you' – was used for countless hymns, the earliest being *O Welt, ich muss dich lassen* – 'O world, I must leave you'. This melody can be found at several points in J.S. Bach's *St Matthew Passion*.

Luther also wrote a number of hymns himself, both words and melody. The most famous must be *Ein' feste Burg* – 'A safe stronghold'. Its original rhythmic scheme makes it more subtle and lively than the version usually sung today. Example 13 is a copy of this hymn in a contemporary hand.

EXAMPLE 13

Not only did Luther recognise the power of music as an aid to devotion, to enhance and to elevate worship, but he was also keenly aware of the need to educate the younger generations into Christian ways. Music had a part to play here too. Young people, he believed, could be encouraged to turn away from music with bad associations by acquaintance with music of a more positive kind:

> And you, my young friend, let this noble, wholesome and cheerful creation of God [i.e. music] be commended to you. By it you may escape shameful desires and bad company. At the same time you may by this creation accustom yourself to recognise and praise the Creator. Take special care to shun perverted minds who prostitute this lovely gift of nature and of art with their erotic rantings...[5]

This did not necessarily mean that the two musics, sacred and profane, had to be entirely separate (as they were for most of the Roman Church's history), but that the profane could be made sacred by encouraging new and more edifying associations. Some four-part Christian songs published in 1571 clearly had secular origins:

> Street songs, knightly and miners' songs, changed in a Christian, moral and ethical manner, in order that the evil, vexatious melodies, the useless and shameful songs to be sung in the streets, fields, houses, and elsewhere, may lose their bad effects if they can have good, useful Christian texts and words.[6]

Not only was it vital for Reformers to make the Bible available in the language of the people, but there was also a ready market for Christian songs in everyday language, even though books would have been too expensive for many parishioners to own.

Luther insisted that the songs should be learned by heart if at all possible. For this purpose, schools attached to the Lutheran churches taught their boys (girls were not part of the educational system!) to lead the congregational singing, at the same time giving the young people a deep familiarity with these new Christian songs.

For the first five years after the Ninety-five Theses there was no music written specifically for the Protestant movement. But with the appearance of Luther's liturgical reforms there began a steady stream of books – the *Etlich Christlich Lieder* (published in Nuremberg, 1524), *Enchiridion geistlicher Gesenge* (Leipzig, 1529), *Geistliche Lieder* (Wittenberg, 1533), *Geystliche Lieder* (Babst in Leipzig, 1545) and many more.[7]

The continuing links with Gregorian chant are the key to understanding how this music was sung. In spite of ornate polyphonic pieces for choir, the basis for the Roman liturgy was still unison singing, emphatically without accompaniment. Organs were being built into many churches for the first time in the fifteenth century, but they made a different contribution to the liturgy from what most people expect today.

There was certainly no feeling that congregations needed the support of an organ in singing of any kind. They and the choir were perfectly capable of enjoying a first-rate tune without the help of any supporting harmony, so most of the early song-collections simply print the melody. It may therefore appear puzzling that Luther's very first publication of songs (the *Neue geistliche Gesänge* of 1523) is in four-part harmony. The explanation for this lies in its presentation, not as a modern hymn-book, with all the harmony parts conveniently laid out for the organist, but as a set of four part-books, each for the use of one voice or group of voices. This book was therefore probably to popularise Luther's music among students and people with a reasonable education.

Musical skills and theory were part of a good education no matter what profession one might enter; some musical accomplishment was an assumed part of a good upbringing. In this era of passive television-watching it may be hard to imagine how in Luther's time students would gather round a table to sing in harmony from part-books just for amusement. The subject matter of these songs was not much more sophisticated than those of the pop world today, so this was another important area where Christian praise could do battle with more worldly pursuits.

In church, the congregation would sing their songs in unison and unaccompanied. The choir, however, might well have been capable of singing in four parts, in which case it often took the responsibility of giving the people a rest and singing every other verse for them. The song would therefore be changing from harmony to unison and back again and alternating between congregation and choir.

The organ (and maybe other instruments if available) was used to support the choir, doubling the voice-parts for security, but it would have been considered quite illogical for the instrument to play parts against the firm unison line of congregational singing. This modern usage only became accepted during the seventeenth century.

The Lutheran reforms spread quickly across Europe, east and north. Lutheran songbooks were published in Bohemia and in Holland, Denmark and Sweden only a few years after their first appearance in Germany. From the seventeenth century onwards, Lutheran immigrants took their faith even further, to the New World. The characteristic musical developments of these communities are discussed in Part 7.

Notes

1. Quoted in O. Chadwick, *The Reformation*, Harmondsworth, 1972, p. 56.

2. Quoted in F. Blume, *Protestant Church Music*, London, 1975, p. 10.

3. For further details of Luther's intentions, see C. Halter and C. Schalk, *A Handbook of Church Music*, St Louis, 1978, chapter 2.

4. Quoted in Halter and Schalk, p. 64.

5. Blume, p. 10.

6. Blume, footnote to p. 33.

7. All these have been published in facsimile this century, at Kassel (1957), Leipzig (1914), Kassel (1954), and Kessel (1929) respectively. See Blume, p. 760.

Chapter 11

The Swiss Reformers – The Calvinist Tradition

Ulrich Zwingli

After Luther, the other great force in the Reformation of Europe came from Switzerland, firstly from Zürich, where in 1518 Zwingli was made people's priest at the cathedral, and then from Geneva through Calvin.

One of the great tragedies of this period of turmoil and questioning is that the great visionaries of Christian reform could not agree on essential matters of doctrine. Instead, they created distinct sects, constantly vilifying and even slaughtering each other. The spirit of the Reformation certainly encouraged a large number of lunatic factions to spring up – Munzerites, Adamists, Devillers and Libertines, to name but a few. Some European towns viewed with alarm the presence of as many as twelve such sects in their midst. But much more regrettable was the fact that Luther and Zwingli met in 1530 and failed to agree on points of doctrine.

Were the bread and wine of the Eucharist literally changed into flesh and blood? Both found the notion abhorrent. But Luther was unable to accept Zwingli's (and later, Calvin's) position that the sacraments were only memorials – symbols of a greater truth. Both Luther and Calvin used the Bible as their authority and refused to give ground. The divisions went deeper, though. Luther believed that the society of which he was a part was still a Christian one. It certainly needed to experience repentance and to know justification by faith; it certainly needed a return to the true ways of Christ, but he saw himself as a reforming spirit within a unified world. So he was happy for the folk-melodies of that world to be reformed and redeemed for use in worship. Zwingli and Calvin held a different position. They understood the true church, defined by the most literal interpretation of the Bible, as being separate from the world. For them, that true church was the only church, and thus an entirely new beginning was needed.

The fact that Zwingli was a highly educated musician (apparently a talented instrumentalist) did not, as in Luther's case, lead to any kind of emphasis on music in worship. On the contrary, his musical experience concerned the sophisticated art-world of polyphony and he had little interest in the simpler fare of congregational singing. In any case, his sensitivity to music was overridden by other more pressing concerns. Eventually, the Christians of the Swiss cantons who adopted Zwingli's reforms and those staying loyal to Rome took to settling their differences by force; Zwingli died in a sectarian battle in 1531.

Jean Calvin

What Zwingli began in German-speaking Switzerland was developed in the French-speaking communities by the most imposing figure of reform, Jean Calvin. He was a French refugee who arrived in Geneva in 1536, the same year in which the city adopted Zwingli's reformed faith. Calvin, like Zwingli, saw the world divided into those destined to be saved and those destined for damnation. The Calvinists were therefore exclusive – they and only they were able to offer salvation.

Calvin, a highly-trained lawyer, established a comprehensive system of state government based on a number of biblical tenets. It was an enigmatic blend of compassion, democracy and harsh discipline. In Calvin's rule, the church leadership was elected by and from its congregations, without, of course, any reference to Rome. The pastorate was required to take its duties seriously, however, and church members would be visited periodically. If irregularities were noted – lapses of morals, superstitious practice, the use of Latin prayers, the visiting of taverns, dancing – then those concerned would be reprimanded in front of their congregation. Depending on the severity of the lapse, they might be banned from receiving communion or driven out of the church. In extreme cases they might be executed, on the authority of the Old Testament Books of the Law.

Calvin's deep suspicion of society at large led to an austerity in worship which excluded any possibility that art or artefacts could distract the people's attention. A Calvinist church was completely devoid of decoration; there were no pictures, vestments, candles or images of any kind. The pulpit, the source of God's Word and the only recognised authority for the elect, was placed at the centre.

In such surroundings the presence of music caused some misgivings. It was, of course, tainted by association with the unacceptable practices of the Roman Church or linked with singing and dancing. In the first case, one's soul was at risk; in the second, one's morals. None of Luther's redeeming of folk-melody would do – music had to be kept on the tightest rein.

As Calvin saw it, the New Testament scriptures only recognised psalms as material suitable for Christian song. Accordingly, the Calvinists absolutely forbade any texts to be sung in church except the Book of Psalms and one or two canticles. Furthermore, Calvin insisted on:

> simple and pure singing of the divine praises, forasmuch as where there is no meaning there is no edification. Let them come from heart and mouth, and in the vulgar tongue. Instrumental music was only tolerated in the time of the Law [the Old Testament] because of the people's infancy.[1]

Singing in harmony and the use of instruments of any kind were therefore expressly forbidden.

The Genevan Psalter

From this artistically barren landscape arose Calvin's great gift to worship. About 1550 Theodore de Beza (1519–1605) had finished translating all 150 psalms into French. A professional musician, Louis Bourgeois (about 1523–1600), was commissioned to set them to music. The result was the Genevan Psalter, completed in 1562.

Such a task might appear a simple one and the results of little interest. In reality, the Genevan Psalter had a profound influence on the Christian world. Paradoxically, the crippling musical restrictions under which Bourgeois had to work were beneficial. The very simplicity and directness of the tunes makes them strong and memorable. They do not have the rhythmic variety of the Lutheran melodies, nor do they ever set more than one note to a syllable (the more decorative elements of Gregorian chant can still be sensed in Lutheran song). Almost all the tunes use only two types of note, long and short. Dotted notes are very rare and lines inevitably begin and end with long notes. Example 14 from a precursor (1542) of the Genevan Psalter illustrates these qualities. With complete lack of harmonic support, this appears to be the musical equivalent of bread and water. But if music has to be this restricted, then the Genevan Psalter, like early Gregorian chant, cannot be bettered.

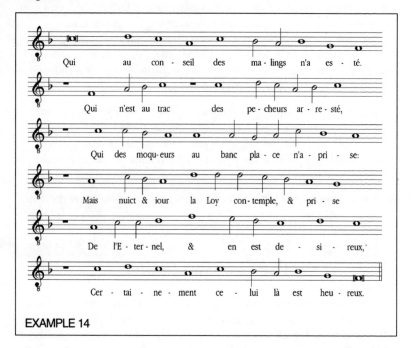

EXAMPLE 14

The tunes were a compilation from a number of sources, as were those of the Lutheran tradition. Some had their origins in Gregorian chant, a few from folk-melodies and some from Lutheran tunes, in spite of the fact that the Calvinists hated the Lutherans as much as they hated the Roman Catholics. Though the musical borrowings are not as easy to spot as those of Luther, it is encouraging to note that music can cross the highest barriers erected by human failings.

Calvin wanted first-rate melodies for his congregations. Music had the capacity *'d'esmouvoir et enflamber le coeur des hommes'* (to move and inflame the heart of humanity)[2] and therefore it should be used to praise God with the qualities of 'weight', 'modesty' and 'majesty' appropriate to such a task.

The impact of the Genevan Psalter in and even beyond the Reformed Christian world was immense. A great many polyphonic arrangements were made of it, many by the finest composers of the day. The composer Claude Goudimel (d. 1572), on the title page of his psalm-collection of 1565 explained that such songs were:

> non pas pour induire à les chanter en l'Eglise, mais pour s'esiouir en Dieu particulièrement ès maisons [not for leading the singing of the church, but for the glorifying of God specifically in the home].[3]

It was common practice for such vocal pieces to be played on instruments, or with instruments and voices mixed. They were also arranged for the popular combination of voice and lute, again for private devotions and therefore still within the realm of music for worship. Outstanding composers continued to make choral arrangements of the Genevan Psalter (Claude le Jeune, for instance) and the Psalter was translated into many languages, including Dutch, German and English before the end of the century. The Genevan Psalter has inspired countless other metrical settings and its melodies have invaded psalters and hymn-books all over the world.

Notes

1. See Calvin in translation in P. Weiss and R. Taruskin, *Music in the Western World*, London, 1984, pp. 107–109.

2. Calvini, *Opera Selecta*, 2:15.

3. Claude Goudimel, *Les Pseaumes mis en rime françoise par Clément Marot et Thide Bèze, mis en musique à quatre parties*, Jaqui, Geneva, 1565.

Chapter 12

The Reformation in England

It would be a mistake to imagine that the common people of the sixteenth century had any freedom of choice in matters of religion. On the continent of Europe that freedom could only be exercised by the rulers of the many small kingdoms into which much of it was divided. Whatever brand of Christianity the rulers adopted, their subjects had to follow, to the point of fighting in the sectarian battles with neighbouring states that happened to choose a different path. Even the aristocracy were by no means protected from trouble if they chose to swim against the tide.

The Anabaptists, members of the one reformed sect which consistently and quietly preached freedom of conscience in religion, were cruelly and inhumanly persecuted from all sides. Only the nobility of Poland made any significant efforts to keep the sectarian arguments peaceful.

Henry VIII and the break with Rome

The Reformation in the British Isles (not Scotland, since it was a separate kingdom) was not so much due to its ruler exercising his freedom of conscience, but rather precipitated by political necessity.

Henry VIII's divorce from Catherine of Aragon could only be achieved at the cost of a break with Rome. At first Henry simply envisaged that he himself would replace the pope as head of the church in England; he was not attracted by the Lutheran ideas of reform. A pile of Lutheran books was burnt outside Great St Mary's Church in Cambridge in 1520 and well after the Act of Supremacy of 1536, when Miles Coverdale published his *Goostly [Spiritual] Psalms and Spiritual Songs* in English, they were still being banned. Possibly the most drastic effect on Christian music during Henry VIII's reign was caused by the dissolution of the monasteries, some of which had maintained the Roman traditions of liturgy and music in splendour. A number of centres of Christian culture were spared, including cathedrals (thirteen of which had schools attached), the Chapel Royal at Windsor and the college foundations at Oxford, Cambridge, Winchester and Eton. Liturgical reforms did not entirely extinguish their medieval traditions, with the result that the style of worship in English cathedrals today has links with a much earlier past.

The reign of Edward VI (1547–52) began with further dissolutions of churches that supported 'vain opinions of purgatory and masses... to be done for them which be departed'.[1] Many of these churches had made considerable provision for music.[2]

All this was achieved with suffering, but with little bloodshed. But only a year after Cranmer's second and more radical version of the Prayer Book, Queen Mary repealed all Acts referring to reforms back to 1529, signalling a return to Roman Catholicism with all the coercion that force could muster. Nearly 300 Protestants were martyred, including Cranmer himself. The anti-Catholic feeling which hardened over these few years has dogged English politics and religious feeling ever since.

Before such political and religious turbulence had its inevitable and drastic consequences for Christian music, the turn of the fifteenth century was the moment for an extraordinary flowering in choral music for worship. The remarkable richness of the music of Europe (Okeghem, Josquin des Prés, Obrecht, Mouton, de la Rue, Isaac) had its parallels in England.

The Eton Choirbook, compiled between 1490 and 1502, well illustrates this peak of sumptuousness for Roman liturgy. The book brings together settings of the *Magnificat* and Marian antiphons. The richness and sophistication of the setting for which this magnificent music was written may have been out of touch with the simple and direct world of the New Testament, but the artistry of the music is breathtaking. Here the Latin text is clearly a vehicle for the music, which is of unprecedented richness and sonority. Choral writing with as many as nine independant voice-parts (the voices ranging from the deep bass to the highest treble) alternate with passages for a few highly-skilled soloists. One remarkable item is a canon by Robert Wylkynson, based on a fragment of plainsong, the words of the creed being allocated to the twelve apostles (Example 15). To perform the canon, thirteen voices are needed, each starting with line one and singing through to the end. Each subsequent voice begins to sing as the previous singer begins the second line.

EXAMPLE 15

Breathtakingly beautiful though this music is, it is in the medieval tradition, old-fashioned even for its time. It was an adornment and elaboration of the liturgy – a mirror of divine order perhaps – but beyond the congregation's understanding. No wonder that Erasmus said of it:

Modern music is so constructed that the congregation cannot hear one distinct word. The choristers themselves do not understand what they are singing, yet according to priests and monks it constitutes the whole of religion… In college or monastery it is still the same: music, nothing but music…[3]

All cathedrals received a Royal Visitation during the first years of Edward VI's reign. The Visitors made sweeping recommendations concerning the liturgy, reducing its great complexity, simplifying the visual spectacle and forbidding the use of the organ, the singing of Latin antiphons, responsories or sequences and sometimes reducing the numbers in the choir. The recommendations were sometimes drastic and must have caused the musicians considerable dismay. At Lincoln Cathedral the Visitors commanded that:

> [The choir] shall from henceforth sing or say no anthems of our Lady or other Saints, but only of our Lord, and them not in Latin; but choosing out the best and most sounding to Christian religion they shall turn the same into English, setting thereunto a plain and distinct note for every syllable one: they shall sing them and none other.[4]

Edward's reign also gave Archbishop Cranmer his greatest opportunities for reform. He had already approved the publication of Coverdale's *Great Bible* in 1539 (though at the price of ten shillings its circulation could not be very wide) and within two years of Edward's accession had produced the first of his two versions of the *Book of Common Prayer.*

The Book of Common Prayer

In 1549 the Act of Uniformity under Edward made the *Book of Common Prayer* compulsory in all places of worship in England, Wales and Ireland. Unlike the sophisticated sets of service-books required for the Roman liturgy and its local variants, this book was all in English, gave little guidance concerning the use of music and was relatively straightforward and simple.

In the 1549 *Book of Common Prayer,* the structure of the Mass, renamed Holy Communion, was maintained in a simplified form, though omitting the Gradual. In a further revision of 1552, however, the other items of the Proper were also cut. Musicians were therefore left with none of the texts that had received the most lavish musical attention. The Daily Office was ingeniously compressed into two services – Matins and Evensong.

Matins was based on the Roman Matins of Salisbury Cathedral – the

Sarum Use. Its canticles were the *Venite* – Psalm 95 – and the *Te Deum* ('We praise you, O God') with a reduced number of readings, the canticle sung at Lauds (the *Benedictus* – Zechariah's song found in Luke's gospel, chapter 1) and sometimes the *Quicumque vult* (the Athanasian Creed) which was a part of Prime. Terce, Sext and None were cut altogether. Evensong married Vespers (with its psalms and *Magnificat*) to Compline (whose canticle is the *Nunc Dimittis*, the song of Simeon in Luke's gospel, chapter 2). These changes were by no means taken up with enthusiasm and many establishments, proud of their time-honoured liturgical traditions, dragged their feet for some time.

Merbecke

In 1550 John Merbecke, a student of the work of Calvin and a keen reformer, published his *Booke of Common Praier Noted*. He intended it as a solution to the difficulties that cathedral churches faced, as Merbecke provided simple music for the Ordinary texts for Communion and for the versicles and responses, psalms, canticles and prayers of Matins and Evensong. Following those of Luther and Calvin, many of his settings use traditional music as their basis, but he chose to keep to the free rhythm of the words and to use a method of notation reminiscent of Gregorian chant.

But Merbecke's music made little headway as further liturgical changes, not to mention storms, rendered his settings unusable. His music is still familiar to Anglicans today because of its revival in the nineteenth century, ironically enough by a group of Anglo-Catholics with motives totally at variance with his own.

During the five years of Queen Mary's bloody attempts to restore the Catholic faith after Edward's death in 1552, many reformers fled to Lutheran Germany or to Geneva. The publication of metrical psalters in English continued in Geneva, such as Sternhold and Hopkins' *One and fiftie Psalms of David* of 1556. These were very much in the Calvinist tradition, with simple and strong tunes and no harmonisation.

Elizabeth's reign

The reign of Queen Elizabeth (1558–1603) was not characterised by revenge but by a careful, sometimes brilliant, diplomacy. Though the country was once more Protestant, Catholics were not punished for their faith. Nonetheless, Queen Elizabeth on her accession once more reversed the religious decrees of Mary and restored the position roughly to that of 1552 and the second version of the *Book of Common Prayer*. While this step led swiftly to her excommunication by Pope Pius V, the Queen determined to avoid further bloodshed and to tread a middle path. The more radical reformists were no more happy with this position than were the Catholics. Both parties found quite different reasons to object to the *Book of Common Prayer*, but both knew relative safety in her realm.

Elizabeth herself enjoyed the ceremonial side of worship and the Chapel Royal continued to employ the services of the finest musicians in the land (though there is plenty of evidence that she did not pay them enough). Reformed clergy were uneasy at the theatrical splendour with which the Queen celebrated St George's Day, 1562, as recorded by a contemporary:

> At Whitehall the Queen's grace went from her Chapel with twelve Knights of the Garter in robes with collars of gold with garters, twenty of her Chapel in copes of cloth of gold... singing the English procession from the Chapel, round the Hall and back again... [the Dean of] her Chapel bore a book and a robe, and Master Norres bore the black rod, in a robe, and Master Garter, all three in crimson satin; the Bishop of Winchester wore his robe of red...[5]

On the other hand, an early seventeenth-century writer recalled that

> not so fewe as an 100 paires organs were pulled down (and many of them sold or imploide to make pewter dishes). And commands were given for short playinge, or none at all, for shortenings or alteringe their songs and service to give place for preachinge, and casting service as it were quite out of doors.[6]

Along with this, ardent reformers attempted to do away with candles, vestments, crucifixes, the practice of kneeling to receive communion and other 'popish' practices. But in spite of this pressure, a Royal Injunction of 1559 permitted that

> for the comforting of such that delight in music... an Hymn, or suchlike song to the praise of Almighty God [might be sung at such times] in the best sort of melody and music that may conveniently be devised, having respect that the sentence [that is, the meaning] of the Hymn may be understanded and perceived.[7]

It is this tolerance that permitted well-endowed churches to benefit from a golden age of music, largely created by the example and talents of musicians in the service of Elizabeth. The Church of England at large was less lucky, however. Where in London early in the century at least two dozen churches had the resources to sing polyphony on a regular basis, after the reforms of the 1540s this provision was steadily reduced as Puritan attitudes took hold. The revisions discouraged organ-playing and choral music, psalm-singing becoming the chief musical content of services which centred on the reading and expounding of the Bible. Sternhold and Hopkins produced metrical translations of all 150 psalms (published by John Day in 1563) followed over the years by many others. Psalm-singing became a popular feature of church-going as the century progressed. The Bishop of Salisbury, writing from London in 1560, was happy to note how worship was once more reverting to the people:

> Religion is now somewhat more established than it was. The practice of joining in church music has very much helped this... You may now sometimes see at St Paul's Cross, after the service, 6,000 persons, old and young, of both sexes, all singing together and praising God.[8]

Notes

1. See W.H. Frere and W.P.M. Kennedy, 'Visitation Articles and Injunctions of the Period of the Reformation', Alcuin Club Collections, 14–16.

2. These included churches and cathedrals at Arundel, Higham Ferrars, Warwick, Beverley and Ripon. See P. Le Huray, *Music and the Reformation in England*, Cambridge, 1978, p. 13.

3. J.A. Froude, *The Life and Letters of Erasmus*, London, 1894, p. 115.

4. See the Lincoln Cathedral Injunctions of 1548; quoted in Le Huray, p. 9.

5. J.G. Nichols, *The Diary of Henry Machyn*, Camden Society Publications, London, 1848, p. 115.

6. *The praise of musicke the profit and delight it bringeth to man and other creatures of God, And the necessity of it in the service & Christian Churche of God*, British Museum MS 18B. xix; quoted more fully in M.C. Boyd, *Elizabethan Music and Musical Criticism*, Pennsylvania, 1940, pp. 19–20.

7. Quoted in H. Benham, *Latin Church Music c. 1460–1575*, London, 1977, p. 165.

8. Letter to Peter Martyr from John Jewel, Bishop of Salisbury, 1560, in H. Robinson, *Zurich Letters*, vol. I, Parker Society, 1845, p. 71.

Chapter 13

The Chapel Royal and Cathedral Music

The Chapel Royal (or Royal Chapel) has been in existence as a musical organisation since the end of the thirteenth century. It still exists today, as it did then, to provide the sovereign of the time with the facilities for worship – vestments, utensils, service books and particularly music. The Chapel moved from place to place as required, adorning the liturgy with a rich tapestry of music.

Comprehensive records concerning the Chapel Royal are first provided by a 'Black Book of the King's House' compiled during the reign of Edward IV (reigned 1461–83). This lists all the officials of the Chapel, priests and musicians, with their duties, privileges and allowances. For instance, the eight Children of the Chapel were taught by a Master of Song – the composer William Cornysh (d. 1523) was one such – and boarded in the King's palace, being supplied daily with:

> two loaves, one messe of great meate, 2 galones of ale; and for wintere seasone 4 candles… 3 talsheids [bunches of firewood] and litter for their pallets [i.e. bedding].[1]

When the King was on his travels, the children received an additional

> 4d… for horsehire daily, as long as they be journeying. And when any of these children come to be 18 years of age, and their voices change… then if they will assent, the Kyng assyneth them to a College of Oxeford or Cambridge of his foundation, there to be at… study… till the Kynge may otherwise advance them.

While the boys were singing for the Chapel they were accompanied by a servant to assist them in dressing for official appearances, and were given a general as well as a musical education by the Clerk of the Grammar School.

As well as the eight boys, at this time there were twenty-four Chaplains and Clerks of the Chapel, who were required to be

> endowed with virtues morolle… shewinge in descante, eloquent in readinge, suffycient in organes playinge…

Tradition gave the monarch the privilege of conscripting any musician for the Chapel, from as far back as the time of Richard III:

> Ric &c To all and every our subjects… greeting… For the confidence and trust we have in our trusty beloved servant, John Melyonek, one of the Gentilmen of our Chapell… [we] give him authority that within all places in this our realm… our College Royal at Wyndesor reserved and except, [he] may take and seize for us and in our name all such singing men and children, being expert in the… science of musique, as he finde, and thinkes sufficient [1485].

One of the more surprising duties of the clerks and boys was to provide entertainment for the court in the form of plays – Cornysh was heavily involved with such presentations, writing a play himself to celebrate the visit of Charles V of Spain in 1522. By the early seventeenth century, however, Puritan reform discouraged the Children of the Chapel from taking part in such 'lascivious and profane exercises'.[2]

The most valuable source of information about the Chapel Royal comes from its Old Cheque Book, covering the period 1561 to 1744. This contains not only the accounts, but details of the personalities, events and problems in the life of the institution. Early seventeenth-century records are particularly full, describing funerals and coronations in fascinating detail.

The regulations and privileges of the Gentlemen of the Chapel also survive: the Gentlemen were required to sing at services throughout the week, but at certain times of the year only for Sundays and holy days (1603); they were to attend dressed

> in decent manner in their gownes and surplyses, and not in cloakes and surplyses, nor with bootes and spurres [1630, repeated in 1663].[3]

There were fines for absence or lateness:

> 9. The check for absence from morning prayers, holy dayes, festivall tymes, and sermon dayes, shalbe 4d, from evening prayer uppon such dayes… 3d, from morning prayer 3d, from eveninge prayer 2d.

10. The check for late cominge, viz. after the *gloria patri* 1d, after the first lesson 2d, after the second as for absent from the whole service.[4]

By 1693 inflation had pushed up the fine for absence to half a crown. The fines collected were redistributed every month to the more worthy members of the choir.

The 1549 *Book of Common Prayer* opens with a compelling preface by Thomas Cranmer which indicates the seriousness of the changes that musicians must have faced during those turbulent years:

> There was never thing by the wit of man so well devised, or so sure established, which in continuance of time hath not been corrupted... These many years passed, this godly and decent order of the ancient Fathers hath been so altered, broken, and neglected, by planting in uncertain Stories, and Legends, with multitude of Responds, Verses, vain Repetitions, Commemorations, and Synodals... The Service... these many years hath been read in Latin to the people, which they understand not; so that they have heard with their ears only, and their heart, spirit, and mind, have not been edified thereby... These inconveniences therefore considered, here is set forth such an Order, whereby the same shall be redressed.[5]

As far as the Chapel Royal and other musically sophisticated institutions were concerned, the change of liturgical repertoire and language necessitated a fundamental reconsideration of the music that clothed them.

Although the Cheque Book and other records (such as the Lord Chamberlain's Papers) do not give much musical detail of the Chapel Royal's liturgy, manuscript collections of music can supply – or imply – much of that missing information. Two Reformation collections of music compiled in response to the 1549 Prayer Book, the Wanley and Lumley books, give an idea of some early solutions – the Wanley books being particularly interesting in their breadth. In this collection the composers are mostly members of the Chapel Royal (though not named) and include composers of the highest standing, in particular Thomas Tallis and John Sheppard. The words set are those approved by the reformers: anthems setting passages of scripture and metrical psalms, with canticles and collects from the new Prayer Book. Evidently the Chapel Royal choir and others continued to be allowed to sing in harmony (Merberke's monodic *Book of Common Praier Noted* was an exceptional, though in a way, perfect solution to

Cranmer's ideals) but homophony was now commonplace. This chordal style, when applied to canticle singing, had important implications for what is now known as Anglican chant (see Example 16).

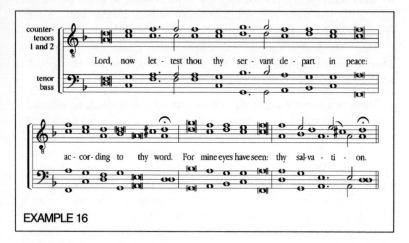

EXAMPLE 16

Like most early Anglican part-music, this is for men's voices only, the tenors singing the pre-Reformation psalm-tone. Canticles were also set in a free style, however, the composers responding to the text line by line and exploiting the capability of each half of the choir, decani (the Dean's side, usually the south) and cantoris (the 'cantor's', or Precentor's side) to provide a simple antiphony.

Groups of canticles set in this way were called 'short' services, mostly syllabic and chordal. But even early on in the Reformation, composers like Robert Parsons were writing much more elaborate and artful settings, called 'full' or 'great'. In Elizabeth I's time, these more extended works, particularly those using the 'verse' structure (alternating sections for solo voices with the full choir), became the musical glory of the Chapel Royal.

Thomas Tallis

Of all composers spanning the Reformation, it was Thomas Tallis (c. 1505–85) who demonstrated the flexibility of true genius. His musical training took place in the final years of the Roman worshipping tradition, but he was appointed a Gentleman of the Chapel Royal in 1543, just at the point when the liturgy was to be entirely rewritten. As a Roman Catholic, Tallis held the post of organist at a Benedictine priory in Dover and at Waltham Abbey until its dissolution in 1540. His appointment to the Chapel Royal came after a short period as a lay-clerk at Canterbury Cathedral. Tallis' earliest works are Latin motets to Marian texts. Tallis anticipated the simplicity of the new English liturgy required under Edward VI in some remarkably straightforward Latin settings of the Mass Ordinary, before he turned his expert hand to English texts. 'If ye love me' is a well-known example of one his anthems for men from the Wanley part-books. Its directness and economy could only come from a composer of far wider experience (Example 17).

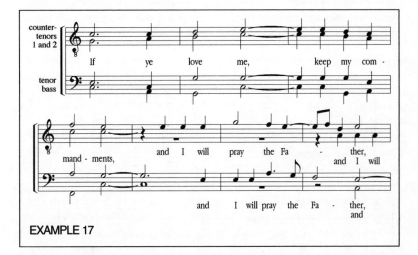

EXAMPLE 17

The reversion to Roman Catholicism characterised by Queen Mary's brief reign (1553–58) allowed Tallis to turn once more to more sumptuous music, writing several responsories on a grand scale (*Videte miraculum* is an impressive example). His later pieces – some in English, some in Latin – include his settings of the Lamentations of Jeremiah for the long-standing Roman tradition of Holy Week services. The dark sonorities of these two sets of Lamentations are extraordinary and unforgettable, and show Tallis able to make profound music out of any liturgical situation presented him by a troubled age.

Anglican chant

Although English was substituted for most of the Latin, evidently music continued to play a vital part in the Chapel's worship; readings and prayers (including the Creed) were intoned on a single note; complex canticle settings were written to the new English translations, and responses and psalms were sung to chants. These were the traditional plainsong formulae of medieval times, often richly and imaginatively harmonised with three or four added parts.

Tallis supplied such settings for psalms and responses from the mid-sixteenth century. They appear printed, along with others, in *The First Book of Selected Church Musick*, an invaluable compilation made by John Barnard, a minor canon of St Paul's Cathedral, in 1641. Gradually the plainsong melodies were forgotten and replaced by newly composed chants, sung to each half of the psalm-verse. This could be called the beginnings of Anglican chant.

EXAMPLE 18

The choir stalls traditionally divided the choir into two (*decani* and *cantoris*) and the psalm-verses were taken alternately by the two sides following the long-established Roman tradition.[6] Over the next hundred years or so the single chants were replaced by double ones, where a musical sentence in two phrases fits two verses of the psalm (Example 18).

A minor canon of St Paul's, James Clifford, published in 1633 some 'brief directions' concerning the practice at St Paul's Cathedral, which describe a liturgy typical also of the Chapel Royal:

The first Service in the morning

After the Psalms a Voluntary on the organ alone.
After the first lesson is sung *Te Deum laudamus*...
After the second lesson *Benedictus*... or *Jubilate*.
After the third Collect is sung the first Anthem.
After that the Litany. After the Blessing...
a Voluntary alone on the Organ.

At Evening Service

After the Psalms a Voluntary alone by the Organ.
After the first lesson *Magnificat*.
After the second lesson *Nunc Dimittis* or *Deus misereatur*...
After the third Collect is sung the first Anthem.
After the Sermon is sung the last Anthem.[7]

At this time the canticle settings would certainly have been those written by the greatest composers of the previous thirty years or so: William Byrd, Thomas Weekes, Orlando Gibbons, Thomas Tomkins and many others. Their dozens of services continued to be used throughout the seventeenth century and still form a vital foundation of Anglican cathedral worship today. The prominent place of solo organ music after the psalm is noteworthy; it continued as a long-standing tradition and was only abandoned during the nineteenth century.

Hymns are conspicuous in their absence from the liturgy of St Paul's, in fact emphasising the largely silent congregation. Hymns had little public part to play except in celebrations of special solemnity, but were instead to be found more in services of private devotion in the houses of the nobility, a context far removed from the populist metrical psalms, The hymn-texts were sophisticated (George Herbert's are among the best examples) and the music sung by professional musicians, perhaps a single voice accompanied by organ or viols. A few of the melodies of these 'devotional songs' have rightly found their way into modern hymnbooks, the best-known of them (such as Song 1 and Song 46) being by Orlando Gibbons, originally intended for George Wither's *The Hymnes and Songs of the Church*. The hymns written by William Byrd to be sung to the accompaniment of viols (also known as consort songs) are practically unknown in worship now, but the viol-playing fraternity know them to be exceptional and precious Christian music.

Anthems

Anthems were the central 'sacrifice of praise' at the Chapel Royal, even overshadowing the sermon. Clifford shows that the 'first' service contained one, the following Eucharist contained another and that a further two were sung at Evensong. Anthems permitted the greatest artistry and invention of which the musicians of the Chapel were capable; they were usually of a complexity that made them performable in few other churches elsewhere. The musical riches of this period of composition have been dealt with thoroughly elsewhere, but it must be said that few other ages have produced music of the integrity and invention of Byrd, Gibbons or Weelkes.

It is fortuitous that one man, Sir William Leighton, should have produced texts for dozens of anthems written by the finest composers of the day. Sir William was jailed for debt in 1609, but being a keen musician and poet, he used the time profitably by writing a large collection of devotional verse, *The Teares or Lamentations of a Sorrowfull Soule*, and then asked composers of the day to set them to music. Those that accepted form a list of the finest composers of his time, including John Bull, William Byrd, Thomas Wilbye, Thomas Weelkes and Orlando Gibbons. Thomas Tomkins is the only conspicuous absentee.

Significantly, the majority of these (and many more) composers wrote with equal facility for other purposes – dance-music for the nobility; songs for devotion or entertainment; instrumental music for recreation. Unlike today, there was no need for a violent change in musical style from the secular to the sacred. It was sufficient, as Thomas Morley wrote, to be aware that for the liturgy the music should have an appropriate solemnity:

you must cause your harmony to carry a majesty... but let it be in long notes, for the nature of it will not bear short notes and quick motions, which denote a kind of wantonness.[8]

Thomas Tudway, Professor of Music at Oxford, and later Composer and Organist Extraordinary to Queen Anne, looked back to this period and found the results admirable:

the Air so solemn, the fugues and & other embellishments so just, & naturally taken, as must warm the Heart of anyone, who is endu'd with a Soul fitted for devine raptures.[9]

Instruments

For special occasions at least, other English cathedrals followed the example of the Chapel Royal, conducting their services on occasion with lavish splendour. In this they were encouraged by John Whitgift (c. 1530–1604), Archbishop of Canterbury from 1586. Whitgift's Calvinist inclinations did not hinder his encouragement of splendid music at Canterbury. During a service at the cathedral in 1589 a visitor observed 'the Deane, Precentors and Preachers in their surplesses and Scarlet Hoods, and heard 'the solemne Musicke with the voyces, and Organs, Cornets and Sagbutts'.[10] The use of instruments was not unusual at this time and continued through the next century. Evidence comes from many cathedrals, including Dublin, Exeter, Durham, York, Winchester and Salisbury. Charles Butler, in his *Principles of Music* suggested that wind instruments were more practical:

because [string instruments] are often out of tune: (which sometime happeneth in the midst of the Musick, when it is neither good to continue, nor to correct the fault) therefore, to avoid all offence... in our Church-solemnities only the Winde-instruments... be in use.[11]

Commonwealth and restoration

In 1640 entries in the Chapel Royal's Cheque Book suddenly cease. Oliver Cromwell's parliament disbanded the Chapel Royal on the execution of its king. The musicians had to find employment elsewhere, which for some meant the continent of Europe. In 1660, however, on the restoration of the monarchy the Chapel Royal was reinstituted with renewed enthusiasm by Charles II, its former living members being offered their jobs back. Thomas Tudway noted:

> The King took great delight in the Service of his Chappell, & was very intent upon Establishing his Choir… as allmost to double the number of Gentlemen, & Children of the Chappell which it consisted of before the Rebellion. His Majesty who was a brisk, & Airy Prince, comeing to the Crown in the Flow'r & Vigour of his Age, was soon… tyr'd with the Grave and Solemn way, And Order'd the Composers of his Chappell, to add symphonys &c with Instruments to their Anthems… In about 4 or 5 years time, some of the forwardest, & brightest Children of the Chappell, as Mr Humfrey, Mr Blow, &c began to be Masters of a faculty in Composing; This, his Majesty greatly encourag'd, by indulging their youthful fancys, so that every month at least… they produc'd something New, of this kind… Thus the secular way was first introduced into the service of the Chappell…
>
> This however did not Oblige the Cathedrals throughout England, to follow such an Example; for indeed such an Example was very improper for their imitation; because they had none of the fine voices, which his Majesty had in his Chappell.[12]

The great diarist John Evelyn attended the Chapel Royal's services from time to time and recorded his impressions, with mixed feelings:

> Instead of the antient grave and solemn wind musicke accompanying the organ, was introduced a Consort of 24 Violins betweene every pause, after the French phantastical light way, better suited to a Tavern or Play-house than a church.[13]

The unfamiliar French manner clearly caused the musicians some difficulty, as another diarist, Samuel Pepys, noted: 'An anthem, ill sung, which made the King laugh…'[14]

Charles II was perceptive enough to see that English composers needed experience and training in the continental styles with which he wished to be surrounded. Accordingly, in 1664 he sent Pelham Humfrey (1647–74) abroad with a considerable sum of money to improve his musical education. The exact details of his travels are not known, but he returned in 1667 'an absolute Monsieur'. His anthems use the rhetoric – the emotional effects of well-matched music and words – of the Baroque style to involve the congregation (or should one say 'audience'?). In a number of anthems violin solos alternate or interweave with dramatic solos for voices (*By the Waters of Babylon*, for example). Humfrey's music displays a wonderful sensitivity to the English language through the Monteverdian technique of recitative (*Hear, O Heavens*).

Humfrey died at the early age of twenty-seven, but John Blow lived well into the eighteenth century and composed such quantities of music that one is right to suspect that quality was sacrificed to speed. His anthems are either of the verse-anthem type, with orchestral *ritornelli* (refrains or interludes) or so-called 'full' anthems, written solely for choirs of up to eight voice-parts.

That the Chapel Royal was happy to hear occasional anthems in Latin is indicated by a dozen or so by Blow (as opposed to the hundred he wrote in English) of which *Salvator Mundi* (Saviour of the world) is deservedly the best known (Example 19).

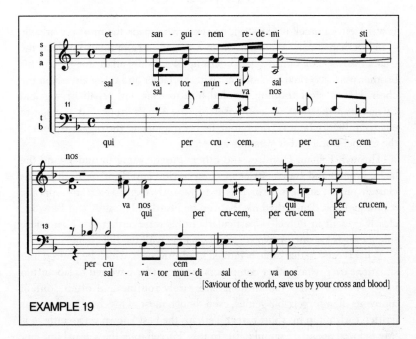

[Saviour of the world, save us by your cross and blood]

EXAMPLE 19

Here waves of harmonic tension and relaxation are created between voices to express as powerfully as possible the plea to Christ the Saviour of the world. His English setting of Jesus' words on the cross 'My God, my God, look upon me, why hast thou forsaken me?' is equally intense and compelling.

The lavish scale of Charles II's musical requirements is no more evident than in a special commission from Matthew Locke (about 1621–77) in 1666. Locke was a court composer already well known for his anthems and Latin motets when the king asked for a 'Song of Thanksgiving for His Majesty's Victory over the Dutch'. In response Locke wrote *Be thou exalted, Lord* for three four-part choirs, larger forces than required by any other English composer of the time and approaching the Italian splendours enjoyed in St Mark's, Venice. In addition, the voices were accompanied by strings, including a consort of viols playing 'in the Gallery'.

Henry Purcell

It was Henry Purcell (1659–95), however, who made the most remarkable – and perhaps final – contribution to a period of sumptuous music at the Chapel Royal. For him it was something of a family affair, for he and his brother were accepted as choristers with his father and uncle already in the choir. His musical training enabled him to tune and repair organs and earned him the post of 'composer for the King's violins' at the age of eighteen. Before he was twenty-one he became one of the organists both of the Chapel Royal and at Westminster Abbey.

Through Pelham Humfrey and others Purcell came to understand the latest French and Italian styles of composition and drew on both for his church music, some of which is extravagantly expressive. The operatic techniques and dance rhythms that can be heard in Humfrey and Blow are clearly evident in Purcell – particularly in his verse anthems, which utilise solo passages for one or two voices alternating with the full choir.

What is most remarkable is Purcell's inventiveness, which he poured into situations over which other composers might not have wished to labour too long. The full and verse anthems are rarely routine and often contain moments of unforgettable genius, even though most of his church music was written early on in his short career. Perhaps the best known verse-anthem is 'My Beloved Spake' (Example 20). In this, Purcell took the sensual imagery of the Song of Songs and reacted with striking and unforgettable musical ideas, such as the ecstatic leaping of the opening solo voices.

EXAMPLE 20

Brilliant though his church music is, it was the semi-operas such as *King Arthur* or *The Fairy Queen* and the songs for dozens of theatre plays that reached the wider public and which led Roger North to observe that 'a greater musicall genius England never had'.[15] At that time, there was, alas, no cause or opportunity for Purcell to write any Christian music for the worshipping public. His Christian music remains, like so much of the music for the Chapel Royal, on a higher level than can be reached by any but the very best choirs and soloists. Indeed, his anthems have been reckoned to be sufficiently long, difficult or controversial for past editors to have mutilated them with cuts and alterations of all kinds.

The Chapel Royal has continued its musical traditions in worship to this day, though its influence and example in the musical world has steadily declined. In this respect it parallels the history of cathedral churches elsewhere in the United Kingdom, a thread followed later on in this volume.

Notes

1. Quoted in E.F. Rimbault, *The Old Chequebook*, New York, 1966, p. iii.

2. Collier's Annals of the Stage, vol. 2, p. 16, quoted in Rimbault, p. ix.

3. Rimbault, p. 78.

4. Rimbault, p. 73.

5. The full text can also be read in the *Book of Common Prayer*, 1662.

6. As one scornful Puritan put it: 'In all theyr order of service there is no edification, according to the rule of the Apostle, but confusion; they tosse the Psalmes in most places like tennice-balles…' (Reverend John Field, *An Admonition to the Parliament*, 1572); quoted in M.C. Boyd, *Elizabethan Music and Musical Criticism*, Pennsylvania, 1940, p. 23.

7. Quoted in E.H. Fellowes, *English Cathedral Music*, London, 1969, pp. 31–32. For a detailed discussion of the music, see P. Phillips, *English Sacred Music 1549–1649*, Oxford, 1991.

8. T. Morley, *A Plaine and Easie Introduction to Practicall Musick*, 1597, edited by R.A. Harman, London, 1963, p. 293. The comment has some resonances years later with the attitudes of the Tractarians of the Victorian era.

9. Quoted in C. Hogwood and R. Luckett, *Music in Eighteenth Century England*, Cambridge, 1983, p. 23.

10. G. Paule, *The Life of the Most Reverend and Religious Prelate John Whitgift, Lord Archbishop of Canterbury*, London, 1612, p. 79; quoted in A. Parrott, 'Grett and Solompne Singing' in *Early Music*, vol. 6, no. 2, April 1978, p. 183.

11. Charles Butler, *The Principles of Music in Singing and Setting*, London, 1636, p. 103.

12. Letter to Lord Harley, 1716; quoted in Fellowes, p. 133.

13. John Evelyn's diary, entry for 21 December 1662.

14. Samuel Pepys' diary, entry for 14 October 1660.

15. J.W. Wilson, *Roger North on Music*, London, 1959, p. 307.

Chapter 14

Catholic Reform

The effects of the Renaissance penetrated the Roman Church's music only slowly. The church was a benevolent employer of the most brilliant composers, allowing them gradually to transform medieval styles to Renaissance ideals without restricting their creative freedom. When serious change was finally imposed on musicians – well into the sixteenth century – the result of the pruning (some say) was a leaner and stronger Christian music, to which the Roman Catholic Church still refers as its musical 'golden age'.

Even before Luther's time there was a desire for reform from within the Roman Catholic Church. The reforming zeal was at first mainly evident in Spain under Cardinal Ximenes (1436–1517), a prelate whose power sprang from both the church and the united Spanish crowns of Aragon and Castile. Under his leadership the Spanish church became disciplined and confident, seeking out and persecuting Moors, Jews and Protestant Christians through the operations of the Inquisition.

Over the same period the Portuguese exploration of the East (Vasco de Gama travelled round the African Cape to India) and the Spanish exploration of the West not only brought wealth and glamour to their countries but also vastly expanded the numbers of converts to the Roman Catholic faith. Their motives for this fresh wave of the crusading spirit were the familiar mixture of altruism and greed:

> to serve God and His Majesty, to give light to those who were in darkness, and to grow rich, as all men desire to do.[1]

The Roman Church's puritan movement gathered particularly around Ignatius Loyola (1491–1556) who adopted an ascetic and disciplined life, regulated by a rigorous course of 'Spiritual Exercises'. Those inspired to follow him called themselves the Society of Jesus, or Jesuits, and became a significant power for reform.

Unlike the Protestants, however, Jesuits pledged themselves with unswerving loyalty to Rome; indeed, they believed that this loyalty was the source of their salvation, rather than the Protestants' justification by faith. Under the influence of this reforming spirit and with the leadership of Pope Pius V, a new and vigorous inquisition was set up against Protestant sects, the celibacy of the priesthood was reaffirmed (the Protestants encouraged their priests to marry) and the Vatican's sculptures and paintings of the human form were adorned with carefully placed fig-leaves.

Music written for the well-endowed Roman monasteries and cathedral churches around this time is undoubtedly a high point in the history of Christian music. It deserves some attention not just because musicians today respect it so deeply but because, in spite of its artistic excellence, it was the very opposite of what Catholic reformers believed Christian music should be.

The beginnings of counterpoint

During the fifteenth century the Ordinary of the Mass (the unchanging texts of the *Kyrie, Gloria, Credo, Sanctus* and *Agnus Dei*) became more and more the focus of musical attention. Guillaume Dufay (1400–74) for instance, set the Ordinary of the Mass at least eight times. His music (especially the music he wrote later in life) sounds different from the medieval music described earlier. The motet style of composition still governed Dufay's settings – that is, they were based on a fragment of traditional chant, two or more voices then weaving an inventive web around it. But it became common practice to use the same chant as the basis for all the sections of the Mass setting.

One of Dufay's Mass settings called *Missa Caput*, for instance, uses the melody of an antiphon *Venit ad Petrum* ('He came to Peter') as the basis for all five sections. The chant basis (called *cantus firmus*) of this type of Mass setting might have some connection with the occasion for which the Mass music was written, but would not have been sung in the service in its original form. What is more, these melodies were so heavily concealed by their musical surroundings that they might very well go unrecognised by the congregation.

Since the best composers of the time were equally occupied with writing music for the glittering and indolent life at court, it was perhaps a small step for Dufay to choose a secular tune as the basis for a Mass setting. So in his *Missa 'Se la Face ay Pale'* Dufay took the melody of one of his own love-songs and used it as a *cantus firmus*. In another, he used the battle-song *L'homme Armé*. This tune was very well-known in the French-speaking world; many other composers used it in Mass settings and its characteristic sound could scarcely fail to be recognised (Example 21). The tune dates from the fifteenth century and the words 'the man-at-arms fills everyone with fear' were probably first sung in a crusade against the Turks.

EXAMPLE 21

Many other composers (Busnois, Ockeghem, Taverner) followed Dufay's example in writing *cantus firmus* or 'parody' Masses. The *cantus firmus* (the melody of the love-song, for example) was distributed from time to time among all the voice-parts and the medieval technique of composing layer upon layer gave way to a greater blend of all parts, each carrying a fair share of responsibility for the overall sense of the music.

Composers of the following generation, Josquin des Prés (1440–1521) and Jacob Obrecht (1450–1505) integrated their music still further by requiring the voices to copy each other melodically. The melodic ideas that begin new sections of the music came to be called *puncta* – 'points'. When voices imitate, the points are set against each other, the technique called counterpoint.

In a book on the history of counterpoint, the composer Vincenzo Galilei (c. 1527–91), father of the famous astronomer, suggested that a group of such composers came together under the patronage of Leo X in 1513. In so doing he lists all the great names in Christian music of the time:

Leo X... so greatly enjoyed that new manner of singing so many melodies simultaneously that in 1513, the first year of his papacy, there came together at Rome from Flanders and from France... all contrapuntists, with large remunerations from the most liberal pope. I do not wish to pass over their names in silence. They are: Josqueno, Lupus, Gian Mouton, Carpentras, Andrea de Silva, P[iet]ro de Terarche, Anton Fevin, Longheval, Hylaire, Brumel, Ricciafort and Divitis.[2]

When this contrapuntal style was at its height, it was described in detail by the theorist and composer Gioseffo Zarlino (1517–90) in *Le Institutione Harmoniche* (1558).[3] The technique began with the simplest textures, moving on to amazing feats of inventive ingenuity. In a 'canon' Mass, for instance, long stretches of one voice-part were made to be identical but out of step with another. Furthermore, imitative sections might be composed proportionally, in such a way that the numbers of beats in each were in simple ratio to one another. The ingenuity required for such an exercise, whilst strictly maintaining the harmoniousness of the music, is difficult to exaggerate. Of course, numerological allusion abounded.

All in all, the music was as much symbolic speculation as aural delight and it is not surprising that one of the earliest pioneers of these techniques, John Dunstable (c. 1390–1453) was as much a mathematician and astronomer as a musician. In short, Renaissance composers had developed music of such profound creativity and ingenuity that few (and not always the singers themselves) were able to appreciate all its subtleties.

By the end of the sixteenth century choirs singing in this tradition had become thoroughly skilled in the part-music required of them. The whole choir was expected to be able to take part in these complex pieces rather than the solo voices of the time of Machaut. Instruments were sometimes used to double with some or all of the choir, as much to add a further element of invention and beauty as to keep the music secure. In 1586 the Spanish composer Francisco Guerrero (1528–99) wrote to the Chapter of Seville. His letter shows not only that highly-skilled instrumentalists were thoroughly integrated into worship, but also that their improvising skills were highly prized:

> First, Rojas and López shall always play the treble parts: ordinarily on shawms. They must carefully observe some order when they improvise glosses [embellishments, that is, divisions], both as to places and to times... Second, the same Rojas and López when they at appropriate moments play on cornetts must again each observe the same moderation in glossing: the one deferring to the other... for both simultaneously to add improvised glosses creates insufferable dissonance. As for Juan de Medina, he shall ordinarily play the contralto part, not obscuring the trebles nor disturbing them by exceeding the glosses that belong to a contralto. When on the other hand his part becomes the top above the sackbuts, then he is left an open field in

which to glory and is free to add all the glosses that he desires and knows so well how to execute on his instrument. As for Alvanchez, he shall play tenors and the bassoon. At greater feasts there shall always be a verse played on recorders. At *Salves*, one of the three verses that are played shall be on shawms, one on cornetts, and the other on recorders; because always hearing the same instrument annoys the listener.[4]

The introduction of instruments to worship did not please a conservative like Bishop Cirillo Franco:

What shall we say of the cornetts, sackbuts, and all the other wind instruments that some religious orders today permit on every occasion? Their use ought to be extirpated. St Thomas expressly condemned such instruments. Religious orders who allow the glossing, the embellishment, the disfiguration, that these and other like instruments frequently add, should blush for shame.[5]

The Council of Trent

The Council of Trent (Trento is an Italian town near the borders of Austria and Switzerland) met intermittently from 1545 to 1563 to discuss and to recommend all manner of reforms in the Roman Church.

One of its original intentions was to see if any reconciliation with the Protestants was possible. But by the time the Council started its meetings, it was far too late for that. There were many other issues before it, however, and although music was not high on the list of priorities (recommendations did not appear till 1562) the Council eventually announced:

In the case of those Masses which are celebrated with singing and with organ, let nothing profane be intermingled, but only hymns and divine praises. The whole plan of singing... should be constituted not to give empty pleasure to the ear but in such a way that the words may be clearly understood by all... and thus the hearts of the listeners may be drawn to the desire of heavenly harmonies, in the contemplation of the joy of the blessed.[6]

The comments about mingling 'profane', 'lascivious' or 'impure' music with the Mass indicate that musicians and clerics had long forgotten the Papal

Bull of 1323 forbidding such practices, and were deaf to the contemporary complaints of Bishop Cirillo Franco. And yet the Mass music by Isaac, Obrecht and Josquin is recognised as unsurpassed in the history of Western Christian music.

Christian worship on the one hand and artistic creativity on the other were, in some people's minds, directly incompatible, a situation more anomalous and tragic when it is remembered that the composers without doubt believed that God himself was the source of their creative gifts.

Palestrina

It was Giovanni Pierluigi da Palestrina (c. 1525–94) whose talents supposedly dissuaded the Council of Trent from taking its revisionist recommendations to extremes. The legends concerning his relationship with the Council centre on one of the best-known of his 104 Mass settings, the *Missa Papae Marcelli*.

Unlike almost any other composer of Christian music, Palestrina has been held in high esteem continuously since his death. Such adulation has not served him entirely well, since over the years his admirers have been tempted to glamorise the slender facts about his life and work.

Palestrina lived and worked throughout his life as organist, singer and composer for the church in Rome. He was deeply involved in the musical traditions of the city's three most venerated churches: San Giovanni in Laterano (where he was *maestro di capella* from 1555 to 1560), Santa Maria Maggiore (he was *maestro di capella* from 1561 to 1566 and had been a choirboy there) and St Peter's in the Vatican. In 1555 Palestrina was invited by Pope Julius to join the Sistine Chapel choir. The official mechanism for appointment was brushed aside, including the entrance examination and the regulation that choir members had to be unmarried. But reform was in the air. Within a matter of months, almost immediately after his own election, Pope Paul IV learned of the irregularities of Palestrina's appointment, dismissing him and two other married singers from his choir. However, Palestrina's reputation ensured that within a month he had been appointed to San Giovanni, where the previous *maestro di capella* had been the young Netherlands composer Orlande de Lasso.

About five years earlier, in 1549, Bishop Cirillo had written an extended letter about church music to a colleague. In it he deplored the inclusion of secular melodies in Mass settings:

> They say, 'Oh, what a fine Mass was sung in chapel!' And what is it, if you please? It is *L'Homme Armé,* or *Hercules Dux Ferrariae* or *Philomena.* What the devil has the Mass to do with the armed man, or with Philomena, or with the Duke of Ferrara?[7]

Having observed that Michelangelo's nude figures on the Sistine Chapel roof were more suitable for the 'loggia of some garden', he complains that composers in the modern style of counterpoint

> have put all their industry and effort into the writing of imitative passages, so that while one says 'Sanctus', another says 'Sabaoth', [and] still another says 'Gloria tua,' with howling, bellowing and stammering...

Ten years later the Council of Trent made its brief pronouncement on music and in April 1565 a significant entry in the Sistine Chapel diary was made:

> At the request of the most Reverend Cardinal Vitellozzi we were assembled in his residence to sing some Masses and to test whether the words could be understood, as their Eminences desire...[8]

The story goes that Palestrina's *Missa Papae Marcelli* was one of the works heard on this occasion, though no evidence has yet been found to prove it. The music may have been written in 1555, when Marcellus was Pope for only three weeks, or as a test case for Cardinal Vitellozzi.

Whatever its background, the *Missa Papae Marcelli* is distinctive. When Palestrina published the music in 1567 along with six other Mass settings in the Second Book of Masses, he explained that his intention was 'to adorn the holy sacrifice of the Mass in a new manner'.[9] The technique of counterpoint is suppressed where there is any danger that the text might be obscured. Thus the *Gloria* and *Credo* are written with almost no imitation between the voices and the most important words are repeated for emphasis. Even in the opening *Kyrie* long melismas (many notes to one syllable) are avoided, the interplay of the parts and the frequent repetition of the words conveying the text with unfailing clarity. Musical variety is preserved by ingenious use of every possible combination of the six available voice-parts.

It seems that Palestrina regarded this type of setting as a particular genre and did not by any means adhere slavishly to the new principles. In a letter to the Duke of Mantua, who had commissioned a Mass from him, Palestrina asks whether it should be rewritten:

> I beg you to inform me how you prefer it – whether short, or long, or written so that the words can be understood.[10]

The later sets of Masses published by Palestrina contain settings in both the new and the old styles (the 1570 collection contains yet another based on *L'Homme Armé*), suggesting that the Council of Trent's pronouncements were by no means universally upheld.

Palestrina was also heavily involved in the revision of Gregorian chant, which the Council found to be full of 'barbarisms, obscurities, contrarities and superfluities'. He was given the task of 'purging, correcting and reforming', the results of Palestrina's work alongside many others being published in 1614 as the so-called Medicean edition of the chant. Large numbers of chants which used tropes (additional and probably unscriptural texts) were pruned away. Of hundreds of sequences, for instance, only a handful were left.

Three hundred years later, scholars – such as the monks of Solesmes described in chapter 23 – would be hard at work undoing Palestrina's efforts and attempting to restore the chant to its earliest known state.

The golden age of Spanish music

One of the most significant contributions to the heritage of Christian music in the sixteenth century was made by Spain, thanks largely to the immense power and influence of the Habsburg dynasty.

The discovery by Christopher Columbus in 1492 of a 'New World' far to the west of Spain and Portugal opened the route for undreamed-of riches to be brought back to Europe within fifty years. The plundering of the civilisations of Mexican Indians and the Incas of Peru helped to make Portugal and the Habsburg empire the most powerful political forces in Europe. By 1535 the two branches of the Habsburg family, Austrian and Spanish, controlled not only the whole of Spain (Granada in the south and Navarre in the north having ceded in 1492 and 1512 respectively) but also Milan, southern Italy, Sicily, Sardinia, Tunis, the Netherlands and parts of Germany and Austria.

One key to ruling successfully on such a scale was to display the wealth that lay behind the throne. The Spanish Habsburgs, Charles V (king of Spain 1516–56) and his son Philip II (reigned 1556–98) were particularly generous patrons of the arts. They fostered and employed the outstanding talent of their country and made sure that Spain's creative excellence was widely known. Spanish musicians and composers accordingly became renowned throughout Europe and the Roman Catholic Church did not hesitate to benefit from their talents.

Cristóbal de Morales

When Cristóbal de Morales (c. 1500–53) was being trained as a choirboy in Seville, the capital of Andalusia, he would soon have become aware that he was living in one of the most cultured cities in the world. Under the influence of the rich musical life of Seville he became one of Spain's most expert church musicians. His baritone voice and compositional talent caught the attention of Pope Paul III and he was invited to join a number of other Spanish singers among the two dozen or more voices of the Sistine Chapel choir in Rome.

Between 1536 and 1543 Morales travelled the cities of Western Europe with the Pope's retinue, enjoying the use of his own horse and servant – perks that went with a job of such high standing. The papal tours gave Morales the chance to introduce his music to the great cathedrals, whose musicians were ready to acknowledge that his church compositions were the finest of their time.

Morales returned in 1545 to take up the post of *maestro de capilla* (choirmaster) at the Spanish cathedral of Toledo. His last few years in his native country were unhappy, marred by disagreements with his superiors. In Toledo Cathedral the musical tradition focused on organ music, whereas Morales had built his reputation on the composition of a more austere unaccompanied music for Mass. Perhaps he was consoled by the fact that two of his pupils, Francisco Oro (1528–99) and Juan Navarro (about 1530–80) were becoming known as the finest Christian composers of their generation.

Antonio de Cabezón

While Morales' fame spread throughout Europe as the result of his patronage by the Pope, the blind keyboard-player Antonio de Cabezón (1510–66) became the most favoured musician of the Spanish king, Philip II. His post as organist of the king's private chapel took him in the king's company to Italy, Germany, the Netherlands and England. His talents as a player and composer excited a great deal of interest, for the compelling expressiveness of his keyboard music suggested all kinds of new creative possibilities to the musicians who had the chance to hear him.

Cabezón made a profound contribution to organ music in worship through pieces of great variety. Some of these wove contrapuntal ingenuity around a known melody such as a hymn, others presented embellished and ornamented versions of such tunes. Still others, the *tientos*, were colourful and free fantasias. Most of this music was printed by Cabezón's son Hernando in a collection called *Obras de música para tecla, arpa y vihuela*.[11]

Tomás Luis de Victoria

Victoria (1548–1611) came from a family with strong Jesuit connections. He was trained from an early age by the *maestros de capilla* at Avila Cathedral near Madrid. After a period at a Jesuit school in the area, at the age of about eighteen he went to a college in Rome (again run by Jesuits) with official duties as a singer. In 1569 he became an organist and chorister at the church of Santa Maria di Monserrato in Rome, later joining a community of lay-priests (who were not in a religious order) and entering the lower ranks of the clergy.

Victoria's increasing wealth during this extended Italian stay and his developing reputation as a composer of unaccompanied choral pieces allowed him to publish several sumptuous volumes of his music. In about 1587 he decided to return to Spain, when Philip II offered him the post of chaplain to the Empress María who was living in retirement in a convent in Madrid.

For the next fourteen years or so, Victoria was able to enjoy writing for and directing the expert convent choir of men and boys (separated from the nuns by a grille). He was offered the most prestigious musical posts of the great Spanish cathedrals, but in vain – the convent of *las Descalzas de Santa Clara* had too much to offer his musical talents.

Almost all Victoria's compositions were vocal music for the liturgy, like those of Morales, Guerrero and Navarro before him. Of his twenty settings of the Ordinary of the Mass, seven are parody Masses – all but one built round music from sacred motets by Guerrero, Morales, Palestrina or Victoria himself. His style is direct, however, and the ideals of the Catholic Reformation are expressed in its simplicity of purpose, albeit controlled by an incomparable intellect.

Some of his most solemn and dramatic works were published in Rome. The 1585 collection contains settings of the Lamentations of Jeremiah and two versions of the Passion story, according to Matthew and John. The Passion story was traditionally required to be sung with other penitential music during Holy Week (leading up to Easter Sunday). Victoria's sonorous Lamentations and his dramatic telling in music of the trial and crucifixion of Jesus are as profoundly moving as his better-known motets.

Victoria's hymns also deserve more attention, though *Jesu dulcis memoria*, which is probably sung more than any other, was not his composition. Victoria's true hymns (of which there are dozens) followed the common practice of setting the even-numbered stanzas in polyphony, the alternate verses being sung to the traditional chant.

Villancicos

One of the intentions of the Catholic Reformation was to introduce a simpler and more populist music into worship with which the common people could identify. In the Spanish-speaking world it was villancicos which best fulfilled that need. Villancico (the word literally means 'peasant') was the name given to a popular song with a refrain. It had early connections with the music of the Arab invaders of Andalusia. By the fifteenth century villancicos were being written and performed for the entertainment of aristocratic audiences: they were courtly love-songs under a rustic disguise.

The reformers encouraged the introduction into worship of villancicos on important feast-days. Well-known tunes were given newly-fashioned texts in Spanish, or wholly new sacred songs were written in the same popular style. In either case, their presence in worship caused consternation to the old guard:

> Villancicos sung in the vernacular are [an]… abuse. The kind now popular mix Castillian, Portuguese, Basque and Galician in an unconscionable farrago. What is more, characters such as Negroes, Moors and others just as hostile to the Christian religion, are introduced solely to divert, to cause laughter, and to turn the House of God into a playhouse.[12]

Villancicos continued to be tolerated in worship for another 200 years, until their operatic style became too much of an embarrassment to conscientious churchmen.

The Hispanic New World

From the very beginnings of the Spanish conquest of the Americas, music was understood to be an essential part of the expression of Christianity among the thousands of new converts. Not only were the Mexican Indians taught plainchant, but the same splendid forms of music from Spain were soon established in the New World. The choral music and villancico tradition of Mexico City Cathedral quickly became the equal of any in Spain, even under its first *maestro de capilla* Canon Juan Xuáres (appointed in 1539).

The Incas of the Andes were found to be highly skilled musicians and were encouraged as part of the process of Christianisation to transfer their playing skills to the accompaniment of choral music in church.

Especially sumptuous music developed in the early seventeenth century in Puebla Cathedral with the encouragement of talented composers: Juan Gutiérrez de Padilla (about 1590–1664) and Francisco López Capillas (about 1615–73) among many others.

In Peru, the administrative centre for the Spanish Americas, Christian music of high quality (such as Morales' Masses) could be heard in the cathedral at Cuzco in the mid-sixteenth century. A rich tradition of liturgical music developed in Lima Cathedral (which was consecrated in 1572) where the Third Lima Council of 1583 recommended the inclusion of instrumentalists in worship. This subject is discussed further in chapter 38.

Reformation and Counter-reformation – a reflection

Many events of the Reformation and Counter-Reformation, especially the sectarian violence, were deep offences to the Christian gospel. This is not the place to reflect at length on that tragedy. But while music was low on the list of critical issues in the violent debate, it nonetheless provides a microcosm of the problems then facing the Christian world.

As far as their music was concerned, the three great churches of Europe – Catholic, Lutheran and Calvinist – demonstrated a triangle of dissension of which there are still echoes in every argument concerning the liturgy and its music: 'The Catholic, in church, listens without singing; the Calvinist sings without listening; the Lutheran both listens and sings — simultaneously!'[13] In other words, for many Roman Catholic worshippers, participation in Christian music was not possible. As in so many other aspects of faith, the church took it upon itself to act as an intermediary between God and his people. The Calvinists, believing that the Christian church on earth had to be begun again, went back to what they could learn of the early church; Christian music had to conform, with everything else, to what they read there. The Lutherans managed to hold a precarious balance between the congregational singing characteristic of the early church and an expression of faith through the art-music of experts.

Such blending of participation and listening might occur even during one hymn, as happened in a special celebratory service in 1659, described by a contemporary:

> the first verse is sung by the congregation, the second is sung as a solo by the cantor, the third is performed by four girls unaccompanied, the fifth is sung by the congregation, the sixth by the schoolboys in the choir, and the last is taken by the congregation, the organ and all the singers.[14]

Such a scenario would be a challenge to any musical director and potentially a recipe for musical chaos. Spiritually, however, it has the attractive possibility of being the outward evidence of a church working as the body of Christ, with its many parts making up a single unit. The majority of Christian denominations today have found that this middle course can reflect the unity of Christ in the diversity of talent which makes up the church.

The Christian approach to the unredeemed world is the other painful issue raised during the years of the Reformation. Church leaders of all persuasions were agreed in their deep suspicion of the ecstatic and physical dimension of music. Luther wrote of the 'erotic rantings' of the secular world and the Council of Trent similarly objected to musical 'things that are lascivious', 'outcries and uproars' and 'seductive and impure melodies'. The humanist tendencies of the Renaissance led musicians to be more aware of the control that music can exercise over the emotions, that is, its rhetorical power. Luther observed music's capacity to comfort, to terrify, to encourage, to humble, and so on. By doing so he emphasised the rhetorical rather than the symbolic property of music, revealing himself as a man of the Renaissance rather than of the Middle Ages.

Calvin also acknowledged music's 'well-nigh incredible power to move us whither it will', but saw in it a serious threat to Christians who wished to keep on the narrow path to eternal life. Not long after, Galileo's suggestion that the sun, not the earth, was at the centre of the galaxy threatened to topple once and for all the church's cosmology and its long-held theories about the God-sustained harmony of the spheres. At just the same time a new humanism seemed to be putting mankind at the centre of the universe. Both were threats to the church's established order and the complaints about a secular element in Christian music were part of the attempts to resist those changes.

The beginning of the seventeenth century heralded an acknowledgment that the rhetorical power of music was of prime importance. The new music it created forms the foundations for present-day Western musical practice. The churches of the time accommodated those changes, but as usual not without difficulty.

Notes

1. B. Diaz, companion to Cortes, quoted in B. Gascoigne, *The Christians*, London, 1980, p. 180.

2. V. Galilei, *Il primo libro della prattica del contrapunto intorno all'uso delle consonanze, 1588–91*, translated in E. Lowinsky, 'A Newly Discovered Sixteenth Century Motet Manuscript at the Biblioteca Vallicelliana in Rome', *Journal of the American Musicological Society*, vol. 3, 1950, p. 178.

3. For an English translation see O. Strunk, *Source Readings in Music History*, London, 1952, p. 229.

4. Quoted in R. Stevenson, *Spanish Cathedral Music in the Golden Age*, Los Angeles, 1961, p. 167.

5. Letter to Ugolino Gualteruzzi from Bishop Cirillo Franco, 1549, quoted in Stevenson, p. 333.

6. The Council's pronouncements on music are quoted extensively in R.F. Hayburn, *Papal Legislation on Sacred Music*, Collegeville, Minnesota, 1979, pp. 25–31.

7. From A. Manuzio, *Lettere Volgari di Diversi Nobilissimi Huomini… Libro Terzo*, Venice, 1564; translated by L. Lockwood in *Palestrina, Pope Marcellus Mass*, New York, 1975, p. 12.

8. From the *Biblioteca Apostolica Vaticana… Diario Sistino*, no. 7, folio 135v, translated by L. Lockwood, p. 21.

9. Dedication of the Second Book of Masses, 1567.

10. Quoted in Lockwood, p. 24.

11. A complete edition is published by the Institute of Medieval Music, edited by C.G. Jacobs, Brooklyn, 1967.

12. Letter of Bishop Cirillo Franco; quoted in Stevenson, p. 333.

13. L. Bianconi, *Music in the Seventeenth Century*, Cambridge, 1987, p. 134.

14. P. Gerhardt, Christmas Matins in Berlin, quoted in C. Halter and C. Schalk, *A Handbook of Church Music*, St Louis, 1978, p. 67.

PART 3

The Flowering of Christian Music

1600–1800

Chapter 15

Italian Splendour

In Venice... I heard the best musicke that ever I did in all my life both in the morning and in the afternoon, so good that I would willingly goe an hundred miles afoote at any time to heare the like... This feast consisted principally of Musicke, which was both vocall and instrumental, so good, so delectable, so rare, so admirable, so super-excellent, that it did even ravishe and stupefie all those strangers that never heard the like... Sometimes there stand sixteen or twenty men together... and when they sung, the instrumentall musitians played also. Sometimes sixteene played together upon their instruments, ten Sagbuts, foure Cornets, and two Violdegambaes of an extraordinary greatness... At every time that every severall musicke played, the Organs... plaied with them.[1]

In this way Thomas Coryat recorded his impressions of worship in the Basilica of St Mark's in Venice at the height of its musical fame. Musicians all over Europe knew something of the splendours created by the line of illustrious composers employed there, from Adrian Willaert of the mid-sixteenth century, through Claudio Merulo, Andrea and Giovanni Gabrieli (uncle and nephew) to the great Claudio Monteverdi (1567–1643).

The design of the building itself profoundly affected the music of these composers. Following the example of Willaert, they developed music which explored the cavernous acoustics of the building, usually placing musicians in the huge wooden *pulpitum magnum cantorum* (great pulpit of the singers) known familiarly as the tub – *bigonzo*.

Occasionally, even larger groups might be spread further afield, the music of opposing groups being made to shift its ground, coming first from one choir, then from another, then creating illusory echo-effects, and finally (in the words of another observer):

at the Gloria Patri, all ten choirs resumed singing together. I must confess to you that I have never experienced such rapture...[2]

The ecstatic words of visitors to such showcase churches of the Catholic faith testify to the church's continual patronage of the finest musicians of the day.[3] Just as people visit King's College Chapel, Cambridge today for a musical feast, so musicians came as pilgrims to St Mark's, Venice. They also made their way to Rome to hear such artists as Girolamo Frescobaldi play at St Peter's. A contemporary account records how Frescobaldi could be heard improvising instrumental fantasies in alternation with the choir, and 'displaying a thousand kinds of inventions on his harpsichord while the organ stuck to the main tune'.[4]

Such musical delights were evidently to be found round practically every street corner. Coryat counted 200 churches in Venice, of which nearly two-thirds had organs, and the Jesuit Gregory Martin found in Rome, that

> It is the most blessed varietie in the world, where a man may goe to so many churches in one day, chose where he wil, so heavenly served, with such musicke, such voices, such instruments, all ful of gravitie and majestie, al moving to devotion and ravishing a man's hart to the meditation of melodie of Angels and Saints in heaven. With the Organs a childes voice shriller and louder than the instrument, tuneable with every pipe: Among the quyre, Cornet or Sagbut, or such like above al other voices. Wherein... they deliver every word and everie syllable so distinctly, so cleane, so commodiously, so fully, that the hearers may perceave al that is sung.[5]

Such musical splendours were, in general, welcomed by the Roman Church and had a profound effect on the musical taste of educated people in the seventeenth century. The church authorities were on occasion sufficiently interested to allow worship to be informally interrupted by visiting musicians. In 1639 the French viol-player André Maugars (something of a musical celebrity at the time) attended a solemn Mass in Rome, instrument in hand:

> The next morning... I decided to go up into a gallery, where after being received with applause I was given fifteen or twenty notes to play [as a basis for improvisation] with a small organ, after the third *Kyrie Eleison*. These I treated with so many divisions [variations] that all were very pleased and begged me... to play again after the *Agnus Dei*.[6]

Maugars was congratulated by the twenty-three cardinals who heard him and went on to play to the Pope a few days later.

Music and emotion

Prompted by the Renaissance rediscovery and emulation of the classical tradition, the rhetorical power of music, extolled so much by the ancient Greeks, became a deepening fascination for composers. Through their music they aimed to exercise that emotional power over their audiences against which Calvin had so solemnly warned.

A group of Florentine intellectuals (they called themselves the *Camerata*) set about a modern re-creation of the long-held ideals of ancient Greek theatre, tragedy in particular. Because the documents and records they had to work from were incomplete their results were little like the dramas of classical antiquity, but through the interest of singers like Giulio Caccini and composers like Claudio Monteverdi, the new musical style they created had a profound impact on Western art-music.

Caccini described in great detail (in *Le nuove musiche* of 1602) the technique and theory of the 'new music'. The intention was 'to move the passion of the mind'. The means was the simplicity of a single human voice, the opposite of the massed choirs of St Mark's. Accompanied by the gentlest of instruments (lute, theorbo, or small keyboard instruments) whose harmonies were governed by the nature of the words being sung, a new kind of intimacy was created.

Music could then draw the audience into a world of intense emotion. The new dramatic medium which used these musical means came to be called *opera*. Naturally enough, the first operas most often and most appropriately drew on the stories of Orpheus, whose legendary musical powers extended even beyond the emotional world to the physical.

The Roman Church welcomed this *stile rappresentativo* (a style representing human emotions) into its worship along with other aspects of new music, in spite of secular origins and associations.

Monteverdi's 1610 setting of music for Vespers is a spectacular example of the possibilities that can be explored by combining the older polychoral and contrapuntal musical styles with the ecstatic element of dance and the rhetoric of *stile rappresentativo*. The music was printed together with a setting of the Ordinary of the Mass in eight partbooks, the full title of which in translation is: *A mass of the most holy Virgin for six voices for church choirs and Vespers to be sung by more voices, with a few sacred songs suitable for the chapels or chambers of princes; a work by Claudio Monteverde recently composed and dedicated to the most holy Pope Paul V. Published in Venice by Riccardi Amadino 1610.*

The *Vespers* settings consist of five psalms, a hymn, a Sonata and the *Magnificat*, beginning with the opening responsory transformed into a toccata-like blaze of fanfares. The psalms are stylistically the most traditional, using at times weighty counterpoint (opening section of *Nisi Dominus* – psalm 127) or opposing blocks of sound from two choirs best positioned some distance from each other in the Venetian style (*Lauda Jerusalem* – psalm 148). Through every psalm (and through the Sonata and *Magnificat*, too) the medieval psalm-tones are present, a reminder that these magnificent settings are only a gloss on the church's traditional music.

The new element arises in the vocal numbers interlaced with the psalms. These have caused some controversy, because they are placed as if they are antiphons to the psalms, yet do not use either the expected texts or the correct modes. Hence a modern English edition in wide circulation misses them out altogether. It appears, however, that these *stile rappresentativo* settings of passages from the Song of Songs acted as substitutes or supplements to the expected antiphons, and the texts are certainly appropriate and powerful expressions of devotion.

Each verse of the hymn (*Ave Maris Stella*) is presented by a different combination of musicians, from a rich eight-part texture to a solo voice and keyboard. Here, in the Sonata and in the *Magnificat* there are interludes of dance music for instruments alone, perhaps the nearest the church had yet approached to the physical and ecstatic enjoyment of music in Old Testament times. The *Magnificat* is the most complex and extensive piece of all. Each short phrase of the canticle generates a musical movement with its own character, using sharply contrasted combinations of voices and instruments and evoking a wide emotional range. The music abounds in magical echo effects, particularly in the final *Gloria Patri*, where they are used with remarkable vocal virtuosity.

Monteverdi's music for *Vespers* is often performed today with a large choir and a substantial orchestra, generating a weighty and impressive sound. It ought to be remembered, though, that even in the best-endowed churches the numbers of choristers was small – St Peter's Basilica in Rome in 1608 used only six boy sopranos, four male altos, four tenors and four basses. The ten separate voice-parts of the *Vespers* could easily be sung by such a small group (or an even smaller one), accompanied by just seven string-players, three cornetti, three sackbuts and an organist. These are the more modest but telling forces that were certainly used for the *Vespers*' early performances, possibly at the chapel of the Ducal court in Mantua, not far from Venice.

Oratorio

Of the new musical styles that invaded Christian music in the seventeenth century, it was opera that had the most profound effect. After all, churchmen had been complaining for generations that music had an exasperating tendency to distract from and obscure the text. Here at last was a type of music whose very purpose was to put across words and their emotional content as clearly as possible. Small wonder, then, that the outstanding composers patronised by the church looked again at the dramatic events of the Bible, seeking to bring them to life through these new operatic means.

The dramatic treatment of biblical narrative found its place, not so much in the liturgy, but in special occasions such as the *Congregazione dell'Oratorio* (the gathering of the prayer-hall). This was a meeting of aristocratic laymen for prayer, to hear the Bible read and commented upon, and for singing. There could be no better place for music to make Bible readings more persuasive.

Giacomo Carissimi (1605–74) has become justly famous for his dramatisations of Latin biblical texts. They became known as oratorios because of their first appearance at the *Oratorio* (prayer-hall). Biblical stories about characters such as Daniel, Jonah and Jephthah were set, as well as episodes such as the Judgment of Solomon and the Deluge. The Old Testament provided plenty of human interest from which simple lessons could be drawn. Some of the more vivid scenes used a chorus and the oratorio was held together by a *testo* (narrator).

André Maugars heard this music in the exclusive setting of the Oratory of San Marcello in Rome in 1639:

This admirable and delightful music is presented only on Fridays in Lent, from three to six o'clock. The church... has a spacial rood-loft at the end with an organ of moderate size, quite mellow in sound and suitable for voices. On the sides of the church, there are two other small galleries, where the best instrumentalists are placed. The singers begin with a psalm motet, and then the players of instruments furnish a very good symphony. Then is sung a story from the Old Testament, in the form of a religious drama... Each soloist represents a character in the story and gives perfect expression to the force of the words. Next one of the most famous preachers delivers a sermon, after which is sung the gospel of the day, such as the story of the Good Samaritan... I cannot praise enough this recitative music.[7]

These Lenten meetings were attended by the high aristocracy of Rome, but oratorio found a much wider following later on in the century when presented in Italian. Legrenze and Stradella were two composers who wrote a dozen such oratorios between them. The high drama of pieces such as Stradella's *St John-the-Baptist* was known to Handel in the next century and helped him in his turn to see how music could bring the Bible to life.

Oratorio is a form of music which has continued to be created down to the present day, even though it may not always be known by that name. Some might argue that it is not music for worship. But it can be a means of teaching Christian truth and can therefore fulfil a vital function in proclaiming Christianity.

Notes

1. T. Coryat, *Coryat's Crudities*, 1611; quoted in T. Dart, *The Interpretation of Music*, 4th edition, London, 1967, p. 104.

2. A. Maugars (1639), quoted in P. Weiss and R. Taruskin, *Music in the Western World*, London, 1984, p. 195. For details of the music, see A.F. Carver, *Cori Spezzati*, 2 vols, Cambridge, 1988.

3. See, for instance, the *Editto sopra le musiche* (Edict on Music) of 1665, translated in L. Bianconi, pp. 108–109.

4. Maugars, quoted in Weiss and Taruskin, p. 196.

5. Gregory Martin, *Roma Sancts*, 1581; quoted in T. Carter, *Music in Late Renaissance and Early Baroque Italy*, London, 1992, p. 102.

6. A. Maugars, *Response faite à un Curieux, sur le sentiment de la musique d'Italie*, Rome, 1639, translated by H.W. Hitchcock, Geneva, 1993, pp. 70–71.

7. Maugars, quoted in Weiss and Taruskin, p. 196.

Chapter 16

The Music of the Lutheran Church

While the Roman Church was enjoying the glories of highly sophisticated polychoral music and the emotionally charged 'new music' of oratorio, the Lutheran Church was benefitting from its own group of brilliantly inventive composers. From the beginning of the seventeenth century the number of outstanding composers is legion: names such as Melchior Vulpius, Michael Praetorius and Johann Crüger appear in present-day hymn-books, but this does no justice to the quantity and quality of their music. Michael Praetorius (1571–1621) was particularly prolific: he wrote more than 1,200 liturgical pieces, many of them hymns and motets. In some of this music he shows a keen awareness of the Venetian polychoral style, but he made it relevant to German congregations by using familiar Lutheran melodies as a basis, in much the same way as earlier composers had used Gregorian chant.

Patronage

Church musicians, of whatever tradition, have for the most part lived (at least until recently) under patronage. This meant that they depended wholly on church or state for their livelihood. They were treated as servants, relying on their own musical reputation and on the honesty and charity of their patrons to keep body and soul together. In a truly Christian society, such patronage should be a guarantee of security and fair dealing. When the patronage failed in its Christian principles, as it often did, the personal results were disastrous.

The horrors of the Thirty Years War which began in 1618 caused serious disruption to church life in Germany. During its course, sectarian warfare between German states and the consequent famines and plagues decimated the population of Germany – by the mid-century it had been nearly halved.

No church musician escaped the effects of such devastation, either in family losses or in the reduction of talented singers and players. Heinrich Schütz (arguably the greatest composer of the seventeenth century) suffered along with the rest. In Dresden, where he was employed as *Hofkapellmeister* (Musical Director) of the Chapel Royal, the court went through periods of being unable or unwilling to pay him or his musicians. Schütz constantly had to write begging letters on behalf of the musicians in his charge:

> I hear that he [Kaiser, a bass in his choir] is lying like a pig in a sty, without a bed and sleeping on straw, and he has already pawned his coat and doublet. His wife came to me yesterday, pleading with me to take them under my paternal wing and help them in their plight... I find it neither laudable nor Christian that in such estimable great lands one cannot or will not support twenty musicians, and I live in the humblest hope that Your Electoral Majesty will reconsider this.[1]

The musicians' duties

In happier times the Lutheran Church was able to boast many brilliant organists and composers who could draw on the talents of well-trained singers and instrumentalists. These were employed by the town council and the imperial power of the area to provide music for worship, for political ceremonies, for conferences, for weddings and funerals. Towns and cities would employ a cantor (whose duties included the organising and teaching of music at local schools), a town organist and a number of singers and players. In Hamburg in 1642 new regulations stated that the cantor had, as part of his duties 'to provide good, suitable music on feast days as well as for every Sunday, for all the town churches'.[2] Although the cantor had a fairly free hand in deciding what music should be provided, there was artistic as well as financial control. He had to

> adhere to the modern, fashionable *stilo modulandi* [operatic style], so that congregations would be able to hear both the old and the new, and both tastes would be pleased. In addition, most people understand the words better in a harmonic rather than a motet setting.[3]

This statement may be compared with the situation that church musicians face today. 'Old' meant the 'point counter point' of the sixteenth century, the learned style of fifty or more years before. The 'new' was the persuasive and emotional music of early opera. Dead tradition in worship, presenting only a museum of past practice, tends to fear and reject the new. But the Lutheran Church of the seventeenth and eighteenth centuries was living and growing, dynamic rather than static, capable of absorbing new musical ideas and changes of attitude without time-honoured elements being threatened:

> In the view of his [the cantor's] employers and the congregation which was his audience there was no more point in repeating music, apart from the familiar hymns, than there would have been in repeating sermons. The cantor was under attack if he did not produce new music in an up-to-date style...[4]

Furthermore, Hamburg expected its cantor to create worship-offerings of a high standard: 'The solo singers are to be experienced and good; more mediocre singers can assist by singing in the full choir.'[5] But 'slovenly, lazy, bad performances' were not permitted; excellence as well as modernity was part of the contract.

Christmas 1659 in the Nikolaikirche, Berlin

A vivid account by Paul Gerhardt (1607–76), hymnwriter and deacon at the Nikolaikirche in Berlin, demonstrates some of the results of the cantor's work. Gerhardt's description of the Christmas morning service in 1659 is clear evidence of a great deal of rehearsal and organisation, from which everyone benefits:

> The church is cold. Candles are being lighted. The people are coming and taking their places. A group of schoolboys is at one side of the gallery and a choir of mixed voices at the other side. Below the pulpit we see a Collegium Musicum, a voluntary musical society composed of tradesmen and craftsmen, who perform on violins and wood-wind instruments, gathered around a small movable organ. Then there is a male quartet, also a military band with trumpets, kettledrums and drums.

After the organ prelude a chorale [Lutheran hymn] is sung… Now three clergymen with white clergymen's bands and black robes have appeared at the altar. The entire liturgy is sung in Latin [the use of Latin or German varied from place to place] by the choirs and the schoolchildren. Next a college student, dressed as an angel with large white wings, sings from the pulpit an Old Testament prophecy, accompanied by the Collegium Musicum below.

More chanting from the altar, and then the principal door of the church opens, and in comes a procession of girls, headed by the teacher, all dressed as angels. They proceed to the high altar, where the teacher sings the first verse of 'Vom Himmel hoch' and the second verse is sung by the girls in two-part counterpoint. The third verse is taken by the organ and the choir in the gallery as a beautiful five-part motet. While the procession has been marching down the aisle, one of the ministers chants a 'Gloria' answered by the electoral court-and-field trumpeters with fanfares and drumrolls.

After the sermon there is more chanting by the liturgist, and the instrumentalists play a boisterous 'Te Deum'. Then follows another Latin anthem by the school-children.

Things now begin to happen in the organ loft: over the railing is raised a cradle with a doll, while some boys with incessant mooing imitate the animals in the Bethlehem stable. The choir and congregation sing a hymn, and at this point high up on the organ façade a Bethlehem star, illuminated and supplied with small bells, is turned round and round, operated by an organ stop.[6] Three wooden images, representing the three Wise Men, with their traditional attributes, solemnly move forward and bow before the doll in the cradle. At the same time we notice two puppets, representing Moors, standing on each side of the central group. One blows a trumpet, and the other beats a drum. Throughout this scene on the gallery railing the Collegium Musicum plays a ritornello [an instrumental refrain].

A boy soprano intones 'In Dulci Jubilo', which is continued by male voices, accompanied by shawms and bombards. The song is scarcely over before a sight exceedingly beloved of the children appears in the centre aisle. It is old Father Christmas himself in his white beard, with pointed cap on his head and a large sack on his back, soon surrounded by 'angels' and children, who vie with each other for the good things that are to be given out. When the large sack is empty and Old Father Christmas has disappeared behind the sacristy door, then is sung as the closing chorale 'Puer natus est Bethlehem'.[7]

As the century wore on, the familiar arguments against complexity and sophistication began again. On the one hand there were those who felt that the excellence and artistry of Christian music was a distraction. The Italianate concerto-style, brought to Germany first by Schütz and then adopted by others such as his pupil Christoph Bernhard (1628–92) or Kasper Förster (1616–73), was a ready target for those who found its virtuosity distasteful:

> In the same way also when in a large church a few boys are placed, who concert with each other in the most artful way possible... in their ornamenting, quavering and trilling rapidly one after another and together, [are] more like the cry of cats and hens than edifying and solemn music... such music would much better be performed in a women's chamber, at a feast, more for human pleasure, than in the church...[8]

Such criticism, which perhaps now has an all-too-familiar ring to it, extended to the other common complaints about musicians: their bad behaviour (drunkenness or immorality) and the inability of the congregation to hear the words being sung. On the other hand these points were interestingly countered by Georg Motz in his *Die verheidigte Kirchen-Music* (Church Music Defended) of 1704. He maintained first that the moral state of the singers was irrelevant, as long as the words they uttered were worthy. And as to the words themselves:

> It is just not necessary... that one always knows what is being sung and played... it is enough that one knows the *genus* of what is being sung, played or performed on the organ, that is to say, sacred, beautiful hymns, psalms and songs of praise that have been composed and created to the praise and glory of God.[9]

The theological divisions between the Orthodox and Pietist Lutherans which lay at the heart of this debate are raised again in chapter 18.

Notes

1. Quoted in H.J. Moser, *Heinrich Schütz*, London, 1967, p. 80.

2. L. Kruger, *Verzeichnis der Adjuvanten… in Beiträge zur Hamburgischen Musikgeschichte*, edited by H. Husmann, Hamburg, 1956, and quoted in H. Raynor, *A Social History of Music*, London, 1972, p. 202.

3. Quoted in Raynor, p. 203.

4. Raynor, pp. 209–210.

5. Quoted in Raynor, p. 203.

6. This facility, called *Zimbelstern*, is available on many German organs today. Paul Gerhardt is quoted extensively in C. Halter and C. Schalk, *A Handbook of Church Music*, St Louis, 1978, p. 68.

7. Quoted in Halter and Schalk, pp. 66-67.

8. J. Muscovius, *Bestraffer Mißbrauch der Kirchen-Music*, Lauban, 1694, p. 38; quoted in G. Webber, *North German Church Music in the Age of Buxtehude*, Oxford, 1996, p. 15.

9. G. Motz, *Die verheidigte Kirchen-Music*, 1703; quoted in Webber, pp. 17–18, where the ideological differences between Orthodoxy and Pietism are discussed.

Chapter 17

Heinrich Schütz

During the Thirty Years War (1618–48), musicians of the time seem to have had a healthy disregard for the sectarianism which caused such bloodshed and turmoil. Heinrich Schütz (1585–1672), for instance, was given permission and financial support by his first employer, the Landgrave of Marburg, to study music in Venice (1609–12) under the then aged Giovanni Gabrieli.

Nearly twenty years later, after much persuasion, the more tight-fisted Elector of Saxony allowed Schütz to visit Venice again, this time to experience the new operatic style of Monteverdi which could by then be heard as much in church as out of it. So it was that a Protestant employed by a Protestant court studied for at least five years under Roman Catholic musicians, absorbing from them the latest in musical fashion and turning it to compelling and brilliant use in his own Christian music.

Schütz' enthusiasm for the latest Italian style in music enabled him to create the greatest music of the century, but the textual foundation for almost all his surviving music is the Bible. He appears to have had little interest in writing instrumental music. Instead, he seems to have been driven by the challenge of bringing the Bible to life.

Schütz' use of the Bible narrative is not so much in its formal liturgical context, but in its ability to instruct on a personal level concerning human and divine relationships. In his motets he frequently uses operatic means to intensify the human drama of God's intervention in the world. Many of these settings are of the psalms and are typified by his first publication, the *Psalms of David*, a striking result of his first Venetian visit.

The twenty-six large-scale settings use all the spectacular techniques of his teacher Gabrieli (as many as four separate choirs are needed for some) but individual vocal lines are designed to convey the psalmist's expression of feeling as strongly as possible. Only on hearing these settings can Schütz' balance of the universal and personal dimensions of the psalms be appreciated fully.

Just before his second Venetian visit (in 1627) Schütz produced another set of psalms. This time they were simpler four-part settings of metrical translations by Cornelius Becker. Their popularity for congregational use lasted at least until the end of the century, but perhaps they proved to be a little too involved rhythmically and harmonically for singers of modest talent. Some of these settings have reappeared in German hymn-books this century and are once more becoming better known.

Sometimes artistic inspiration and sheer necessity come together to produce something exceptional. To suggest that composers need a free rein to create what their inspiration dictates is a romantic fiction. On the contrary, practical restrictions are absolutely necessary to provide a framework for creativity.

In Schütz' age of patronage the restrictions were those of circumstance and necessity rather than of choice – those who paid the piper definitely called the tune. There were two driving forces behind the motets that Schütz composed after his second visit to Venice. Firstly, he was deeply impressed with the new music he heard there (particularly that of Monteverdi, with whom he studied) and he sought to put that highly expressive and emotional style to good use in his biblical settings. But secondly, as the preface to his *Kleine geistliche Konzerte* (Little Sacred Concertos)[1] makes clear:

> honourable music... has not only decreased as a result of the persistent dangers of war around us... but in many places has been completely subdued [by] other general ruins and violent disorders.[2]

There was a clear necessity to write music for small forces for the depleted choirs of war-torn Germany, reasonably straightforward to sing and using sometimes as few as one or two voices accompanied only by a bass instrument and small organ. Yet this necessary reduction in scale was just what was needed to make the new style work best; it created intimacy and could draw the listener not only into biblical scenes, but also reveal their human passion, such as Mary's meeting with Jesus outside the tomb on the first Easter Sunday morning. Schütz' Resurrection Story includes the touching scene of Example 22, where Jesus' words to Mary ('Woman, why are you weeping? Whom do you seek?') are sung by two voices accompanied by a bass instrument (such as a viola da gamba) and organ. The figures under this instrumental bass line instruct the organist which chords to play. The dissonance in bar 3 stresses the humanity of the encounter through the traditions of rhetoric.

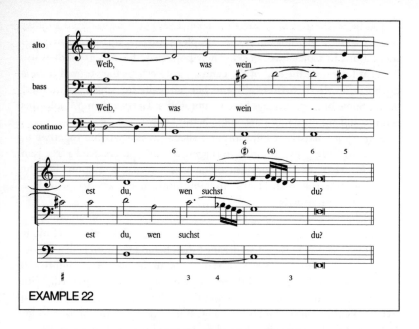

EXAMPLE 22

Schütz' interest in the Bible extended beyond the countless motet-settings of the *Cantiones Sacrae* (Sacred Songs), *Symphoniae Sacrae* (Sacred Symphonies)[3] or *Geistliche Chormusik* (Sacred Choral Music) for later in life he also found opportunities to set dramatic biblical scenes on a much larger canvas. This was nothing new: musical settings of the drama of Jesus' trial and crucifixion (his 'Passion') or of the Easter or Christmas stories were traditional in the Roman and Lutheran churches. But Schütz takes a particular interest in these stories, setting first the narrative of Jesus' resurrection (*Resurrection Story*, 1623), then the Seven Words of Jesus on the Cross (1657), the Christmas story (*Christmas Oratorio*, 1660) and finally three settings of the Passion according to Luke, John and Matthew (all in 1666).

The variety of approach in these dramas is an object-lesson for composers today who may consider setting biblical texts. In the *Resurrection Story* the narrative is given to an evangelist who sings in a kind of recitation which lends drama and intimacy to the words, at the same time surrounded by a halo of sound from four viols. Unusually, some characters such as Mary or Jesus are sung by two voices in harmony.

The *Christmas Story* uses instrumental forces to intensify characters in the drama. Herod, for instance, is accompanied by clarini (high-sounding trumpets) and four scribes are complemented by two trombones.

In complete contrast the settings of the Passion use no instruments at all, but return to the comparatively austere world of the sixteenth century – the evangelist and the characters in the story sing by themselves, unsupported by any harmony. But the whole choir takes the part of the crowd in short but incisive outcries. Characteristically, Schütz avoids any commentary or elaboration in the form of hymns or songs. In these last works he penetrated to the heart of the Christian faith simply by turning to the Bible.

Notes

1. 'Concerto' here is not used in the modern sense. See glossary.
2. Quoted in H.J. Moser, *Heinrich Schütz*, London, 1967, p. 63. See also H. Raynor, *A Social History of Music*, London, 1972, p. 205.
3. 'Symphony' is used here in the general sense of a 'sounding together'.

Chapter 18

J.S. Bach

The great stream of outstanding composers in the Lutheran tradition of the seventeenth and early eighteenth centuries finds its final and most complete expression in Johann Sebastian Bach. Here the three dimensions of Christian music discussed in the introduction – symbolic, rhetorical and ecstatic – are uniquely integrated.

The Lutheran Church's continuing demands for an extensive musical contribution to worship, as well as the developing possibilities of the Baroque[1] style, created music of superb quality. The current interest in early music is encouraging both church choirs and professional groups to explore the rich creativity of this period. The work of Johann Pachelbel (which extends far beyond the beautiful *Canon in D*), Johann Krieger, Franz Tunder, Dietrich Buxtehude, his pupil Nickolaus Bruhns, Johann Kuhnau, Georg Telemann and many others marks a period of excellence in Christian music which has probably never been surpassed.

At the end of an era and at the head of them all stands J.S. Bach (1685–1750), the greatest composer that Western culture has produced. Strong words perhaps, but many of the greatest figures of Western music – Haydn, Mozart, Beethoven, Wagner, Schoenberg, Stravinsky – have all said as much and have freely acknowledged their indebtedness to his music.

Bach the craftsman

Yet Bach's contemporaries saw him from a very different perspective. He was known only locally as a composer, but more widely as a performer. As an organist he was clearly phenomenal. Plenty of anecdotes have survived which typify reactions to his playing:

> When he was called from Leipzig to Cassel to pronounce an organ properly restored [a task he was frequently called to perform], he ran over the pedals with the same facility as if his feet had wings, making

the organ resound with such fullness, and so penetrate the ears of those present like a thunderbolt, that Frederick... Prince of Cassel, admired him with such astonishment that he drew a ring with a precious stone from his finger and gave it to Bach as soon as the sound had died away.[2]

Such descriptions project the uneasy feeling that Bach was admired less for his artistry and creativity than for his mental and physical agility, but he certainly was uniquely respected as a player and improvisor by organists throughout Europe. His music, however, was not universally welcomed:

When in a large town [Bach's] Passion Music was done for the first time, with twelve violins, many oboes, bassoons, and other instruments, many people were astonished and did not know what to make of it. In the pew of a noble family in church, many Ministers and Noble Ladies were present, who sang the first Passion Chorale out of their books with great devotion. But when this theatrical music began, all these people were thrown into the greatest bewilderment, looked at each other and said: 'What will come of this?' An old widow of the nobility said: 'God save us, my children! it's just as if one were at an Opera Comedy.' But everyone was genuinely displeased by it and voiced just complaints against it. There are, it is true, some people who take pleasure in such idle things...[3]

Bach did not always have an easy relationship with the church that employed him. At the age of twenty, he was given his first full-time post as organist at the New Church in Arnstadt. In 1706 members of the church Consistory (an ecclesiastical court) firstly reproved him for visiting Lübeck for sixteen weeks where he had only been given permission to go for four (he had gone to visit Buxtehude). Then they went on to

reprove him for having hitherto made many curious variations in the chorale, and mingled many strange tones in it, and for the fact the Congregation has been confused by it.

and later observed:

the organist Bach had previously played rather too long, but after his attention had been called to it by the Superintendant, he had at once fallen into the other extreme and had made it too short.[4]

Any organist is aware that the post includes a measure of tedium; Bach seems only too human in this youthful clash with authority. His later disputes with the town council of Leipzig concerned a continuing problem of lack of funds and inadequate support for his choirs and musicians.

The overall picture is certainly not one of a creative artist fêted for his prodigious talent. Instead, Bach was regarded as he regarded himself: as a craftsman following in a long family tradition. His task was to glorify God by the composition of music, working to the best of his ability and for a reasonable wage.

Unlike Handel and many other better-known musicians of his day, he never travelled far from home, was only once given well-publicised attention by the nobility (when as an old man he visited Frederick the Great's Prussian Court in Potsdam) and published very little of his music. Bach was therefore known and appreciated chiefly in the small area of Germany where he lived and worked. He expected his fate as a composer to be that of any other in the same position – he would hear his music performed on the occasions for which he wrote it, to be supplanted in due course by the music of his successor. His position was akin to that of many musicians of the Middle Ages, content in relative anonymity and satisfied in the exercising of a God-given craft.

It would be a great mistake to imagine that the craftsman-like attitude of Bach, or others in his position, inevitably created well-meaning but arid music. On the contrary, one of Bach's most remarkable talents was his ability to shed new light on a time-worn formula. He was well acquainted with all the fashionable musical styles of the day and did not hesitate to adopt them. But his remarkable mind enabled him to go far beyond his contemporaries, breathing new life into a conventional task. The six Brandenburg Concertos, for instance, are an incomparable summary of everything a composer could possibly do (and rather more) within the confines of a Baroque concerto. The imagination which he brought to bear on even the smallest task did not endear him to those who wished music (especially Christian music) to be straightforward and without too much intellectual or emotional challenge. This was undoubtedly the cause of the adverse reactions to his Passion music.

Bach – symbolism and rhetoric

The recurring tensions between Bach and his employers and congregations might suggest that he was frustrated by the lack of appreciation due to him as an outstanding artist. But there are many signs in the few scattered records of Bach's own words that he was driven to artistic creativity by stronger forces than a need for fame or even for a decent wage. In his letter of resignation to his employers at Mühlhausen in 1708 he expressed the simple desire: 'to work towards the goal, namely, a well-regulated church music, to the Glory of God'.[5]

This could easily be taken as rather uninspiring diplomacy were it not in reality a rebuke to his employers (one of many) for the lack of support he received for such a task, for the sentence begins: 'I should have liked…' Then in a commentary to a short book on musical theory, he stated that

> The aim and final reason, as of all music… should be none else but the Glory of God and recreation of the mind. Where this is not observed, there will be no real music but only a devilish hubbub.[6]

As an orthodox Lutheran Bach here echoes Luther's own views on the edifying power of music and makes no distinction between secular and sacred. God sees and hears all: humankind must therefore strive to please him in all. Bach strove to 'make a well-sounding harmony to the Glory of God' by an unceasing exploration of the possibilities of traditional musical grammar that for him represented order.

His collection of keyboard pieces under the general title of 'Clavier-übung' ('keyboard practice') is a perfect example of highly persuasive music under a forbiddingly intellectual exterior. The third volume is a collection of organ works which contains, as the title-page reads: 'various preludes on the Catechism and other hymns for the organ, for music lovers and especially for connoisseurs of such work, to refresh their spirits…' The pieces are based on traditional Lutheran melodies (some of them are Gregorian chant) and are presented in a cycle reflecting the themes of the church year. To symbolise the Greater and Lesser Catechism (Luther's essentials of the Christian faith for adults and children) Bach presents two settings of each traditional melody, one on a grand scale and one in simple form and without pedals.

There is also a trinitarian symbolism in the three massive settings of the traditional *Kyrie* – one addressed to the Father, one to the Son and one to the Holy Spirit. Furthermore, the whole collection is framed by an opening prelude and closing fugue, both in the key of E flat (requiring three flats in the signature), the fugue having three sections with three melodies, much of it in triple time. These are impressive symbols, but a sympathetic hearing is all that is needed to convince a listener that they are far more than mere intellectual games.

But there is something symbolic in the very nature of Bach's music, built as it is from layers of melodies which copy and confront each other in a ceaseless web of counterpoint. Marco Pallis likens the interactions of these voices to human relationships:

> To speak of a world is to speak of contrast and opposition, for the distinction of one being from another inevitably imposes this condition... These beings may either converge or diverge or, for a brief space, move parallel with one another... and this will from time to time bring the beings into contact or even collision... What does this picture suggest but a counterpoint which, by its continual interplay of tensions and releases, expresses that unity out of which all its constituent elements have arisen and which they are all for ever seeking to regain... The musical parallel is self-evident and it is this, in fact, which confers on contrapuntal music its strange power to move the soul.[7]

Is it therefore too fanciful to suggest that Bach's music invites an emotional response because horizontal diversity (the many voices) is brought into vertical unity (the 'well-ordered harmony') in a way that symbolises the waywardness of human relationships and a longing for the stability and unity of the kingdom of God?

Bach's music was not merely symbolic, but also intended as a powerful expression of feelings. In common with his contemporaries, Bach had a firm belief in the power of music to move its hearers. Music had the capacity to be expressive, not just of pain and joy, but also of anger, love, jealousy and hate. These emotional states were called *Affekten* ('affects' or moods) and each was associated with a specific musical idea:

> Since *joy* is an expansion of our vital spirits, it follows that this affect is best expressed by large and expanded intervals. *Sadness,* on the other hand, is a contraction of those same subtle parts of our bodies. It is, therefore, easy to see that the narrowest intervals are most suitable.[8]

Bach, like every other musician of his day, adopted these theories wholeheartedly. The difference is that he used them with more imagination and subtlety than others, not only providing vocal arias with the accompaniment that exactly complemented the 'affect' of the words (as other composers did in opera), but also using these same methods to resonate with the words of a particular hymn which would be in the mind of the congregation for whom he played it. The prelude on *Durch Adams Fall* (Through Adam's Fall) in his *Orgelbüchlein* (Little Organ Book) surrounds the hymn melody with heavy and dissonant descending intervals in the bass, not only a standard gesture for the affect of despair, but also symbolic of falling and of fear.

Pietism

Bach found himself at odds with some sectors of his congregation, who objected to his rhetorical methods. They also objected to his setting non-biblical texts to music. The trouble sprang from divisions within the Lutheran Church itself. Orthodoxy had for some time been failing to satisfy the emotional needs of Lutheran Christians and a powerful evangelical movement developed during the seventeenth century, initiated by P.J. Spener (1635–1705). This movement was known as Pietism, a name which comes from his influential book *Pia desiderata* ('Holy desires') published in 1675. Spener suggested that spiritual rebirth and the beginnings of a personal relationship with Jesus Christ were the prerequisite for church membership, and furthermore, that the church's priesthood was not and should not be specially privileged. On the contrary, all true believers were themselves the priesthood. This idea was particularly threatening to orthodox Lutherans. Spener instituted Sunday afternoon meetings for Bible study and prayer first of all in Frankfurt and then further afield. These groups he called *collegia pietatis*, fellowships of the saved.

Spener felt that the church had become ensnared in complex tradition. As he wrote in his *Pia desiderata*:

> When men's minds are stuffed with such a theology which, while it preserves the foundation of faith from the Scriptures, builds on it with so much wood, hay and stubble of human inquisitiveness that the gold can no longer be seen, it becomes exceedingly difficult to grasp and find pleasure in the real simplicity of Christ and his teaching.[9]

The Pietists had much in their favour, however: a new sense of the 'priesthood of all believers', a renewed appreciation of the Bible, a sensitivity to the needs of the poor and a missionary zeal. But they had a negative side. In their rejection of orthodox Lutheranism they also set their face against

much that could be wholesome, including the creative instincts of which
Luther approved. Luther himself had said: 'I would like to see all arts in the
service of Him who made them.'[10] This the Pietists firmly rejected and, as a
result, sought to curb the activities of musicians like Bach. Pietism certainly
lay behind some of the church authorities' reluctance to support Bach in his
repeated requests for a reasonable number of skilled players and singers.
And yet Bach himself had strong Pietist sympathies, to judge from items in
the inventory of his personal library made at his death:

> Rambach's *Reflection on the Tears of Jesus*
> Müller's *Flame of Love*
> His *Hours of Refreshment*...
> Gerhard's *School of Piety,* 5 vols
> Neumeister's *Table of the Lord*
> Spener's *Zeal against Popery*...[11]

Further evidence of Bach's Pietist leanings can be found in the texts that he
set to music so persuasively. These concern the individual's relationship with
Jesus, the personal response of the believer. The texts he set were often
highly emotive and his musical response to them was equally strong. Had the
Pietists penetrated beyond their prejudices and listened attentively to Bach
they would have found much to edify them in their spiritual lives.

The most far-reaching effects of Pietism were felt through the spiritual
revival of the Moravian Church, whose history could be traced back to the
early reformation of the Bohemian Church under Jan Hus, a contemporary
of Wycliffe. Count Nicolaus of Zinzendorf (1700–60), Spener's godson,
encouraged the hymn-singing traditions of the Moravians in what he called
'hours of song' which were first introduced in the town of Herrnhut[12] in
the 1720s. Zinzendorf described this song-centred worship in a letter to the
King of Prussia:

> The cantor takes up the subject of the sermons that have just been
> given and chooses whole and half verses from twenty or thirty songs
> that illustrate the subject in a clear and orderly fashion: and cantor,
> organist, teacher, and audience are so practised that no one is
> permitted to hesitate, nobody may consult a book... During public
> prayers, however, I first have a familiar song recited before [the
> sermon]. After it, however, if I do not find a song in the hymnal that I
> would like to have sung to emphasise the subject matter of my sermon

to the audience and to offer it to the Saviour as a prayer, I invent a new song of which I knew nothing before and which will be forgotten as soon as it has served its purpose.[13]

Over about thirty years, the Moravians published thousands of hymns and songs, many of them the result of spontaneous singing, some no doubt by the prompting of the Holy Spirit. The quality of many of the songs reflected their ephemeral and transitory nature, like many Christian songs today, but some became influential. John Wesley met some Moravians while on a boat crossing to America and was much impressed by the spiritual power of their song; the experience awoke him to the efficacy of hymn-singing.[14] Zinzendorf's hymns may occasionally be found in evangelical hymn-books today.[15] They are often concerned with personal salvation and with self-examination before God. The English translations are usually by John Wesley.

The Moravian Brethren established themselves in the British Isles, the New World and elsewhere, their constantly renewed repertoire of hymns becoming known in many languages.

Bach's cantatas

Nowhere is Bach's music more obviously expressive of his personal faith than in his cantatas. The word 'cantata' was first used in the context of Lutheran church music by the pastor and poet Erdmann Neumeister (1671–1756), whose texts Bach set in abundance. Neumeister explained his intentions in his foreword to a collection of cantata texts that he wrote for all the Sundays and feast-days of the church year:

Having properly performed my official duties on Sundays in the church, I attempted to transform the most significant thoughts that were treated in the sermon into poetic language for my private devotional use.[16]

Neumeister then produced these poems specifically for setting to music, probably with the guidance of the composer Johann Krieger (1649–1725) who also first set them to music. The cantata was strategically placed between the Gospel reading and the sermon, to have the greatest chance of reinforcing the message of both.

The musical methods of opera were the natural choice for giving expression to the spiritual content. Church ethics would not have allowed cantatas to be staged, but with such emotionally vivid music this was no great loss. Another composer of the time wrote:

> These... 'cantatas' have completely replaced the former German songs. Their invention, however, originated in opera. As I became aware of the pleasantness of their mixed styles, namely recitative and aria, which are at one moment happy, the next sad, one moment in this mood, the next in that, I turned from the old type of long ode with many verses... to a poem that mixes recitatives and arias.[17]

These cantatas are therefore a significant departure from earlier Lutheran music like that of Schütz, whose texts were almost always directly biblical. A move away from God's word might be seen as a move for the worse, but the use Bach makes of his cantata-texts is so compelling that they remain unsurpassed as musical expression of Christian truth. Bach's use of familiar words and melodies from the great heritage of Lutheran chorales reinforced the congregation's awareness of the cantata as worship, even if they were not expected to participate.[18]

Performance

Even in this age of authenticity in performance, it is worth being reminded of the circumstances in which cantatas were created. During his employment at Leipzig (from 1723 till his death) Bach was not in charge of the music of a single church, but of the music of a school (St Thomas) which supplied the musicians for four churches in the town. The abilities of these 55 boys and men varied from the most brilliant, capable of singing the most complex 'figural' music, to those who could barely read the notes of simple chorale. The former were called 'concertists' and were given the responsibility of singing in Bach's cantatas, which were regularly sung on feast-days by the best choir in either the Thomaskirche or the Nikolaikirche. A second choir of less able singers alternated with the first and sang simpler cantatas and old-fashioned motets (not by Bach). Bach explains the system in his numerous letters of complaint to the Leipzig town council, who by their lack of support appeared not to understand the demands of his job:

> The musical church pieces which are done in the first choir, and
> which are mostly of my own composition, are incomparably harder
> and more intricate than those which are performed in the second
> choir – and then only on feast-days – when I am obliged to choose the
> [cantata] by the capacité of those who are to execute it.[19]

The second and other choirs were graded in competence and given music
appropriate to their abilities. Thus the concertists in the first choir sang all
the music of Bach's cantatas (arias and chorusses) as soloists. Bach also
explains that less able singers (ideally another two to each of the four parts
and called 'ripienists') would be added to fill out the sound in the chorusses.
The same practice applied to the performances of the Passions. Thus the
numbers of voices involved in Bach's Leipzig cantatas was small – twelve at
most, often fewer – and the concertists were not separated from the choir as
they are now, but formed the nucleus of it.[20] Bach also trained his
instrumentalists in the Thomasschule, some of the instruments being played
by the abler choirboys.

Bach put more of his creative energy into his cantatas than into any other
form. During his lifetime he may have completed five year-cycles of
cantatas, one cantata for each Sunday and holy day. Out of these 300 or so,
about 200 now survive. Altogether they are a unique legacy in Christian
music, created by the requirements of orthodox Lutheranism, but
expressing a Pietist's faith in God and testifying to the joy of a personal
relationship with Jesus Christ.[21]

The ecstatic dimension in Bach's music

The dire warnings and deep suspicions of the Church Fathers concerning the
ecstatic dimension of music – its ability to bypass the intellect and evoke a
physical response, such as dance – are repeated constantly across the history
of Christianity. Nevertheless, the many celebrations of strongly rhythmic
music and dance described in the Old Testament suggest that an ecstatic
dimension is a central part of musical experience. Outside the Christian
church and in other cultures this has been celebrated and accepted freely.

The sophisticated world of Baroque music, of fugues and figured basses,
does not seem a likely place to find ecstatic music. But Wilfrid Mellers
suggests that Bach's Christian music is capable of precisely that:

It's an apotheosis of the dance if ever there was one; and this despite the fact that Protestantism, far more oppressively than Catholicism, had banished dance from worship in accord with its denial of the flesh; certainly his music, whatever dogma he intellectually subscribed to, reinstates dance as 'a play of Powers made visible' (Langer)... In this sense sensual dance is a sacral act, and Bach's blood, nerves and sinews were wiser than his church. In this chorus [*Cum Sancto Spiritu* from the B Minor Mass] he responds to an older rhythm, which Bernard of Clairvaux referred to when he wrote:

> Jesus the dancers' master is,
> A great skill at the dance he is,
> He turns to the right, he turns to the left,
> All must follow his teaching deft.

In order adequately to perform the 'Cum Sancto' and the many comparable passages in Bach, we must learn to swing no less than do, in our own day and world, black and brown North and South Americans as they worship God in the corybantic revel of gospel song and dance. It's worth noting that Gesner, rector of St Thomas's School and sometime critic of Bach's management of his academic duties there, remarked of Bach's direction of a rehearsal that 'the rhythm takes possession of all his limbs. I believe that my friend Bach must have many men like Orpheus within him!' ...For those who have ears to hear and limbs to cavort Bach's Gloria is a present excitation far more powerful than anything our jaded world can offer.[22]

The debt that much modern Christian music owes to Baroque composers has many dimensions. But one outstanding feature is the preference, then and now, for music with a strong pulse. Underpinning the music of Bach, for instance, is a beat, to be sensed most strongly in the commonplace 'walking' or 'running' bass, a restriction of the bass line to notes of equal value. Bach's interest in the music of Vivaldi and Corelli undoubtedly sharpened this quality in his music. The theory of affects, discussed earlier, encouraged a strong pulse to be firmly established for a substantial period, contributing to and sustaining the affect, or mood, of the piece.[23] The technique is akin to jazz and its very similar treatment of double-bass or bass guitar. What is more, both Baroque music and jazz have important roots in dance. From the humble tavern to the theatre, from the village hall to the aristocrat's palace, dance was an essential social grace in eighteenth-century Europe. Art-music – music for performance – was by no means set apart from dance-music; on the contrary, many suites of dances (not least by Bach himself) were written for the harpsichord, for stringed instruments and for orchestra.

Calvinists may have protested against dance-music in church worship, but on the whole they readily accepted its place in the secular world. It is worth noting that between 1717 and 1723 Bach was employed by Prince Leopold at the Calvinist court of Cöthen. Consequently, during that time Bach had practically no church-music duties whatever, but he wrote much instrumental music – extensive collections of dance-movements (Allemandes, Sarabandes, Gigues, Minuets) and countless other pieces which are dances in all but name. When he returned to writing music for the church, he did not hesitate to borrow material for his cantatas from the instrumental concertos he had originally written years before. Just as dance was present in courtly music, it was equally evident in Bach's music for the church.

The eternal truths

Thus Bach's music holds the symbolic, the rhetorical or emotional and the ecstatic or physical in perfect balance. Almost any work could be cited as an example, but the *Mass in B minor* is surely one of the most potent. In the *Crucifixus*, for example, the 'unlucky thirteen' repetitions of the ground bass (Example 23 gives two of them) symbolise the temporary triumph of evil when Jesus 'was crucified also for us under Pontius Pilate'; the mournful rhetoric of the exceptionally poignant harmony is extraordinary for its time, and yet the whole piece dances with the gentle ecstasy of a sarabande.

In its embodiment of every facet of musical experience – the symbolic, the rhetorical, the ecstatic – Bach's music finds a response with almost anyone. It can resonate with those who are sensitive to music on almost any level. It is compelling to the casual listener who expects immediate musical satisfaction. But equally it reveals unfathomable depths to those prepared to study its symbolic nature.

Cultural change gradually alters the perspective of succeeding generations on music of the past, but since Bach's music inhabits such a broad arena it

EXAMPLE 23

cannot fail to continue to delight its hearers with revelations of beauty, whatever their expectations. That beauty is of eternal and abiding truths: created order and human relationships, the perfection of God's universe and the agonies and joys of humanity's struggle to find its place within it.

If Bach was in many ways a typical product of his generation, what has been said of him can also apply to many other composers of that time. But it is significant that those who looked for wide recognition did not spend so much of their time writing Christian music. Telemann (1681–1767), although a church musical director in Hamburg for many years, made a bigger reputation from his forty operas than from his church music. Handel (1685–1759), also from Hamburg, built his personal and financial success in the world of secular music, again chiefly through opera.

Bach was perhaps the last truly great musician who owed his living almost entirely to the church. Many others have since been employed by it, but the opportunities and expectations of musicians in this position have on the whole gradually declined since Bach's time. Indeed, Lutheran church music suffered a particularly rapid and painful collapse at the end of the eighteenth century, revival having to wait until the twentieth and a renewed interest in its Baroque heritage.

Notes

1. The word Baroque has its origins in the Portuguese term 'barroco', meaning wild or untamed. In jewellery it referred to an uncut stone and in music to a style which used rhetorical methods to reflect the changing moods of human behaviour.

2. Constantin Bellerman, 1743, quoted in H. David and A. Mendel, editors, *The Bach Reader*, London, 1966, p. 236.

3. Christian Gerber, 1732; quoted in David and Mendel, pp. 229–230.

4. The Consistory records are quoted in David and Mendel, p. 52.

5. Quoted in David and Mendel, p. 60.

6. Quoted in David and Mendel, p. 33.

7. M. Pallis, *The Metaphysics of Musical Polyphony*, in *Studies in Comparative Religion*, vol. 10, no. 2, p. 106.

8. Quoted in P. Weiss and R. Taruskin, *Music in the Western World*, London, 1984, p. 218. For the complete work from which this extract is taken and an invaluable treatise on musical thought in Germany, see E.C. Harriss, *Johann Mattheson's Der Vollkommene Capellmeister* (1739), Ann Arbor, Michigan, 1981.

9. J. Spener, *Pia Desiderata*, Frankfurt, 1675, translated by T.G. Tappert, Philadelphia, 1964, p. 56.

10. *Works of Martin Luther*, vol. 7, Philadelphia, 1915–32, p. 284; quoted in A.K. Swihart, *Luther and the Lutheran Church*, London, 1961, p. 142.

11. See David and Mendel, pp. 195–96 for the complete list. Orthodoxy and Pietism in Bach's life are discussed in P. Spitta, *Johann Sebastian Bach*, London, 1884, vol. 1, p. 358 on, and summarised in G. Herz, *Essays on J.S. Bach*, Ann Arbor, 1985, pp. 2, 57–58.

12. The name means 'under the protection of the Lord'.

13. Quoted in F. Blume, *Protestant Church Music*, London, 1975, p. 601.

14. See also chapter 20, section on 'John and Charles Wesley'.

15. 'Jesus, thy blood and righteousness' is an example.

16. From E. Neumeister, *Geistlichen Cantaten statt Einer Kirchen-Musik*, 1704; quoted in L. Schrade, *Bach, the Conflict Between the Sacred and the Secular*, New York, 1973, p. 60.

17. Reinhard Keiser, *Gemüt sergötzung*, Hamburg, 1698, and quoted in H.E. Samuel, *The Cantata in Nuremberg*, Michigan, 1982, p. 72.

18. The extent to which congregations participated in the chorales of Bach's Passions and Cantatas is unknown. See M. Boyd, *Bach*, London, 1983, p. 144.

19. W. Neumann and H.J. Schulze, editors, *Bach-Dokumente*, Kassel, 1963, vol. 1, p. 88.

20. The likely performing circumstances of Bach's cantatas are elaborated in A. Parrott, 'Bach's chorus: A "brief yet highly necessary" reappraisal', *Early Music*, vol. 24, no. 4, November 1996.

21. An introduction can be found to Bach's cantatas in J.A. Westrup, *Bach Cantatas*, BBC Music Guides, London, 1966.

22. W. Mellers, *Bach and the Dance of God*, London, 1980, pp. 209–10.

23. The opening of the *Magnificat* or the so-called 'Air on a G-string' (the *Adagio* from Orchestral Suite No. 3), are only two examples from thousands.

Chapter 19

Turmoil in England – Commonwealth and Restoration

The time when, was in the year 1644, the Place where, was in the stately Cathedral Church of the Loyal City York. The occasion of it was, the great and close Seige which was then laid to that City, and strictly maintain'd for eleven weeks space... By this Occasion, there was shut up within the City abundance of People... who all or most of them came constantly every Sunday, to hear Publicke Prayers and Sermon in that spacious church. And indeed their Number was so exceeding great, that the church was even cramming or squeezing full.

They had a custom in that church... that always before the Sermon, the whole Congregation sang a Psalm, together with the Quire and the Organ; And you must know, that there was then a most Excellent-large-plump-lusty-full-speaking Organ, which cost (as I am credibly informed) a thousand Pounds.

This organ... being let out, into all its fulness of Stops, together with the Quire, began the Psalm. But when the Vast-Conchording-Unity of the whole Congregation came thundering in, even so, as it made the very ground shake under us; (Oh the unutterable ravishing Soul's delight!) In the which I was so transported, and wrapt up into High Contemplations, that there was no room left in my whole Man for anything below divine and heavenly Raptures; Nor could there possibly be any Thing in Earth to which That very Singing might be truly compared except That glorious and miraculous Quire, recorded in the Scriptures, at the Dedication of the Temple... where at their Singing of Psalms, Praises or Thanksgivings, the Glory of the Lord came down among them.[1]

This eyewitness account by Thomas Mace, a committed Christian and a staunch Royalist, gives an idea of the spiritual intensity that metrical psalm-singing could generate. Yet Mace had political as well as musical reasons for recording his experiences at York. He was in a city loyal to the Crown and under siege from Cromwell's armies. He was probably not aware that this was one of the last occasions that York Minster was to be used for worship for years. That same year, Parliament issued

> Two Ordinances of the Lords and Commons assembled in Parliament for the speedy demolishing of all organs, images and all matters of superstitious monuments in all Cathedralls, and Collegiate or Parish-Churches and Chapels, throughout the Kingdom of England and the Dominion of Wales; the better to accomplish the blessed reformation so happily begun, and to remove all offences and things illegal in the worship of God...[2]

Worship during the Commonwealth

Already the Puritans had dissolved the traditional hierarchy of the Church of England and within three years cathedrals became redundant, turned instead into ammunition dumps and staging posts for the army. In addition, Christian feasts (including Christmas) were no longer to be celebrated; marriage ceremonies in church were forbidden. Mace, in common with many, saw all this as a compound tragedy: political, social and religious.

Use of the *Book of Common Prayer* was made illegal in 1645 and about one-third of the ten thousand or so parish priests felt forced to resign. They were replaced by Presbyterian ministers in tune with the Puritan cause. The organisation of the church was supposedly democratised through new provincial and national assemblies, but the poet and political commentator John Milton noted the reality: 'New Presbyter is but old Priest writ large.'

Forms of service were very straightforward, stripped of any adornment, spectacle, ritual or set prayers:

> introductory prayer
> readings
> psalm
> prayers

sermon
prayers
(optional) psalm
blessing.[3]

This simple structure will be familiar to many non-conformist worshippers today. In Cromwell's Commonwealth, Anglicanism and Roman Catholicism were abhorred to the same degree that non-conformists were encouraged, the latter including the Baptists, Congregationalists and Quakers, and also Jews.

The Puritans were highly suspicious of music and its trappings – psalm-singing was the only form of Christian music which was approved. Psalms were sung metrically, very much in the manner of the European Calvinists, to verses often little more than doggerel, as this doxology shows:

> All glory to the Trinity,
>   that is mightes most,
> The living father and the Sonne,
>   and eke the holy ghost.
> As it hath bene in all the time,
>   that hath bene heretofore:
> As it is now and so shalbe,
>   henceforth for evermore.

The century-old translations of the psalms by Sternhold and Hopkins remained popular in spite of other recommended versions. Scotland had an official psalter imposed in 1650.

Lining out

The Puritans took a number of measures to try to ensure that the form and content of services was understood by the most humble parishioner, even when it meant overturning valued traditions. In 1644 one recommendation had a startling and widespread effect on the singing of psalms:

> In singing of psalms, the voice is to be tunably and gravely ordered; but the chief care must be to sing with understanding, and with grace in the heart, making melody unto the Lord… Every one that can read is to have

a psalm-book... but for the present, where many in the congregation
cannot read, it is convenient that the minister, or some other fit person...
do read the psalm, line by line, before the singing thereof.[4]

The results of this injunction were simple but bizarre. Each line of the psalm
verse was recited – and often sung – by the leading voice, which the
congregation would then follow. However, there was little or no musical
expertise in the leadership: the minister received no musical training and in
all probability neither did his clerk.

The result, which came to be called 'lining out', was wayward to say the
least. Both leader and individual members of the congregation tended to take
their own time (and a very long time indeed it was – perhaps half a minute
for each line!). Where harmonisation was attempted it was unsupported by
any organ or instruments, probably improvised and most unlikely to conform
to the four parts of a printed book. The slow pace of the singing allowed the
possibility of decoration and ornamentation of the melody by extra notes,
though these might be spontaneously and simultaneously created by several
singers at once. The result was a kind of semi-improvised chaos, undoubtedly
very remote from what trained musicians could tolerate, but with the heady
excitement of the musically ecstatic.

For a time lining out became a significant folk tradition, persisting in
England into the eighteenth century. Remarkably, the tradition is still just
alive today and can be heard in remote Gaelic-speaking areas of Scotland (in
the Isle of Lewis, for example) and in about 200 small Baptist churches in
the Southern States of North America.

The Restoration – crisis in parish church and cathedral

With the defeat of Cromwell and the restoration of Charles II to the throne
in 1660 the Church of England was reinstated. The Act of Uniformity of
1662, together with severe punishments for dissenters, required the revised
Book of Common Prayer to be used once more throughout the Church of
England. Nonetheless, the Puritans' demolition of worshipping traditions,
of organs, and most of all, the destruction of the irreplaceable contents of
church and cathedral choir-libraries, were body-blows to Christian music

from which recovery was very slow. Indeed, the annihilation or dispersal of choir-books meant that musicians have remained ignorant of much pre-Restoration church music right up until the research of twentieth-century scholars. From a trained musician's perspective, musical standards in the parish church fell to the lowest level. Because the landed gentry and other educated people no longer supported the country parishes with their resources, the churches became places of worship where music was uniquely the province of ordinary people.

In spite of the fact that metrical psalms had no official place in the Anglican liturgy, they were forced upon the local parish priest by their popularity – it was the only kind of music the congregations knew and in which they could join. The parish priest himself probably did not sing these psalms. Indeed, most educated people found such primitive music excruciating:

> For when we Sing unto God, we ought to Sing chearfully, and with a loud voice, and heartily to rejoyce... 'Tis Sad to hear what whining, toting, yelling, or Screeking there is in many Country Congregations, as if the people were affrighted, or distracted.[5]

Meanwhile, the cathedrals were suffering very serious financial troubles and good musicians could not be found for the fees they offered, made paltry by inflation. As Thomas Tudway noted, in 1716:

> Deans & Chapters, since the Reformation, tyeing their Clerks down to the same allowance now, when money is not a 5th part in value to what it was then, have brought generall neglect of the service & a very mean and lame way of performing it, for want of encouragement... This insufficient provision, I take to be, the sourse of the decay of Cathedrall Service with us; and what makes this yet more evident is that where there is encouragement, or a maintenance, as at the Royall Chappell, St Pauls, Westminster Abby &c, they abound in good voices, and the service is perform'd with decency & solemnity that God is truely worship'd, as of old, in the beauty of Holines...[6]

According to Roger North, another contemporary musical observer:

> The Cathedral churches in the North... have the ordinary wind instruments in the Quires, as the cornett, sackbutte, double curtaile and others, which supply the want of voices...[7]

These instruments were those associated with the town bands, the city waits, and presumably were allowed to participate in Christian worship only under these desperate circumstances.

Parish churches and Independent chapels fared even more badly in their musical provision, with no organ or other musical talent to lead them. Their musical fare was extraordinarily limited, no more than a universal adherence to the metrical psalms – either the old way of Sternhold and Hopkins, or the new of the Tate and Brady Psalter first published in 1696.

Notes

1. T. Mace, *Musick's Monument*, London 1676, in facsimile, Paris, 1966, part 1, chapter 10, pp. 18–10.

2. Quoted in K.R. Long, *The Music of the English Church*, London, 1972, p. 206.

3. From N. Temperley, *Music of the English Parish Church*, Cambridge, 1979, vol. 1, p. 78.

4. From *A directory for the publicke worship of God throughout the three kingdoms of England, Scotland and Ireland*, London, 1644, in P. Hall, *Reliquiae Liturgicae*, vol. III, Bath, 1847.

5. Mace, chapter 5, p. 9.

6. Tudway (c. 1716); quoted in C. Hogwood and R. Luckett, *Music in Eighteenth Century England*, Cambridge, 1983, p. 43.

7. Roger North, *Lord Keeper North*, 1676; see J.W. Wilson, *Roger North on Music*, London, 1959, p. 40.

Chapter 20

Congregational Music

It is no surprise that seventeenth-century styles of worship should reflect the hierarchical nature of a class-based society. Attitudes to the new and the adventurous were also sharply differentiated by class. At one extreme, traditions of worship in the country areas, once established by the reformers, changed very slowly and with great reluctance. The old version of the psalter existed side by side with the new version of Tate and Brady for years; indeed, the new never wholly replaced the old, which clung on in places till the mid-nineteenth century. On the other hand, the Chapel Royal encouraged, for a time at least, the production of several new anthems a month in the latest continental styles.

Does a slow rate of change indicate sterility? Do congregations cling to tradition for the illusion of safety it may bring? Or does the excitement of the new and the colourful blur a sense of the enduring truths of the Christian faith? These questions are still relevant today, for English cathedrals cling to the old ways while patterns of parish worship, together with their musical content, are changing with bewildering rapidity. Perhaps resistance to such change and a desperate need for it are both signs of a faith under threat – for the coming eighteenth century was an Age of Reason not unlike the present.

The Anglican Church was guilty of providing the outward image of worship, without being too concerned about the spiritual welfare of its congregations. The abject poverty and the pitiful quality of life for the masses were matters of no consequence for the very wealthy; sharply differentiated musical styles in worship typified the two extremes.

Not until the arrival of the Methodists and Evangelicals in the mid-eighteenth century did compassion seem once more to return to Christianity, and with it came a renewed awareness of the need and the possibility of redemption, expressed in a great surge of hymns. With them returned the corporate expression of faith in God which lies at the heart of Christian worship.

Early hymns

In the seventeenth century hymns did not at first exist as an expression of worship for everyone, for the public singing of texts not directly from the Bible was still regarded by many as an 'error of popery'. Instead, they were written for the aristocracy and performed in their private chapels by professional musicians. Some of the most beautiful hymn-tunes from the earlier seventeenth century, and still included in English hymn-books were created under these circumstances.

One of the earliest moves towards congregational hymn-singing came from a minister of the Particular Baptists, Benjamin Keach, who in about 1673 persuaded the majority of his congregation in Southwark, outside London, to sing a hymn at the end of Communion, remembering the Gospel account of the Last Supper: 'And when they had sung an hymn, they went out into the Mount of Olives...'

The practice caused much controversy and threatened the Particular Baptists with schism. Twenty years later Keach published the decisive *The Breach Repaired in God's Worship; or, Singing of Psalms, Hymns, and Spiritual Songs, proved to be an Holy Ordinance of Jesus Christ* and in 1697 he published a collection of thirty-seven hymns.[1] Hymns also began to appear in supplements to collections of psalms, such as the *Divine Companion* published by Henry Playford in 1701.

What did Keach and his contemporaries mean by 'hymn', as opposed to psalm or spiritual song? A hymn was considered to be a devotional poem 'of human composure', intended for corporate worship. The writer who began the new era of the Christian hymn was Isaac Watts (1674–1748) whose hymns refreshingly cross denominational divides and are a part of Anglican, Roman Catholic and free church worship today.

One of the reasons for the widespread use of Watts' hymns down the ages was his ability to summarise universal Christian experience – sentiments with which all worshippers could identify. Since he composed his hymns in the standard metres of the psalms (short, common and long) they were easily married to any number of familiar tunes.[2]

Watts wrote well over 400 hymns and psalm paraphrases, but he stood only at the start of a veritable explosion of hymn-writing. More than 450 different metrical psalters and at least 250 different hymn-books were published during the eighteenth century. The very nature of the hymn makes it impossible to count the number of poems or tunes these figures might represent. For it is a mistake to regard a hymn as a fixed and final creation. Like the church buildings they are sung in, they are subject to continual alteration. Firstly, the tunes to which the words were matched were constantly changing from one publication to another. Secondly, both words and tunes were frequently altered from the first time they appeared. Perhaps those who baulk at present-day revisions would do well to consider how many changes their favourite hymns may already have suffered before reaching the pages of a modern hymn-book.

This apparent lack of respect for the original or the 'authentic' gives an important clue to the true nature of hymn-writing. With few exceptions, it is best understood as a folk-art. Even sophisticated thinkers like Isaac Watts or John Wesley were aware that hymns could not be poetry fully-fledged. Isaac Watts said of himself: 'I make no pretences to the name of poet or polite writer... I am ambitious to be a servant to the churches and a helper to the joy of the meanest Christian.'[3]

Watts was certain of the need to be simple and straightforward, to avoid the expression of sentiments more involved than a singing congregation could grasp: 'I would neither indulge any bold metaphors, nor admit of hard words, nor tempt the ignorant worshipper to sing without his understanding.'[4] This would be a challenge to any writer and Watts admitted its difficulties: 'It was hard to sink every line to the level of a whole congregation, and yet to keep it above [critical] contempt.'[5]

Some of the best-known English hymns of the Christian church stem from Watts' desire to interpret the psalms afresh in the light of the New Testament. These he collected in *The Psalms of David imitated in the Language of the New Testament, and apply'd to the Christian State of Worship*. In its introduction he implied adverse criticism of Tate and Brady:

> Would I encourage a parish clerk to stand up in the midst of a country church and say, 'I will praise Thee upon a psaltery'? I have chosen rather to imitate than to translate, and thus to compose a Psalm-Book for Christians after the manner of the Jewish Psalter.

It was evidently Watts' intention to imitate the psalms in his contemporary language, like so many authors today. He would not have been aware in his lifetime of the degree of success these psalm 'imitations' eventually had, for texts like *Jesus shall reign where'er the sun* (part of Psalm 72) or *O God, our help in ages past* (Psalm 90) only became widely known in the later nineteenth century. Their continuing success has necessitated further alteration; they are sung nowadays much shortened, and John Wesley changed the original *Our God, our help* to *O God*... Further changes would be needed nowadays to passages like the one below to accommodate shifts in the meaning of words:

> Here every bowel of our God
> With soft compassion rolls.

The melodies to which such hymns were sung were published in a great variety of ways, reflecting the differing situations in which they were sung. The simplest (and for a long time the commonest) congregational singing had no accompaniment or harmonisation at all. The older psalm-tunes have a simplicity and strength that is imposing without harmony. But such tunes would have been profusely decorated by the singers, and in a country church probably 'lined out' with the help of the parish clerk, who would say or sing each line in turn with the people echoing him.

Music in the town

In the eighteenth century Anglican churches in towns and cities began to aspire to a more refined style of music. Efforts were made for the first time to find groups of singers that might be trained to assist the congregation to sing better. The Society for the Promotion of Christian Knowledge was founded in 1698 to campaign for the establishment of religious societies and charity schools. The schools existed to give free education to the poor of the parish, but the inmates in their turn began to receive some musical training in order to assist in parish worship.

Some of the more well-to-do town parishes might have boasted a choir of charity children and a recently installed organ. The money for these facilities had to be raised locally and the school-children were instructed to be grateful:

At Chelsea a charity school was founded in 1707 by William Petyt, and the school building included a special 'cloister' or covered arcade, three arches in length, facing the street. Here the scholars were to stand after service twice each Sunday 'with their caps off... until the congregation passed by', and were to 'be given to understand who are their benefactors and instructed that as often as they pass by any of them they pull off their caps and make them a bow.'[6]

For those who could afford them, the presence of choir and organ transformed the musical content of the worship, though not to everyone's pleasure. It was not always accepted that the choir should sing anything by itself, nor that it should sit apart from the congregation. The organist often took the opportunity to play over the tune in a highly decorated way and then to provide interludes between verses and even between lines.

Organ improvisations ('voluntaries') after the morning psalm were performed for many years in urban areas. For the benefit of the organist, hymns were printed with a bass line, perhaps with figures to indicate the accompanying harmonies. Other books added a middle line for those who might be able to harmonise – Playford's *The whole book of psalms... compos'd in three parts* (1677) was particularly successful. Although tunes did appear in the familiar four-part layout of present-day hymn-books, it would be at least a century before a significant number of choirs were capable of leading congregations in this way.

Some Anglican churches in towns and cities even aspired to imitate the cathedral style on special occasions. The charity children might be encouraged to sing on their own (perhaps at the annual 'charity sermon') and anthems were composed for treble voices and organ in the tuneful Italian style that owed something to Purcell and later to Handel. It was also expected, as a matter of good performance, that the melodies would be embellished with expressive ornaments, as prefaces to many psalters instructed:

> Nothing is more common than for practitioners in plain Psalmody not
> to be taught the use of the Appoggiatura, which was invented to adorn
> the Arts of Singing, and is a little note placed immediately before a
> great one, for the arriving more gracefully to it.[7]

Today classical musicians are generally exceedingly wary of departing from the printed page and provide no ornaments at all, which, judging by Example 24, does not represent the spirit or the letter of the Baroque age. These pages are from *A New and Easie Method to Learn to Sing by Book... Design'd chiefly for, and applied to, the promoting of PSALMODY*.[8] The left-hand page here presents the unadorned psalm-tune as usually printed (note that it is the Middle Part, not the Treble) with bass line and accompanying treble voice added. The right-hand page shows the 'usual' and 'better' style of embellished singing. As such it might be acceptable to a trained musician sung by a competent soloist, but *corporate* embellishment by a congregation (which was undoubtedly practised) produced results that cultured musicians abhorred.

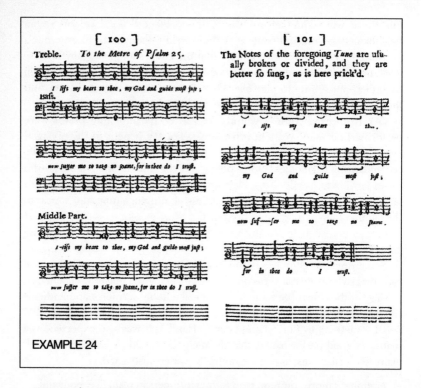

EXAMPLE 24

However, at St Thomas' Church in Southwark (where there was no choir and no organ till 1879)[9] and in many churches:

> the cause was almost hopeless. The clerk commences his stave, and goes through it almost wholly unaccompanied, or perhaps joined towards the close, by the feeble efforts of a single voice or two.[10]

Music in the country

The countryside in the eighteenth century did not have the easy accessibility that car-owners now expect of it. Villagers could rarely afford to travel and their life was largely isolated from the rapidly developing world of urban commerce and industry. Worship in country churches therefore tended to develop in distinctive ways, often very different from the town. There was no money to build organs, and there were few educated people in the congregation able or willing to raise musical standards.

The old way of psalm-singing remained popular and the parish clerk continued to have his way. Gradually it was accepted that a choir could help to improve matters. The choir usually won for itself a place in the old west galleries of Gothic parish churches. In other places they sometimes had a gallery provided for them. Such choirs sometimes became very keen, spending nights during the week practising together. They received a rudimentary musical training from travelling singing-teachers, who found some sort of living by offering instruction to anyone who could pay for it:

> There are men who travel, and style themselves professors of, and instructors in, psalmody; they are furnished with books of their own selection which are seldom correct, and these are disposed of in every place where they go. While such measures are countenanced, it is impossible to expect that their disciples should ever arrive at any degree of perfection.[11]

A uniquely primitive kind of music developed under these circumstances. As west-gallery choirs became more confident, they attempted to sing in harmony, usually with the hymn-tune taken by the tenor voices and up to three more voices added around them. They even embarked on anthems circulated by the singing teachers, written in a vivid and ungrammatical style by composers such as William Tans'ur (1706–83) and George Ffitch.[12] Unfortunately, the musical results were sometimes distressing, and not always edifying for the congregation which was excluded from taking part in such pieces.

In the latter half of the eighteenth century musical instruments became accepted as a means of reinforcing the choristers in the gallery. Churches even bought instruments for their use. The bass was the part that most obviously needed bolstering and the most lowly choirs might use a vamphorn – simply a long megaphone – to amplify the voice! Otherwise bassoon and cello were found to be the most useful. Other treble instruments (wind instruments tended to carry better) played along with the upper voices to create some kind of harmony. Even so, the secular associations of some instruments caused misgiving:

> The violin is very properly excluded, since, beside its weakness as a solitary instrument, its continued use to wait upon the drunken

ditties, trolled forth in the ale house, or to regulate the dances that grace a village festival, renders it a very unfit medium for Sabbath praise.[13]

A number of printed books were produced with music to help such players, but mostly the instrumentalists played from the voice-parts or by ear. George Eliot's novel *Adam Bede* (1859) contains a detailed and sympathetic evocation of worship in a country parish church, of which this can only be a glimpse:

> Presently the sound of the bassoon and the key-bugles burst forth; the evening hymn, which always opened the service, had begun... The interior of Hayslope Church... was free from the modern blemish of galleries. The choir had two narrow pews to themselves in the middle of the right-hand row, so that it was a short process for Roshua Rann [the parish clerk] to take his place among them as principal bass, and return to his desk when the singing was over... None of the old people held books – why should they? not one of them could read. But they knew a few 'good words' by heart, and their withered lips now and then moved silently, following the service without any clear comprehension indeed, but with a simple faith in its efficacy to ward off harm and bring blessing.

The isolation of some country parish churches and especially of non-conformist chapels encouraged congregations to develop their own music. The Baptists at Lumb, in the moors and forests of Rossendale north of Manchester, built up an enthusiastic tradition of hymn-singing and composition under their minister, John Nuttall. These 'Larks of Dean' were Lancashire farmers and gradually

> developed into a strong local society of musical composers, of whom John Nuttall's two sons James (1745–1806) and Henry (1747–1810) both excelled in composing hymn tunes. James's tunes bore such names as Bocking Warp, Friendship, Lark, Sampson, Spanking Rodger and Temple... Like many late eighteenth-century composers elsewhere throughout England, they revelled in Handel's oratorios and so far as their resources allowed tried imitating his style. Their tunes invariably go with a swing, teem with runs and repetitions, and often finish with a few bars of rousing chorus. Dauntless enthusiasm and robust joyousness were the keynotes of their religion... [14]

The performance practice of such groups makes colourful reading, albeit recorded by a critic:

> The evils that require a reforming hand are chiefly these: singing out of tune, frequently too flat, with a nasal twang, straining the voice to an unnatural pitch, introducing awkward drawls and tasteless ornaments... Trilling upon each syllable is no uncommon vice among country singers... But the evils, however glaring, are all redeemable... the scream, the pert snap, the buzzing bass, the rude and violent pronunciation, the deafening thump of the timekeeper, which resembles that of the tilt-hammer of some furnace, might be kept in subjection to a sounder judgment.[15]

Recently, interest in this rough-hewn Christian music has intensified, particularly around the parish church of St Mary in Puddletown, Dorset, where the family of the novelist Thomas Hardy worshipped for many years. A number of other churches are now recreating their own forgotten west-gallery traditions, evidently far more widespread than previously supposed. There is now evidence of such bands in a number of Welsh churches, one (at the Baptist church in Upper Rhymney) surviving up to the Second World War.[16]

John and Charles Wesley

For the Wesleys, questions of decorum in worship were a distraction from the fundamental aim, which was to proclaim that, through Christ, everyone, and not simply the Calvinist elect, had the right to salvation and eternal life. To proclaim that message, both John (1703–91) and his brother Charles Wesley (1707–88) made a unique contribution to Christian hymnody, in words and music, that severed denominational boundaries.

In 1735 John Wesley, already involved with developing the spiritual life of Oxford undergraduates (the 'Oxford Methodists' so called because they were following a method of dividing time between work and devotion), accepted an invitation to travel with his brother as a missionary to Georgia on behalf of the Society for the Propagation of the Gospel. They found themselves travelling with some Moravian Christians whose expression of faith through their hymn-singing made a deep impression. The Wesley brothers' experiences in Georgia were traumatic, but for John they especially helped him to understand 'what I least of all suspected, that I, who went to America to convert others, was never converted myself'.[17]

In 1738, partly through the study of Luther, both he and Charles experienced true conversion profoundly and personally, finding themselves 'at peace with God'. In the words of Charles' journal: 'I saw that by faith I stood.'

John Wesley then visited the Moravians at their Herrnhut community to experience their Christian living for himself. His love for their music led him to translate a number of their hymns and to encourage the use of a number of German melodies then unknown in England.

Apart from preaching, Charles Wesley's special gift was to encompass his Christian experience in hymns. They are 'songs of individual experience, marking the successive stages of penitence, conversion, justification, pardon and sanctification in the life of the Christian pilgrim'.[18] The impact on countless lives of many of Charles Wesley's 6,500 hymns need not be re-emphasised here. But his hymns were a challenge to musicians, too, for they were cast in a far greater variety of metres than those of Isaac Watts. Clearly, their music often needed to be composed specially, allowing the possibility of a more intimate relationship between words and music. In the late 1740s Handel wrote three melodies for texts by Charles Wesley ('Sinners, obey the gospel word', 'O love divine' and 'Rejoice, the Lord is King'). Another composer of the time and a convert to Methodism, J.F. Lampe, provided many more.

The Wesleys had very clear ideas of the role of music in worship, both John and Charles having a strong musical awareness (and modest musical skills) through a cultured family. Charles was later blessed with two sons of considerable musical talent: Charles (1757–1834) and Samuel (1766–1837). Some of his Methodist friends disapproved of his encouragement of their music, but it seems that Charles regretted his own lack of formal training in the art:

> Who would not wish to have the skill
> Of tuning instruments at will?
> Ye powers who guide my actions, tell
> Why I, in whom the seeds of music dwell,
> Who most its power and excellence admire,
> Whose very breast itself a lyre
> Was never taught the happy art
> Of modulating sounds...[19]

John Wesley closely supervised the content of the dozens of Methodist hymn-books published during his lifetime, to be set down exactly as they were sung by their congregations. In the preface to *Sacred Melody* (1761) he wrote:

> I have been endeavouring for more than twenty years to procure such a book as this. But in vain: Masters of music were above following any direction but their own. And I was determined, whoever should compile this, should follow my direction. Not mending our tunes, but setting them down, neither better nor worse than they were...

The Methodists insisted that the music to their hymns should be accessible to all and where possible sung by all. Gone (or almost gone) were the old metrical psalms, gone also was the involved part-singing of some country churches, gone was the separation of choir from congregation. Like Luther, John Wesley was happy to adapt popular tunes from any source (much to the disapprobation of high churchmen).

Above all, strenuous efforts were made to educate congregations into singing well. John Wesley provided musical advice to the congregation in a number of his hymn-books:

I.   LEARN *these* Tunes before you learn any others; afterwards learn as many as you please.

II.   Sing them exactly as they are printed here, without altering them or mending them at all...

IV.   Sing *lustily* and with good courage. Beware of singing as if you were half dead, or half asleep; but lift your voice with strength...

V.   Sing *Modestly*. Do not baul, so as to be heard above, or distinct from the rest of the congregation, that you destroy the harmony; but strive to unite your voices together, so as to make one clear harmonious sound.

VI.   Sing in *Time*: whatever time is sung be sure to keep with it. Do not run before nor stay behind it; but attend close to the leading voice, and move therewith as exactly as you can; and take care you sing not too slow. This drawling way naturally steals on all who are lazy; and it is high time to drive it out from among us, and sing all our tunes just as quick as we did at first.

VII.   Above all sing *spiritually*. Have an eye to God in every word you sing. Aim at pleasing Him more than yourself.[20]

Quite apart from the excellent sense these rules would make for present congregations, points V and VI are revealing as counterblasts to the tradition of lining out – which undoubtedly used 'open-throat' singing, a coarse and rough sound to classically-trained musicians, and which involved the heterophony of many individuals deliberately singing out of time with each other.

When a Methodist congregation had developed the capacity to sing with heart and soul (in a way that is rarely experienced nowadays) then a number of musical elaborations were possible. Women and men occupied different parts of the chapel and were asked to take alternate verses. A more sophisticated scheme was for the men to sing the bass to the women's melody, as minutes from the 1740s indicate:

(9)   Let the women constantly sing their parts alone. Let no man sing with them, unless he understands the notes, and sings the bass, as it is pricked down in the book.[21]

Hymns with independent parts for men and women naturally developed as a result. Instruments, however, were viewed with caution in the early days of the movement. There is evidence that John Wesley used an oboe to assist singing in the open, but otherwise 'the organ and bass viol were apparently the only instruments that the Conference sanctioned'.[22] Where John Wesley was ambivalent about the organ, he was certain about anthems. They included 'vain repetition':

The repeating the same words so often (but especially while another repeats different words, the horrid abuse which runs through the modern church-music)... shocks all common sense, so it necessarily brings in dead formality.[23]

Formality was the deadening force in music most to be resisted. The Wesley's would interrupt the singing of a hymn to challenge the congregation to recall the meaning of the words they had just that moment uttered. Later on in the movement, such formality did return: the organ, instrumental groups, even anthems.

Partly through the example of the Methodists, singing in Anglican churches may have made some improvements in the nineteenth century, but the west-gallery choirs and bands continued in country parishes to perform their 'formal' anthems and hymns with raucous enthusiasm, to a seated congregation. They, too, benefitted from the repertoire of Methodist tunes, sung to metrical psalms. As Thomas Hardy recounts in *The Return of the Native*:

> One Sunday I can well mind – a bass viol day – and Yeobright had brought his own. 'Twas the hundred and thirty-third to Lydia, and when they'd come to
>
> > Ran down his beard and o'er his robes
> > Its costly moisture shed,
>
> neighbour Yeobright, who had just warmed to his work, drove his bow into them strings that glorious grand that he e'en a'most sawed the bass viol into two pieces.

Handel's *Messiah*

For the congregations of most country churches, the music for which the eighteenth century is now remembered was almost unknown – but not altogether. Following his arrival in England in 1710, Handel (1685–1759) had increasingly dominated the art-music of Britain: his Italian operas became highly fashionable in London till about 1728 and he wrote the most splendid church music for state occasions, as Purcell had done before him (*Zadok the Priest* and the Utrecht and Dettingen settings of the *Te Deum,* for instance). For the London opera audiences he provided biblical oratorios to be performed during the Lenten closed season. These were operas in all but name – performed in the manner of opera, by opera singers and in their theatres. Only the staging was missing.

All this did have some effect on Christian music, albeit indirectly. Firstly, a number of English composers of the time (Maurice Greene, John Stanley, William Boyce) admired Handel and his achievements and were able to transmit something of his style to the more humble musical surroundings of Christian worship. Secondly, the work that he wrote in 1741 called *A Sacred Oratorio, Messiah* had an effect eventually reaching far beyond the circumstances of its first performances.

Messiah was originally written for a charity concert at the New Music Hall, Fishamble Street in Dublin, on 13 April 1742. The idea of presenting it in a

London theatre caused some initial unease. As *The Universal Spectator* put it, on the date of its first performance in London, on 23 March 1743:

> How will this appear to After-Ages, when it shall be read in History, that in such an Age the People of England were arriv'd to such a Height of Impiety and Prophaneness that the most sacred Things were suffer'd to be us'd as publick Diversions, and that in a Place, and by Persons, appropriate to the Performance not only of light and vain, but all too often prophane and dissolute pieces?

Clearly, the secular and sacred had to be kept strictly apart. What is more, *Messiah* was unlike any of Handel's other oratorios. Not only was it contemplative of its theme rather than vividly dramatic, but the subject was Christ himself, unlike the other oratorios based almost exclusively on Old Testament figures. For some liberal thinkers, its serious Christian message was an uncomfortable intrusion into worldly and high-class entertainment.

From its composition, *Messiah* has been performed incessantly, and often on a grand scale even in its early days. In 1784, for instance, a centenary performance was given in Westminster Abbey by more than 500 performers (including an orchestra of 95 violins, 26 violas, 21 cellos, 15 double basses, 26 oboes, 27 bassoons, 30 brass and four drummers). The Dutch composer J.W. Lustig was in the audience and confessed it had an 'indescribably beautiful effect'. The exercise was repeated often and successfully in subsequent years.

Messiah in its entirety had no place in church worship. Nonetheless, its effect on Christian music (albeit delayed) was profound, for local choirs and their instrumentalists, particularly in the north of England, began to join together to perform oratorios, *Messiah* in particular. The Ellenbrook Monthly Meeting was one such society, made up largely of handloom weavers, who, in the early nineteenth century

> became good performers, and had a large experience and knowledge of Handel's music, Dr Croft's, Dr Greene's, Dr Boyce's... and other anthems. At the quarterly meetings the proceeds were divided between the four choirs, with which they generally bought a score copy of some oratorio... and from this the instrumental parts were copied.[24]

This was an early stage of the widespread development of choral societies in the nineteenth century, many of which are still thriving today. More importantly, contact with music of high professional excellence gave the choirs involved an idea of what might be achieved in the music of their local churches. Cathedral musicians, who felt this sophisticated music to be their province, were not all happy with this development:

> These [village practitioners], since the rage of oratorios has spread from the capital to every market town in the kingdom, can by no means be satisfied unless they introduce chants, services, and anthems, into their parish churches, and accompany them with... scolding fiddles, squalling hautboys, false-stopped violoncellos, buzzing bassoons... in place of an organ.[25]

Notes

1. *Hymns in Commemoration of the Sufferings of Our Blessed Saviour Jesus Christ, compos'd for the celebration of his Holy Supper.*

2. See glossary under 'psalm metre'.

3. Quoted in E. Houghton, *Christian Hymn-Writers*, Bridgend, 1982, p. 57.

4. Quoted in D. Davie and R. Stevenson, *English Hymnology in the Eighteenth Century*, Los Angeles, 1980, p. 10.

5. Davie and Stevenson, p. 10.

6. From the London County Council's *Survey of London XXII*, London, 1950, p. 103; quoted in N. Temperley, *Music of the English Parish Church*, Cambridge, 1979, vol. I, p. 102.

7. William Riley, *Parochial Psalmody Corrected*, 1762; quoted in R.G. Woods, *Good Singing Still*, Telford, 1995, p. 97.

8. Published anonymously in London, 1686, but almost certainly by Captain Simon Pack. I am grateful to Robert Spencer for this information and for the musical example.

9. See Temperley, vol. I, p. 123.

10. W. Vincent, *Considerations on Parochial Music*, London, 1787, p. 23.

11. Preface to Thomas Billington, *The Te Deum etc, page XI* (1784); quoted in Temperley, vol. I, p. 161.

12. The American counterpart of this type of music is discussed in chapter 33.

13. J.A. La Trobe, *The Music of the Church Considered in its Various Branches*, London, 1831; quoted in Woods, p. 74.

14. A. Buckley, *History of the Providence Baptist Chapel*, Lumb, Rawtenstall, 1928; see R. Elbourne, *Music and Tradition in Early Industrial Lancashire*, Wodbridge, Suffolk, 1980, Appendix 1.

15. J.A. La Trobe; quoted in Woods, p. 96.

16. A West Gallery Music Association exists to encourage interest in the music and social life of eighteenth-century country church musicians.

17. H. Davies, *Worship and Theology in England*, Princeton, New Jersey, 1961–75, vol. III, p. 234.

18. J.S. Curwen, *Studies in Worship-Music*, London, 1880, p. 12.

19. F. Baker, *The Representative Verse of Charles Wesley*, New York, 1962.

20. From *Select Hymns with Tunes Annext: Designed chiefly for the USE of the people called Methodists*, 1761; quoted in C.R. Young, *Music of the Heart*, London, 1995.

21. *Minutes of the Methodist Conference*, London, 1862–64, vol. 1, 'Large' Minutes in answer to question 39.

22. Young, pp. 89–90.

23. 1768 Bristol Conference Minutes, section 6, in J.T. Lightwood, *Methodist Music in the Eighteenth Century*, London, 1927, p. 35.

24. W. Millington, *Sketches of local musicians and musical societies*, Pendlebury, 1884; quoted in Temperley, vol. I, p. 199. See also D. Burrows, *Handel: Messiah*, Cambridge, 1991.

25. W. Mason, *Essays on English Church Music*, York, 1795; quoted in Temperley, vol. I, p. 200.

Chapter 21

Wales – Land of Song

The Welsh have a respect for the art of singing that the English delight to caricature. It shows itself in all sorts of ways: the roaring song of the rugby crowds at Cardiff Arms Park, the continuing excellence of some male-voice choirs... On another level comes the bardic tradition of *Cerdd Dant*, in which exacting poetic and melodic structures must be improvised against a folk-tune. In all this there is perhaps a distant race memory of the role music used to play in an isolated and agrarian society – a memory which has faded more quickly and completely in England.

Like Italian, the Welsh language is a wonderful vehicle for song: its strong stresses and lilting quality are already half-way to music. The exceptional hymnody of Wales has benefitted from it as much as the folk-song: tunes such as *Olwen* or *Crugybar* have repetitive rhythmic patterns related to the language.

Celtic traditions of worship flourished in Wales till the eighth century, but although some of the liturgical detail is known, the music that beautified it is lost – almost certainly for ever – through the failure of the melodies to be passed on to an age that took the trouble to write them down. Only the words to some unique local hymns are preserved in the *Bangor Antiphoner*, dating from the seventh century. The combined pressures of Pope Gregory and later of Charlemagne on churches to conform to the Roman tradition in their liturgies eventually squeezed the Celtic traditions out of Wales.

Little evidence remains of medieval musical traditions. Giraldus Cambrensis in his travels around Wales at the beginning of the twelfth century commented on the Welsh love of singing in harmony:

> When they make music together, they sing their songs not in unison, as is done elsewhere, but in parts, with many simultaneous modes, so that in a crowd of singers... you would hear as many songs and different intervals as there were heads; yet, they all accord in one consonant polyphonic song.[1]

This tantalising glimpse suggests that some monastic music also might have been harmonised by capable Welsh musicians – and perhaps some items in the Worcester Fragments, a manuscript dating from the thirteenth century, represent a style not unlike Gerald's description (Example 25). It must be said that these are also typical of English music of the time, some *conducti* yielding a rich three-part sonority.

EXAMPLE 25

The bleak isolation of parts of Wales was attractive to monastic communities such as the Cistercians, an Order established in France in 1098 to recover the original traditions of St Benedict. The remote Abbey of Valle Crucis in North Wales, for example, was the heart of a Cistercian community established by Madog ap Gruffydd Maelor at the beginning of the thirteenth century. The Cistercians favoured the study of literature and music, but no records survived the Reformation.

The first printed church music of Wales is the psalter of Edmond Prys. This is the Welsh-language equivalent of Sternhold and Hopkins' *Whole*

Booke of Psalmes of 1569. As a book of metrical psalms in the Welsh language, it appeared late, in 1621, when psalters in most other European languages had been long established. It uses twelve English psalm-tunes, but a mystifying characteristic of the *Llyfr y Psalmau* is that every other line of the psalm-texts has seven syllables, one too long for the melodies, for example, the beginning of Psalm 51 as shown here:

> Trugaredd dod i mi
> Duw o'th ddaioni tyner,
> Ac ymaith tyn anwiredd man,
> O'th drugareddau lawer.

Prys' translations are at a much higher literary level than the doggerel of its English equivalents.

Of the cathedral churches after the Reformation, only St David's managed to maintain a continuity of church music. It was here that one of the most famous of Jacobean composers, Thomas Tomkins, was born (in 1572) into a musical family, his father being vicar-choral and subsequently organist and master of the choristers at the cathedral. Tomkins was in his twenties when the family moved to Gloucester; he became a key musical figure at Worcester Cathedral and later with the Chapel Royal. Llandaf Cathedral, outside Cardiff, had its choir suppressed during this period; it is possible that the Tomkins family moved from Wales because musical life could no longer support them there.

It was the spiritual revival of the eighteenth century that once more stirred the embers of Welsh church music, although travelling singing teachers had been at work to raise the standard of parish music for some time. Charles Wesley toured Wales several times in the 1740s, where he enjoyed passionate and enthusiastic singing:

> *Journal, Friday July 17th, the Castle, Cardiff*: The voice of praise and thanksgiving was heard in this dwelling-place. Before, at, and after supper we sang, and blessed God with joyful lips. Those in the parlour and kitchen were continually honouring, by offering him praise.

Clearly the emotional effect of the singing was powerful:

> I preached in the afternoon to the prisoners... above twenty were felons. The word melted them down. Many tears were shed at the singing of 'where shall my wondering soul begin', 'Outcasts of men to you I call' etc.[2]

A few days before this, Charles Wesley had met an influential figure in the Christian life of Wales, Howel Harris (1714–73). Harris was by this time at the head of a significant Christian revival in Wales, on a parallel course to the Methodist movement. Though the leadership of this Welsh Calvinistic Methodism was marred by disagreements between Harris and his colleague Daniel Rowland, Harris managed to fulfill his dream of building an almshouse and school as the nucleus of a new Christian community at Trefeca, near Brecon. Although the Trefeca community came to an end in 1839, the house, chapel and grounds remain an important Christian centre for Wales and a permanent landmark of the revivals of their time.

The third key figure of the eighteenth century was the hymn-writer William Williams of Pantycelyn (1717–91). His high productivity and standards in both Welsh and English hymnody encouraged new hymn-melodies to be published in increasing numbers towards the end of the century. Their tunes reflect the powerful influence of the Methodist movement and its love of hymn-singing, especially in the provision of rousing refrains which could be sung 'competitively' in parts, as in Example 26.

Although this period and the earlier years of the nineteenth century were a rich period for nonconformist hymnody in Wales, it would be misleading to think that the quality of singing was then as high as legend now has it. A strong Calvinist element disapproved of music in four-part harmony, let alone accompanied by organ or instruments (it was in the established churches that west-gallery choirs and instruments were sometimes found). The lining-out of psalmody continued in Wales well into the nineteenth century.

It was John Roberts ('Ieuan Gwyllt', 1822–77) who helped to give Wales its present reputation as a singing nation. Although he was a solicitor's clerk and journalist, two other qualities – a passion for congregational singing and musical literacy – drove him to campaign for better music in church and chapel. He lectured on the subject, published pamphlets, and edited and promoted his own congregational tune-book *Llyfr tonau cynulleidfaol* (1859). Its success was such that a number of regional societies appeared, fired with the task of learning its tunes with the help of Curwen's tonic *sol-fa* notation. Their meetings were the beginning of *cymanfaoedd ganu* (singing meetings not unlike the German *Kirchengesängfeste* of the same period), local events held to develop the quality of congregational singing. The revival of Christianity late in Victoria's reign added further impetus to the resulting musical changes: the expanding congregations were housed in fine new churches and

EXAMPLE 26

Calvinist opposition finally gave way to the irrepressible call for organ
accompaniment. Following the ancient example of the parish clerk and
encouraged by the more emotional leadership of the American evangelists

Moody and Sankey, the singing of the *cymanfaoedd* continued to be led by an individual, the *codwr canu* or 'song-raiser'. The festive atmosphere was observed by John Curwen (the son of the pioneer of tonic *sol-fa*) near Swansea:

> This Welsh singing makes straight for the heart, and plays upon the spirit like the sound of storm or cataract... Our English choirs, both in church and out, are generally deficient in basses, and their singing sounds in consequence thin and unsubstantial. These Welsh basses have voices that make the furniture vibrate as they sound, just as do the pedal stops of an organ. While they were singing, especially in the loud passages, I could see the sheet of paper I held in my hand tremble...[3]

Clearly, these were moments when Wales truly became a 'land of song'.

The musical legacy of such singing is in the hymns, whose passionate quality is typified by *Aberystwyth*, written in 1876 by Joseph Parry (1841–1903) and which English congregations usually sing to the words 'Jesu, lover of my soul'. Its obsessive minor mode is briefly lightened towards the end of each verse, only to sink back to its dark-toned opening. A number of other powerful tunes follow this pattern: *Trewen* by Emlyn Evans, *Llef* by Griffiths Jones and *Ebenezer* by Thomas John Williams. There are, of course, major-key tunes of great power, such as *Hyfrydol* by R.H. Prichard, *Blaenwern* by William Penfro Williams (dating from the revival of 1904–5), and above all, *Cwm Rhondda* by John Hughes. All have a breadth and solemnity in keeping with the large and enthusiastic crowds who originally sang them.

With the gradual collapse of the communities that supported the chapels, these and other great hymns have been kept alive through the continuing tradition of *Cymanfa Ganu*. Sadly, these have developed a life largely separate from the worship of the churches from which they sprang. Like other traditions in Wales they are now being preserved rather than growing and living. With few exceptions (such as Arwel Hughes' *Tydi a Roddaist*) the hymn-writing tradition has largely died out. But there are signs of change: the worship song, sung both in Welsh and English, has rekindled a spark of Christian music in a younger generation, but it will need plenty of fanning before it resembles the roaring flames of previous generations.

The cathedrals of the church in Wales (more numerous since disestablishment from the Church of England in 1921) all host choirs well able to sing the traditional Anglican repertoire, usually in English. The presence of competent – and in the case of William Mathias (1934–94) sometimes inspired – composers in Wales has created a repertoire of indigenous modern liturgical art-music, but it is not large enough yet to make Welsh cathedral worship musically distinctive. Brecon Cathedral has specialised in the provision of instrumental accompaniment for baroque cantatas on special occasions, but this facility is rarely found elsewhere and is not usually applied to new music.

Notes

1. From *Descriptio Cambrae,* 1198, translated in Gerald of Wales, *The Journey through Wales and the Description of Wales*, Harmondsworth, 1978, p. 242.

2. Journal, July 14th and 17th, 1741.

3. J.S. Curwen, *Studies in Worship-Music*, 2nd series, London, 1885, pp. 20–21.

PART 4
The Path Divides

1750–1900

Chapter 22

Music in the Courts of Europe

As the Protestant churches struggled to create simple music that would edify their local congregations, the Roman Catholic Church continued throughout the eighteenth century to deepen its embrace of modern music. This did nothing for the common people worshipping at parish level, but it pleased musical connoisseurs such as Charles Burney (1726–1814) who visited city churches and cathedrals not so much to worship, but to savour and to compare their music. He was particularly pleased with Vienna:

> There is scarce a church or convent in Vienna, which has not every morning its mass in music: that is, a great portion of the church service of the day, set in parts, and performed with voices, accompanied by at least three or four violins, a tenor and base, besides the organ.[1]

The restless sumptuousness of eighteenth-century church architecture was matched by the frank theatricality of the worship:

> Music spread its gorgeous mantle over the whole Mass, so that the other details of the rite had scarcely any significance... the liturgy was not only submerged under this ever-growing art but actually suppressed... the new age sought not the sight of the holy, but the beautiful in art and universe. And so the church became a great hall, its walls shimmering with marble and gold.[2]

In such splendid surroundings, instrumental music was often heard, not only in the form of glittering and colourful accompaniments to motets and the Mass Ordinary, but by itself. A Polish dictionary entry of 1701 points out the original use of pieces called Sonatas:

> *Sonada* or *Sonata* is a grave and imposing musical work for any combination of instruments. Some years ago such works were performed in a solemn manner during the Mass after the Epistle.[3]

The composer Heinrich Biber (1644–1704), for many years organist at the Cathedral of Salzburg, wrote many instrumental pieces evidently intended for worship. His Sonatas of 1676 were entitled *tam Aris, tam Aulis servientes*, 'appropriate to the altar or the court'. Some of these are lavishly scored for trumpets and strings. His impressive *Sonata Sancti Polycarpi à 9*, for eight trumpets and kettledrums was written for the installation of a new provost of Salzburg Cathedral in 1673. Writing such pieces formed an important part of the duties of a number of other composers working in Austria such as J.H. Schmelzer (c. 1620–80) and Georg Muffat (1653–1704). Later, Mozart (1756–91) contributed to this instrumental tradition with his delightful Church Sonatas, short movements mostly for strings and organ to be played at Salzburg Cathedral after the Epistle and substituting for the Gradual. Such music could also be played in place of the Offertory and to begin and end the service.

In Vienna today the Michaelerkirche, Augustinerkirche and St Stephen's Cathedral among others continue to play the best of the orchestral mass settings, chiefly those of Joseph Haydn (1732–1809) and Mozart. At the end of the eighteenth century, though, composers since eclipsed by these familiar names would have been equally well known, such as Georg Reutter (1708–72), Michael Haydn (Joseph Haydn's brother, 1737–1806) and Anton Salieri (1750–1825).

Such breathtaking displays of temporal and artistic riches symbolised the long-established alliance between the Roman Catholic Church and European courts. In France the immensely powerful régime of the Sun King, Louis XIV (reigned 1661–1715) required low Mass (*Messe basse solennelle*) to be celebrated regularly at Versailles, but with the addition of *grands motets* composed by his favourite musicians Henry Du Mont (1610–84) and Jean Baptiste Lully (1632–87).

One of the most impressive of these was Lully's 1677 setting of the *Te Deum*. Since it was performed by at least 120 musicians it was bound to overshadow the main text of Matins. Hundreds of such motets on a more modest scale were composed for the Chapel Royal at Versailles by Michel-Richard de Lalande (1657–1726), Marc-Antoine Charpentier (c. 1650–1704), the fashions of Versailles being copied elsewhere in France wherever resources permitted. The latter's fine setting of the *Te Deum* is today the best known of this neglected French music. To be fair, Louis XIV did not always require music on such a scale.

The sublime intimacies of François Couperin's *Leçons de Ténèbres* for two sopranos, bass viol and organ make them among the most compelling liturgical music of the period. Couperin was organist of the Chapel Royal, but wrote the Leçons for the nuns at Lonchampt outside Paris, well-known for their singing during Holy Week. The pieces are settings of the Lamentations of Jeremiah, where what were originally the initial Hebrew letters of an alphabetical poem (Aleph, Beth, Gimel…) are set like the ornate capitals of an illuminated manuscript (see Example 27).

EXAMPLE 27

The practice of substituting organ music for sections of the Mass Proper was the chief duty of Roman Catholic organists of this period (see appendix). French composers in particular produced fine music for the purpose, such as Louis Couperin (about 1626–61) and his nephew François (1668–1733), Nicolas de Grigny (1672–1703), Louis-Nicolas Clérambault (1677?–1749) and Louis-Claude Daquin (1694–1772). The pieces were often compiled into what are called Organ Masses (for example, François Couperin's *Messe des paroisses* and *Messe pour les convents*). A fashion among

French organists was for the writing of *Noëls*, charming and light pieces based on

> tunes intended for certain canticles which the people sing at Christmas: these... should have a rustic and pastoral character consistent with the simplicity of the words and of the shepherds who were supposed to have sung them while paying homage to Christ in the crib.[4]

Clamour for reform

Celebrations of temporal power became an embarrassment to an age of growing egalitarianism, for the winds of change were sweeping across Europe. In France, the Revolution of 1789 ended the commissioning of music of such lavish splendour in the Roman Catholic Church.

In Vienna, reform came from the Emperor. Joseph II, who reigned jointly with Maria Theresa from 1765 and alone from 1780–90, curbed the wealth of the Roman Church by dissolving monasteries and building parish churches and schools with the proceeds. He gave Protestants and Jews freedoms and human rights hitherto denied them. Above all, he put severe restrictions on the ceremonies that symbolised the power of the church: processions, candles, statues and the operatic settings of the Mass with orchestra and soloists that the Viennese upper classes had come to love.

In Spain, where the church was still the most powerful patron of the arts, Francisco Fajer, *maestro di capilla* of La Seo in Saragossa from 1756 to 1809, persuaded many cathedrals to return to an entirely Latin liturgy and to ban the singing of villancicos, recitatives and arias in the style of Italian opera.

Notes

1. C. Burney, *The Present State of Music in Germany, the Netherlands and United Provinces*, London, 1775, vol. I, pp. 226–27.

2. J.A. Jungmann, *The Mass of the Roman Rite*, revised edition, New York, 1959, pp. 111–12.

3. T.B. Janovka, *Clavis ad thesaurum*, Prague, 1701, p. 119; quoted in W.S. Newman, *The Sonata in the Baroque Era*, New York, 1972, p. 24.

4. Jean-Jacques Rousseau, *Dictionnaire de Musique*, Paris, 1768.

Chapter 23

The Romantic Movement

It was in the nineteenth century that the modern 'cult of personality' emerged. Composers in the ages of patronage had certainly been praised for the magnificence or the craftsmanship of their work. But they were not expected to step too far out of line. After all, they were working for patrons – church or state – who had very precise requirements of them. Too great an originality was likely to put them out of work.

The cult of the artist

In the nineteenth century, individuality was expected, even praised. The arts became for many people a means of spiritual enlightenment, even the source of revelation. Painters, poets and musicians came to be revered as vessels for these revelations, the 'supreme discerners of transcendent truth'.[1]

The adulation Richard Wagner received during and after his lifetime epitomises this Romantic spirit: over 10,000 biographies of him were written before his death in 1883. People searching for spiritual fulfilment tended, as literally as possible, to fall in love with his music, with all the passion and adoration that the phrase implies.

No case was more celebrated than that of King Ludwig II of Bavaria, who wrote to Wagner after a concert of his music in 1864:

Beloved and only Friend!
Overwhelmed... I must... tell you how indescribable is the happiness which you have brought me. I was transported into superterrestial spheres, I breathed immeasurable bliss. But how can I begin to describe to you my ecstasy?[2]

With such encouragement, artists became less concerned with pleasing their public than with expressing their true selves in their art, for better or worse. As a result, the nineteenth century is the first where the composers' individuality becomes a priority. It is difficult for instance to mistake a composer like Berlioz for any other, even after short acquaintance with his music.

The new middle class

The momentous changes of the industrial revolution were already deeply rooted by the beginning of the nineteenth century. While this revolution brought new wealth, it also left the vast majority of the population in a worse state. In the rapidly expanding cities (and especially in London) there was abject poverty in the appalling lifestyle of the 'climbing boys' (chimney sweeps aged as young as four, bought and sold like slaves), in the teenage prostitution and in the danger and exploitation faced by factory- and mine-workers as yet unprotected by unions. The benefits of the revolution were certainly not for these pitiful masses but for an increasing minority who could now afford material comforts and education.

This middle class was large enough and rich enough to create a new market for cultural entertainment. In the world of music, public concerts had been popular from the 1720s. Concert promoters became wealthy enough to be able to invite the most famous composers from abroad. It was the entrepreneur Salomon who invited Haydn to London in the 1790s. In 1813 the Philharmonic Society was formed in London, a fully professional body both able and willing to commission new music and now (as the Royal Philharmonic Society) the second oldest concert organisation in the world.

One of the Philharmonic's guests of honour in 1820 was Louis Spohr, a composer in his day much better known than Beethoven. He was the first in London to take up the rôle of conducting:

> I then took my stand with the score at a separate music desk, [i.e. not that of the leading violin, who would would at that time have led the orchestra] drew my baton from my coat-pocket and gave the signal to begin. Alarmed at such a novel procedure, some of the directors protested against it at first... Immediately after the first movement of the symphony, the orchestra were impressed by the new method of

conducting... In the evening the results were even more brilliant than
I could have hoped.[3]

Since Spohr's first efforts, conductors have become enmeshed in the cult of
personality which is as characteristic of the present as of the Romantic era.

The Romantics' inspiration drew from another source too – from the
past. Again, this is an attitude too familiar to make a clear perspective easy. It
was only in the 1770s that the Academy of Ancient Music was formed, the
first club with a specific interest in the 'music of the ancients'. For its
members, 'ancient' meant the music of forty or fifty years previously, the
equivalent of a present-day society unearthing the music of Berg or Webern!
Even long after the Academy's formation, musical interest generally was in
the latest and most modern creations, very much more like the present-day
pop culture (though even that is now making money from nostalgia). So
when in 1728 Roger North discussed music of a hundred years before his
time, he could hardly bear to call it music:

> It is a sort of harmonious murmur rather than musick; and in a time
> when people lived in tranquillity and at ease, the enterteinement of it
> was agreeable, not unlike the confused singing of birds in a grove.[4]

In sharp contrast, the educated public of the nineteenth century came to
look on the past with new respect. The span of history lent an atmosphere
of mystery to crumbling buildings and to ancient manuscripts. Scholars
began in earnest to catalogue, to restore and to copy. As architects found a
new interest in the Gothic style and expressed it in their buildings,
musicians started to unearth the forgotten music of the past.

The decline of Christianity

For Christian music, the consequences of these attitudes were profound and
by no means beneficial. The most significant was their implication that the
spiritual dimension to existence was separate and distinct from everyday
living.

Christianity and its music, responding little to the objective enquiries of
science which were exciting so much interest, was gradually relegated to the
peripheries of culture. A number of churchmen rationalised the move by
stressing the distance between the sacred and secular worlds:

Neither [Christians'] joy nor their sorrow can be expressed, with propriety, in quite the same tones as if related to things of this world. There should be a quality about them showing our consciousness of the infinite distance between us and our Maker...[5]

By the end of the nineteenth century such sentiments had become suffused with a Romantic view of the past which attributed antiquities with spiritual and numinous qualities just by reason of their age:

Our fine old cathedrals and their music ought to go together – the music should suggest worship as much as the roof and arch and window. A stranger listening at a distance and unable to catch the words, should be able to say, 'that is sacred music'.[6]

But a faith that does not inform daily living further than the occasional visit to the hallowed walls of a cathedral will command diminishing attention. In confirmation, the number of self-confessed Christians in Europe declined steadily through the century.

The Mass as performance

For composers, public concerts were now able to provide wages which were viable alternatives to commissions from church or state. Consequently the most talented composers were able to decide on more personal grounds whether they wished to write music for the liturgy. Many decided against it.

The Roman Catholic Church too, was less inclined and less able to support the sumptuous and spectacular services which had been served so well by high-art music. The operatic style of Mozart's and Haydn's liturgical music was copied well into the nineteenth century by the next generation of composers – Schubert in Vienna, Cherubini in Paris, Weber in Dresden and many others, for whose music a diminishing European royalty still provided a market:

Ecclesiastical discipline was almost a dead letter in the ducal or grand-ducal establishments for which Haydn and his successors wrote their Masses. Their princely patrons kept a stud of opera singers and players, who were turned loose in the church on Sundays, to perform music identical in character with that which had occupied them during the week in the Opera House... No-one in that easy-going age worried about its breaches of liturgical laws. It was a fine 'musical programme' and that was all that mattered.[7]

But these composers would hardly have made a living or be remembered today if that is all they had written, however admirably or compellingly they fulfilled their patrons' requirements. Beethoven's two Masses – the *Mass in C* (1807) and the *Missa Solemnis* (1819–23) – were written in the same tradition, but their scale and highly personal manner (the *Missa Solemnis* in particular) has generally precluded their use in the liturgy, though when they are heard in worship, it can be a memorable experience:

> His *Missa Solemnis*, heard within the context of the celebration of the Mass, as it occasionally is in Austria, does not dwarf the liturgy, even though it prolongs the service unduly, but it proclaims throughout a personal belief so God-centred, so enriching and sublime, that it enters into the universal and deepens the belief of the worshipping community.[8]

The striking originality of so much music of the nineteenth century makes its relationship with the liturgy one of controversy, the most flamboyant musical personalities creating the greatest tensions. Berlioz' *Grande Messe des Morts* (1837) and *Te Deum* (1849) are works of arresting individuality, of which their vast scale is only one aspect (the *Te Deum* was intended for a thousand performers). But they reflect the nature of the state occasions for which they were intended rather than a desire to write music sympathetic to liturgical needs.

Franz Liszt (1811–85) is a more complex case, for while wholeheartedly embracing Romantic ideals he was also a trained priest. In consequence perhaps, his Christian music (of which he wrote a great deal) is either startlingly akin to his dramatic works for the concert-hall (the *Christus* of 1855–67, for instance, or the *Hungarian Coronation Mass* of 1867) or it is self-effacing on the smaller scale and uneasy in its lack of character. Liszt himself was aware of the limited public success of his Christian music, and complained in a letter to a friend:

> Everyone is against me. Catholics, because they find my church music profane, Protestants because to them my music is Catholic, freemasons because they think my music is clerical...[9]

There is an air of apology in Liszt's explanation of his need to write for the general public and an open admission of the gulf between the sacred and secular worlds:

> Nowadays when the altar is trembling and tottering, when pulpit and religious ceremony serve as subject matter for the mockers and sceptics, art must forsake the holy of holies, expand itself, and seek a stage for its magnificent manifestation in the world outside. How often – indeed, how much more than often – music must acknowledge both people and God as its springs of life. It needs to hasten from one to the other, in order to ennoble, comfort, and chasten mankind as well as to bless and praise God.[10]

'Hastening from one to the other' also characterised the career of Charles Gounod (1818–93), though his intention to take holy orders never became reality:

> Both composers wavered eternally between the secular life and the religious. The excitements of the theatre for Gounod and the easy triumphs of the concert platform for Liszt often muffled the call of the monk's cell. And then, at the height of the applause and the glory, a sudden stab of conscience would send them hurrying away... to bury themselves in pious austerity... They were alike in their religiosity, in their yearnings for the holy life and in their ambitions to write sacred music which they fondly, and vainly, believed to be greater than their other works.[11]

Charles Gounod was unlike many other well-known composers of his time in his enthusiasm in writing for the church. Following the extraordinary though short-lived success of his cantatas *Redemption* (1882) and *Mors et Vita* (1885), he turned increasingly to writing Christian music. Towards the end of his life

> religious music... was all that really interested him... Masses, prayers, motets and canticles dripped from him as the rain from heaven... There is no doubt that Gounod wrote with sincerity and belief in the religious content of his music. But sincerity is not enough to ensure a great work of art...[12]

In turn, Gounod's style became the *lingua franca* for hundreds of other composers of even more modest talent, whose efforts were confined to the specific needs of the church, needs defined more by the simple tastes of congregations and priests rather than by papal decree.

In Italy, for instance, the operatic style of liturgical music has been long popularised to the extent that tunes from operas (by Donizetti or Bellini for example) were adapted to the Ordinary of the Mass, a practice decried by the authorities to little avail.[13] After an entertaining description of excruciating music during High Mass in the Sistine Chapel, Berlioz observed during his stay in Rome in 1831–32:

> I often heard in other churches the overtures to *The Barber of Seville, La Cenerentola* and *Otello*. These pieces seemed to be particular favourites of the organists. They gave an unusual flavour to divine service.[14]

The Cecilian Movement

The Romantics' rekindled interest in the past had strong resonances in the Roman Church which had so richly patronised artists, architects and musicians through the ages. The Cecilian Movement was a direct result of this new historical perspective. Its aim was to reform music in the Roman Catholic Church (an exercise clearly long overdue) by looking to its past glories – the sixteenth century being regarded as the golden age. It was inspired initially by Karl Proske (1794–1861), a canon and choirmaster of the cathedral at Ratisbon (now called Regensburg) but later dominated by the composer Franz Xaver Witt (1834–88). On his initiative the *Allgemeiner Deutscher Cäcelien-Verein* was founded in 1869, St Cecilia being the patron saint of music. The society encouraged and co-ordinated reforms by establishing branches in Germany, France, the Netherlands, North America, Poland, Austria, Ireland, and finally Italy, where the *Scuola Gregoriana* of Rome was founded in 1880. These societies held meetings, published articles and issued lists of music approved for use in worship, much of it by Witt himself. They campaigned vigorously against the use of instruments apart from the organ and for the restoration of choral music.

Witt's own music was written very much under the spell of composers of the sixteenth century – but like reproduction furniture it lacks the creative touch of a master. Some musicians, like the composer Claude Debussy, were not content with mere imitation. In a letter to Prince Poniatowski, he wrote:

By way of consolation I recently had the most rewarding musical experience. This was at Saint-Gervais [in Paris], a church where an intelligent priest has the idea of reviving some beautiful ancient religious music. An unaccompanied Mass of Palestrina was a marvel. Written in a very severe style, this music is extremely pure; its feeling is not conveyed by shrieks of any kind but by melodic arabesques which combine to produce unique melodic harmonies... When one hears such music one wonders how it came about that this beautiful art developed in such an unfortunate manner.[15]

Debussy had heard this sixteenth-century music, probably for the first time, some eight years earlier in Rome. The music affected him enough for him to declare it 'the only church music I can allow. That of Gounod and company seems to me to derive from a hysterical mysticism and produces the effect of sinister farce.'[16]

Unfortunately, when the Cecilian Movement asked composers to write new music for it, it generally attracted people of small talent – especially under the editorship of Witt's successor, Franz Haberl (1840–1910). Even composers of high standing among concert audiences (such as César Franck and Camille Saint-Saëns) suffered from the same difficulty as so many other composers of the age: in making concessions to the needs of Christian music they trivialised their musical ideas.

Two composers stand out as exceptions. One was Gabriel Fauré (1845–1924), whose few liturgical works rise head and shoulders above the efforts of all other French composers of the time. His *Requiem* (1886), *Cantique de Jean Racine* (1873) and a few other motets are among the handful of French pieces written for the liturgy whose style is inward and contemplative rather than over-persuasive and sentimental.

The other was Anton Bruckner (1824–96) who, as a deeply committed Christian, dedicated himself without compromise to God's service and to writing for the liturgy. Even his symphonies are, in a sense, wordless extensions of the large-scale mass-settings he was writing in the 1860s. They were preceded by an arduous apprenticeship, not only in musical theory but in writing for the modest talents of Upper Austrian church choirs. His obvious model should have been the operatic style – with orchestra and soloists – still to be heard in the cathedrals of Salzburg and Vienna. But it was the comparative austerity of sixteenth- and eighteenth-century music, whose technique he had to study intensively, that led Bruckner to write with a discipline and restraint unusual for his time.

While Bruckner's reputation now rests securely on the vast canvasses of his symphonies, the choral motets are just as valuable. Many of them are in only four parts and usually unaccompanied. Their simple and direct presentation of Latin texts central to the Christian faith show the composer's deep understanding of the needs of an attentive congregation. In *Vexilla Regis*, for instance, the voice-parts almost always move together in homophony, any gentle imitation between them serving to animate the words and not to obscure them. The impressive architecture of buildings such as the cathedral at Linz, where he was organist, led him to provide silences after the frequent shouts of exultation, when the acoustic spaces are left to make their own contribution to the music.

Bruckner was well aware of the need for simplicity in Christian music and was keen to meet the challenge. In 1879 he wrote to Ignaz Traumihler, a choirmaster and supporter of Cecilian ideals, to whom he had just dedicated his motet *Os Justi*:

> I should be very pleased if you found pleasure in the piece. It is written without sharps or flats, without the chord of the seventh, without a six-four chord [a three-note chord with its fifth in the bass] and without chordal combinations of four and five simultaneous notes.[17]

The Cecilian Movement published a *Pange Lingua* of Bruckner's, but autocratically and shortsightedly Witt censored some of its most poignant moments, an act which confirmed Bruckner's fears that the Society's extreme views were stifling Christian musical creativity.

Bruckner set the Ordinary of the Mass seven times, from the *Mass in C*, written when he was seventeen, to the *Mass in F minor* of 1868. Perhaps the most remarkable is the *Mass in E minor*, commissioned by the Bishop of Linz in 1866, for it avoids the usually obligatory solo singers altogether and only uses wind and brass instruments in a restrained and simple accompaniment. As in the motets, the words are the springboard for every musical idea and are never submerged by their musical surroundings. It is a rare example of how the Cecilians' ideals of a return to the 'extremely pure' Christian music of the sixteenth century could be compatible with the expressive manner of the nineteenth.

The continuity of Bruckner's music with Roman Catholic tradition is further reinforced by his respect for plainsong. His music was sung in its context and he often quoted its melodies in his own music or adapted them.

Chant

The plainsong that Bruckner and his contemporaries knew had been given little respect or attention for years. He was probably unaware that it had suffered all kinds of corruptions over the previous four or five centuries. For, along with the drastic changes that music had undergone since medieval times, the chant itself had been significantly transformed. A disinterest in ancient manuscripts and a desire to conform to modern tastes had created a very different type of music, rhythmically rigid (more like a present-day hymn-tune) and with highly substantial changes both to melodies and in word-setting.

An idea of the unfortunate musical practice then surrounding chant is provided, surprisingly enough, by Berlioz' remarks on the musical instrument called the serpent, reminiscent of its use in the west galleries of English churches:

> The truly barbaric tone of this instrument would be much better suited for the bloody cult of the Druids than for that of the Roman Catholic Church, where it is still in use – as a monstrous symbol for the lack of understanding and the coarseness of taste and feeling which have governed the application of music in our churches since times immemorial...[18]

The so-called Medicean version of the chant was published in 1614 as a result of the revisions Palestrina had been required to make by the Council of Trent. Further alterations to the chant had been made in eighteenth-century versions, rendering the original shape of the medieval melodies barely recognisable.

Long before the Cecilians, a centre for chant research was already in existence. In 1833, the Benedictine monastery of St Pierre was built in Solesmes on the banks of the River Sarthe, near Le Mans. The monks there researched all the earliest manuscript versions of the chant available to them and collated them in a new edition. They hoped this would become once more the universal Christian music of the Roman Catholic Church. The process took far longer than they had expected. It was partly hindered by Friederich Pustet who, in 1871 (and backed by the Cecilians!) republished the corrupt readings of the chant yet again. But Pius X, a pope of exceptional musical understanding and with a background of parish life, issued his *motu proprio* of 1903 which sanctioned the use of the Solesmes versions of the chant throughout the church. They have been published by the Vatican ever since.

Example 28 shows the gradual *Justus ut Palma* as published by Pustet in 1871 set against the Solemnes edition of the same music, published in 1908. The differences accumulated over hundreds of years are striking. The Pustet edition cuts sections from the medieval chant, alters the word underlay, and in particular the characteristically medieval melismas on final syllables are axed. To prepare this edition of *Justus ut Palma* the Solesmes scholars compared over 200 manuscripts.

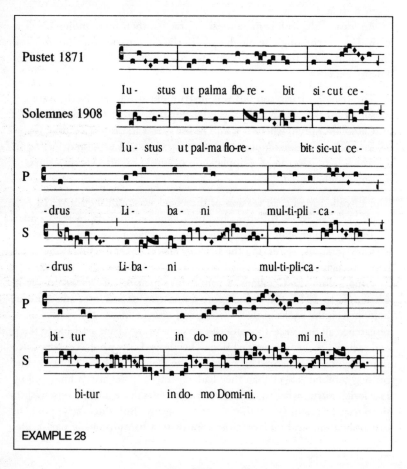

EXAMPLE 28

The way the chant is sung is as important as the books themselves. The received tradition of the nineteenth century encouraged a rhythmical style which did serious damage to the fluid beauty of the melodies. Worst of all, keyboard accompaniment was the palliative that made the chant acceptable to modern taste, a practice which persists nowadays. The French composer Olivier Messiaen accompanied the chant for most of his working life and it is therefore not without a certain irony that he should have asked: 'Why is it necessary today to accompany Gregorian chant with the organ, embellishing it with a harmony which, however skilfully handled, at one stroke totally destroys its character?'[19]

Solesmes is today an important teaching centre for the authentic performance of the chant and its research still generates lively scholarly debate. But the aspirations of the Solesmes monks for the universality of the chant have never quite been realised, even early this century when it had many admirers. Today its future looks gloomy. Perhaps the most significant moment for this ancient Christian music was the Eucharistic Congress of 1960 in Munich, where the chant joined together a gathering of over a million voices from across the world. Ironically enough it was also the very moment when the Second Vatican Council was initiating changes that have since destroyed the place of Gregorian chant in the church's liturgy.

Notes

1. W.J. Gatens, *Victorian Cathedral Music in Theory and Practice*, Cambridge, 1986, p. 49.

2. Quoted in W. Blunt, *The Dream King*, London, 1973, p. 38.

3. H. Pleasants, *The Musical Journeys of Louis Spohr*, Norman, Oklahoma, 1961, p. 205. Spohr was also a composer of numerous oratorios and sacred works, now largely forgotten.

4. Roger North, *Memoires of Musick*; see J.W. Wilson, editor, *Roger North on Music*, London, 1959, p. 340.

5. R. Druitt, *A Popular Tract on Church Music*, London, 1845, p. 36.

6. George Elvey, in M. Elvey, *Life and Reminiscences of George J. Elvey*, London, 1894, p. 320.

7. R.R. Terry, *The Music of the Roman Rite*, London, 1931, pp. 47–48.

8. A. Robertson, *Requiem*, London, 1967, p. 30.

9. Quoted in P. Merrick, *Revolution and Religion in the Music of Liszt*, Cambridge, 1987, p. 99.

10. Quoted in P. Weiss and R. Taruskin, *Music in the Western World*, London, 1984, p. 367.

11. J. Harding, *Gounod*, London, 1973, p. 152.

12. Harding, pp. 213 and 211.

13. See for an example, H. Berlioz, *Memoirs*, translated by D. Cairns, London, 1987, p. 161.

14. Berlioz, pp. 136–37.

15. For another translation, see Lesure and Nichols, *Debussy Letters*, London, 1987, p. 42.

16. Letter to Vasnier, 24 November 1885; see F. Lesure and R. Nichols, p. 14.

17. Letter to Traumihler, 25 July 1879; quoted in H.F. Redlich, *Bruckner and Mahler*, London, 1963, p. 72.

18. H. Berlioz, *Treatise on Instrumentation*, translated by Theodore Front, New York, 1948, p. 348.

19. O. Messiaen, *Musique et Couleur (nouveaux entretiens avec Claude Samuel)*, Paris, 1986, p. 30.

Chapter 24

The Decline of the Lutheran Chorale

In the German-speaking Lutheran Church, support for the lavish orchestral and choral music of Bach and his contemporaries had waned steadily as the nineteenth century approached. Lutheran town councils were more and more reluctant to continue to support the choir schools which were the churches' musical life-line. The age of Pietism also heralded a backlash in the form of 'enlightened' thinking, a questioning of the fundamental tenets of Christianity. As Kant proclaimed in 1781, 'Our age is the true age of criticism, to which all must be subjected.'

Such attitudes led to a new emphasis on general education, alongside which the choral duties of choir schools became a nuisance. Expert choirs were run down, leaving the responsibility for the singing more with the people. This could have been a positive step, but these congregations were also left without dedicated musical leadership and the results were sometimes lamentable. Chorales were sung so slowly that 'each song of praise or thanksgiving in performance became a hymn of penitence and death'.[1]

The historian Charles Burney visited the Domkirche in Bremen in 1772, and gives this account of the worship:

> I visited the Thomkirche or cathedral [in Bremen], belonging to the Lutherans, where I found the congregation singing a dismal melody, without the organ. When this was ended, the organist gave out the hymn tune, in the true dragging style of Sternhold and Hopkins. The instrument was large, and has a noble and well-tuned chorus, but the playing was more old-fashioned, I believe, than any thing that could have been in our country towns, during the last century. The interludes between the line[s] of the hymn were always the same. [Burney's examples are given in Example 29.] After hearing this tune,

219

and these interludes, repeated ten or twelve times, I went to see the town, and returning to the cathedral, two hours after, I still found the people singing all in unison, and as loud as they could, the same tune, to the same accompaniment. I went to the post-office, to make dispositions for my departure; and, rather from curiosity than the love of such music, I returned once more to this church, and, to my great astonishment, still found them, vocally and organically performing the same ditty, the duration of which seems to have exceeded that of a Scots Hymn, in the time of Charles I.[2]

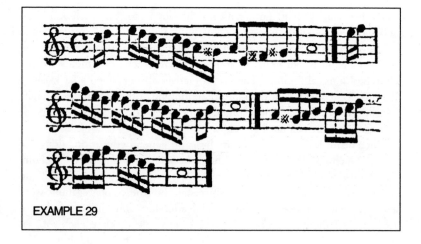

EXAMPLE 29

It is difficult to accept that this story is not exaggerated, unless it was that several hymns were sung during the service to the same tune. This is certainly a possibility, since the number of tunes congregations knew had very much reduced. As many as ninety hymn-texts were habitually sung to one popular tune (*Wer nur den lieben Gott*). Precentors, who often led the singing in the manner of the English parish clerk, embellished the pauses at the ends of lines with vocal ornaments. These decorations (with the slow pace of the melody) were also incorporated into the tune itself. Thus, with lack of musical (and perhaps spiritual) encouragement, many of the characteristics of English congregational singing in the eighteenth century were repeated in Germany well into the nineteenth.

Recovery from the poor state of Lutheran Christian music was slow. Indeed, a steady decline in church attendance precluded any return to the church's earlier strength, for Christianity was losing its hold on people's imagination, at parish and at diocesan level. Its music was relegated to the peripheries of cultural expression and the general public who sought some culture went instead to concert parties, to house soirées or to the opera.

Reforms

There were moves for reform, chiefly a desire to return to the past and to first Lutheran principles. Logically, this required liturgies to be in German, but with unaccompanied Lutheran hymns and Gregorian chant.

The establishment in Berlin of a superb and salaried choir by King Wilhelm IV in 1843 fulfilled these Romantic ideals: it used boys and men only, they sang entirely unaccompanied and, to add to 'the distance between us and our Creator',[3] out of sight! This move, where it was adopted elsewhere, caused much argument and trauma. It was a drastic change with which people of habit could not identify. In any case, it was only ever a compromise, as organists were unwilling to give up their central place in worship: a strict return to mid-sixteenth century practice would have put a complete stop to their accompanying the congregation. Furthermore, cantors and choirs were simply not available to take an effective lead in such reforms.

Just the same, there were steady changes throughout the century. The efforts of the Cecilians to encourage unaccompanied choral singing in the Roman Church had their counterparts in the Lutheran. The music of the sixteenth-century composer Johann Eccard (1553–1611) became popular as a German parallel to the revered Palestrina.

Church choirs were gradually re-established – though without the support of the old choir schools. A strong amateur tradition of choral music gradually evolved which still thrives today. Much of its activity was outside the routine of church worship, culminating in occasional choral festivals (*Kirchengesängfeste*), but it was bound also to have a beneficial effect on church singing.

The complexity and drama of Bach's music prevented it from playing much part in the Lutheran revival till at least half-way through the century (Mendelssohn's famous performance of Bach's *St Matthew Passion* in 1829 was not at a service, but in a concert-hall – the *Singakademie* in Berlin), but gradually Bach's organ music, chorales and last of all the cantatas began to return to Lutheran worship. Similarly, Schütz' unaccompanied music was revived at an earlier stage than his music with instruments.

By the end of the nineteenth century, a more relaxed and sympathetic attitude to the whole history of Christian music encouraged Lutheran musicians to look to anything from the past that was worshipful and excellent, even if it lay outside the traditions of their denomination.

Notes

1. J.E. Hauser, 1834; quoted in F. Blume, *Protestant Church Music*, London, 1975, p. 341.

2. C. Burney, *An Eighteenth-century Musical Tour in Central Europe and the Netherlands*, vol. 2 of P. Scholes, editor, *Dr Burney's Musical Tour in Europe*, London, 1959, pp. 222–23.

3. The music at the Domkirche was described in great detail by the American hymn-writer Lowell Mason in April 1852. See L. Mason, *Musical Letters from Abroad*, New York, 1854, reprinted in 1967, pp. 105–08 and 111–15.

Chapter 25

The Church of England and the Tractarians

The Church of England at the beginning of the nineteenth century reacted slowly to the desperate spiritual needs of the country at large. It was hardly surprising. Those in high authority were simply not trained or competent to hold their offices, but still enjoyed unbelievably high salaries for being absent from their work. The novelist Anthony Trollope memorably portrayed this 'high-and-dry' churchmanship in the character of Archdeacon Grantley, a pen-portrait based on Henry Philpott, Bishop of Exeter (1778–1869). Queen Victoria was once pleased to refer to Philpott as 'that fiend, the Bishop of Exeter'. The clamour for reform became loud in pamphlets such as *The Black Book, or Corruption Unmasked* of 1823. The Rev. John Jebb wrote a bitter exposure of the plight of the cathedrals that summarised the situation: 'The whole aspect of the church plainly indicated the mechanical performance of a burthensome duty.'[1]

The malaise of the Anglican Church needed political as much as spiritual solutions. Parliament set up the Ecclesiastical Commissioners in 1835 which recommended that all senior cathedral posts had to be residential, limited in number and that their salaries should be reduced to release more funds for the parish clergy. These drastic changes imposed from outside were complemented by changes from within. A number of high churchmen, including John Henry Newman, John Keble and Edward Pusey expressed new ideals of integrity for the Anglican Church in a series of *Tracts for the Times*.

The first tract, by Newman, appeared in 1833 and the ninetieth and last (also by him) in 1841. The contents of the Ninetieth Tract and the furore it caused led to Newman's conversion to Roman Catholicism, followed in due course by a number of others, including H.E. Manning (later Archbishop of Westminster from 1865). The group have been called the 'Tractarians' or 'Puseyites' and their ideas usually termed the Oxford Movement (Keble and Pusey were Oxford professors).

The movement was the product of a Romantic age. It recommended a return to the past, to a time when the ritual and symbolic aspects of worship were fundamental. Indeed, a too-precise return to the pre-Reformation tenets of the Roman Catholic Church was the difficulty that lay behind the Ninetieth Tract. The daily ritual of public worship, conducted in a formal and reverent fashion, was at the centre of the Tractarians' ideals for church life, just as it had been in medieval times.

At the same time the Tractarians strongly resisted the liberalism which was closing the door on a simple Christian faith. They believed firmly in the authority of the Bible and showed deep concern for individual spiritual welfare. Where they differed from the Evangelicals of the Church of England and from the dissenters was in the way they expressed those concerns. For the Tractarians believed that (as in former times) the divinely appointed church could speak on spiritual matters with God's authority. The dissenters, on the other hand, acknowledged no authority but the Bible. The Bishop of Oxford wrote in 1840:

> [The Tractarians] are forming at this moment the most remarkable movement, which, for three centuries at least, has taken place among us... The system in question, instead of being an easy comfortable form of religion, adapting itself to modern habits and luxurious tastes, is uncompromisingly stern and severe – laying the greatest stress upon self-discipline and self-denial – encouraging fasting, alms-deeds and prayer, to an extent of which the present generation, at least, know nothing – and inculcating a deference to authority which is wholly opposed to the spirit of the age.[2]

All this was symbolised by a return to the daily and timeless ritual of worship. The Tractarians took full advantage of the surviving medieval architecture by putting their choirs in the chancel with the priest, placing candelabra and symbolic silver vessels on the altar, which itself was adorned with cloths whose colours were changed with the church's year. Symbolic white robes were worn by priest, acolytes and choir, who were encouraged to process and recess before and after worship.

The choir was therefore visually associated with the priest and not with the congregation. In cathedrals, such theatrical rituals were not out of place in an architecture originally created with them in mind. But the parishioners of country churches found them disconcerting: services would sometimes be interrupted by cries of 'no popery' and even by violence. Tractarians were taken to court by fellow Christians for kneeling or prostrating themselves before the elements, for using incense or for mixing water with the wine during communion. An 1852 cartoon headed 'the Papal Invasion', conveys the hostility many felt at the practices of the Oxford Movement and the defection of Anglican leaders to Roman Catholicism only seemed to confirm their fears. Nonetheless, the movement grew in influence to the point where churches were altered or newly built to a Gothic medieval plan, complete with chancel and screen, to create the English parish church of present popular imagination.

The music of the Oxford Movement

The musical consequences of the Oxford Movement were considerable. In 1841 Leeds built the first parish church whose building and worship was modelled on the cathedral tradition. Even in country parishes there was a new desire for solemnity, in pursuit of which it was reckoned that the gallery musicians were nothing but a nuisance. Money was raised for the purchase of organs in parish churches, many of which had probably never housed one before. Gallery musicians were almost immediately dismissed in favour of the organist, though there was often real difficulty in finding a competent player. One solution to this problem was the barrel organ:

> After the construction of the organ at St Paul's Church, Walden, in 1850... a difficulty arose as to who could play it, and to get over the difficulty a dumb-organist [an automatic barrel-organ attachment] was used.[3]

After about 1850, churches unable to afford any kind of pipe organ could purchase a harmonium. These became widely used in churches and chapels throughout England and Wales. All except the rare French instruments of real quality were (and still are) hopelessly inadequate to lead congregational singing. Many are still mouldering in vestries today. West-gallery choirs and players were indignant:

> 'But I don't care who hears me say it, nothing will spak to your heart wi' the sweetness o' the man of strings!'
> 'Strings for ever!' said little Jimmy.
> 'Strings alone would have held their ground against all the new

comers in creation.' ('True, true!' said Bowman.) 'But clar'nets was death.' ('Death they was!' said Mr Penny.) 'And harmonions,' William continued in a louder voice, and getting excited by these signs of approval, 'harmonions and barels'organs' ('Ah!' and groans from Spinks) 'be miserable – what shall I call 'em? – miserable – '

'Sinners,' suggested Jimmy...

'Miserable dumbledores!'

'Right, William, and so they be – miserable dumbledores!' said the whole choir with unanimity.[4]

Anglican chant

As Tractarian ideals took hold metrical psalms were gradually abandoned in England and Wales and a number of alternatives were adopted in their place. The Oxford Movement encouraged the use of Gregorian chant, but the necessity of fitting the melodies to English caused problems and Anglican chant became the solution for most parishes. In the reformed stronghold of Scotland, however, the singing of metrical psalms remained a deeply-engrained national characteristic and is still a valued part of the worship of many Scottish churches. In the remote Highlands and Islands the old style of 'lining out' is still practised in the Free Churches (see chapter 19).

Anglican chant was of course only an elaboration of Gregorian chant and had been in use since Elizabethan times in the Chapel Royal and intermittently in cathedrals. But now it was being proposed for the first time as a vehicle for corporate worship. The problem of this type of chant, unsolved to this day, is that it requires prose verses of varying length to be fitted to a musical formula that feels as if it should proceed in strict rhythm, for classical harmony in general creates a very clear association of chord progressions with a regular beat.

The problem of fitting the square musical peg in the textual round hole was traditionally solved on an *ad hoc* basis, as is evident from a suggestion in 1808 by J.C. Beckwith, the organist of Norwich Cathedral:

Suppose the organist and choir were to meet every morning and afternoon for one month, and agree on the proper place in each verse of the psalms, where the reciting should end in both the first and last parts of the chant, and under that particular word or syllable place a conspicuous red mark; if one were thus marked, the others might be rendered similar to it. The benefit would be, all the members of the choir might recite as one person.[5]

The inference is that Norwich Cathedral choir did not habitually recite 'as one person'.

The introduction of local festivals which joined a number of choirs together created the need for published systems of 'pointing' – an indication of word-setting by signs. One of the first was Dibb's *Key to Chanting* of 1831. But, as J.S. Curwen observed in 1880:

Nothing can be more admirable than the directions which the editors of countless psalters have given to choirs and congregations: nothing can be more universal than the disregard with which those directions are received.[6]

As little Western music asks for chordal progression to be set to an irregular or haphazard rhythm, to ask a humble congregation to perform the task is to require the unnatural, if not the impossible. Expert choirs can overcome the problem with rigorous training, but having arrived at perfection, they become indignant if the congregation starts to sing with them and spoil their efforts.

Other chants were eagerly revived, such as Merbecke's (see chapter 12), but now accompanied by organ. The versicles and responses which open Morning and Evening Prayer were harmonised, as might be the intoning of the Lord's Prayer and the Creed.

Cathedral music

The composers of Anglican cathedral music were specialists, that is, they were not generally known for their compositions outside Christian liturgy. Almost all of them were deeply involved in the life of the church, mostly as organists and choirmasters. They became excellent at providing what the casual listener would recognise as 'sacred music', but little of their work would stand up to critical listening today.

Thomas Attwood (1765–1838) was in an unusual position. He had the enviable status of having been one of Mozart's favourite pupils. On his return from study in Vienna in 1787 he was able to move into high musical circles, finally being appointed organist of St Paul's Cathedral and composer to the Chapel Royal. But even a Mozart can only stimulate and direct if his pupil has imagination. Attwood is best remembered for pieces that did not demand of him a sustained creative effort, miniatures such as *Turn Thy Face from My Sins* or *Enter Not Into Judgment*.

Attwood was one of the few composers of Christian music to have contact with the musical profession outside the church. Through the rest of the century and among his successors Christian music became a closed world: John Goss (1800–80) and T.A. Walmisley (1814–56) were pupils of Attwood, J.B. Dykes (1823–76) was a pupil of Walmisley and all three worked exclusively in cathedral surroundings.

The reward of these hardworking men was to see a steady improvement in the standards of cathedral music. In turn this set an example to parish church choirs who were encouraged to emulate the musical world of the cathedral through diocesan choral festivals, the first of which was held in Lichfield Cathedral in 1865.

Some of these musicians made special contributions which easily overshadow their composing talent. Sir Frederick Ouseley (1825–89) used his considerable means to found and to staff the church and College of St Michael at Tenbury. Its purpose was to set an example to the Anglican world at large of what could and should be done in the training of church musicians and in the reverent performance of cathedral music. John Stainer (1840–1901) was one of the first organists appointed to Tenbury (at the age of seventeen!) and his tireless work for the same cause eventually took him to St Paul's Cathedral and a knighthood.

These are only a few of the musicians whose names still appear regularly on the service sheets of English cathedrals. Little of their music is worthy of the place it occupies today. A few pieces deserve attention simply because they are excellent, and others are sung because of their local connections. The settings of the *Magnificat and Nunc Dimittis in D minor* by Walmisley are impressive because they avoid some of the distressing general weaknesses of this music, as do some of the works of S.S. Wesley (a grandson of Charles Wesley).

As parish church choirs strengthened, cathedral works were used as yardsticks by which to measure the creation of simple and accessible music for local choirs. A huge market for anthems and canticle settings developed, fed by the ease and speed with which music could be printed. The dusty cupboards of churches and chapels throughout England and Wales are still full of damp copies of this musical doggerel, composed to fill a need as quickly as possible by composers of poor talent.

Tradition encourages a diminishing number of choirs to sing this music today and even to exhume some, such as J.H. Maunder's *Olivet to Calvary*. One piece, Stainer's *Crucifixion,* has never been forgotten. It is not even liturgical music, strictly speaking, but it has been used so often as an occasion for Christian contemplation that it should be considered as such. What is most remarkable is its perennial staying-power. It has been spectacularly criticised:

> Sparrow-Simpson's appalling doggerel set to Stainer's squalid music is a monument to the inane. It is almost frightening that such a piece should remain so popular since it proves that most people will accept whatever they hear in church quite uncritically; indeed, they regard criticism as a form of sacrilege.[7]

The piece indicates the extent to which some church music fell short of Tractarian ideals of excellence and solemnity. Stainer regretted having written it.

Hymns

Alongside the enormous quantities of anthem-books, canticle settings and oratorios produced for the parish church choir were equally vast quantities of hymns for the congregations. They formed important focal points in worship for Anglicans and non-conformists alike, and were shared by many denominations. While both tunes and words of many hymns were instantly forgettable (Henry Gauntlett, who wrote the tune to *Once in Royal David's City* wrote 10,000 others) a very few of them have a rightly valued place in the spiritual life of almost every English-speaking Christian. By far the most influential hymn-book was *Hymns Ancient and Modern* published in 1861: 60 million copies had been sold by the end of the nineteenth century. The title is significant, for it reflects the Tractarians' respect for the past. One of the striking features of the collection was the inclusion of medieval Latin hymns and sequences, many translated with great imagination by J.M. Neale.

The Tractarians themselves contributed – John Keble (*Blest are the Pure in*

Heart) and John Henry Newman (*Praise to the Holiest in the Height* and *Lead Kindly Light*) among many others.

One of the intentions behind *Hymns Ancient and Modern* was to create a collection suitable for occasions throughout the church year. Modern tunes for these new hymns were obviously plentiful, but the immense popularity of the book married tunes to words much more firmly than in the past, partnerships which in many cases are indissoluble even today (such as Sullivan's ghastly tune St Gertrude set to *Onward Christian Soldiers* or Dykes' sublime melody Nicaea to *Holy, Holy, Holy*).

Notes

1. Rev. J. Jebb, *The Choral Service of the United Church of England and Ireland*, London, 1843, p. 63; much of this is challenging and readable, and quoted at length in K.R. Long, *The Music of the English Church*, London, 1972, p. 320.

2. *Charge of May 1840 to the Clergy of the Oxford Diocese on Tractarianism and Tract 90*; quoted in S. Neill, *Anglicanism*, Oxford, 1977, p. 257.

3. A.T. Robinson, *Reminiscences of an Old Organist*; quoted in K.H. MacDermott, *The Old Church Gallery Minstrels*, London, 1948, p. 42; see also N. Boston and L.G. Langwill, *Church and Chamber Barrel Organs*, Edinburgh, 1967.

4. Thomas Hardy, *Under the Greenwood Tree*, 1873. A 'dumbledore' is dialect for bumblebee.

5. Preface to J.C. Beckwith (1750–1809), *The First Verse of Every Psalm of David with an Ancient and Modern Chant*, London, 1808. See also J. Wilson, *Roger North on Music*, London, 1959, p. 269.

6. J.S. Curwen, *Studies in Worship Music*, London, 1880, p. 113; quoted in R. Box, *Make Music to Our God: How We Sing the Psalms*, London, 1996.

7. Long, p. 365.

Chapter 26

Revival in the Nineteenth Century

Hand in hand with North America, Britain experienced further spiritual awakening in the mid-nineteenth century. On both sides of the Atlantic the Christian gospel was proclaimed by evangelists to the huge populations of the urban areas and there were conversions by the thousand.

The meetings took place in tents, halls and in the open air as much as in churches and chapels. It was gospel songs that had the ability to reach large numbers powerfully and effectively with a simple message. The melodies were instantly memorable, their sentiments direct and their effect strong and immediate:

There is no reasoning, nor are the lines made heavy with introspection. 'Tell the story simply, as to a little child.' The feelings are touched; the stiffest of us become children again.[1]

These songs sprang partly from the increase during the century of Sunday School training among children and the establishment in 1844 of the Young Men's Christian Association.

Sankey and Moody

Following their first visit to England in 1872, Ira D. Sankey (formally a YMCA worker in America) and Dwight L. Moody published a pamphlet of the songs associated with their missions called *Sacred Songs and Solos*. It was expanded constantly in the following years – by 1903 it contained 1,200 items. Its sales in Britain matched those of *Hymns Ancient and Modern* (80 million by the 1950s) and are indicative of the powerful influence of the American evangelical movement of the time. Moody and Sankey even persuaded some Scots to reconsider the musical habits of several lifetimes.

As a professor of the Free Church College in Edinburgh commented:

> It is amusing to observe how entirely the latent distrust of Mr Sankey's 'kist o'whistles' [chest of whistles, that is, an organ] has disappeared. There are different ways of using an organ. There are organs in some churches for mere display, as someone has said, 'with a devil in every pipe,' but a small harmonium designed to keep a tune right is a different matter, and is seen to be no hindrance to the devout and spiritual worship of God.[2]

The team-work of preacher (Moody) with song-leader and soloist alongside (Sankey) proved highly effective and is still being repeated to this day. The creation of one of Sankey's best-known songs, *There were Ninety and Nine* (Example 30) gives a glimpse of the spiritual atmosphere of their meetings. In Edinburgh in 1874 Moody had just given an impassioned sermon on the Good Shepherd and turned to Sankey to invite him to sing a song on the subject. All Sankey had to hand were the words of a hymn that had just appeared in a newspaper, but no music:

> The impression came strongly upon me that I must sing the beautiful and appropriate words I had found the day before, and placing the newspaper slip on the organ before me, I lifted my heart in prayer, asking God to help me to so sing that the people might hear and understand. Laying my hands upon the organ I struck the key of A flat, and began to sing. Note by note the tune was given, which has not been changed from that day to this... As the singing ceased a great sigh seemed to go up from the meeting and I knew I had reached the hearts of my Scotch audience. Mr Moody was greatly moved. Leaving the pulpit, he... leaned over the organ... looked at the little newspaper slip... and with tears in his eyes said: 'Sankey, where did you get that hymn? I never heard the like of it in my life.'[3]

The Salvation Army

When the Salvation Army first came into being in 1878 (following a number of years' work as the Christian Mission) it followed the same pattern. Its priorities in Christian music were typical of the evangelists of the time, its first *Orders and Regulations for Field Officers* stating that, in song:

EXAMPLE 30

One voice alone is always much to be preferred... because the words can be heard with so much greater distinctiveness.[4]

As the founder of the Salvation Army, General William Booth, recommended:

Let us have a real tune, that is, a melody with some distinct air in it, that one can take hold of, which people can learn, nay which makes them learn it, which takes hold of them and goes on humming in the mind... That is the sort of tune to help you; it will preach to you, and bring you believers and converts.[5]

Booth looked on choirs with suspicion:

Merely professional music is always a curse and should you ever find a choir in connection with any hall or mission, I give you my authority to take a besom and sweep it out, promising that you do so as lovingly as possible.[6]

The fear that choirs 'confine the singing to the few, instead of making it the servant of many' kept the soloist as the sole musical leader in Salvation Army meetings till the turn of the century when the Songster Brigades developed.

The frank emotionalism of these songs and their imitation or borrowing of secular pop music for their purposes was offensive to more aesthetically-minded observers. It even caused some hesitation among Evangelicals. But General Booth was certain of his ground:

Music is to the soul what wind is to the ship, blowing her onwards in the direction in which she is steered... Not allowed to sing that tune or this tune? Indeed! Secular music, do you say? Belongs to the devil, does it? Well, if it did, I would plunder him of it... Every note and every strain and every harmony is divine and belongs to us.[7]

The wholesale exchange of popular music between Britain and America had a profound effect on gospel song in Britain. Stephen Foster's songs served the Salvation Army well: 'Poor old Uncle Ned' became 'O what battles I've been in' and 'Poor old Joe' was transformed into 'Gone are the days of wretchedness and sin'. These are no more nor less than *contrafacta*, or text substitutions, common at many points in Christian history.

During the twentieth century, the music of the Salvation Army has become more sophisticated. Highly trained groups such as the International Staff Songsters have developed alongside a network of local bands and choirs. These come together from time to time at International Congresses featuring musical contributions from Songster Brigades from all over the world. The massed bands and choirs of the final concerted items at these meetings make spectacular music.

The Path Divides

During the nineteenth century a problem which had beset Christian music for centuries came to a crisis. The rhetorical and forward-looking art-music of the eighteenth century had profane associations that proved too much for many Christians to tolerate.

Its most characteristic form, opera, was peopled with characters who generally made decisions about their behaviour and their relationships without reference to God or to the church's moral teaching. The clergy were therefore uneasy at the reappearance in the liturgy of this tainted secular music and enthusiastically supported the Cecilians and others in their efforts to oust such modernity. Their partial success led to a widening rift between the musical idioms of the concert hall and of the church. A writer of the time observed the result, that Christian music became:

> the handmaid of religion, and no longer an art which soared free, breathing alike the joys and sorrows of men, but an art which sought to shadow forth that heavenly calm which exists beyond the fever and fret of human life.[8]

A composer's natural inclination to write for the church on the one hand and his identity as a modern and highly trained musician on the other were therefore set on a collision course. The Victorian composer Joseph Barnby (1838–96) experienced the dilemma keenly when writing Christian music:

> You may imitate and plagiarise the old tunes to an extent, and in all probability you will be spoken of as one who is 'thoroughly imbued with the truly devotional spirit of the old ecclesiastical writers', but you are not permitted on any account to give your natural feelings fair play; or, in short, to write spontaneously.[9]

The church's loss of contact with art-music in the nineteenth century had serious consequences for compositional standards in the Christian music of city churches and cathedrals across Europe, whether Roman Catholic, Lutheran or Anglican. Recovery from some very low points was slowed by the cartel of the cathedral organ-loft, protecting its members like a cocoon from the concerns of professional music outside.

The influence of the Tractarians

An apparent solution was offered by the Tractarians, who led the Anglicans' rediscovery of the potency of symbols in worship. The visual focus of the altar, the symbol of the cross, the priestly garments and a hundred other details all conveyed messages about the nature of worship and about the relationships of the people involved – priest, choir and congregation.

It seemed as though worship that encouraged a personal and individual response (expressed through rhetoric) was giving way once more to contemplation of universal truths (expressed through symbols). But Western culture at large was no longer medieval, no longer grounded in a profound sense of God as sustainer and synchroniser of the cosmos. In an age of industrial and social revolution the restoration of symbols could not bring back these old certainties.

The balance between the past and the present created by the Tractarians was therefore an uneasy one. In music the desire to restore the symbolic and contemplative elements was uncomfortably overridden by modern rhetorical expectations. Anglican chant makes the point. In its constant repetition of the same melody for every psalm-verse its contribution is ritualistic and impersonal, like the Gregorian psalm-tones of the Middle Ages. The music seems to offer the ancient and simple benefits of emphasising the parallelism of the Hebrew text and symbolising the unity of all believers through a song common to all. But Anglican chant contributes an additional element: it uses the powerful and rhetorical tool of harmony. Its chord progressions carry a much more modern and very different message from the unison of plainsong, for they are the essential vehicle for emotional expression.

It is therefore contradictory to attempt to convey the narrative of a psalm, with its dramatic emotional contrasts, by the same rhetorical messages incessantly repeated in the music. Changing the chant in mid-psalm or the organist's changes of registration (full swell for the 'bulls of Bashan', fanfare of trumpets for 'the Lord strong and mighty') are only crude attempts to improve the expression of a psalm's emotional content.

In spite of such machinations the problem remains – the music masquerades as a symbol while its true nature is rhetorical or emotional.

In all this the losers were – and to a certain extent, still are – the established churches. Their traditions of musical excellence were deprived of the stimulus of truly inventive minds by the churches' rejection of full-blooded Romanticism. What Christians were left with was a diluted and anodyne modern music which gained diminishing respect and attention from the educated public.

The evangelical churches had no such difficulties. For them, music was a means of emotional persuasion like the sermon – its artistic excellence was less important. The straightforward musical rhetoric of the march, the drawing-room ballad and the music-hall song was already part of popular culture and evangelical churches did not hestitate to adapt it to the Christian cause.

It is these churches, such as the Salvation Army or the Elim Pentecostals, which were able to express their faith in music of spontaneity and enthusiasm. The striking contrast between their confidence on the one hand and the unease of the established churches in allowing serious composers to 'write spontaneously' on the other is equally evident today.

Notes

1. J.S. Curwen, *Studies in Worship Music*, second series, London, 1885, p. 40.

2. W.R. Moody, *The Life of Dwight L. Moody*, New York, 1900, p. 186; there is further discussion in R.M. Stevenson, *Patterns of Protestant Church Music*, Cambridge, 1953, p. 151 and following.

3. I.D. Sankey, *My Life and Sacred Songs*, London, 1906.

4. *Christian Mission Magazine*, August, 1877; quoted in B. Boon, *Sing the Happy Song*, London, 1978, p. 5.

5. William Booth, quoted in Boon, p. 5.

6. William Booth, quoted in Boon, p. 5.

7. William Booth, quoted in Boon, p. 115.

8. F.W. Joyce, *Life of Sir F.A.G. Ouseley*, London, 1896, p. 247.

9. J. Barnby, preface to his collected *Hymn Tunes*, London, 1897; quoted in W.J. Gatens, *Victorian Cathedral Music in Theory and Practice*, 1986, p. 78.

PART 5
Eastern Traditions

Chapter 27

The Orthodox Churches

It is impossible not to be profoundly moved by the liturgy of our own Orthodox Church. I also love vespers. To stand on a Saturday evening in the twilight in some little country church, filled with the smoke of incense; to lose oneself in the eternal questions, whence, why and whither; to be startled from one's trance by a burst from the choir; to be carried away by the poetry of this music; to be thrilled with quiet rapture when the Royal Gates of the Ikonostasis are flung open and the words ring out, 'Praise the Name of the Lord!' – all this is infinitely precious to me! One of my deepest joys![1]

So wrote Tchaikovsky in 1877. To enter an Orthodox church, to experience its music, is to enter another world. Orthodox Christians have a long and sometimes turbulent history, full of divisions and schisms, yet their music has a timeless quality and a changeless beauty.

Constantine and Christianity

It was the new status of Christianity as a state religion in the fourth century that first caused serious problems. The conversion of the emperor Constantine and the spread of Christianity as a state religion throughout the Roman empire brought into focus issues of doctrine and uniformity. This led to the setting up of the Council of Nicaea (325) and further councils in the fourth and fifth centuries, eventually leading to the division of the Roman Church from the Orthodox.

Following Emperor Constantine's adoption of Byzantium as the centre of his new Christian empire (he renamed the city Constantinople) the city quickly became the centre of Orthodox Christianity. Relations with neighbouring Armenia (whose king, Tiridates III, was converted to Christianity even earlier than Constantine, in 301) were good until the Chalcedon Council of 451, to which the Armenians were unable to send representatives. The Armenians disagreed with the decisions made in their absence and were thereafter branded as heretic by the Orthodox bishops. The same Council failed to reconcile the Coptic and Ethiopian churches to orthodoxy and they also broke away.

The five patriarchs

By the fifth century authority in the Christian world was in the hands of five patriarchs whose centres were Rome, Constantinople, Alexandria, Antioch and Jerusalem. Their jurisdiction extended to numerous districts presided over by metropolitans. The intention was for the patriarchs' authority to be equal, but the constant rivalry between them strengthened their frontiers, particularly between East and West. Through the turbulence in the East – the many divisions and sects, the adherence to heresy – Rome, by contrast, proved to be a centre of some stability, to whom other patriarchs could appeal for dispassionate advice over local disagreements.

The patriarchs of Rome grew ever more aware of the importance of their apostolic succession through St Peter and believed more and more in the additional authority that this gave them over the other patriarchies. This supremacy was eventually claimed to be absolute and has never been recognised by the East.

The saddest aspect of this most serious division is the issue that lay at its heart. As before at the earlier councils, it was a question of creed. John's gospel states that the Holy Spirit, the third member of the Trinity, 'comes from the Father'. Western Christians were required to accept a creed which stated that the Holy Spirit proceeds from the Father 'and the Son' (*filioque*). On this difference and the question of authority was built a controversy which finally (in 1054) became the chief justification of a permanent schism between the Church of Rome and the churches of the East. The incessant arguments over doctrinal matters may seem trivial, but they had very real consequences in the appalling suffering of the common people caught up with one faction or another.

The Crusades proved to be a further disaster both to the credibility and unity of the Christian faith. They began both as pilgrimages and holy wars, bent on rescuing the most precious Christian sites from the Muslims. In the First Crusade of 1095, a Christian army from the West wrested control of Jerusalem from the Muslims after great bloodshed in 1099. But the Fourth Crusade (1202–4) was disastrously directed against Constantinople – Western Christian fighting Eastern Christian. During Holy Week of 1204, Constantinople was sacked and looted by a Christian European army. Many of the spoils found their way back to Europe, where they contributed to the fabulous wealth of such cities as Venice.

Although the reunion of East and West was discussed again, the Eastern Church was too exasperated by the forcible occupation of Constantinople to be able to negotiate. Such carnage, based ultimately on greed, turned the gospel on its head.

The strength of Orthodoxy

Constantinople was restored as the centre of Eastern Christendom and the Byzantine empire in 1261, but it was much weakened and gradually gave way to the Turks over the next two centuries. During the fourteenth century the emperor unsuccessfully implored the assistance of the West, hoping that the offer of reunion with Rome could be exchanged for the Western church's help. Nothing was forthcoming. The gradual decline of the Byzantine empire led eventually to the conquest of Constantinople by the Turks in 1453.

Curiously enough, the downfall of Constantinople temporarily increased the authority of the Orthodox Church under its patriarch, for the Turks who now ruled allowed them freedom to worship, if not to make converts or to display Christian symbols (like the cross) on their churches. And the Turks naturally identified religious leadership with national identity.

Under these conditions the patriarchs of Constantinople retained – and even gained – power and respect. But on the other hand they lived through five centuries of Turkish rule which proved to be perilous. Many patriarchs were driven from their thrones by the Turks, some abdicated, some were murdered. But the Christians clung to the faith with remarkable tenacity through their example and through the pastoral care of the country priests.

The people of the Orthodox Church have also had the advantage of a liturgy which has remained in a language well understood by them and of a church in which they feel truly at home.

Orthodoxy today

Of the four ancient Orthodox patriarchies, only that of Constantinople has been discussed so far. But the other three, established at the very beginnings of the Christian faith, are still in existence, though their sphere of influence is not what it once was. The Orthodox patriarchy of Alexandria (established by St Mark) is now small (perhaps 250,000) as most Christians in Egypt are members of the independent Coptic Church. The region of this patriarchy also covers countries like Saudi Arabia and Libya which are nowadays almost wholly Muslim.

Antioch at the time of its conversion was an immensely important centre, politically and economically. Its patriarchy was established at a very early stage in Christian history (earlier than AD45) but down the ages Christians in the region have become independent (such as the Church of Cyprus) or heretical (such as the Jacobites and Nestorians). Many Christians in the region are now Uniate (that is, they owe their allegiance to Rome). All this has eroded the influence of Antioch as a centre of Orthodoxy.

Jerusalem is such a vital and emotive centre for Jews, Christians and Muslims that its Orthodox patriarchy has inevitably seen great turbulence. This is the church whose traditions Egeria described at the start of the fifth century (see chapter 4). Even then the city was a centre of pilgrimage for many faiths and the church in Jerusalem has striven to keep the peace under these most difficult circumstances.

The Orthodox Church also consists of a number of other branches, all of whom are now independent, though they use a very similar liturgy in their appropriate languages. The Church of Cyprus became independent in 431, the Church of Russia in 1589. Greece remained under Turkish rule with only one interruption (1684–1718) from the fifteenth century to the nineteenth.

Modern Greece came into being in 1829, following the defeat of the Turks by Britain, France and Russia in the naval battle of Navarino. Shortly after, in 1833, the independent Orthodox Church of Greece was created, with its metropolitan in Athens. In the later nineteenth century the Orthodox churches of Bulgaria, Serbia and Romania also became independent.

Worship in the Orthodox churches

Orthodox Christians have rich and varied musical traditions, which retain a sense of identity through the ancient liturgy. Art historians have worked hard to introduce the West to the visual glories of Byzantine civilisation. Looking at the richness of expression, it seems reasonable to suppose that the musical traditions of the Byzantine empire must have been equally impressive.

Western traditions of early Christian music and especially those of its chant have been well documented and researched. Now the ancient Byzantine music is being studied as avidly as Western chant was a century ago. But the present-day music of the Orthodox Church is its living relative and it is not hard to find a church in most countries where the traditional music of the Orthodox liturgy is sung.

In most Christian denominations, the style of worship varies according to the type of church and local tradition. Anglican churches, for instance, may be 'high' or 'low' and resources in a cathedral differ greatly from those of a small parish church. To some degree the same is true of Orthodox churches. A monastery on Mount Athos in Greece will express the full musical heritage of the Orthodox traditions in services lasting many hours, whereas a small village church will not even be able to boast a choir. But the sense of tradition within the Eastern churches generally is so strong that there is a close relationship between the worship of any of its member churches that is rare in the West.

To enter an Orthodox church is to be aware of a long-established and revered tradition of worship. It is a place apart. The building itself is often in the shape of a cross surmounted by a dome, creating a broad open space, the inside of which at first gives no obvious focus of attention. But however plain the exterior, the interior is richly decorated with carvings, frescoes and ikons.

Ikons may not necessarily be old, but they have been created by artists working within strict confines laid down by tradition and informed by a precise understanding of their nature. They are not religious paintings so much as 'prayers enshrined in painted wood'. Two of the ikons most prominently displayed will be to the saint after whom the church is named and to the saint who is being honoured at that particular feast, depending on the time of year.

One of the first acts of a Christian entering an Orthodox church may be to place a lighted candle in a stand, either in prayer for the living or in memory of the dead. There are few chairs in the church – most of the congregation will stand while much of the service is conducted by the priest or priests in the chancel, behind the *ikonostasis* (a word literally meaning 'picture-stand').

There are sensory experiences of all kinds: the light of candles, the rich colour of the frescoes, ikons and vestments, the scent of incense, the taste of the bread and wine perhaps, and the sound of the chant. All these are part of a worship which intends to bring heaven to earth and in which all bodily senses are caught up in a corporate and joyful experience of the love of God.

It is important not to judge these essential features of Orthodox worship by Western standards. The deep interest in ritual might, for instance, suggest an authoritarian attitude to the congregation; or that the church exerts discipline on its congregations through its clergy; or that its firm and unerring commitment to tradition means a rigidity of thinking. In reality these are false conclusions. Instead, the ritual and symbols encourage the worshipper to be aware not only of celebrating God's presence with the congregation, but also of the closeness of heaven (right above in the vault of the dome), of the availability of salvation (through the open doors to the chancel) and of the presence of the saints of the church (depicted in the ikons, which are often greeted by a kiss on first entering the building).

It is vital to understand the unique place that art – and especially music – occupies here. Unlike Western Christianity today which is seeking to absorb back into the church idioms and styles in the arts which have long developed an independent life in the world outside its walls, Eastern Christians have their own unique traditions which are largely self-sustaining. In the world of art, for example, the use of symbols in the paintings of ikons is strictly controlled, along with aspects of their design and the techniques used to create them. Orthodox Christian art sprang directly from the contemporary practice of the Middle East in the early years of the Christian church (though with important changes of emphasis) and gradually parted company with the changing fashions of secular life.

The arts of the Orthodox churches are therefore not just a precious window onto the past, but at the same time an essential element of the Eastern church's present-day worship. There is none of the turbulence and questioning that surround art (and particularly music) in the Christian worship of the West.

Notes

1. Letter to Nadejda von Meck, quoted in V. Volkoff, *Tchaikovsky*, London, 1975, pp. 169–70.

Chapter 28

The Greek Orthodox Church

Music is uniquely integrated into the worshipping traditions of the Eastern churches. In the Orthodox churches music and liturgy are interdependent. In well-endowed churches the singing is by choirs, or by the priest and people in a humble village church. Following the injunctions of the Church Fathers, musical instruments have never been accepted. The sound of the human voice raised in song is central. As Basil the Great wrote as far back as the fourth century:

> A psalm is tranquillity of soul and the arbitration of peace; it settles one's tumultuous and seething thoughts... A psalm creates friendships, unites the separated and reconciles those at enmity. Who can still consider one to be a foe with whom one utters the same prayer to God! Thus psalmody provides the greatest of all goods, charity, by... joining together the people into the concord of a single chorus.[1]

The church year and its fasts, feasts and celebrations dominates national and home life in a way that is difficult for the Westerner to appreciate:

> Nobody who has lived and worshipped among Greek Christians for any length of time but has sensed in some measure the extraordinary hold which the recurring cycle of the church's liturgy has upon the piety of the common people. Nobody who has kept the Great Lent... who has shared in the fast which lies heavy on the nation for forty days... who has known the desolation of the holy and great Friday, when every bell in Greece tolls its lament and the body of the Saviour lies shrouded in flowers in all the village churches... who has been present at the kindling of the new fire and tasted the joy of a world released from the bondage of sin and death – none can have lived

through this and not have realised that for the Greek Christian the Gospel is inseparably linked with the liturgy that is unfolded week by week in his parish church.[2]

Monastic traditions of worship are very strong in the East and the twenty monastic foundations on Mount Athos in Greece form its cornerstone. For them, life is governed by Daily Offices similar to those of the Western monastic tradition, but for churches in towns and villages only extracts from the full monastic liturgy are celebrated. The most important of these is the Divine Liturgy (that is, Mass or Communion), the central act of worship on Sundays and feast days, and the people do not receive communion without initial preparation and fasting.

The Divine Liturgy

There are three liturgies used by the Orthodox churches today. The Liturgy of St John Chrysostom is in common use throughout the year; the Liturgy of St Basil is rather more elaborate and is used only on Christmas Eve and at Epiphany; the Liturgy of St James (the oldest of the three) is heard only rarely.

The Divine Liturgy of the Orthodox Church follows the pattern of worship that has changed little in 1,500 years. It may be interesting to compare the outline given below with that of Egeria's experience of Mass in fifth-century Jerusalem (see chapter 4) and the outline of the later Roman Mass (chapter 6).

It cannot be stressed enough how important a role music plays in the liturgy. Apart from the sermon, the silent prayers and perhaps the creed, everything is sung.

Divine liturgy begins with the *prothesis* (preparation), an elaborate private ceremony preparing the bread and wine. For the participants, the service begins with the *enarxis* (opening), consisting of:

An opening blessing

The Greater Litany
Petitionary prayers

First Antiphon
Varies according to the feast-day

Short litany

Second Antiphon
Ends with the *troparion*
'Only-begotten Son'

Short litany and concluding prayer

This is followed by the *synaxis* (assembly), originally the part of the service where the clergy entered, but now 'upstaged' by the *enarxis*. The *synaxis* parallels the Western 'liturgy of the Word' and follows a similar pattern:

The Little Entrance
During this the book of the Gospels is carried to the altar

Third Antiphon

Troparia and *Kontakia*
Hymns of the day

The *Trisagion*
Hymn addressing God three times as 'holy'
Followed by a silent prayer
No Old Testament reading

The *Prokeimenon*
A psalm-verse and refrain which parallels the Roman Gradual

The New Testament reading

Psalm-verse with Alleluia

The Gospel reading

The Sermon
In Greece often preceding communion but in Russia usually delivered at the end of the service

Litanies of fervent prayer
For the departed and for the catechumens (candidates for baptism)

The central part of the service that follows is the Eucharist, or liturgy of the faithful:

Litanies of the faithful

The Great Entrance
A long private prayer of the celebrant, censing of the altar,
intercessions, censing offerings and placing them on the altar,
all accompanied by the singing of the *Cheroubikon,* the Cherubic
Hymn

The Creed

The *Anaphora* (offering)
The eucharistic prayer, said silently, overlaid by the choir's
sung responses

The *Sanctus*
The narrative of the institution of the Eucharist at the Last
Supper. Sung by the priest, with concluding 'Amens' from the
choir

Hymn to the *Theotokos* (Mary, of whom God was born)
Sung over silent prayers commemorating saints, prayers for the
departed and for the living

The Breaking of the Bread
During this a hymn is sung

The Communion
During the invitation of the people to communion, the choir
sings verses 26–27 of Psalm 118. During communion itself,
anthems are sung, followed by a further two after communion.

The Conclusion
Final prayers, the Litany of Thanksgiving, dismissal and a final
blessing with responses .

Chanting

The simplest type of chanting can be heard in the scripture readings,
declaimed to a single note with deviations related to the punctuation, in a
manner already described (see the music of the synagogue and the Roman
Church in chapters 2 and 4). Between about the eighth and thirteenth

centuries a simple but unique method was used to indicate the way in which the pitch of the reader's voice had to be raised or lowered. This *ekphonetic* (exclamatory) notation consisted of signs written above the beginnings and endings of sentences, although their meanings are still not completely understood. Today ekphonetic notations are still used in some Eastern churches and in the Jewish synagogue.

The psalms used in the Divine Liturgy and those which also form the backbone of the Daily Office, are sung to chants belonging to one of eight modes. These modes are similar to those of Western medieval music, being scale-systems whose finals (like key-notes) are the notes D, E, F and G. Psalm-singing is elaborated to a similar degree to Western chant. More interestingly, the eight modes are incorporated into the church's year.

For symbolic reasons buried in antiquity the modes of Byzantine chant are governed by an eight-weekly cycle, the eight modes being changed Sunday by Sunday until the cycle is begun afresh. The systematic organisation of all chants into the eight modes is called the *oktoechos*.

Perhaps the most interesting feature of the modes is the tendency of music written in any one mode to develop a unique character through the use of stock melodic ideas or formulae, a practice known as centonisation. This is a feature of many types of music which are created aurally rather than composed on paper. There is evidence of centonisation in Gregorian chant and it is an essential part of Indian classical music, where a *ràg* is given its character not just by the notes of the scales used, but by the melodic ideas used as the basis for improvisation. African master-drumming is based on the same principle and it is inherent in contemporary jazz.

Hymns

One of the most striking musical features of Orthodox worship must be its hymns, which have been composed in huge numbers from the fourth century onwards. One compilation lists at least 60,000.[3] Byzantine hymns have traditional structures which all have their proper place in the liturgy. The simplest hymns are one verse long and called *troparia* (singular *troparion*). Originally these were short poetic prayers inserted between the verses of a psalm and set to simple music easily memorised by a congregation. *Kontakia* are much more extended hymns, being built up of many verses – it might be thirty or more. They are based on a number of traditional patterns (called *hirmoi*) which govern the numbers of lines for each verse and the number of syllables and their stresses in each line. The beginning letters of each verse make an acrostic which may spell out the name of the author, or the day and feast for which the *kontakion* was intended or perhaps the musical mode to which it was sung. Each verse has a short refrain suitable for participation by choir or congregation. Many *kontakia* were composed by Romanus in the sixth century.

Kanones became the most complex of all Byzantine hymns and replaced *kontakia* around the eighth century. In full they consist of nine sections (called odes), the subject of each being based on nine biblical songs:

Exodus 15:1–19
Deuteronomy 32:1–43
1 Samuel 2:1–10
Isaiah 26:9–19
Daniel 3:26–45 and 52–56 (including the deuterocanonical section)
Daniel 3:57–88 (ditto)
Jonah 2:3–10
Habakkuk 3:2–19
Luke 1:46–55 (*Magnificat*)
Luke 1:68–79 (*Benedictus*)

As with the *kontakia*, the odes consist of a verse from a traditional source (the *hirmos*) followed by a number of *troparia* modelled on it.

Each ode is sung to a different melody. In practice, *kanones* in their full form are very long and are only heard nowadays at the important yearly feasts and then only in monasteries and cathedrals. They are sung during the Morning Office and split into three parts (odes 1 and 3, 4 to 6 and 7 to 9).[4] Between these parts are inserted hymns and a reading. Usually *kanones* are drastically shortened so that only the initial *hirmoi* are sung.

Stichera were a later development of the *troparia* – hymns sung after a verse of a psalm. In this respect they are similar to Western antiphons. They are divided into different categories according to their subject and the feast for which they are appropriate.

In the last few centuries of the Byzantine empire, expert singers and composers – *maistores* – developed a highly elaborate style of *kalophonic* singing, 'beautifying' the already elaborate chant. The names and compositions of these *maistores* are known today, Joannes Koukouzeles (about 1280–1370) being the most revered (he is a saint of the Greek Orthodox Church). This unique singing tradition even had a competitive element, *maistores* rivalling each other in their spectacular elaborations of a given text. The *kalophonic* tradition lasted until the nineteenth century, when Chrysanthos of Madytos revised and simplified the chant to bring it back into closer touch with the common people.

The Greek Orthodox chant today

How is Byzantine chant performed today? The answer of course depends on where it is performed, but under no circumstances will it be heard with musical instruments. In a village church there may very well be no choir and the chanting will be undertaken by the local priest. If the priest himself is not available, a lay-reader will be able take the role of *psaltes* (cantor), for the music will be very familiar to regular church-goers.

In a few city churches in Athens it is still possible to hear Byzantine chant harmonised in a manner developed in the seventeenth and eighteenth centuries, but in most monasteries and cathedrals this is not the case. Here the music will be sung in the long-established manner by two choirs standing either side of the chancel, the left-hand choir led by the *lampadarios* and right-hand by the *protopsaltes*. The right-hand choir tends to have the more skilled singers and handles more complex music, though much of the music is antiphonal, the music moving from one choir to the other and back again. Highly skilled cantors will sing the most complex chants (such as the *prokeimenon*) as solos.

In many monastic choirs (such as that of the Monastery of Saint Simon on Mount Athos) a tradition of two-part singing is preserved. In reality the second part is not melodic but consists of held notes rather like a drone, a practice dating from about the seventeenth century. The upper part keeps to the traditional chant.

The language used by the church for its traditional music is the Greek of the very earliest years of Christianity, very different from modern Greek, but nonetheless understood and revered by church-goers. The music of course has changed since its creation in those early times. How much it still resembles the music of the ancient Byzantine Empire is a difficult question which cannot be answered easily.[5] But considering the enormous time-span from their composition to modern times the correspondence between ancient manuscripts and the present-day chant is remarkable.

Notation in the Greek Orthodox Church

From the tenth century onwards a comprehensive and elaborate method of writing down Byzantine chant was developed, more sophisticated than the Roman neumatic notation and with a completely different basis.

Instead of indicating pitch by placing symbols on a grid of parallel lines, the signs indicate changes of pitch from a given starting-point. The following table lists some of the more common signs in Byzantine round notation of the thirteenth century which still form the basis of choir-books in the Greek Church today:

⌣	stay on the same note
⌣⟩	ascend one note of the scale
⟩	descend one note of the scale
⌣⌐	ascend two notes
⌢⟩	descend two notes
⸗⟩	descend three notes

This is a simplified explanation of a system which originally indicated the way the chant should be sung with great precision. There were, for instance, at least six different ways of descending by one note indicated by six different signs. Even the notation today can instruct cantors to execute specialised inflexions of the voice known only to singers of the East. Example 31 shows the beginning of a *troparion* (a one-verse hymn) in Byzantine and Western notation. It comes from the first week of the Octoechos. The final of the mode, D, is stated in the heading (in Greek, Pa). The sign above the first syllable of 'Kyrie' indicates that the tune starts one note above the final, that is, on E. Subsequent signs tell the singer where to move relative to the previous note. Every few bars a cautionary sign appears naming the note just sung, reassuring the singer that he is still on the right track. Modern chant often has a perceptible rhythmic pulse, probably a fairly recent development. The vertical slash in the notation is the equivalent of a bar-line. Signs also show notes of twice or half the normal length (the equivalent of minims or quavers) and of more complex durations such as triplets.

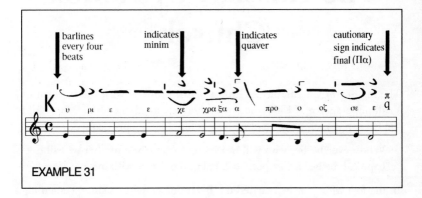

EXAMPLE 31

Notes

1. J. McKinnon, *Music in Early Christian Literature*, Cambridge, 1987, pp. 65 and 66.

2. R. Hammond, *The Waters of Marah*, London, 1956, pp. 51–52.

3. Follieri, *Initia hymnorum ecclesiae graecae*; quoted in the *New Grove Dictionary of Music and Musicians*, London, 1980, under 'Byzantine Rite'.

4. A glance at the subject matter of the second canticle will suggest why it is usually only included during Lent.

5. But see M.P. Dragoumis, 'The Survival of Byzantine Chant' in E. Wellesz, editor, *Studies in Eastern Chant*, Oxford, 1966, vol. I, p. 9.

Chapter 29

The Russian Orthodox Church

The history of Christianity in Russia began properly with the baptism of Vladimir, emperor of Kiev, into the Orthodox Christian faith in 988. As did the Roman emperor Constantine long before him, he proclaimed:

> Whosoever he be, who will not come to the river tomorrow to be baptised, be he rich or poor, will fall into disgrace with me.[1]

In the following year he married the Byzantine emperor's sister, cementing a relationship with the empire at the height of its power.

The history

For some time the metropolitans of the Russian Church were mostly Greeks appointed by the patriarch of Constantinople and only in the fifteenth century did the Russian Church begin to make decisions for itself. By this time, the Byzantine liturgy was firmly established with little alteration except for its translation into Slavonic, which is the language still used by the Russian Orthodox Church today.

During the period of the Tartar occupation of Russia (1240–1461) Christianity survived, for in 1272 the Tartars embraced the Islamic faith in which – like the Turks' later occupation of Byzantium – they were tolerant of Christian 'People of the Book' (the Old Testament). A century after the fall of Constantinople and the end of the Byzantine empire, the Russians appointed their first patriarch in Moscow in 1589.

From that time the Russian Church had to face constant difficulties. Among them was the Time of Troubles, a civil war which followed the death of the emperor, Boris Godunov, in 1605. Worse, perhaps, were the failed ambitions of Nikon (Patriarch from 1652–66) for the supremacy of the church over the state, resulting in the Great Schism and leaving the church under the thumb of tsarist rule.

The most recent catastrophe was the Bolshevik Revolution of 1917. The long history of the church's allegiance to the tsar inevitably marked it out for special treatment by the Bolsheviks, who worked hard to diminish the church's authority as much as possible. Sadly, they were assisted by some church leaders prepared to further the Communist cause. Patriarch Tikhon was arrested in 1923, and determined attempts were made to undermine the church economically (church valuables and buildings were confiscated by the state) and spiritually (monasteries were dissolved, restrictions were placed on religious gatherings, religious teaching in schools was forbidden and more than a thousand priests were martyred in the first years of the Revolution). World War II gave the Communists a short-lived awareness of the church as a useful patriotic focus, but the Khrushchev era renewed the pressures and penalties to open confession of the Christian faith. In spite of the constant oppression, the collapse of Communism in the early nineties has revealed the churches of Russia and Eastern Europe to be very much alive and rejoicing in a new-found freedom of worship.

The music of the Russian Orthodox Church

The liturgy of Russian Orthodoxy is closely allied to that of the Byzantine Church; many of the general remarks made about the worship of Greek Orthodox Christians in the previous chapter apply equally to the Russians. The music, however, is very noticeably different. The story that lies behind it is complicated by the loss or corruption of early chants and by the church's current perception of traditional or 'canonical' music, as it is termed.

The ancient chant of the Russian Church, like the Greek, was written down in a notation similar in principle to the Byzantine and manuscripts go back as far as the eleventh century. From these it is clear that the chant was a single melody just like Gregorian or Byzantine chant, and to begin with (according to the scholar Preobrazhensky) the melodies were Byzantine too. The translation of the Greek liturgy into the Slavonic language and its transplantation into a different culture rapidly changed its music to something unlike any other tradition. The name given to this collection of chant was *znamenny raspev* (chanting by signs), now known simply as *znamenny.*

Although the old books still exist in great numbers, the symbols used in the notation are ambiguous and the earliest versions of these ancient melodies cannot yet be sung with accuracy. During the seventeenth century the now-familiar Western notation was brought to Russia (together with many other Western innovations) and a few of the traditional melodies were copied out. Unfortunately, the incentive at the time was for drastic reform, imposed by the Patriarch Nikon. The changes included the adoption of a new and Western style of music, sung in a Baroque harmonic style. This so incensed a number of Christians that they annexed themselves from the church altogether in order to continue the old traditions.[2]

Miraculously, adherents to the old way are still worshipping today and are known as the Old Believers. Their many sects are widely distributed (with representatives in Moscow) and many of them are priestless. They have also emigrated to Canada and the United States and continue their worship there. The Old Believers are the only Christians who still sing the *znamenny* chant in anything like its true form, reading it from a notation similar to the Byzantine. Another type of chant, now even less accessible than *znamenny*, was *demestvenny*, a highly decorative chant for solo voice used for special feast-days. In its elaboration it paralleled the *kalophonic* chant of the Byzantine Church.

From the seventeenth century on, Russian church music is much more akin to the West than the East. Nikolai Diletsky (about 1630–90) was a musician from Kiev who had studied in Poland (where Italian music was well known). He promoted Western styles of church music through his own compositions and text-books. The following generation of Diletsky's pupils included Kalashnikov, who wrote sumptuous settings of texts for Vespers which he called Sacred Concertos. These are pieces for up to four choirs and in as many as twenty-four parts; their imitative effects are reminiscent of the polychoral music of Gabrieli and Monteverdi in Venice a century earlier. In such pieces all connection with the tradition of *znamenny* chant is lost.

By the close of the eighteenth century Italian opera had been firmly established in Russia with its consequent importation of skilled and professional foreign musicians. Conversely, Russian musicians of the Court Chapel such as Maxim Berezovsky (1745–77) and Dmitri Bortniansky (1751–1825) had the opportunity to study in Italy. While they did not use

Italian operatic styles in their Christian music, they nonetheless brought the technical skills of counterpoint and harmony to bear on it. Many of their works are settings of psalm texts and are masterpieces of concentrated economy and intensity in choral writing.

But the character of Russian church music today owes more to the nineteenth century than to any other period. It was dominated by Fyodor L'vov and his son Alexey (1798–1870, and musical director of the Court Chapel for twenty-five years), Pyotor Turchaninov and many others. They created the sonorous and somewhat sentimental style of singing associated with Russian liturgical music, often dubbed the 'St Petersburg style'.

An idea of the extent to which *znamenny* has altered down the years can be seen in Example 32, which puts some Kiev chant from 1709 alongside an edition of 1906. The lower line is taken from *Tserkovnoje Prostopinije* (*Plainchants of the Church*) while the upper is a transcription from the printed *Irmologion* found in the monastery of Lviv, west of Kiev. These latter chant-books are among the oldest transcribable sources of *znamenny*. The Lviv chants are quite clearly the same melodies as those of the modern *Prostopinije*, but show the 1906 book to be a recent tradition. The additional sharps and flats of the 1906 chant book have been put in to allow harmonisation and modulation in Western classical style. The earlier version reveals its ancestry through its modality.

The chants used in the Court Chapel were simplified and shortened versions of traditional melodies and these romantic and rhetorical harmonisations of them were published in an edition of the *Obikhod* (canticles of the Ordinary) in 1848. They were thus disseminated throughout Russia and are still the basis of Russian Orthodox music today.

It is most unfortunate that the Russian Church has come to identify its musical traditions so closely with these chants (and, even worse, with the wooden and uninspiring contributions of Bakhmetyev). At that time Russian art-music was beginning a most exciting period of natural development, beginning with Glinka and culminating in the music of the Russian Five – Rimsky-Korsakov, Borodin, Cui, Balakirev and Mussorgsky. Tragically, none of these composers made any impact on the music of their national church.

The difference between the sentimental harmonies of L'vov and the spectacular world of Russian symphonies and ballets must have seemed an unbridgeable gap. Only one great composer of that time made a serious and single-minded contribution to Orthodox church music, and he was taken to court for doing so.

EXAMPLE 32

Tchaikovsky's *Liturgy*

On 30 April 1878, Tchaikovsky wrote to his confidante Nadejda von Meck:

> If the favourable mood lasts long enough, I want to do something in the way of church music. A vast and almost untrodden field of activity lies open to composers here. I appreciate certain merits in Bortniansky, Berezovsky and others; but how little their music is in keeping with the Byzantine architecture, the ikons, and the whole spirit of the Orthodox liturgy!... It is not improbable that I shall decide to set the entire liturgy of St John Chrysostom.[3]

The Court Chapel held a monopoly on the publication of all church music (a fact that contributed greatly to its musical sterility) so, having gained approval from the Ecclesiastical Censors of his new setting of the *Liturgy of St John Chrysostom,* Tchaikovsky published abroad. Bakhmetyev, the director of music of the Court Chapel, immediately protested and the publisher Jurgenson was taken to court. After two years, Tchaikovsky and his publisher won the case and litigation finally forced Bakhmetyev to resign.

Tchaikovsky's *Liturgy* is a work of simplicity and restraint, artistically far in advance of anything of which the Chapel composers were capable. At the same time it takes no imaginative steps outside the conventionally rhetorical world of diatonic harmony nor does anything distinctive 'in keeping with the Byzantine architecture'. Certainly Tchaikovsky used none of the old *znamenny* chant, nor showed that he was aware of its true nature.

Rachmaninoff's *Liturgy of St John Chrysostom* and *All-Night Vigil*

Only one composer of the following generation and of similar stature to Tchaikovsky in the world of art-music made musical settings of the Orthodox liturgy – Sergei Rachmaninoff (1873–1943). This might come as a surprise, not least because his legendary reputation as a pianist and the popularity of his own music for the instrument have given a distorted impression of the breadth of his talent.

Although Rachmaninoff had expressed an interest in setting the liturgy of St John Chrysostom in 1897, it was not until 1910 that he composed his *Liturgy*, opus 31. He too, was deeply attracted to the traditions and the music of Russian Orthodox worship, a sympathy which spills over into his music for the concert hall. Like Tchaikovsky, he wanted to write music specifically for use in worship. His setting of the *Liturgy* accordingly sets all the required passages and makes due allowances for the cantillation of readings and prayers.

Like Tchaikovsky's *Liturgy*, though, the music has been ill-fated, and for similar reasons. Unaccompanied choral music lacks the dramatic rhetoric that concert-hall audiences expect and is a taste they are rarely encouraged to acquire. On the other hand, the Orthodox Church found the music too compelling, too reminiscent of opera. Early concert-hall performances of the music generated considerable enthusiasm, but for one perceptive observer of the time, the music was 'absolutely wonderful, even too beautiful, but with such music it would be difficult to pray; it is not church music'.[4]

Rachmaninoff seems to have recognised these unsolved (and perhaps insoluble) difficulties but was drawn once more to the liturgy, this time that of Vespers and Matins – known collectively as the *All-Night Vigil*, as they run together as a preparation for Divine Liturgy the following day. His profound respect for the old *znamenny* chant prompted him to use a number of ancient melodies as the basis for his settings and they give a unique character to the music, a flexibility that is hard to describe.

Rachmaninoff must have realised that liturgical use of his music was unlikely (it seems that the *Liturgy* was never used in worship) and perhaps wrote his *All-Night Vigil* (opus 37) more as an expression of personal faith. This puts the work (apart from extracts like *Nyne Otpushchayeshi*, the *Nunc Dimittis*) into the category of art-music. For some, its restraint effaces the composer's public identity (a hindrance to an artist in an age of individualism) and as a result its extraordinary beauties are only now beginning to be discovered.

The first performances of the *All-Night Vigil* took place in 1915, only two years before the Russian Revolution which completely overturned the world of the arts (Rachmaninoff was among many artists forced to flee to the West). As the church was forced into hiding, Christian music could no longer enjoy any creative life.

Notes

1. See N. Zernov, *Eastern Christendom*, London, 1961, p. 112.

2. The transition to the new music during the seventeenth century is well documented in A.J. Swan, *Russian Music and its Sources in Chant and Folk-song*, London, 1973, p. 48 and following. For a study of *znammenny*, see J. Gardner, *Russian Church Singing*, New York, 1980 and J.L. Roccasalvo, *The Plain Chant Tradition of Southwestern Rus'*, New York, 1986.

3. R. Newmarch, editor, *The Life and Letters of P.I. Tchaikovsky*, London, 1906, pp. 298–99.

4. Quoted in B. Martyn, *Rachmaninoff*, Aldershot, Hants, 1990, p. 222.

Chapter 30

The Coptic and Ethiopian Churches

The churches of the East can be divided into three groups: first the Orthodox churches of the four Ancient patriarchies (Constantinople, Alexandria, Antioch and Jerusalem) already described, together with the now independent churches still in communion with each other: Cyprus, Greece, Russia, Bulgaria, Yugoslavia and Romania. Second are the Uniate churches, in union with the Church of Rome although following an Eastern rite. These owe their existence to Roman Catholic missionary work in the seventeenth and eighteenth centuries and are to be found in small numbers all over Eastern Europe and the Middle East, including the Melkite and Maronite Christians.

The third group of churches are what the Orthodox Church would call heretical. That is, they broke away from the Orthodox, mostly at the time of great doctrinal struggles in about the fifth century. These are the Nestorian Church (the Church of East Syria) and the Monophysite Christians consisting of the Jacobite Church of Antioch, the Armenian Church, the Coptic Church and the Church of Ethiopia. These last two are particularly good illustrations of the wonderful riches in the Christian music of the area.

The Coptic Church

The words 'Egypt' and 'Copt' are really the same and refer to the geographical area around the Nile. The older form, Copt, has become attached to the language spoken in Egypt before Arabic became commonplace about six centuries ago. Even so, Coptic continued to be spoken in remote villages in Southern Egypt until the nineteenth century. It is therefore a language that dates back, through the Bohairic dialect, to the ancient Egyptian period.

There may be as many as seven million Coptic Christians in Egypt today, living in reasonable harmony among at least forty million Muslims. Some Muslims are becoming more militant and look for an Islamic revolution as a reaction to the increasing poverty and hardship in the country. On the other hand, the Muslim and Christian communities in Egypt have lived in mutual co-operation for centuries and at present that seems set to continue.

Coptic Christians are keenly aware of their ancient ancestry. They revere the apostle Mark as the saint who established the Christian church in Alexandria before his martyrdom there in AD68. They particularly treasure the story of Joseph and Mary's flight to Egypt with the young Jesus. Many ancient Coptic churches were built to commemorate the various resting-places of the Holy Family.

Egypt became one of the great centres of Christian monastic life from the fourth century onwards. Antony (about 251–356) is held to have been the first and finest example of a Christian following a world-renouncing life in the desert. Many others followed. By the fifteenth century there may have been as many as 300 monasteries and nunneries in Egypt. At present there are seven, supporting some 300 monks.

When the Coptic Church separated from the Orthodox in the schism of 451, its sense of spiritual and national identity was brought into a sharp focus which has never been lost. As a consequence, the traditions of worship have been less subject to change than in most other Eastern churches. A visitor to a Coptic church today is immediately aware of being put in touch with very ancient customs which words can only attempt to describe:

Perhaps nowhere in the world can you imagine yourself back in so remote an age as when you are in a Coptic Church. You go into a strange dark building; at first the European needs an effort to realise that it is a church at all, it looks so different from our usual associations... In a Coptic Church you come into low dark spaces, a labyrinth of irregular openings. There is little light from the narrow windows. Dimly you see strange rich colours and tarnished gold, all mellowed by dirt... Lamps sparkle in the gloom [and] before you is the exquisite carving, inlay and delicate patterns of the *haikal* [chancel] screen. All around you see, dusty and confused, wonderful pieces of wood carving. Behind the screen looms the curve of the apse; on the thick columns and along the walls... are inscriptions in exquisite lettering – Coptic and Arabic.[1]

As with the Orthodox churches, the Divine Liturgy is central to Coptic worship – even services of baptism will end with communion. The liturgy generally used is that of St Basil the Great, the liturgies of St Gregory of Nazianzus and St Mark being reserved for special occasions. There is a dramatic shape to the service which is made very evident by the involvement of everyone present. The participation is practical, too.

The historic continuity of the music of the Coptic Church has been under threat. Unlike the Byzantine, its music has always been an oral tradition. During the 1920s the British musician Ernest Newlandsmith undertook the huge task of transcribing the heritage of Coptic music into Western notation. This collection, added to and with a parallel archive of the chant on tape, is intended to help preserve a body of chant threatened by the social pressures of the modern world.

The antiquity of Coptic chant is indicated by the practice of cheironomy, hand-gestures which the church's cantors still use while singing. A German scholar, Hans Hickmann (1908–68), discovered some remarkable parallels between the signs used by Coptic cantors and the heiroglyphics found on ancient Egyptian tombs. He showed that the signs used are essentially the same, enabling him to propose a tentative transcription of the musical notation on Egyptian tombs as much as 4,000 years old, an amazing period of continuity. The cheironomic signs are used today for teaching Coptic chant – effectively an alternative to written notation. The use of the 'Guidonian hand' in teaching choir-boys to sing in medieval times is a parallel case.

As in the Orthodox Church, music is an inseparable part of the liturgy and the whole service is sung from beginning to end – the music being not so much a *way* of worshipping, but worship itself. Indeed, a would-be priest or deacon cannot be ordained unless he has mastered the traditions of Coptic worship music. Unlike the Orthodox however, the congregation are emotionally and vocally involved in the refrains of the litanies.

The pace of the liturgy can be very slow (depending on the priest) and the intonations have a hypnotic quality, using a very narrow range and intervals of a semitone or smaller. The responses are congregational and vocally strongly committed. A choir, or *schola*, will lead the singing at large gatherings. Choirs are made up of theological students, for knowledge of the music is inseparable from study of the liturgy. They accompany some chants with cymbal and triangle, a practice introduced during the Middle Ages and somewhat akin to the vocal drones of the Greek monks. The chanting is always in unison and the percussion instruments keep time with a fairly fast and syncopated beat. The *Sanctus*, an emotional high point in the Divine Liturgy, is much enhanced by this style of accompaniment.

This ancient liturgical music is quite different from the popular music of modern Egypt, which is often played by Western instruments such as the electric guitar and synthesiser. It can also be something of an endurance test for the younger generation – but they still attend. In Sunday School, though, there is music of a more relaxed and folk-song style. Here the children and young people sing a different collection of Christian songs, some of which may be chants adapted from the liturgy. Instruments can be used that could never be brought into church, such as violin, flute, piano and drums. Like Middle Eastern folk-music, the melody instruments decorate and play along with the vocal melody and do not provide additional lines or harmonies.

Since most Christians attend church three times a week the liturgy and its music becomes familiar and much treasured. It is at once one of the most ancient of all musical traditions but at the same time a vital and living force in Christian music, remarkable for its variety and richness.

The Ethiopian Church

The instruments of Musick made use of in their rites of Worship are little Drums, which they hang about their Necks, and beat with both their Hands; these are carried even by their Chief Men, and by the gravest of their Ecclesiasticks. They have sticks likewise with which they strike the Ground, accompanying the blow with a motion of their whole Bodies. They begin their Consort [that is, music-making] by Stamping their Feet on the Ground, and playing gently on their Instruments, but when they have heated themselves by degrees, they leave off Drumming and fall to leaping, dancing, and clapping their Hands, at the same time straining their Voices to the utmost pitch, till at length they have no Regard either to the Tune, or the Pauses, and seem rather a riotous, than a religious, Assembly. For this manner of Worship they cite the Psalm of David, 'O clap your Hands, all ye Nations'.[2]

So wrote a Jesuit priest, Jerome Lobo, in 1627. By any standards, Ethiopia is an inhospitable place to live. It has been beleagured recently by catastrophic famine due to repeated failures of the rains, a disastrous locust plague in 1986 followed by a malaria epidemic in 1988. The government has until recently been constantly in conflict with people fighting for independence. It is not surprising that Ethiopia is described as 'economically one of the least developed countries in the world'.

In spite of all this, it is a country of lively culture and strong spirituality, both of very long standing. The story goes that the Ethiopians adopted the Christian faith in about AD328 as the result of the shipwreck of two Coptic Christians, Frumentius and Aedesius, on their shores. From this early stage they have maintained strong links with the Coptic Church, siding with it in the Chalcedonian schism of 451.

The Ethiopian Church also developed a desert monastic tradition from the fifth century onwards. Many of the Ethiopian monks were highly educated and by the seventh century had translated the Bible from Syriac, Coptic and Greek into the language of Ge'ez, which is still used in the Ethiopian Church today. Like Coptic, this liturgical language is now quite different from the locally-spoken Amharic.

In its Christian history, Ethiopia has had very little contact with the West and although it has been evangelised by Jesuits and more recently by Protestant missionaries, it is unique among African countries in having a Christian church which was established before the conversion of most of Europe. That church is strongly supported by at least 22 million members, divided among 20,000 parishes and led by about 250,000 priests! This represents nearly half the population, the rest being Muslims or followers of traditional animist religions.

The statistics alone show a support for the Christian faith unmatched by any European country. If the number of priests suggests that their title is a nominal one, then the intensity and thoroughness of their training tells a different story. There are several categories of clergy, collectively referred to as the *kahinat* (priests, deacons and monks) and the *debteras*, men who have either elected not to enter the priesthood, or who are ritually unclean (for example as the result of divorce). All of these have a deep knowledge of their Christian music, for it is bonded to the liturgy as closely as in other Eastern churches. Where the chief duties of the priests is to celebrate the Eucharist and to hear confessions, to the *debteras* is given the responsibility of preserving the artistic traditions of church worship. After an elementary schooling, a *debtera* undergoes an intense training in traditional music (*zema*), dance (*aquaquam*), poetry (*qene*) and perhaps in theology and church history too. The task is a huge one and may take twenty years.

In music, the *debtera* faces a rigorous study of the traditional hymns and anthems, of which there are many hundreds. The study is sufficiently intensive for the *debtera* to memorise them all. As part of this process he must make his own copy of the whole vast collection, manufacturing his own parchment and coloured inks, binding the books and making leather cases to preserve them. This task alone may take him seven years, during which time he must also practise the chant daily.

Then the *debtera* must study the sacred dances and how to accompany them. The third study, ecclesiastical poetry, is by all accounts a highly sophisticated art, resembling (and probably surpassing) the most demanding of Western disciplines. The poems first and foremost have to be a perfect fit to one of the traditional chants, for they will be heard in worship as a commentary on scripture. The poem has to be written in the ancient church language of Ge'ez and conform to strict rules of grammar. Most important of all, the poems use a host of scriptural symbols which the congregation understand very well. The poet is judged on how subtly and cunningly he handles these symbols and the technicalities of their expression.

Ethiopian Christians treasure their faith and its traditional enactment. By this rigorous training it is handed down accurately from generation to generation, but at the same time there is room for creativity and a place for new work within its confines. As if this was not enough, *debteras* may also act as herbalists, fortune-tellers and scribes for those who cannot read.

Notation

Although the sacred music is committed to memory almost in its entirety, the Ethiopian Church has its own unique form of notation, a kind of *aide-memoire*. A large number of traditional texts have their own music attached to them, just as the tune and words of 'Happy Birthday to You' are inseparable. This tune is well known and so could be codified simply by the first letter of the text: H. This is the equivalent of the Ethiopian system of musical signposts, or *meleket* letters. The signpost (a single letter) is put at the beginning of a text (such as 'praise the Lord all the earth') thereby instructing the *debtera* to sing this text to the traditional musical phrase 'H'. The melodies that the *meleket* letters represent all have to be learnt, but once that is done, there is no need for staves or neumes, crochets or quavers.

In addition, there are *meleket* signs which show the singer with great precision how the melodies should be sung. Here are a few examples:

•	(*yizet*)	stop, pause or breathe
⌣	(*deret*)	drop the voice to a deep chest register
—	(*heedet*)	quickly, get faster
⌐	(*kurt*)	cut the note short
•••	(*rikrik*)	repeat the note several times very quickly on the same syllable

Signs at the beginning of each chant indicate to which of the three distinct styles of chanting (*zema*) it belongs: the *ge'ez* (fairly unadorned and simple), *'ezl* (deep-sounding and chromatic, solemn, appropriate for fasts, vigils and funerals) or *araray* (lighter, more decorative).

Unfortunately for the *debtera*, the alphabet used for the *meleket* letters has over 200 signs, and combinations of these are made to represent as many as 1,000 musical phrases. Memorising them all is an amazing feat strongly reminiscent of the practice of ancient Greek and early Christian cultures.

The reverence in which all these traditions are held is delightfully illustrated by the legends which describe their origin. Ethiopian Orthodox Christians believe that all their sacred chant was created by Yared, a saint of the sixth century:

> At this time, there were no rules for the famous *zema*, or liturgical chant. The offices were recited in a low voice. But when the Saviour wanted to establish sacred chant, he thought of Yared and sent three birds to him from the Garden of Eden, which spoke to him with the language of men, and carried him away to the heavenly Jerusalem, and there he learnt their chant from twenty-four heavenly priests.

Back on earth, Yared set to work composing and singing the sacred chants:

> And when the king and queen heard the sound of his voice they were moved with emotion and they spent the day in listening to him, as did the archbishop, the priests and the nobility of the kingdom. And he

appointed the chants for each period of the year... for the Sundays and the festivals of the angels, prophets, martyrs and the just. He did this in three styles: in *ge'ez, 'ezl* and *araray*; and he put into these three nothing far removed from the language of men and the songs of the birds and animals.[3]

These stories are recorded in a fourteenth century *Synaxarium* (*Lives of the Saints*) called the *Senkessar*, but in reality the chant is likely to be even older than the time of Yared. It is probable that some direct link exists with the temple music of Jerusalem.

This connection is reinforced by some remarkable circumstantial evidence. For instance, the characteristic shape of many of the churches is circular and inside are three sections, one inside the other. The outer passage is open to anyone and is where the *debtera* sings. The middle section is where the baptised take communion, but the innermost chamber is only for the priests; it houses the *tabot*, an altar very much like the ark of the covenant, made of wood and draped with highly decorated cloth. Even the name of the innermost chamber (*keddusa keddusan*) is clearly connected to the Hebrew *kodesh hakkodashim* – the 'holy of holies'. It is significant that it is the ark that is consecrated, not the church building in which it stands.

The dance is of course the most striking link with the Old Testament:

The veneration accorded to the *tabot* in Abyssinia [Ethiopia] up to the present day, its carriage in solemn procession accompanied by singing, dancing, beating of staffs or prayer-sticks, rattling of *sistra* and sounding of other musical instruments remind one most forcefully of the scene in 2 Samuel 6:5, 15 and 16, when David and the people dance round the ark. The entire spectacle, its substance and its atmosphere, has caused all who have witnessed it to feel transported into the times of the Old Testament.[4]

Notes

1. A. Fortescue, *Lesser Eastern Churches*, London, 1913, p. 288.

2. Father J. Lobo, *A Voyage to Abyssinia*, translated by Samuel Johnson, London, 1735.

3. M. Powne, *Ethiopian Music*, Oxford, 1968, p. 91.

4. Quoted in Powne, pp. 98–99.

Chapter 31

Christianity East and West – Worlds Apart?

The cult of the individual has formed the cornerstone of Western culture since the Renaissance in fifteenth-century Italy. The sanctity of personal rights, aspirations and freedom of expression are humanist ideals deeply embedded in every aspect of society – in politics, ethics, religion, social life and art.

The emphasis placed on the value of the individual fits so comfortably into Western culture that it generally goes unnoticed. Occasionally it draws attention to itself by reaching absurd levels. By what yardstick, for instance, is the fabulous price on a picture by Vermeer being measured? Its value can be demolished by the news that it is a fake, even if the fake and the original are indistinguishable to any but the expert with the microscope. The breathtaking price put on such works of art does not measure their excellence, but the significance of the artist's individuality.

In the realm of music, the composers who are most revered are those with a striking identity. Beethoven epitomises the artist-hero, at odds with society in general, fighting for his place within it without making concessions to its expectations. But this has not always been the case. In medieval times, the priorities of Western culture were different. According to the psychiatrist Anthony Storr, the Middle Ages had

> a generally agreed conception of how an individual ought to behave. The idea that anyone should pursue his personal economic ends to the limit, provided that he kept within the law, was foreign to the medieval mind, which regarded the alleviation of poverty as a duty, and the private accumulation of wealth as a danger to the soul. The Reformation made possible the growth of Calvinism, and the establishment of the Protestant work ethic. It was not long before poverty was regarded as a punishment for idleness or fecklessness, and the accumulation of wealth as a reward for the virtues of industry and thrift.[1]

In other words, before the Reformation, survival depended on conformity to a prevailing social order with rigid codes of behaviour. Expressions of individuality, whether from witches, revolutionaries or mere eccentrics, were a serious threat to medieval society, which reacted promptly and viciously against them.

In the light of this, the dissimilarity of Eastern and Western Christendom is understandable, for the East has preserved attitudes overturned in the West by the European Renaissance and Reformation. For example, Eastern churches place little emphasis on the sermon, which in reformed Western churches is a personal exhortation addressed to individuals. Instead, ancient ceremonial expresses continuity with the past and with timeless truth, through the veneration of places and people associated with the great events of Christian history. Small wonder, then, that Christianity for Eastern countries provides a strong basis for collective identity and is strongly bound up with national sentiment.

Music of the East

Music contributes vitally to the Eastern churches' sense of tradition through its great antiquity. A number of their greatest musicians are revered as saints and their music preserved with care and reverence. Change, on the whole, has been through steady evolution.

The musical dimension most important to Eastern Orthodoxy is undoubtedly that of symbol, as it was to all Christians in medieval Europe. Eastern chant does not convey the meaning of its text in a rhetorical, or emotionally expressive fashion, but symbolises it by mode and structure. The music is a corporate gesture not only in the sense that it draws all voices and minds together in one building, but also through its simultaneous experience by worshippers throughout the land. Eastern psalmody still provides, as Basil the Great pointed out in the fourth century, 'a bond of unity... by joining together the people into the concord of a single chorus'.[2]

When ecstatic music is experienced in the Eastern church, it is a further product of tradition, in this case stretching back as far as the Old Testament. The music of the Ethiopian Christians in particular is sufficiently old to have preserved the ancient Israelites' physical dimension of dance and the heartbeat of their rhythmic accompaniment.

Symbol and rhetoric in conflict

It is rhetorical music, music that intends to persuade and to evoke feelings, that is fundamentally out of place in Orthodox worship. When in the seventeenth century Russia embraced Western culture, the Russian Orthodox Church followed suit by abandoning the old *znamenny* chant in favour of the rhetoric of harmony and polyphony. At the time, a substantial number of Christians found the new music wholly inappropriate for their worship and left the church altogether in the Great Schism.

More recently, when composers such as Tchaikovsky and Rachmaninoff offered their outstanding gifts in the service of Russian Orthodoxy, they were turned down. The *Liturgies* they set are now their least performed works, neglected by both church and concert-hall: too rhetorical and expressive for one and too austere for the other. Present-day composers are almost never invited to write music for the Orthodox Church. In one rare instance of such an invitation, the sympathies of the composer for the Eastern church are complemented by an antagonism towards Western culture.

John Tavener

Tavener is an English composer (distantly related to the sixteenth-century composer of the same name) who embraced Russian Orthodoxy in 1977. His compositions have been increasingly influenced both by Christian mysticism and by Orthodox traditions, while his attitudes to Western culture and the art it produces have become less and less sympathetic:

> It sounds very extreme, but I think sacred art has gone downhill since the Middle Ages. I feel I've come into contact with what ikon painting is, with the primordial kind of Orthodoxy that the West has never had; the fact that the Byzantine tone system is practically unchanged, the fact that Greece never had a renaissance. I think a lot of people are feeling the importance of this... however impressed I am by Michelangelo, the simple Greek peasant ikon means much, much more to me. Or to give a musical example, I'm deeply moved by the very simple harmonic music they sing at the Russian Orthodox cathedral...[3]

Tavener's dissatisfaction with Western culture is expressed by his desire to compose symbolically, 'in the manner of an ikon painter'. He would also prefer the anonymity of a craftsman:

> If only the church was the wise patron she once was! I would love to have lived in Byzantine Greece at its height. I would have been part of the community of ikon painters and writers of texts, and been much more anonymous.[4]

A brief opportunity for John Tavener to join the community of Orthodox artists came from Metropolitan Anthony of Sourozh as an invitation to write music for the English Liturgy of St John Chrysostom. The result, completed in 1978, is music of extreme simplicity. For the most part it avoids the sonorous harmonies typical of the Russian Church and presents the text once more as a single line, only occasionally adorned by a drone or by the simple two-part singing of the Greek monasteries. Since then Tavener has set the complete Orthodox *Vigil Service* (1984), but as far as the concert-going public is concerned this is overshadowed by a number of epic works on Christian spiritual themes, mostly for choir and orchestra, such as *The Annunciation* (1992), *We Shall See Him As He Is* (1992), *Hymns of Paradise* (1993), *The World is Burning* (1994) and *The Myrrh-Bearer* (1995). The piece that has made the greatest impression since the enormously popular *The Protecting Veil*, however, is *Akathist of Thanksgiving*, first performed to a packed Westminster Abbey in 1988 and written to celebrate the millennium of the Russian Orthodox Church. An 'Akathist' is a hymn of supplication or thanksgiving, used on special occasions. The text was written in a Siberian prison camp in the 1940s by a Russian Orthodox priest.

While such large works cannot be incorporated into an existing liturgy, they certainly bring some elements of such an experience to a paying audience. But a critic's remark (not Tavener's) that '*Akathist of Thanksgiving . . .* is not just the music for an Orthodox service but the service itself' goes too far in equating a concert with an act of worship. Christian liturgy (as opposed to an evangelistic meeting) surely springs from a *community* of believers and does not put a ticket price on admission.

Arvo Pärt

Arvo Pärt (b. 1935) is another composer with an Orthodox background, whose music shares some of the qualities of Tavener's. Pärt comes from

Estonia, although he has lived in the West since 1980. His life under a Communist régime did not prevent him from developing a profound Christian faith, and his attitude to his art produces a unique music (much of it settings of biblical texts) which is intriguing to Western musicians because it seems to differ so profoundly in intention from their own. Rather than emotional self-expression, Pärt believes that musicians should concern themselves more with 'pauses and reflection, and evoke this reflection and this condition of stability for the people for whom we create our art'.[5]

Pärt's setting of the Ordinary of the Mass for the Western church, *Missa Sillabica*, is informed throughout by his sense of stability and reflection. Its methodical simplicity stems from the shape of the music being governed by the syllable count of phrases, not directly by their meaning – an extension of the symbolic technique of cantillation. The result is music that can carry worship with great effectiveness and without technical difficulty.

Even these contemporary composers of the Orthodox faith show that Eastern Christianity has maintained a consistency and unanimity which were lost to the West even before the Reformation. The active presence of Eastern Orthodoxy in the Christian world today is a valuable reminder not only that culture and upbringing colour perception of the faith, but that the Western approach is not the only or even the ideal one.

The attention that Pärt has been paid in the last ten years has placed his music in concerts of contemporary music all over Europe. Many of these have taken place in churches, whose acoustic and ambience are far better suited to them – especially the choral works. The Hilliard Ensemble has championed Pärt's work consistently and has sung or commissioned a number of works suitable for church performance. Its tours of the *St John Passion* (1982/88) surprised and delighted large audiences with a contemplative storytelling without histrionics. While the length of the *Passion* precludes its inclusion in a set act of worship, Pärt's shorter settings of biblical texts are eminently suitable in the context of formal worship as meditations on gospel events. The recent *And One of the Pharisees* (1992) could introduce a new seriousness of purpose to art-music in worship, for here is music sufficiently self-effacing and impersonal to allow undistracted contemplation of the words (Example 33 gives a short extract). Three voices recreate the dialogue (in English) between Christ and the pharisees about the woman who anointed Christ with ointment (see Luke 7:36). The style is reminiscent of Schütz' *Resurrection Story* and even of the plainsong dramas of *Quem Queritis* or the Rouen Ceremony of the Shepherds. The Western church could embrace Pärt's music and its musicians learn from it.

EXAMPLE 33

Notes

1. A. Storr, *Solitude*, London, 1989, p. 79; note also the chapter on 'The Significance of the Individual'.

2. Quoted in J. McKinnon, *Music in Early Christian Literature*, Cambridge, 1987, p. 65.

3. P. Griffiths, *New Sounds, New Personalities*, London, 1985, p. 106.

4. John Tavener in discussion with Basil Ramsey in *Music and Musicians*, December 1989, vol. 38, no. 4, p. 7.

5. *Musical Times*, March 1989, p. 132.

PART 6

The African Genius

Chapter 32

Africa and the Influence of Western Music

The Christian ancestry of Ethiopia is unique in Africa, but in the last few decades Christianity has blossomed in many other areas of the continent, with a higher percentage of followers in some African countries than in Western Europe, the area that first evangelised them. Africa is a huge continent and a survey of its Christian music here cannot even begin to be exhaustive. Through brief and selective views, therefore, the following chapters trace the steady climb that Christianity is making there away from Western trappings and dogma to a faith that expresses African priorities, fully absorbed into African life. The musical consequences of this change are dramatic.

It is comparatively recently (around 150 years ago) that Western missionaries became fired with the task of converting 'pagan' Africa to the Christian faith:

> However anxious a missionary may be to appreciate and to retain indigenous social and moral values, in the case of religion he has to be ruthless... he has to admit and even to emphasise that the religion he teaches is opposed to the existing one and one has to cede to the other.[1]

The traditional religions have certainly ceded. In Kenya estimates are that in 1900, 95.8 per cent of the population adhered to traditional religions and only 0.2 per cent were Christian. By 1962 the figures were respectively 37 per cent and 54 per cent; by 1972, 26.2 per cent and 66.2 per cent. Although these figures refer to one country, they reflect the general trend.

Western lifestyle

Along with these changes in religious persuasion have come imported lifestyles which have found their natural habitat in the big cities. With them come all the trappings – good and bad – of Western lifestyle: the cars, the clothes, the fast food, the ghetto-blasters. It is in such surroundings that churches with a European style of worship are to be found in great diversity, with their Western liturgies, languages and music.

But unlike Europe and North America, the majority of Africans still live in a rural setting, where traditions established over centuries, even millennia, continue to exert a powerful influence. In the cities an adapted Western culture has long been accepted and has replaced many local customs, but it is in village life that the collision of European Christianity and established tradition is still an issue.

The place of music in these societies provides one indication of the cultural gulf to be bridged, for it plays a far more active part in the consciousness of Africans, penetrating deeply into traditional upbringing:

> The African mother sings to her child and introduces him to many aspects of music right from the cradle. She trains the child to become aware of rhythm and movement by rocking him to music, by singing to him in nonsense syllables imitative of drum rhythms. When he is old enough to sing, he sings with his mother and learns to imitate drum rhythms by rote... Participation in children's games and stories incorporating songs enables him to learn to sing in the style of his culture, just as he learns to speak its language. His experience, even at this early stage, is not confined to children's songs, for African mothers often carry children on their backs to public ceremonies, rites and traditional dance arenas... sometimes the mothers even dance with their children on their backs...[2]

These are qualities of life, along with strong religious awareness, to which the early missionaries were blind. As the nineteenth-century missionary Robert Moffat wrote:

> Satan has employed his agency with fatal success, in erasing every vestige of religious impression from the minds of the Bechuanas, Hottentots and Bushmen; leaving them without a single ray to guide them from the dark and dread futurity, or a single link to unite them with the skies.[3]

Europeans believed that the minds of Africans were empty of any sense of religion or culture and were waiting to have these instilled into them. Desmond Tutu summarises the result:

> These poor native pagans had to be clothed in Western clothes so that they could speak to the white man's God, the only God, who was obviously unable to recognise them unless they were decently clad. These poor creatures must be made to sing the white man's hymns hopelessly badly translated, they had to worship in the white man's unemotional and individualistic way, they had to think and speak of God and all the wonderful Gospel truths in the white man's well-proven terms.[4]

Establishing trade with Africa was high on the European agenda in the nineteenth century and a prime reason for converting the continent to Western ways:

> In the Buxton expedition of 1841... the first aim was to discover the possibilities of legitimate trade with Nigeria... But the spreading of the Gospel was regarded as essential and integral to this. It was widely believed that, in order to have legitimate trade, one must have a people of developed culture, reliable and industrious habits... Christianity was confidently regarded as the foundation for all of these and all the virtues of social and commercial intercourse...[5]

The signs of a change of attitude among the missionary churches are evident in a hymn-book like *Africa Praise*, published in 1956 for use in English-speaking schools. It contains many of the best-loved Protestant hymns of the past two centuries, but also a large number of African songs to English words in tonic *sol-fa* (very few Africans have a musical training that allows them to read Western notation). The hymn-book is an indication of a desire to narrow the gap between the African and European cultures, but it was only a first step.

The Western legacy

In a few city cathedrals, resources are channelled to the provision of printed books and to musicians who know how to get the best out of them; outside their walls the music of the many churches founded by the West is in a sorry state. Without the provision of music books with stimulating contents of high quality and without the training to use such material, the Western legacy of Christian music has become a dead weight, even a millstone. Norman Warren described his experience of Christian music in Uganda after a visit in 1985:

> Generally speaking, we found the life of the church at a low ebb. All too common was the desire to ape the west... I was disappointed in coming across so little original music in worship. In most instances the music was rather formal and old-fashioned...

He noted the use of *Hymns Ancient and Modern* (standard version) at Kampala Cathedral, Moody and Sankey in a suburban church in Kusoga and *Africa Praise* at Arua Church in the north. The musical facilities available even in Mukono Cathedral were very slender:

> The organ is a pedal harmonium that has not worked for months. All the music was unaccompanied and led with great gusto by a small choir. The hymn-tunes were, without exception, Victorian... and, quite frankly, I would never want to hear them again.[6]

The language of the people

The musical legacy of the missionary churches in Africa is not wholly depressing, however. The Roman Catholic Church world-wide adopted a dramatic and new attitude to its liturgy in Vatican II (the second Vatican Council) of 1962. The abolition of Latin and the adoption of the language of the people was its most radical step.

A 'coming-of-age'

Vatican II coincided with the independence of many African countries and a powerful awareness of national identity and heritage. The feelings of Catholic African bishops were summarised in a report in 1974:

> The 'coming-of-age' of the churches signifies a turning point in the history of the church in Africa. It is the end of the missionary period.

This does not mean the end of evangelisation. But it means, in the words of Pope Paul VI during his visit to Uganda: 'You Africans may become missionaries to yourselves.' In other words, the remaining task of evangelisation of Africa is primarily the responsibility of the African Church itself. This fact implies a radically changed relationship between the church in Africa and... the other churches in Europe and North America.[7]

One important consequence of this new attitude is the reduction of the numbers of missionaries from the traditional societies and churches working in Africa and alongside that, the development of new styles of worship more in harmony with African culture and lifestyle.

Cameroun – African Christian music

The Catholic Church in Cameroun began exploring the possibility of Christian music in local languages even before Vatican II, indeed, it was such widespread experimentation that forced the Council to address the problem. The first step was to take pre-existing Western melodies and simply to overlay them with words of the appropriate local language. This was easier said than done, for many languages in Cameroun (and in Africa generally) are tone-based, where the meaning of words is dependent on the pitch at which they are uttered. As a consequence, melodies take control of the meaning of the words set to them. The marriage of language and music of differing cultures can be an unhappy one, and in Cameroun was quite clearly a failure. So was the singing of Latin to Camerounian tunes.

The only solution was to marry Camerounian texts to Camerounian music, which has since become the life's work of Abbé Pie-Claude Ngumu. The reaction of congregations was evident in their enthusiasm and in the early 1960s the Abbé founded the choir *Maîtrise de la croix d'ébène* at Yaoundé Cathedral. The style of this music and the colour and excitement it brought to the liturgy led to further developments:

Our melodies are always rhythmic; while they are being played, those present have the greatest difficulty in stopping themselves from beating time with head, finger, or foot. So then we asked why this movement that people had so much difficulty in restraining should not be given free rein. Yielding to our requests in this matter was the starting-point of that liturgy... that is the pride of Cameroun.[8]

The reactions of authorities and outsiders to this style of Roman Catholic worship were not always favourable:

Since it was launched, this experiment has met with a varied reception: for some it constitutes an attempt to paganise Christianity; for others it is one of the finest achievements of post-conciliar Christianity.[9]

Cameroun already boasts one of the most lively scenes in African popular music, and for the Roman Catholic Church to move towards the people's needs in that area was new.

In the Protestant tradition, new and challenging music has occasionally arisen from the collision of cultures. By the 1970s, for instance, Namirembe Cathedral in Uganda had developed a competent choir able to sing in four-part harmony, accompanied by a reasonable pipe organ. Alongside the perennially-loved Victorian English hymns has developed a fascinating repertoire of anthems in local languages: Luganda, Lumasaba and Swahili. The compositions of Wassanyi-Sserukenya are particularly compelling in their simplicity and directness. *Ssimunanyi!* (*I do not know him*), for example, not only brings Peter's denials of Jesus to life, but, like Lutheran music of the Baroque age, personalises their significance for the listener.[10]

Harcourt Whyte

A more detailed picture of the musical collaboration of Western and African cultures is provided by the life and work of Ikoli Harcourt Whyte (c. 1905–77). Although wholly Nigerian (from Abonnema near Port Harcourt in the south) Harcourt Whyte was strongly influenced by Western culture through his contraction of leprosy at the age of fourteen. From that time he was wholly cut off from the outside world by his confinement to mission hospitals, chiefly the Uzuakoli Leprosy Hospital, a project supported jointly by the Methodists and the government. It was not until thirty years later that the drug Dapsone was discovered (through research in Uzuakoli) and through its application Harcourt Whyte was pronounced cured in 1949.

His seventeen-year-long stay at Uzuakoli brought Harcourt Whyte a resilient Christian faith:

> Leprosy isolated me into a place where I could see no other books to read than the Bible and religious books. I read and read, and they transformed me... Instead of feeling bitter that all was lost, I discovered that 'all things work together for good to them that love God'.[11]

As well as a profound understanding of the language of the Ibo people and of its folk-music, he developed an acquaintance with Western music through the English missionaries at the hospital. His contact with European music was limited almost entirely to the hymns and songs of Methodist worship of the time – *Sacred Songs and Solos* of the evangelists Sankey and Moody and the *Methodist Hymnbook*.

From fairly early on Harcourt Whyte taught in the hospital school and developed his musical talents by forming choirs in the school and chapel. His self-taught musical talents became evident in the music he created for these groups and established a pattern from which he deviated very little for the rest of his life.

Apart from a few political songs, Harcourt Whyte's music is almost all Christian, consisting of hundreds of songs in Igbo, the language of the Ibo, all unaccompanied and almost all in four-part harmony. The idea of creating music for a trained group of singers, music to be listened to rather than participated in, is rare in African tradition. The harmony of his music is unusual too. It is a unique adaptation of European tradition, blinkered by Harcourt Whyte's limited knowledge of it, but coloured by African music and particularly by Igbo.

Harcourt Whyte was surrounded for most of his life by Igbo. It is a tone language, like many in Africa, and therefore poses the problems of music-setting that had caused such difficulty for European missionaries.

The Igbo word 'oke', for instance, has many meanings according to the way it is pronounced. Two syllables high in the voice give the meaning 'male of an animal', high in the voice then low would mean 'boundary', low-low means 'share' and low-high means 'rat'. Take the Igbo for 'word' – 'okwu'. It must be pronounced high in the voice on both syllables – like two relatively high notes. But if the tone of the voice on the second syllable is lowered, another word altogether is created, meaning 'heap'. Missionaries thoughtfully provided translations of Western hymns into Igbo and translated 'Thou whose Almighty Word' correctly as 'Chineke okwu Gi'. But when the phrase is put to the tune 'Moscow', the word 'okwu' receives a lowered pitch on the second syllable, which now conveys the meaning 'Thou whose almighty heap'! The crazy meanings created by subsequent verses and the entirely different melodic contours of the alto, tenor and bass lines quickly reduce the text to utter gibberish.

Harcourt Whyte addressed this problem early on. He realised that Igbo words needed melodies which (as in their folk-song) were wholly sympathetic to the language. The restrictions under which he worked were considerable, especially when he chose to set several verses to a given melody. His solution was to write his own words, but to start the creative process with a melody:

> What I mostly do first is the melody. Then the words of the first verse. After this the harmony. Lastly, the words of the following verses. It is this part of the composition that takes more time due to the rise and fall of the tonal expressions of the Igbo language as one tries to bring into conformity all the verses with the melody.[12]

Although Harcourt Whyte always wrote in four parts, always used major keys, almost always tied the voice-parts together in homophony and never used chromaticism, there is plenty of variety in his songs. The words of his songs are strongly biblical, either quotations, paraphrases or commentaries and deeply moving to their hearers:

> [On Good Friday, 1954, at Uzuakoli] the choir... moved into and up the chapel in slow march to Harcourt's *E gburu Nwa Chuku* (*The Son of God was Crucified*), a composition he wrote specially for... that day. By the time the choir had got to the middle and front of the chapel and taken their seats... everybody —preacher, layman, men, women and children, patients and the healthy – was already either weeping or sobbing... So powerful... are his texts and music that Sunday after Sunday people troop to that great chapel to hear him...[13]

Example 34 is an extract from *Kayafasi kwuru si* (*Caiaphas Spoke and Said*), an early piece but typical of Harcourt Whyte's style. It dramatises an episode in Jesus' Passion, recorded in John 18:4. The music interferes as little as possible with the tonal inflections of the Igbo language.

Towards the end of his life Harcourt Whyte's music became widely known in churches where Igbo is the language of worship. As far as is

EXAMPLE 34

known, his texts have not been translated into other languages and his music has not circulated beyond parts of southern Nigeria. This is a great shame, for his songs are a unique bridge between Western and African cultures, and they have created something new. Harcourt Whyte commented:

Just as European harmony is more developed than African harmony, so is African rhythm more developed than European rhythm. That I do not have what you have or as much of anything you have does not make me inferior to you, or does it?... In your studies, you must try to learn both European and African musics so that you can understand better what I am driving at. I take from European music what I find good in it and use it. As rice is different from beans, so is African music different from European music... if any of them can be called superior, I think it is the product of the mixture...[14]

Notes

1. D. Westermann, *Africa and Christianity*, Oxford, 1937, p. 94.

2. J.H. Kwabena Nketia, *The Music of Africa*, London, 1982, p. 60.

3. E.W. Smith, *African Ideas of God*, London, 1961, p. 83.

4. D. Tutu, 'Whither African Theology?' in *Christianity in Independent Africa*, edited by Fashole-Luke, Gray, Hastings and Tasie, London, 1978, p. 365.

5. A.D. Galloway, 'Missionary Impact on Africa', in *Nigeria*, Independence issue of *Nigeria* magazine, Lagos, October, 1960, p. 60.

6. *Music in Worship* magazine, no. 33, September/October 1985, pp. 6–7.

7. 'Report on the Experiences of the Church in the Work of Evangelism in Africa'; the African Continent's report for the 1974 Synod of Bishops on 'The Evangelisation of the Modern World', p. 16.

8. P. Abega, 'Liturgical Adaptation', in *Christianity in Independent Africa*, p. 599.

9. Abega, p. 599.

10. See Discography.

11. A.K. Achinivu, *Ikoli Harcourt Whyte, The Man and His Music*, no. 7, Beitrage zur Ethnomusikologie, Hamburg, 1979, vol. 1, p. 84.

12. Achinivu, p. 228.

13. Achinivu, p. 322.

14. Achinivu, pp. 50–52.

Chapter 33

The Independent Churches

Another development in the recent history of African Christianity is the pronounced and dramatic growth of indigenous independent churches. The Kimbanguist Church of Zaire is one of hundreds founded as the result of the inability of the established missionary churches to understand African needs and aspirations in the faith. As a member of the Kimbanguist Church has written:

> The arrival of the missionaries, accompanied by colonisation, obscured the new knowledge of Christianity. The preaching of Christ was seen as another means of helping colonisation to alienate men completely from their African identity. It was in this situation that Christ turned his face towards his people and chose the prophet Simon Kimbangu as his messenger...[1]

Kimbanguist music

In common with many indigenous churches in Africa, the Kimbanguists value the Bible and its teachings highly and their practices are founded on biblical principles. They also denounce the traditional animist religions with vigour, but remain close to many local customs. Music is an important aid to worship, from the simple unison singing of the thrice-daily services of prayer through to the choral and instrumental sounds of Sunday worship and the colourful festivals of the church year. The beginning of the Kimbanguist musical traditions is indicative of the failure of the established missions in colonial times to understand the needs of the Christian community in Africa:

> At the start of the prophet's mission at N'Kamba, the songs utilised to accomplish the work of Christ were those of Protestants. But the

Protestants refused to sell their hymn-books to the followers of the prophet. Saddened, Simon Kimbangu went apart to pray, laying before God this poverty, so deeply felt by his congregation. From that was born the gift of 'catching' the songs.[2]

The musical tradition that has developed is perfectly attuned to a society where it is memory rather than the written word that provides cultural identity and continuity:

> Kimbanguists catch songs in various ways: in dreams, and in visions in which they hear angels singing. As a general rule, once they have been caught, the songs are sent to an office, set up by the church called the Directorate of Kimbanguist Songs, where they are studied and to some extent modified to give them a good meaning. Other songs are deleted, if the meaning of the song is not clear. The songs have to be examined to avoid those that may be inspired by the Devil.[3]

The songs have all sorts of functions – some are songs of praise, others are 'living lessons, explaining and clarifying biblical teaching', still others are prophetic. After approval these songs are learnt by a regional choir of leaders whose members then pass them on to the local choirs. One regional choir, the Kimbanguist Theatre Group, travels round the churches using singing and drama to bring Bible stories and the church's history to life.

Aladura churches

The Kimbanguist Church is only one of the hundreds of indigenous Christian organisations thriving in Africa today. Because there are no Europeans involved and little sign of Western culture, they can make an impact in areas hardly touched by the older missionary churches. The Aladura churches, for instance, which are very popular among the Yoruba and Ibo people in southern Nigeria, have also become established in the Muslim north of that country.

In political terms, these churches have generally been treated in a friendly manner by emerging nationalist governments, in contrast to the previously open suspicion of the colonialists. Among people of all walks of Nigerian life, the Aladura churches are supported enthusiastically. Where the Kimbanguists are reminiscent of seventeenth-century Puritans in their restrictions on smoking, drinking and dancing, the Aladura celebrate their faith with hand-clapping, dancing and traditional instruments. They have incorporated other elements of traditional worship too – instantaneous healing of the sick, raising of the dead, prophecy and exorcism. As one Aladura Christian puts it, it is in their liturgy that 'the unfulfilled emotional needs in the western-oriented churches have found ample fulfillment'.[4]

An indication of the popularity of the Aladura churches in city and country is provided by their choirs' and solo singers' great following; an American-style network of gospel music is developing fast. The guitarist Patty Obassey is one of the best known, scoring an enormous success with *Nne Galu* in 1984. Among the many choirs who have produced a number of albums are Imole Ayo and the Christian Singers, the Choir of the Eternal Sacred Order of Cherubim and Seraphim and Erasmus Jenewari and his Gospel Bells.

The balance of European and African influences on the practice of Christianity is still on the move in favour of the African, but this does not mean a wholesale eradication of Western culture. The style of vestments worn by Aladura priests is only one element borrowed from the Protestant and Catholic churches. On the other hand, the independent churches have taught the older mission churches valuable lessons in liturgy and Christian music.

Ecstatic music

There is a growing number of indigenous churches where the style of worship is difficult to distinguish from the traditional animist religions. The African Apostolic Church, founded in 1932 by John Maranke, is an example. It is based in Eastern Zimbabwe but its influence has spread far and wide. Where the Kimbanguist Church approves and disseminates its songs in a highly organised manner, spontaneity and improvisation are the most striking elements of Apostolic worship.

The main meeting of the African Apostolic Church is held on Saturday – the Sabbath – and may last several hours. Worship begins with an invocation *'kerek! kerek!'* which is the name given to the ecstatic state the group will later experience. Then hymns are sung, which are formal not in the sense of being read out of a book, but by being commonplace among many churches in Africa:

> Mwari Komborera Africa, Alleluia
> Chisua yemina matu yedu
> Mwari Baba Jesu utukomborera
> Jesu, turi branda bako
>
> *Refrain:* O mueya, hoanna mueya utukomborera

In translation, this means:

> God save Africa, Alleluia
> Hear our prayers
> God, Father, Jesus, bless us
> Jesus, we are your servants
>
> *Refrain:* O come Holy Spirit, bless us.

The words are in Chishona, a language reserved for religious ceremony. The invocation of Father, Son and Holy Spirit (the latter is emphasised) is a sign to the people of a spiritual presence among them which is to become almost tangible.

The men are seated on the open ground separately from the women and all are addressed by preachers (there may be three or more) and the chief evangelist. Between them they will have agreed beforehand on the biblical topics most appropriate for the day. After the opening hymns the preaching begins, but members are free to interrupt with songs of their own choosing at any point. They are particularly likely to jump in and lead off with a song whenever the preacher hands over to a reader. As in the Kimbanguist Church, instruments and dancing are not allowed, but their place is taken by the use of *ngoma* – vocal sounds which imitate drumming – and swaying while standing or sitting.

The call-and-response form so commonplace in African music demonstrates the relationship between a song-leader and the rest of the congregation, who respond with their refrain even before the leader's improvised verses have ended. These songs exert a powerful emotional influence on the meeting and may very well develop into the repetitive chanting of a short refrain, such as 'God in Heaven' (*Mambo wa ku denga*):

> During chanting, the rhythmic shape of the song is transformed as worshippers put increasing emphasis on strongly accented beats…
> While the rhythm is accentuated, the harmonies of the chorus tighten. The loose collection of voices [of the call-and-response]

becomes a tight, single unit. The overall effect is hypnotic. The rhythmic and harmonic ramifications push the singers into a state of maximum spiritual involvement. As the chant proceeds, individuals moan, yodel, and insert *ngoma*... and glossolalic utterances [the gift of tongues]. The entire congregation sways to the rhythm...[5]

It is sometimes difficult for the preacher to regain control of the service unless the chanting dies out naturally. If it does not, then he may attempt to break the spell by shouting a greeting. These songs are nevertheless regarded by the preachers as a valuable reinforcement of their message and the success of the meeting depends on the degree to which the members have experienced 'possession' by the Holy Spirit.

The congregation's sense of participation is absolute, even extending to the improvisation of songs expressing discontent – perhaps expressing disagreement with one of the church leaders or with the way in which a decision has been made. Even if problems are aired through song during the service, the sense of peace of unity after a long *kerek* is very evident.

The true Christian music of Africa

Christian music in Africa this century has gradually moved further and further away from the European styles of worship which were first introduced by the missionaries. The music of Harcourt Whyte or of Namirembe Cathedral is a unique half-way point in that process of change and could therefore become a rich source of Christian music especially for the West, accessible because it can be written down and because the style it adopts has some Western characteristics. It only remains to be translated and published in Western notation.

But it is the indigenous churches that demonstrate most dramatically how the African musical sensibility differs from the European, above all in an emotional abandon and a delight in participation. The Westerner, after all, reads from books or newspapers, whereas the African habitually relies for cultural continuity on memory and improvisation. European music has developed relationships of counterpoint and harmony where the African thrives on a dialogue of rhythms; Western classical music is founded on narrative structures, in which the listener is taken on an emotional and dramatic journey by means of musical rhetoric. African tradition, however, has always created music of immediate and compelling physical impact, static when compared with Western expectations, ecstatic in its own right.

As Harcourt Whyte pointed out, each way is an expression of a culture, highly revealing of the priorities and make-up of certain strata of their respective societies. But in the realm of Christian worship, the Western musical style that most missionaries brought to Africa sprang from nineteenth-century sub-cultures held back from the liberation of true worship by debilitating social attitudes. There was fear that music might become a real force in the lives of those involved in it. It was, for instance, wholly reprehensible to allow music to become rhythmic and exciting enough to invite a bodily response, so its physical dimension was banned from worship. Then, as intellectual challenge in general was threatening for evangelicals, Christian music which possessed any real rhetorical power – music that is emotionally penetrating or challenging – was not allowed any space either.

The permissible Christian music that remained was (and unhappily still is) a narrow and poverty-stricken offshoot from the main cultural stem of Western culture, reflecting and tainting the Western style of Christian worship. Small wonder then, that Desmond Tutu should reject the white man's 'unemotional and individualistic' attitude to his faith and that the thriving churches in Africa are those encouraging a commitment in worship which is both spiritual and physical, wholehearted and corporate.

Westerners may find the emotionalism and the trance-like states of ecstasy disturbing, but for the many African churches they are the sign of God's presence with them. Where many missionary churches have denied the existence of demons, witches and evil spirits, indigenous churches recognise them, but exercise the power of God over them with the help of agencies such as music. It is in these latter churches that the true Christian music of Africa is to be found. As an Aladura Christian has written:

A spiritual revolution was necessary... and this was promptly provided by the Aladura churches. The Holy Spirit descended, as on Pentecost day, to proclaim afresh the Gospel message in languages which Nigerians understood and so through revelations manifested in trances, dreams, visions and prophecies, established the universality and the all-embracing, and all-saving power of Jesus Christ... the obvious conclusion that one can logically reach is that the Aladura way of worship is the true African expression of the Christian religion.[6]

Notes

1. D. Ndofunsu, 'The Role of Prayer in the Kimbanguist Church', in *Christianity in Independent Africa*, edited by Fashole-Luke, Gray, Hastings and Tasie, London, 1978, p. 578.

2. Ndofunsu, p. 590.

3. Ndofunsu, p. 590.

4. A. Omoyajowo, 'The Aladura Churches in Nigeria since Independence', in *Christianity in Independent Africa*, p. 110.

5. B. Jules-Rosette, 'Ecstatic Singing: Music and Social Integration in an African Church', in I.E. Jackson, editor, *More than Drumming*, London, 1985, p. 134.

6. Omoyajowo, p. 109.

PART 7

Music in
North America

Chapter 34

Christianity Comes to the New World

A census of citizens of North America in 1790 revealed that only 5 per cent professed any religious affiliation. Today that figure is 95 per cent, of whom nearly half worship regularly in a Christian church. These simple statistics represent a growth that might be the envy of Christians in Western Europe, whose numbers have suffered a steady decline over the same period.

The story of the development of Christian music in the United States is a complex and colourful one, additionally important for the impact that it has had on the world at large. For North Americans do not keep their faith to themselves. In 1985, Protestant Christian missionary societies alone spent more than $500 million in supporting overseas missions and that figure is rising yearly. The 20,000 missionaries that the sum sends out world-wide take the hymns and songs of America with them.

The American heritage

Compared with Europe, Christianity in the United States has developed over a mere few hundred years, without the support of the wealth and traditions of an established church. These two facts may have some bearing on the present strength of faith there.

The first Christian settlement, in Jamestown, Virginia, was only established in 1607. These English settlers and the immigrants who followed them from other parts of Europe arrived with none of the resources which those they had left behind could take for granted. Their life in the New World began with the poverty and hardship that had driven them there in the first place. There was no church wealth built up over centuries, no Christian traditions of worship. They had nothing except what they carried with them in books, probably no more than a Bible and a metrical psalter. Christianity in North America has grown since those times as a fire grows from a spark. But a healthy suspicion of ecclesiastical power has remained. The style of worship still valued most highly is one of directness and simplicity, without undue ceremony.

Life in North America is too easily known by its urban side, the extraordinary blend of decadence and deprivation which is supported by the technology of instant communication. For between the huge cities there are vast and sparsely-populated areas of countryside in which small communities enjoy a continuity of traditions in life and faith. Here a different Christian music of North America is to be found. It is a folk-art, which in its formative years had no chance of being influenced by music as an art-form, for classical music remained undeveloped in North America until the mid-nineteenth century. Even today it remains largely untouched by the sophistication of European traditions, a window onto the past.

Establishing a new tradition

The Christian music sung by the early white settlers was that of the metrical psalms. Indeed, the pilgrims left their European homes with the psalm-tunes ringing in their ears:

> They that stayed at Leyden feasted us that were to go at our pastor's house, being large; where we refreshed ourselves, after tears, with singing of Psalms… and indeed it was the sweetest melody that ever mine ears heard.[1]

For the French Huguenots in Florida or the English and Dutch Puritans of New England, psalm-singing was at the heart of their musical expression of faith. Its importance to the early Christian communities is evident from the first publication of any kind in America, the *Bay Psalm Book*. Remarkably, it was published in Boston as early as 1640 and its pioneering spirit is evident from the preface:

> God's altar needs not our pollishings: for wee have respected rather a plaine translation… and so have attended Conscience rather than Elegance, fidelity rather than poetry… that soe wee may sing in Sion the Lords songs of prayse according to his own will; untill hee take us from hence, and wipe away all our tears, & bid us enter into our masters joye to sing eternall Halleluiahs.

The *Bay Psalm Book* did not contain any music, but recommended the tunes of Ravenscroft's *Whole Book of Psalms* 'collected out of our chief musicians' (1621).

The practice of 'lining out' (described in some detail in chapter 19) was established early in North America, as the Rev. John Cotton made clear in 1647:

> For the present, where many in the congregation cannot read, it is convenient that the minister, or some other fit person... do read the psalm line by line before the singing thereof.[2]

The results for American psalmody were as extraordinary as for the Old World:

> The same Person who sets the Tune, and guides the Congregation in Singing, commonly reads the Psalm, which is a task too few are capable of performing well, that in Singing two or three Staves, the congregation falls from a cheerful pitch to downright Grumbling, and then some to relive themselves mount an Eighth above the rest, others perhaps a Fourth or Fifth, by which Means the Singing appears to be rather a confused noise, made up of Reading, Squecking and Grumbling...
>
> In many places, one Man is upon this Note, while another is a Note before him, which produces something so hideous and disorderly, as is beyond Expression bad... and besides, no two Men in the Congregation quaver [decorate the tune with extra notes] alike, or together; which sounds in the Ears of a good Judge, like Five Hundred different Tunes roared out at the same time...[3]

By the early eighteenth century, some ministers were beginning to clamour for a more 'Regular' way of singing, causing 'Heats, Animosities and Contentions' among the old guard. Typically, it was the country areas that resisted any suggestion of change:

> Tho' in the polite city of Boston this design [the new way] met with general acceptance, in the country, where they have more of the rustic, some numbers of elder and angry people bore zealous testimonies against these wicked innovations, and... not only... call the singing of these Christians a worshipping of the devil, but also they would run out of the meeting-house at the beginning of the exercise.[4]

In New England, new ways of singing eventually supplanted the old, but not in other parts of North America. Extraordinarily enough, there are still isolated parts of Appalachia and the South East where the old technique of lining-out is still practised, particularly among remote Baptist churches. It is an oral tradition – just as it was 300 years ago – where the congregation relies on its memories of the tunes and sings in heterophony ('500 different tunes roared out at the same time') and at an extremely slow pace.

The singing schools

The 'New Way' of singing was really only a return to what today's church musicians would call normality; the Americans called it 'Singing by Note'. But education had to be provided for such a change. As a minister observed as early as 1720:

> Would it not greatly tend to promote singing of psalms if singing schools were promoted?... Where would be the difficulty, or what the disadvantages, if people who want skill in singing, would procure a person to instruct them, and meet two or three evenings in the week, from five or six o'clock to eight, and spend their time in learning to sing?[5]

These singing schools sometimes provided more than they were originally intended, as a student at Yale revealed in a letter to a friend:

> At present I have no inclination for anything, for I am almost sick of the World & were it not for the Hopes of going to the singing-meeting tonight & indulging myself in some of the carnal Delights of the Flesh, such as kissing, squeezing &c. &c. I should willingly leave it now.[6]

These singing schools had their parallels in English country parishes. They were set up on a temporary basis in a schoolhouse or a tavern with the blessing of the local church, and worshippers were encouraged to enrol for a course of singing lessons (provided that they brought their own candles with them). The lessons were based on instruction in solmisation, a system of pitching adapted from the invention of Guido d'Arezzo whereby the notes of a scale are identified by names. Where Guido used a different name for each note of the scale, the pioneers of the singing-schools used a simplified system using only four: *fa, sol, la* and *mi*. Thus an upward major scale would have been sung to the note-names *fa, sol, la, fa, sol, la, mi, fa*. Such a system might seem over-simplified to the point of confusion, but the standard of singing in many churches improved noticeably. As Samuel Sewall wrote in his diary in the early 1720s: 'House was full, and the Singing extraordinarily Excellent, such as has hardly been heard before in Boston.'[7]

Gradually, other systems to help people to read notation developed, from the crude system of the Rev. John Tufts, which placed letters indicating the *sol-fa* names in the appropriate positions on a five-line stave, to the shape-note systems of the turn of the eighteenth century, where shapes corresponded with the four *sol-fa* names – a triangle for *fa*, a circle for *sol*, a square *la* and a diamond *mi*.

The many new tune-books appearing from the 1750s onward catered for the developing interest in part-singing: *Youths Entertaining Amusement* (1754), *Urania* (1761), *Royal Melody Complete* (Boston, 1767, containing music by the British composer William Tans'ur) and others. The music of some of these books contained pieces complicated enough to be called anthems rather than psalmtunes. Example 35 shows a setting of Psalm 96 from James Lyon's *Urania, or A Choice Collection of Psalm-Tunes, Anthems, and Hymns, From the most approv'd Authors, with some Entirely New*. When Lyon, a Princeton graduate, announced *Urania* in the Philadelphia press, he called it the 'first Attempt of any kind to spread the Art of Psalmody in its Perfection, thro' our American Colonies'.

EXAMPLE 35

Such pieces testify to the musical ambitions and even the success of some of the singing masters who, when their course of lessons was complete, would move on to the next town to start again. Nonetheless, the instructors themselves were self-taught. There were no colleges teaching the rudiments of music, let alone the conventions of counterpoint and harmony. All that was picked up by the very imperfect example of oral tradition and through printed music.

William Billings

Of all the singing teachers of eighteenth-century America, there was none more endearing and inspiring than William Billings (1746–1800). He was born in Boston where he himself learned music at a singing school and spent his life in incessant and enthusiastic labour for Christian music, composing, conducting and teaching. The absence of copyright laws meant that he earned nothing from his published music, although some of it became immensely popular. Instead, he had to earn his living from time to time as a street cleaner or as a hogreeve (whose responsibility was to keep pigs off the streets). He was clearly something of an eccentric, described as:

> a singular man, of moderate size, short of one leg, with one eye, without any address [ie manners], & with an uncommon negligence of person. Still he spake & sung & thought as a man above the common abilities. He died poor and neglected...[8]

Billings was convinced of music's ability to express emotion, whether of praise or supplication. In the preface to his songbook, *Continental Harmony* (1794) he wrote:

> how enraptured should we be to hear the sharp key [i.e. major-key music] express itself in such lofty and majestic strains as these: 'O come let us sing unto the Lord, let us make a joyful noise...' Do I hear the voice of men, or angels! surely such angelic sound cannot yet proceed from the mouths of sinful mortals: but while we are yet warm with the thought, and ravished with the sound, the musicians change their tone, and the flat key [i.e. minor-key music] utters itself in strains so moving, and pathetic, that it seems to command our attention to such mournful sounds as these: 'Hear my prayer O Lord, give ear to

my supplication…' O how these sounds thrill through my soul! how agreeably they affect my nerves! how soft, how sweet, how soothing…

Billings wrote well over 200 songs, and in an age of rebellion some were strongly nationalistic:

> Let tyrants shake their iron rod,
> And Slavr'y clank her galling chains,
> We fear them not, we trust in God,
> New England's God for ever reigns.[9]

His songs were divided into two types: 'plain', where the four parts moved together in homophony like a hymn; and 'fuging', a style of writing of which he was particularly fond. In a preface to one of his songbooks he provided his own definition of 'fuge', more enthusiastic than academic:

> Notes flying after each other, altho' not always the same sound. N.B.
> Music is said to be Fuging, when one part comes in after another; its
> beauties cannot be numbered…[10]

Such a definition would not have satisfied European composers of the time, who received a strict and prolonged training in the rules to be followed when 'one part comes in after another'. Billings was refreshingly ignorant of the Baroque techniques of counterpoint. But it is his very independence of spirit that has gained him an increasing following, especially among modern American composers. As he wrote in *Continental Harmony*:

> For my own Part, as I don't think myself confin'd to any Rules for
> Composition laid down by any that went before me, neither should I
> think (were I to pretend to lay down Rules) that any who came after
> me were any ways obligated to adhere to them, any further that they
> should think proper: So in fact, I think it is best for every Composer
> to be his own Carver.[11]

Billings' music is now beginning to receive the attention it undoubtedly deserves, but largely from the music schools of universities rather than from churches. In many ways, it parallels the Christian music of the west galleries of English country parishes. That hearty but rough-hewn music was swept aside by Victorian reform, and in New England expectations and tastes were moving in a similar direction before the eighteenth century was out.

At the end of the eighteenth century ministers and their more educated congregations started to look for a more refined style in their Christian music. They were becoming aware of the difference between the music of the self-taught Yankee tunesmiths and the refined poise of European classical music. Musicians came to scorn the shape-note notation as 'dunce notes' and in New England the music printed in this way gradually fell out of favour, to be replaced by a European and 'educated' style of Christian music: 'The harshness of our singing must be corrected. Our voices must be filed. Every note must be rendered smooth, persuasive and melting.'[12]

The 'genteel correctness' which resulted can be sensed in the hymn-tunes of Thomas Hastings (1784–1872) and Lowell Mason (1792–1872). Mason's *Olivet* and *Missionary* (perhaps his best-known tunes in Britain) are a thousand miles from the sturdy music of Billings and his generation.

In America, however, the shape-note music survived. The vastness of the continent and the comparative isolation of country communities once again preserved a folk-like Christian music in areas of the South, whence it had spread during the eighteenth century. Thus two distinct traditions in Christian music exist today in North America, one of grammatical correctness, 'rendered smooth, persuasive and melting' and the other an uneducated and imperfect music sung at full volume and with an infectious enthusiasm which is hard to resist when Billings describes it:

> While each part is… striving for mastery, and sweetly contending for victory, the audience are most luxuriously entertained, and exceedingly delighted; in the mean time, their minds are surprisingly agitated, and extremely fluctuated; sometimes declaring in favour of one part, and sometimes another. – Now the solemn bass demands their attention, now the manly tenor, now the lofty counter [i.e. alto], now the volatile treble, now here, now there, now here again. – O inchanting! O ecstatic! Push on, push on ye sons of harmony…[13]

Changing tastes in the expanding urban populations gradually ousted this rough-hewn music from city churches, but in the South and at the westward-advancing frontiers it remained popular. Nineteenth-century music collections continued to print the music of the singing-school pioneers of a century before: *Virginia Harmony, Kentucky Harmony* (1816) *Knoxville Harmony* (1838), *Union Harmony* (Tennessee, 1837), *Southern Harmony* (1835) and many others.

These collections also show quite clearly how folk-tunes, originally wedded to secular words, came to be accepted in church worship with Christian texts. From these sources come a number of folk-hymns whose melodies have penetrated the consciousness of the English-speaking world: in *Southern Harmony*, for instance, can be found *Wondrous Love*, and the tune to *Auld Lang Syne* put to a hymn by Isaac Watts. The best-loved of all, perhaps, is *Amazing Grace*, originally set to 'There is a land of pure delight' in *Virginia Harmony*. Example 36 shows it notated in the four-shape system, as it appeared in *Southern Harmony*. Note the raw harmony of fourths and fifths (inherited by many folk-singers today) surrounding the centrally-placed melody.

A collection of 1844 called *The Sacred Harp* has a special significance, having given its name to the annual Sacred Harp Conventions which still meet today to celebrate this Christian folk-music – clear evidence that it is still known and well-loved in the Southern states.

Moravians and Shakers

Two traditions of worship established in North America in the eighteenth century created Christian music of particular richness. The cultures from which they sprang were opposites, but both for a while chose isolation rather than integration with the societies around them. Such insularity was necessary for something exceptional to grow, but it also prevented such music finding its way into the worship of other denominations.

As they travelled to North America on an evangelistic mission in 1737, John and Charles Wesley found that they were sailing with a group of Moravian Brethren with the same intentions. These Moravians had come from Herrnhut, a settlement in north Germany, but the origins of their movement, the 'Unitas Fratrum', lay in the reforming zeal of Jan Hus in sixteenth-century Bohemia. The revival of the Moravian Church in 1722 sent missionary expeditions to the Virgin Islands, then to Greenland, South Africa, Jamaica and North America. Communities of Moravians were founded in Bethlehem in Pennsylvania and in parts of North Carolina.

For the German-speaking Moravians, as for the Lutherans, music generally held a treasured place in life. They brought instruments with them from north Germany, and there were instrument-makers among them. Thus bands were available for ceremonial occasions of all kinds, such as weddings or christenings.

EXAMPLE 36

The Moravians had a knowledge of the European music they left behind them which was rare in eighteenth-century America. Their Christian music lay at the centre of this activity and only quite recently has the true extent of this music been uncovered. Not only did they have their own hymn-writers, but they also boasted choirs which, judging by the music composed for them, must have possessed skills quite beyond those of the New Englanders. Example 37 gives the beginning of a motet by the Moravian composer Johann Peter (1746–1813) who emigrated to Pennsylvania in

1770. His style resembles that of his contemporary, Joseph Haydn. The finesse of this music was to remain unique in North America for at least another hundred years.

EXAMPLE 37

The Shakers, 'The United Society of Believers in Christ's Second Appearing', started life as a small English sect to which Ann Lee had been attracted at the age of twenty-two in 1758. She was a humble woman from the slums of Manchester, who became convinced that she was 'Ann the Word' and 'the Bride of the Lamb'. Some of her converts emigrated to North America, where, in the early years of the nineteenth century, the Society's membership grew to about 6,000, settling mostly in areas of the north-east, such as New York, Massachusetts and Connecticut.

One of her converts described Mother Ann Lee:

Mother Ann Lee was sitting in a chair, and singing very melodiously, with her hands in motion; and her whole soul and body seemed to be in exercise. I felt, as it were, a stream of divine power and love flow into my soul, and was convinced at once that it came from Heaven, the source and fountain of all good. I immediately acknowledged my faith, and went and confessed my sins.[14]

The believers lived in small, exclusive and self-sustaining villages. Their very strict moral sense kept the sexes apart, even by providing separate entrances and staircases in homes and meeting-houses – though women and men had equal status. They built their own dwellings and churches, grew their own food, made their own furniture (now highly prized and much copied), everyone covenanting their wealth to a central fund.

Most Shaker songs were created as a spontaneous act of praise and under the control of the Holy Spirit, whether in a worship meeting or outside. A Shaker pamphlet of 1782 described the spontaneity of their worship, clearly related to charismatic meetings today:

> One will begin to sing some odd tune, without words or rule; after a while another will strike in; and then another; and after a while they all fall in, and make a strange charm – some singing without words, and some with an unknown tongue or mutter, and some with a mixture of English... [15]

In the earlier days these songs were passed down in oral tradition, as the Shakers initially resisted the idea of notating their music. The first printed collections of Shaker tunes did not appear till the 1830s, but surviving manuscripts and notebooks show the true scale of their creativity, containing as many as 10,000 tunes. Example 38 shows a notated Shaker song, 'The Harvest' which symbolises in actions the sowing, watering and reaping of spiritual seed. The sweeping sign directs the singers to make a seed-sowing gesture. As an eye-witness of the ceremony wrote:

> It was a most beautiful sight to see such a devoted company all moving over the ground with such simplicity and eagerness to gather a full share of blessing. [16]

The music, with its use of a pentatonic mode, has all the artless simplicity of folk-song. Shaker music is a uniquely refreshing reminder of the directness of much Christian music in America. In country areas around and beyond the Shaker communities, where education was even harder to come by and illiteracy was high, music was still being handed down orally from one generation to the next. It was largely a folk-art, recalled as much as read, each performer adding new flavour to an old song.

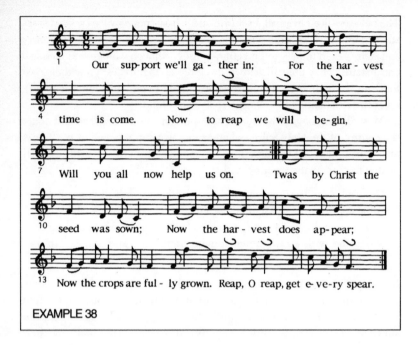

Our sup-port we'll ga - ther in; For the har - vest

time is come. Now to reap we will be-gin,

Will you all now help us on. Twas by Christ the

seed was sown; Now the har - vest does ap-pear;

Now the crops are ful - ly grown. Reap, O reap, get e- ve-ry spear.

EXAMPLE 38

Notes

1. Edward Winslow, 'Hypocrisie Unmasked', and quoted in W.S. Pratt, *The Music of the Pilgrims*, Boston, 1921, p. 6.

2. Cotton Mather, *Singing of Psalmes a Gospel-Ordinance*, 1647; quoted in P. Scholes, *The Puritans in Music*, London, 1934, p. 265.

3. T. Walter, *The Grounds and Rules of Music Explained*, Boston, 1721.

4. K. Silverman, *Selected Letters of Cotton Mather*, Louisiana University Press, 1971, p. 376.

5. Quoted in H.W. Hitchcock, *Music in the United States*, New Jersey, 1974, p. 7.

6. Quoted in I. Lowens, *Music and Musicians in Early America*, New York, 1964, p. 282.

7. M.H. Thomas, editor, *The Diary of Samuel Sewall*, New York, 1973, vol. III, p. 285.

8. W. Bentley, *The Diary of William Bentley, D.D.*, Salem, 1905–14, vol. II, p. 350.

9. 'Chester', from *New-England Psalm-Singer*, Boston, 1770.

10. Preface to the *Singing Master's Assistant*, 1778.

11. W. Billings, *Continental Harmony*, facsimile edited by N. Nathan, *Harvard*, 1961, p. 28.

12. Andrew Law, *Musical Primer*, Philadelphia, 1793, p. 8.

13. Billings, p. 31.

14. S.Y. Wells, editor, *Testimonies Concerning the Character and Ministry of Mother Ann Lee and the First Witnesses of the Gospel*, Albany, 1827, p. 101; quoted in D.W. Patterson, *The Shaker Spiritual*, Princeton, 1979, p. 18.

15. *Some Brief Hints, of a Religious Scheme, Taught and Propagated by a Number of Europeans, living in a place called Nisqueunia, in the State of New York*, Salem, 1782; quoted in E.D. Andrews, *The Gift to be Simple*, New York, 1940, p. 10.

16. Musical example and commentary from Patterson, p. 214.

Chapter 35

Africans in America

A glance down the 'for sale' columns of eighteenth-century American newspapers would reveal dozens of small-ads such as this:

> TO BE SOLD a valuable young handsome Negro Fellow about 18 or 20 years of age; has every qualification of a genteel and sensible servant and has been in many different parts of the world... He lately came from London, and has with him two suits of new clothes, and his French horn, which the purchaser may have with him.

Slavery had begun two centuries earlier – the first slaves were brought to America by Sir John Hawkins in 1563. The plantations that developed in mid-America in the eighteenth century increased the demands for slaves enormously, bringing the number by the 1750s to 300,000. By the end of that century this figure had tripled. One estimate suggests that altogether 15 million black slaves were brought to the continent (including the West Indies and South America) before Abraham Lincoln's Proclamation of Emancipation in 1863.

The music of Africa

The wonderful musicality of Africa came with the slaves. It could be heard even in the appalling and life-threatening conditions of the slave-ship:

> [the slaves on the ship] sang songs of sad lamentation... They sang songs expressive of their fears of being beat, of their want of victuals, particularly the want of their native food, and of their never returning to their own country.[1]

The slaves on board had to make music whether they liked it or not, being forced to dance for the entertainment of the sailors: 'and if they do not, they had each of them [the boatswain and his mate] a cat to flog them and make them do it...'[2]

The many musical traditions brought over from Africa were transformed by the conditions of slavery and by the arbitrary mixing of peoples of differing cultures (this was a specific policy believed to make the slaves less rebellious) but they were not eradicated. On the contrary, music and dance remained, as in Africa, far more than a diversion from the hardship and injustice of slavery. They were vital expressions of identity occasionally permitted in a life of almost unremitting labour.

Dancing and music-making using traditional instruments were celebrated at festivals such as 'Pinkster Dagh' (a corruption of 'Pentecost Day') when white spectators could look on at a great carnival of ecstatic dancing and music lasting several days. It was also possible to hear the musical expression – the hollers – of black slave-workers in the fields and open spaces:

> Suddenly one raised such a sound as I never heard before, a long, loud, musical shout, rising and falling, and breaking into falsetto, his voice ringing through the woods in the clear, frosty night air, like a bugle call. As he finished, the melody was caught up by another, then by several in chorus.[3]

The conversion of the blacks to the Christian faith went ahead slowly, for by no means all whites felt it appropriate for their slaves to know for themselves the privileges of their faith. But in such scraps as the slaves could pick up, they discovered the God who ignores human barriers, who delivers people from oppression and in whose sight everyone is equal. These were messages of hope and eventual liberation which came to be celebrated in music and dance of great power:

> it was musicking and dancing... with their unique power to weld into a higher unity the contradictory experiences of sorrow, pain, joy, hope and despair, that were at the centre of their religious expression.[4]

Hymns

So when the slaves adopted Christianity and began to sing the psalms and hymns in the white churches (albeit segregated) they brought a life and vigour to the music which the whites could not fail to notice: 'all breaking out in a torrent of sacred harmony, enough to bear away the whole congregation to heaven'.[5]

This skill and passionate sincerity in Christian music-making was brought into the homes of white Christians. In 1755 the Rev. Samuel Davies described his slaves singing from their psalters and hymn-books:

> Sundry of them have lodged all night in my kitchen, and sometimes when I have awaked about two or three o'clock in the morning, a torrent of sacred harmony has poured into my chamber and carried my mind away to heaven... I cannot but observe that the Negroes, above all the Human species that I ever knew, have an Ear for Musicke, and a kind of extatic Delight in Psalmody...[6]

By now it will be evident how significant are those last few words, for through their continued celebration of 'extatic delight', the black community in America has proferred a great gift to the legacy of Christian music.

It was not until the 1770s that blacks were permitted to form their own churches.[7] The first hymnal for black churches was published in 1801, the *Collection of Spiritual Songs and Hymns Selected from Various Authors*. The hymns, with texts by Isaac Watts, Charles Wesley and others, were selected by Richard Allen, minister of one of the first independent black denominations, the African Methodist Episcopal Church (his church was in Philadelphia). The many editions of this influential hymn-book (right up to recent times) are a touchstone for the changing tastes in hymn-singing of many black congregations. The early editions, for instance, contain simple, folk-like tunes popular at the revival meetings of the late eighteenth century. Subsequent editions contained the most popular spirituals of the next hundred years.

The folk-tunes of the early editions were not to everyone's taste. A Methodist Minister, J.F. Watson, wrote in 1819 of

> a growing evil, in the practice of singing in our places of public and society worship, merry airs, adapted from old songs, to hymns of our [the whites'] composing: often miserable as poetry, and senseless as matter... most frequently composed and first sung by the illiterate blacks of the society.[8]

Camp meetings

By far the most dramatic spiritual developments in North America came with the Great Awakening at the end of the eighteenth century. The numbers of people caught up in the sweep of renewal were so great that buildings could not house them. Instead, huge throngs, black and white, would gather outdoors to worship for days on end. The scenes were sometimes so extraordinary that only eye-witness accounts can do justice to them. This scene took place in Kentucky, 1801.

> The noise was like the roar of Niagara. The vast sea of human beings seemed to be agitated as if by a storm. I counted seven ministers, all preaching at one time... Some of the people were singing, others praying, some crying for mercy in the most piteous accents, while others were shouting most vociferously... I stepped up on to a log... The scene... was indescribable. At one time I saw at least five hundred swept down in a moment as if a battery of thousands had been opened upon them, and then immediately followed shrieks and shouts that rent the heavens.[9]

By the 1830s, the camp meetings were more carefully organised, though no less emotional:

> About an acre and a half was surrounded on the four sides by cabins built up of rough boards; the whole area in the centre was fitted up with planks, laid about a foot from the ground, as seats. At one end... was a raised stand, which served as a pulpit for the preachers... Outside the area... were hundreds of tents pitched in every quarter... One of the preachers rose and gave out a hymn, which was sung by the congregation, amounting to about seven or eight hundred... more than twenty men and women were crying out at the highest pitch of their voices, and trying apparently to be heard above the others... When it was at its height, one of the preachers came in, and raising his voice high above the tumult, intreated the Lord to receive into his fold those who now repented and would fain return... some fell on their backs with their eyes closed, waving their hands with a slow motion, and crying out – 'glory, glory, glory!'[10]

The black slaves flocked to these camp meetings and large numbers of them were converted. They were allowed to set up their tents in the area behind the preacher's stand. Their own celebrations could be enthusiastic enough even to drown out the preaching of the whites' meeting nearby. Indeed, many whites would join in the blacks' singing, picking up Christian songs which would then get sung in their own white churches, a process not always condoned by the elders. J.F. Watson wrote in *Friendly Christian Advice, to Those Methodists, Who Indulge in Extravagant Religious Emotions and Bodily Exercises*:

> Here ought to be considered, too, a most exceptional error… In the blacks' quarter, the colored people get together, and sing for hours together, short songs of disjointed affirmations, pledges or prayers, lengthened out with long repetitious choruses… in the merry chorus-manner of the southern harvest field… the example has already visibly affected the religious manners of some whites.[11]

However uneasy it might have made some people feel, the final moments of camp meetings literally broke down the barriers that kept blacks and whites apart. Joint worship followed with a free exchange of Christian music in a final march round the camp, as an onlooker observed:

> accompanied with leaping, shuffling and dancing, after the order of David before the Ark when his wife thought he was crazy; accompanied by a song appropriate to the exciting occasion…[12]

Spirituals

Camp meetings were an important basis for the growth of what are now known as spirituals. These songs, whether sung by blacks or whites, were essentially music of the countryside. The blacks brought special qualities to their spirituals, a background of field hollers (see above) and the ecstatic character of their African musical heritage. The words of the spirituals were directly biblical, drawn especially from passages which speak of liberation (Moses, Daniel and the book of Revelation were favourites) and perhaps adapted from popular English hymns, for example, the popular hymn by Isaac Watts:

> When I can read my title clear
> to mansions in the skies,
> I'll bid farewell to ev'ry fear,
> And wipe my weeping eyes.

This became the basis for several spirituals, such as the following:

Good Lord, in the mansions above,
Good Lord, in the mansions above,
My Lord, I hope to meet my Jesus
In the mansions above.

My Lord, I've had many crosses,
and trials here below;
My Lord, I hope to meet you,
In the mansions above.

The music tended to be of the call-and-response type. This simple structure, so common in African traditional music, allows great freedom: no books are needed, for the chorus is easy to pick up and the solo calls can be improvised on the spot. All this was accompanied by hand-clapping and foot-stamping, creating a Christian protest music of distilled and concentrated ecstasy.

White spirituals of the same period often adapted the texts of hymns in the same kind of way, perhaps repeating lines or adding a short refrain (like 'Glory, hallelujah!') between them, just like the blacks. The music was often borrowed or adapted from well-known folk-melodies.

Conversely, black Christians were well aware of the songs that the whites were singing in the camp meetings and were happy to sing tunes from white traditions. There were more pragmatic reasons for white ministers' disapproval of the wild conduct of black worship in the South. The words of their songs had layers of meaning which were as much earthbound as spiritual:

    . . .
    no more slavery in de kingdom
    no evil-doers in de kingdom
    all is gladness in de kingdom[13]

There's no doubt that 'de kingdom' was as much the North, where an escape from the bondage of slavery was possible, as it was a spiritual home in 'the heavens above'.

One organisation to assist slaves to flee their masters was called the Underground Railroad. A black slave, Frederick Douglass, became involved with it in 1835 in an attempted escape and later explained the coded messages embedded in spirituals:

We were, at times, remarkably buoyant, singing hymns and making joyous exclamations, almost as triumphant in their tone as if we had reached a land of freedom and safety. A keen observer might have detected in our repeated singing of 'O Canaan, sweet Canaan, I am bound for the land of Canaan,' something more than a hope of reaching heaven. We meant to reach the north – and the north was our Canaan.[14]

Many whites felt that the preaching of the Christian gospel of justice and liberty for all men was dangerous. It seems they were right.

Dance

The population of the industrial areas of North America grew rapidly during the nineteenth century and with the inexorable move towards the abolition of slavery, more and more black churches were established which did not have to suffer the strict control of the white Episcopal Church. They reflected a number of traditions, from an orderliness which emulated the atmosphere of many white congregations, to an ecstatic and physical abandon characteristic of African tradition.

Frederika Bremer visited some black churches in Cincinnati in 1850. The Episcopal Church left her with the impression of a service that was 'quiet, proper and a little tedious'. But the African Methodist Church was quite a different matter:

I found in the African Church African ardor and African life. The church was full to overflowing, and the congregation sang their own hymns. The singing ascended and poured forth like a melodious torrent, and the heads, feet and elbows of the congregation moved all in unison with it, amid evident enchantment and delight in the singing…[15]

Another report comes from William Faux who visited a black church in Philadelphia in 1820:

After sermon they began singing merrily, and continued, without stopping, one hour, till they became exhausted and breathless… While all the time they were clapping hands, shouting and jumping, and exclaiming, 'Ah Lord! Good Lord! Give me Jasus! Amen.'[16]

Although many black Christians acknowledged secular social dancing to be sinful, they claimed it could be sanctified when it became part of worship. Black Christian dance came to be known as a 'shout'. The first recorded use of the word is by an Episcopal clergyman in 1860, in terms of emphatic disapproval:

> 'Heathenish! quite heathenish!... Did you ever see a shout?' I responded in the negative, and inquired what it was. 'Oh, a dance of negro men and women to the accompaniment of their own voices. It's of no particular figure, and they sing to no particular tune, improvising both at pleasure, and keeping it up for an hour together.'[17]

A fuller description is given by Maria Waterbury, who observed it in the Sea Islands off Georgia, where the practice was already widespread:

> It usually began when the preaching was nearly done. Aunt Chloe, or Dinah, would get blest, and seemed unable to contain the blessing, and would spring to her feet, and begin shaking hands with the nearest one to her, and in a moment the example would be contagious, and two-thirds of the congregation would rise to their feet, each shaking hands with some other, the men on one side of the church, the women on the other, and soon all would swing into the center of the church, in front of the pulpit, and shouts of some would rend the air, while those who could sing would sing as though their life depended on their making a noise, all the time swaying their bodies up and down and circling among each other, shaking hands, and moving feet as if keeping time to the music. The preachers would come down out of the pulpit, and stand ready for the hand-shaking... Perhaps after twenty minutes of such exercise, the pastor would lift his hand, when instantly the noise would cease, while he pronounced the benediction, and the worshippers would pass out of the church.[18]

Such descriptions are evidence that informal dance was a central part of much black worship. Paradoxically, it was the suppression of dance by influential Puritan whites (such as Increase Mather in his *An Arrow Against Profane and Promiscuous Dancing Drawn out of the Quiver of the Scriptures*)[19] that encouraged its development when the black churches became independent.

The abolition of slavery

By the 1840s the ideological split between the Northern and Southern states was affecting every aspect of life. The white Southerners no longer holidayed in the North, nor sent their sons to be educated in the famous Northern universities of Yale, Princeton and Harvard. The issue that polarised North and South was the exercise of slavery, to which the Southerners clung as to a right. The Northern states, better educated and more liberal than the South, had long accepted its abolition as inevitable, but the Southern states refused to comply. The issue split the church: in 1840 the Methodists in the South were unable to agree with those in the North over the morality of slavery, Baptists dividing on the same issue a year later. (The rift between the Methodists was not formally settled until 1936.)

The issue was finally settled in the Civil War of 1863, where the eventual defeat of the Southern forces allowed Congress to pronounce freedom from slavery in all states in 1865. Tragically, this victory did not necessarily improve the lot of the ex-slaves, many of whom found themselves worse off than before. In an atmosphere of vengeance the South established Black Codes and 'Jim Crow' laws which made segregation almost universal. Blacks were still dependent on whites for their livelihood and given no chance to improve their position. Slavery had at least created a framework for black and white to exist together, but after the Civil War the deprivation and suffering of ex-slaves was very great and made worse still by the activities of white gangs such as the Ku Klux Klan, who attempted to preserve white supremacy by merciless terrorism.

The exodus of liberated slaves from the South therefore continued for the rest of the century. Gradually the spirituals of the countryside were replaced in the minds of migrant freedmen by music of the growing city churches. A schoolteacher in Tennessee noted this change after the Civil War:

> How I wish you could hear my children sing their strange, wild melodies, that bring back so vividly the old slave life with its toil and servile ignorance. Yet their old plantation songs are falling into disuse, and in their stead we hear chanted daily the hymns and psalms so familiar to Northern ears.[20]

But the spirituals were preserved in invaluable collections, the first and most important of which was *Slave Songs of the United States*. They were also popularised world-wide by black singing groups, such as the Fisk Jubilee Singers at a time when the slave culture that produced their music was rapidly disappearing.

The Fisk Jubilee Singers

A number of organisations had been working for the cause of black emancipation; the American Missionary Association, founded in 1846, was typical. By 1871 it had acquired for the education of freedmen a number of churches, schools and a few 'institutions of learning' in the South, one of which was the Fisk University of Nashville, Tennessee. In response to a desperate need to raise money, George White, the treasurer and musical director, trained a small choir of student ex-slaves and suggested a tour of the Northern states. Their musical repertoire was varied to begin with, including anthems, ballads, patriotic and sentimental songs and a few spirituals. They sang to sophisticated and increasingly enthusiastic audiences who, by all accounts, found the spirituals moving and strange. According to a letter written to the New York Tribune, they sang:

> a... collection of the most weird and plaintive hymns sung in the plantation cabins in the dark days of bondage... the very embodiment of African heart music... The harmony of these children of nature and their musical execution were beyond the reach of art.[21]

The respectful but patronising tone of this letter emphasises the cultural gap between the performers and their white audiences, in spite of the singers' education and musical training.

Their two American tours, in 1871 and 1873/4 were great financial and popular successes and led to a tour of Britain in 1874, during which the Singers raised $50,000. Their success was copied by countless other 'Jubilee Singers' across Canada and North America, introducing spirituals to audiences world-wide.

The Fisk Singers' spirituals were published in several editions, the first of which was called *Jubilee Songs* (1872). The songs were copied down into notation by T.F. Seward, who insisted in the introduction to the collection that 'no line or phrase was introduced that did not receive full indorsement from the Singers'. Part of a song from this collection is given in Example 39.

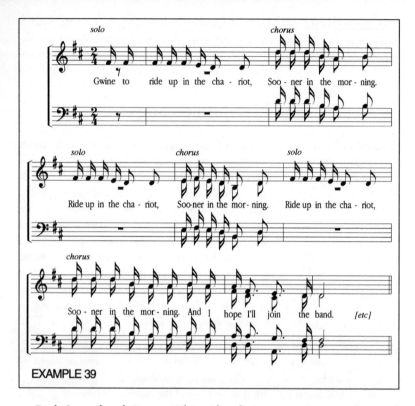

EXAMPLE 39

Both Seward and George White (the choir's trainer) were white and valued a European style of musical education. This gave them what they felt to be a justifiable superiority over a group that Seward reckoned were 'without culture', 'having no knowledge whatever of the rules of art' and with 'wholly untutored minds'.[22] Probably White trained the Singers in the use of major and minor scales (rather than the modes characteristic of true folk-music) and corrected their harmony. And Seward was accused by Thomas Rutling, one of the original Singers, of falsifying their music:

> the musician (all due respect to him) who took down the melodies
> from the singing of the Jubilee Singers, made so many errors in many
> of them that the singers did not recognise their own songs.[23]

True folk-music (like the original spirituals) is a delicate plant. Its transportation away from its natural surroundings and the popular acclaim that follows inevitably changes and probably diminishes it. It seems that the essential qualities of the slave spiritual cannot be sensed from even the earliest collections of the music, let alone from more recently published versions. Its clearest evocation may only lie in the recorded eyewitness accounts of the culture that produced it.

Notes

1. Ecroyd Claxton, *Minutes of the Evidence... respecting the Slave Trade*, 34, pp. 14–36, House of Commons; quoted in D.J. Epstein, *Sinful Tunes and Spirituals: Black Folk Music to the Civil War*, Urbana, Illinois, 1977.

2. James Towne, *Minutes of the Evidence... respecting the Slave Trade*, 34, pp. 14–36, House of Commons; quoted in Epstein, p. 8.

3. F.L. Olmstead, *Journey in the Seaboard Slave States*, New York, 1856, vol. 2, p. 19; quoted in E. Southern, *The Music of Black Americans*, 2nd edition, New York, 1983, p. 156.

4. C. Small, *Music of the Common Tongue*, London, 1987, p. 87.

5. S. Davies, *Letters from the Reverend Samuel Davies and Others...*; quoted in C. Hamm, *Music in the New World*, New York, 1983, p. 128.

6. Davies; quoted in Hamm, p. 128.

7. See Southern, 2nd edition, pp. 73–75.

8. J.F. Watson, *Methodist Error*, Trenton, 1819.

9. Quoted in C.A. Johnson, *The Frontier Camp Meeting*, Dallas, 1955, pp. 64 and 65.

10. Captain C.B. Marryat, *A Diary in America*, New York, 1839, pp. 136–138.

11. Watson, pp. 29–31.

12. Robert Todd; quoted in E. Southern, *The Music of Black Americans*, New York, 1971, p. 99.

13. Verses from the Spiritual 'Dere's No Rain'; quoted in Southern, p. 159.

14. F. Douglass, *My Bondage and My Freedom*, New York, 1855, p. 87; quoted in Southern, 2nd edition, p. 143.

15. A.B. Benson, editor, *America of the Fifties: Letters of Frederika Bremer*, New York, 1924.

16. W. Faux, *Memorable Days in America...*, London, 1823, p. 420.

17. See Southern, 2nd edition, p. 169.

18. M. Waterbury, *Seven Years Among the Freedmen*, Chicago, 2nd edition, 1891, pp. 195–96; quoted in Epstein, p. 287.

19. Boston, 1684. See J.E. Marks III, *The Mathers on Dancing*, New York, 1975.

20. L.W. Slaughter, *The Freedmen of the South*, Cincinnati, 1869, p. 134.

21. *Tribune*, 17 January 1872; quoted in L.D. Silveri, 'The Singing Tours of the Fisk Jubilee Singers', in S.V. Martin and G.R. Keck, editors, *Feel The Spirit, Studies in Nineteenth-Century Afro-American Music*, Connecticut, 1988, p. 109.

22. See D.J. Epstein, 'Theodore F. Seward and the Fisk Jubilee Singers', in R. Crawford, R.A. Lott, and C.J. Oja, editors, *A Celebration of American Music*, Ann Arbor, Michigan, 1990, p. 40.

23. T. Rutling, *Tom: An Autobiography*, Torrington, Devon, UK, 1907; quoted in Epstein, 'Theodore F. Seward and the Fisk Jubilee Singers', p. 41.

Chapter 36

Gospel Music – White and Black

The spirituals sung by the Fisk and other 'Jubilee' singers became immensely popular in the concert- and music-hall, but were only selectively adopted as songs for worship in the years after the Civil War. White Episcopal churches would not have considered slave songs appropriate company for the hymns of Lowell Mason or the Wesleys.

Very few collections of spirituals for use in worship were published after Richard Allen's *Hymns and Spiritual Songs* of 1801. The singers of shape-note music (even in the black churches) continued to sing their traditional *Sacred Harp* songs without the invasion of spirituals. But in the growing black congregations of city churches spirituals were adopted, but very much changed in the process. The Evangelical and Pentecostal churches (especially those where instruments were welcomed as an accompaniment for singing) decorated and embellished spirituals with foot-stamping, hand-clapping and melodic improvisation. The old spontaneity was thus returned to them and the way paved for a new type of Christian music.

White gospel music

The first use of the term 'gospel music' in print was probably by Philip P. Bliss (1838–76) in a collection of his music published in 1874: *Gospel Songs, A Choice Collection of Hymns and Tunes, New and Old, for Gospel Meetings, Sunday School.* The title suggests the importance that popular music still held in Christian music in America. Through the increasing influence of the Sunday School movement (The American Sunday School Union was founded in 1824), the Young Men's Christian Association (established in Boston in 1851) and many other organisations, increasingly large numbers of white Americans were experiencing conversion. From the 1870s, huge meetings were held in football stadia, tents, meeting houses and even railway depots to hear a new era of evangelists proclaim the personal significance of the Christian faith.

In 1873 Dwight L. Moody and Ira D. Sankey formed the earliest evangelistic team of preacher and musician. As one of their slogans put it: 'Mr Moody will *preach* the gospel and Mr Sankey will *sing* the gospel.' The formula was successfully taken up by many others: from John W. Chapman and the singer Charles Alexander, William A. Sunday ('Billy' Sunday) and Homer Rodeheaver, to the tele-evangelists of the present.

The 'gospel songs' of these meetings conveyed the simplest of Christian messages through music of emotional directness to huge numbers of people. The style of the music was a familiar one, closely related to the music halls and the sheet music of Tin Pan Alley. As one newspaper reported, Sankey's hymns

> while written to religious words, are made attractive by many secular contrivances... a circus quickstep, a negro sentimental ballad, a college chorus, and a hymn all in one...[1]

The twentieth-century singers (Alexander and Rodeheaver for instance) emphasised even more the informality of the meetings through the influence of ragtime and early jazz, Rodeheaver sometimes playing the trombone in meetings as well as singing.

The influence of the music of these evangelistic teams has had an equally strong impact in Britain, indeed, gospel song has over the years penetrated deep into the consciousness of all English-speaking countries. Much of it is still in print and available in collections such as *Sacred Songs and Solos* or *Alexander's Hymns*. As the twentieth century has progressed, the successful strategy of 'circus quickstep' and 'sentimental ballad' established by *Brighten the Corner* or George C. Stebbins' *Out of My Bondage, Sorrow and Night* was repeated with little change for fifty years, and there seemed little desire on the part of evangelists to keep pace with the rapidly changing trends in popular music.

White Southern gospel

At the big gospel music conventions in the South today there are still traditions which go back to the shape-note singing of the early nineteenth century. Music using the shape-note system continued to be published right up to the 1940s, much of it in the form of periodicals, which formed the basis for 'old book singings' (Sunday evening meetings around the *Sacred Harp* book) or 'new book singings' (using the seven-shape system). Since then, sheet music has gradually taken over the circulation of songs and nowadays white gospel music reaches its public through recordings and radio.

While the gospel sound has become thoroughly commercialised (well over 1,000 radio stations are dedicated to it, promoting all the latest albums) it still has an important base in the independent churches of the Southern states – the Baptists, Methodists and the Pentecostal and Holiness churches.

Black gospel

Black gospel music took on a different character from the beginning, though its identity was not fully established until the 1920s. Its roots lay much further back than those of the gospel music of the white evangelists. The black churches had their own traditions of Christian music whose unique character was, if anything, sharpened by the Civil War and its aftermath.

The African roots of the spirituals and shouts once more found their true home in the Holiness and Sanctified movements of black churches towards the end of the nineteenth century. Here the intensity of Christian revival was expressed in the exercise of the charismatic gifts of the Spirit, particularly those of prophecy and singing in tongues. Christopher Small gives a vivid description of the inseparability of music and worship in these Pentecostal churches today:

> when the Holy Ghost descends, sometimes immediately after the ceremony begins, sometimes only after prolonged searching, the intensity of emotion has to be felt to be believed, most especially in the feeling of unity and common purpose between all present. Speech, music and dance are the tools by means of which the Holy Ghost is invoked and brought into the midst of the congregation – not as separate arts but as aspects of the one great performance art of celebration. A gifted black preacher's... performance... will grow through stages of excitement in which the sense of his words gives way to more ecstatic musicality, his often reiterated words and phrases being taken up by the congregation and thrown back to him with cries

of affirmation and with Amens. Finally... the whole congregation are singing, clapping their hands, often in marvellously complex inter-locking rhythmic patterns, and moving their bodies each in his or her own idiomatic way. The level of ecstacy thus attained is a matter for each individual... but the overwhelming feeling is of a singing, dancing, praying *community*.[2]

Ancient African traditions of music-making are central to this spontaneous Christian music – a call-and-response structure between preacher and congregation is commonplace and the ecstatic qualities of music are very evident in the body-movement and hand-clapping that accompanies it. As the gospel singer Mahalia Jackson (1911–72) recalled of her childhood:

> These people had no choir and no organ. They used the drum, the cymbal, the tambourine and the steel triangle. Everybody in there sang, and they clapped and stomped their feet, and sang with their whole bodies. They had a beat, a rhythm we held on to from slavery days, and their music was so strong and expressive. It used to bring tears to my eyes.[3]

Such expressive intensity came partly through extravagant and wild coloration of the voice – moaning, growling, shouting – and the deliberate bending of pitch to create a musical scale quite different from the Western major or minor. In particular, the third, seventh and sometimes sixth and fifth degrees may be flattened by a semitone, causing ecstatically painful collisions with an accompaniment of more conventional Western harmony.

The endlessly expressive possibilities of these techniques were already indigenous to the blues singers, the poorest unemployed blacks, singing on street corners for their next meal. The passionate sound of these half-improvised melodies is quite distinct from the Jubilee singers' spirituals, which were influenced – even corrupted – by European traditions of harmony. The composer of the *St Louis Blues*, W.C. Handy (1873–1958) wrote of his childhood:

> The Baptists had no organ in their church and no choir. They didn't need any. The lusty singers sat in the amen corner and raised the songs, raised them as they were intended to be raised, if I'm any judge. None of the dressed-up arrangements one sometimes hears on the concert stage for them. They knew a better way. Theirs was pure rhythm. While critics like to describe their numbers as shouting

songs, rhythm was their basic element. And rhythm was the thing that drew me and other members of our home town quartet to attend the Baptist services.[4]

Charles A. Tindley

The essential stepping-stone to the establishment of black gospel music was Charles Tindley (about 1859–1933), a Methodist preacher and song-writer. His church in Philadelphia (East Calvary Methodist Episcopal Church – rechristened the 'Tindley Temple') developed a reputation for powerful music from its foundation at the turn of the century. Tindley wrote both the melodies and the words of his songs (like almost all gospel songs, black or white, the words and music are inseparable).

In the true tradition of the spiritual his songs give reassurance to the poor and the disadvantaged. The word 'overcome' seems especially important:

> By and by when the morning comes,
> When the saints of God are gathered home,
> We'll tell the story how we've overcome:
> For we'll understand it better by and by.[5]

The refrain of his song ('I'll overcome some day') seems to have been the inspiration for the universally known 'We shall overcome'.

Tindley was unusual in copyrighting and publishing his music (an anthology, *New Songs of Paradise* was printed in 1916). Where the gospel music of the white evangelists was published in vast quantities, black gospel songs were still a folk-art and rarely found their way into print. Not long after, the National Baptist Convention published *Gospel Pearls* (1921), a collection of traditional hymns alongside gospel songs, with a number of Tindley's among them.

Thomas A. Dorsey

The most influential of all black gospel singers and writers was Thomas A. Dorsey (1899–1993, not to be confused with the band-leader Tommy Dorsey). In spite of a strict Christian upbringing as the son of a travelling

Baptist minister, Dorsey at first sought opportunities to make music wherever he could find them, making a name for himself in his 'teens as the dance pianist 'Barrelhouse Tom'. In 1921 he heard the singing and preaching of Rev A.W. Nix at the National Baptist Convention:

> He was great! He was powerful! He rocked that convention: shouts, moans, hollers, screaming… That's where I first got the gospel word, and I was converted at that meeting.[6]

The hysterical quality of Nix's preaching may be sensed from a sleeve-note to one of his most famous sermonettes, *Black Diamond Express to Hell*:

> Here she comes! The Black Diamond Express to Hell, holding the throttle wide open; Pleasure is the Headlight, and the Devil is the Conductor. You can feel the roaring of the Express and the moanin' of the Drunkards, Liars, Gamblers and other folks who have got aboard. They are hell-bound and they don't want to go. The train makes eleven stops but nobody can get off…[7]

In spite of his experience at the National Baptist Convention, Dorsey continued to make his reputation in secular music. With the singer Ma Rainey and his own Wildcats Jazz Band he was the first to make blues into big business with the record companies.

In the early thirties he decided to turn wholeheartedly to writing and singing for the church; *Precious Lord*, a song written after the death of his wife and baby daughter, was a turning point (see Example 40). But the expressive blues style and its secular associations caused consternation, especially with the older generation. As the singer and contemporary of Dorsey, Willie Mae Ford Smith (1904–94), recalled:

> They said I was bringing the blues into the church… When I first started out singing gospel they said 'We don't want that coonshine stuff in here, we don't want that ragtime singing in here,' but that didn't stop me. I kept going because that's what the Lord wanted.[8]

As well as writing over 800 songs Dorsey did much to promote gospel music, through his founding of the Chicago Gospel Choral Union and the National Convention of Gospel Choirs and Chorusses in 1932. He set black gospel music firmly on the road to big business in the same year by creating the Dorsey House of Music, the publisher of some 500 of his songs and the first business whose sole concern was the commercial cause of black gospel.

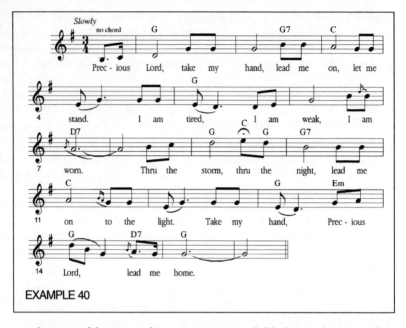

EXAMPLE 40

The powerful impact of Dorsey's music took black gospel into another dimension. Where Tindley's songs have an immediacy and directness which spring from straightforward melodies and the simple and slow harmonic rhythms that accompany them, Dorsey's songs are linked closely to the harmonic tensions and complexities of the expressive language of the blues. He sang with breathtaking intensity, turning a simple song (such as 'Amazing Grace') into a kind of vocal sermon lasting many minutes, heightening the emotional impact of every significant word with extravagant vocal decorations. The congregation would respond to these with spontaneous applause, gasps and cries of encouragement and praise, exactly paralleled by spontaneous and wild arpeggios from the accompanying piano and Hammond organ.

Solo singers and quartets

Churches did not always accept this new music without misgivings: Dorsey spent three years advertising his sheet music before sales began. Soon enough, however, the new gospel music won pride of place over the older songs – usually next to the sermon. Dorsey's innovations then created and inspired a new generation of music for various vocal combinations. Soloists, duets, trios and quartets were established earliest – Sallie Martin, Clara Ward (1924–73), Marion Williams (soloists), the Gay Sisters (duet), the Soul Stirrers (male quartet) and the Original Gospel Harmonettes (female quartet) representing only a fraction of the burgeoning talent of the 1930s and 1940s. At this time gospel radio stations started broadcasting in the United States – there are now hundreds. The balancing of a lead singer against other voices resonated with the relationship of preacher and congregation – indeed, the lead vocalist would be expected to preach as well as sing.

New situations invited new styles – 'hard' or 'hot' gospel of the 1950s and 1960s replaced the lighter crooning style of the previous decades (epitomised by the singer Claude Jeter of the Swan Silvertones) with an altogether wilder delivery, especially from the lead voice, with thigh-slapping and screaming top notes. At this point gospel artists found they had aspiring rock'n'roll singers in their audiences looking for inspiration. Indeed, the great debt that current commercial music owes to gospel starts here. Elvis Presley provides one of countless examples:

> We were a religious family, going around together to sing at camp meetings and revivals. Since I was two years old, all I knew was gospel music – that *was* music to me… The preachers cut up all over the place, jumping on the piano, moving every which way… I guess I learned from them. I loved the music. It became such a part of my life it was as natural as dancing, a way to escape from problems and my way of release.[9]

Choirs

More recently gospel choirs have created new musical possibilities, providing an 'orchestral' backdrop to a soloist or a punchy 'big-band' style of delivery. In North America massed choral sound is a special attraction. The best known is perhaps the Mississippi Mass Choir established in 1988 by Franklin Williams (1947–93), who was a member of a family quartet called the Williams Brothers. The huge recording sales of the choir contribute (along with other mass choirs – Dallas-Fort Worth, Wilmington-Chester, Florida and New Jersey) to a commercial income for gospel music which in 1990 exceeded $500 million.

In Britain the commercial interest is nothing like as great – a brief glance of the stock of gospel music in a local record shop or library will make this clear – but among black churches themselves there is often vibrant and lively activity in music. Almost every church will have its gospel choir, local choirs joining forces to heighten the musical and spiritual impact. Rev. John Francis, for instance, is a young black pastor with churches in Brixton (London) and Birmingham. The choirs from these churches act as a nucleus for larger groups which can heard in both cities; the Saturday afternoon music to be heard outside Brixton tube station has acted as a witness to the city round about, illustrating the radical discipleship that lies behind gospel music:

> The watchword is relevance… [The congregation] want to hear things relating to their real-life situation. They want worship which is vibrant and exciting… If a church can get its message, its music, its good methods right, ministering to the poor, dealing with social issues… people will respond.[10]

Just as the earlier quartets were led by a soloist, so these choirs usually act as a vibrant backdrop to a guest singer who is still expected to preach when the occasion demands.

The debt that secular music owes to this immensely powerful mixture – this collision of African and Western cultures – is immense. Every potent musical expression of emotion today, the very basis of rock music, seems to have its roots in gospel:

> All rock's most resilient features, the beat, the drama, the group vibrations derive from gospel. From the rock symphonies to detergent commercials, from Aretha Franklin's prototechnique to the Beatles' harmonies, gospel has simply reformed all our listening expectations. The very tension between beats, the climax we anticipate almost subliminally is straight out of the church. The dance steps that ushered in a new physical freedom were copied from the shout, the holy dance of victory. The sit-ins smoothed by hymns, the freedom marches powered by shouts, the brother and sister fraternity of revolution: the gospel church gave us all of these.[11]

But the wonderful gift of gospel music, its free expression of feeling and its invitation to an unfettered physical response, has been adapted and distorted in its secular forms. By taking the physical and emotional qualities of the music, but rejecting its spiritual basis, the worship of God through ecstatic music has been transformed into a worship of feeling and sensation itself, a change reflected by the materialist and selfish lifestyles of some of the people involved.

Mahalia Jackson made an important distinction between these two worlds, the spiritual and the secular, symbolised in her day by gospel music and blues. She rejected the latter, not because it did not suit her voice, but because

> blues are the songs of despair, gospel songs are the songs of hope. When you are singing gospel you have a feeling there's a cure for what's wrong. When you're through with the blues you've got nothing to rest on.[12]

Many black gospel singers seem to have led lives like Dorsey, uneasily poised between the Christian and the secular world. As the music business has become more and more interested in the commercial potential of gospel singers, its temptations have sometimes become irresistible. In the mid-1950s Sam Cooke was a lead singer with the Soul Stirrers vocal quartet:

> I was happy enough on the gospel trail and making myself a nice living... But the more I thought about the pop field the more interesting it became... I wanted things for my family, and I wanted nice things for my own. Making a living was good enough, but what's wrong with doing better than that?[13]

His success as one of the earliest singers of soul was cut violently short by his murder in 1964.

Black Voices

Black Voices is an *a capella* group which attempts to keep its Christian integrity yet reach an international audience. The five women who make up the group are based in Birmingam, where Black Voices was established in 1989. Their background is a strict Christian upbringing:

My first singing experiences started in church... that was all we were allowed to listen to as children. My dad never allowed 'worldly' music, as he called it, to enter the household. As he would often preach from the pulpit... anything that didn't acknowledge Jesus Christ as Lord in terms of a song was really not welcome in our household. Our family has ten children and my dad brought an old banjo with him from the Caribbean, so we were all sat around him and he would play his banjo, and that's often how a lot of the chorusses entered the church... There were children's choirs... there were plays going on at the church that turned out to be mini-operas, and then there were the church choirs, junior, adult, young people and... quartet-groups forming. So I really was fulfilled in terms of singing through the church.[14]

Black Voices certainly sing the traditional gospel songs of their childhood – the songs (like *In the Upper Room*) made famous by Mahalia Jackson – but they are not defensive about moving into commercial music (Stevie Wonder *Love's a Need*), blues and exploring their ethnic roots:

Just because you are a Christian doesn't mean that you can't appreciate music that speaks to wholesome experiences... fun, laughter, or even sexuality... so Black Voices was forced to broaden its repertoire. To deliver the kind of concerts it does internationally, it has to cater for a much broader taste than just the church. Sam Cooke realised that he couldn't live being a gospel singer, so he had to seek other ways of earning his money with his voice.[15]

That broadening has involved going back – physically and emotionally – to African roots, through visits to Ghana and Kenya. Where traditionalists may say that a gospel group is not defined by the singing of African freedom songs or the blues, to reach a wide audience Black Voices must, it seems, address contemporary multiculture. This way a door is open to bring the good news into the concert-hall.

The success of Black Voices would not be possible without the springboard of a thriving gospel scene. While the following comment from the pastor of the Celestial Church of Christ in East London may be somewhat oversimplified, it shows that the freedom in African worship observed in the eighteenth century still endures:

In Africa we are a bit loud and joyous. In an English, Anglican church they are very conservative and very quiet, cool, but that is not our way.

Our way is jubilation, shouting, dancing and expressing the joy of life. So we beat the drum and we dance and we enjoy ourselves...[16]

The reasons for the striking difference between European and African traditions of worship are complex, but they partly have to do with social acceptability. What is acceptable has in turn been shaped by history, for Western society imposes its restraints on worship as the result of the evolution of thought over centuries:

Black people, wherever you find them, have not been as much influenced by the ideology of the Enlightenment... One of the effects of the Enlightenment on white people and their culture is the split between body and soul and [between] Reason and Faith, the things of God and the things of this world — politics and economics on one side, religion on the other.[17]

Perhaps black Christians are as a result better defended against the potentially corrupting influence of commercialism than their white counterparts. If European dualism is of less consequence in their culture, then God may be seen in places where he may otherwise be difficult to recognise.

Notes

1. *The Nation*, March 1876; quoted in E. Sanjek, *American Popular Music and its Business*, New York, 1988, vol. 2, p. 251.

2. C. Small, *Music of the Common Tongue*, London, 1987, pp. 103–4.

3. Quoted in V. Broughton, *Black Gospel*, Poole, 1985, p. 53.

4. W.C. Handy, *Father of the Blues*, New York, 1970, p. 157.

5. The music may be found in the *New Grove Dictionary of American Music*, London, 1986, vol. 2, p. 256.

6. Quoted in Broughton, p. 36.

7. Quoted in Broughton, p. 37.

8. From the sound-track of the film *Say Amen Somebody*, 1982.

9. Quoted in Peter Guralnick, *Lost Highway*, Boston, Ma., 1979, p. 120.

10. Quoted in *Africa to Britain, a Journey of Religion*, BBC Radio 4, December 1995.

11. A. Heilbut, *The Gospel Sound*, New York, 1971, p. 10.

12. Quoted in Broughton, p. 52.

13. Quoted in Broughton, p. 95.

14. Interview on *Kaleidoscope*, BBC Radio 4, December 1996.

15. Interview on *Kaleidoscope*.

16. Quoted in *Africa to Britain, A Journey of Religion*, BBC Radio 4.

17. Quoted in *Africa to Britain*.

Chapter 37

The United States and the European Classical Tradition

A German composer noted irritably in 1849, after an extended visit to America, that

> in all departments of the fine arts – but especially in music – [the American] is behind all, and is therefore not capable of enjoying instrumental music. It is a matter of course, that only the so-called anti-classical can, in any degree, suit the taste of the American public: such as waltzes, galops, quadrilles – above all, polkas.[1]

Cultured Americans were only too aware of the low standing in which their musical education was held by Europeans and in order to improve it, any classical musician from Boston or New York was expected to go to study in Europe, if he had the means. William Mason (1829–1908), youngest son of the hymnodist Lowell Mason, John Paine (1839–1906), Dudley Buck (1839–1909), Horatio Parker (1864–1919), who was Charles Ives' teacher at Yale, George Chadwick (1854–1931) – all these composers trained in Germany or Austria and returned to America to write music in imitation of their Teutonic masters. The recognition that these composers received by critics of classical music was measured by their ability to write in the European tradition:

> in this work Mr Paine has shown himself strong in all the qualities which one expects to find in a great composer. In his easy mastery of the minutest details of counterpoint we recognise the devoted student of Bach. His work is distinguished by a clearness and conciseness of form which Mendelssohn has hardly surpassed...[2]

Paine, like most of these composers, was also an organist, and the Christian music of the episcopal churches around Boston reflected the attitudes of such men, known as the Boston classicists, who encouraged the performance of the church music of classical European composers as well as writing much of their own. Most churches were unable to find a well-trained choir to sing such music and instead made do with a paid solo quartet who also satisfied the congregations' interest in an operatic vocal style. The singers occupied a side-gallery or were placed above the pulpit, singing excerpts from 'sacred' works by Rossini or Gounod and even adaptations of opera (such as the sextet from Donizetti's *Lucia di Lammermoor* sung to 'Guide me O thou Great Jehovah'!). Dudley Buck wrote a great many anthems for such quartets in both Latin and English, easy-going music with more than a touch of sentimentality.

Opportunities to write Christian music on a much grander scale increased towards the end of the century. Both Paine and Buck showed some ability with large choral and orchestral forces, for instance Buck's *46th Psalm* (1872) and Paine's *St Peter* (1873), but none of these could be compared to Horatio Parker's *Hora Novissima* (1893) which still receives an occasional performance, other pieces of the time having been long forgotten.

Charles Ives

Horatio Parker would have had no idea that one of his pupils, Charles Ives, (in his opinion probably his worst) was to become of far greater significance than himself. The Christian background of the two men could not have been more different. As Charles Ives, the American composer, recalled:

> I remember how the great waves of sound used to come through the trees when things like *Beulah Land*, *Woodworth*, *Nearer My God to Thee*, *In the Sweet Bye-and-Bye* and the like were sung by thousands of 'let-out' souls... Father, who led the singing, sometimes with his cornet or his voice, sometimes with both voice and arms, and sometimes in the quieter hymns with a violin or French horn, would always encourage the people to sing their own way. Most of them knew the words and music (their version) by heart and sang it that way. If they threw the poet or composer around a bit, so much the better for the poetry and the music. There was power and exaltation in these great conclaves of sound from humanity.[3]

For Charles Ives (1874–1954), such childhood memories of camp meetings were vivid and enduring. His recollections are more than just a window onto a colourful past: they were also a fundamental influence on his music, which itself often recalls the fervour and passion of those 'thousands of "let-out" souls'.

The thick, swirling textures of his orchestral pieces suggest mass participation in some great emotional enterprise and are delivered with the stormy rhetoric of the preaching – ebbing and flowing between emotional extremes. Some pieces are a direct evocation of Christian worship, such as the *Third Symphony* (1904), subtitled 'The Camp Meeting'. Its three movements have specific associations, as their titles show: 'Old Folks Gatherin'', 'Children's Day' and 'Communion'. The music is shot through with revivalist hymn-tunes. *Woodworth* ('Just as I am, without one plea') occurs in all three movements, binding the whole work together.

Compared with other works, Ives' *Third Symphony* is gentle in expression and modest in scale, but the few musicians of his time who came across it found it incomprehensible, along with most of the rest of his music. Much of the *Third Symphony* was arranged from organ pieces Ives had written some three years earlier and which a fellow student of his pronounced 'hideously modern'.[4]

Indeed, Ives' visionary creativity took him into realms of modernity and experiment utterly at odds with the music and musicians of his day. Not only that, but the appearance of so much music of the common folk – not just the sentimental hymn-tunes, but Stephen Foster's parlour-songs and all that trained musicians called 'cheap trash'[5] – would have been wholly unacceptable to critics of art-music, had they even had the chance to hear it.

From the age of fourteen till 1902 when he was twenty-seven, Ives was church organist in his home town of Danbury and later in New Haven and New York. His remarkable mind must have startled his congregations from fairly early on. At seventeen, he wrote the now well-known set of organ variations on *America* (the same melody as the British National Anthem). This shows a refreshing and humorous enthusiasm for music-making; the tune is forced into all kinds of eccentric shapes over oompah accompaniments and the final variation demands a lunatic tirade of semi-quavers for the feet 'as fast as the pedals can go'.

Apart from a number of organ pieces in every one of which there are surprises of some kind,[6] he also wrote choral music for his churches. The most moving and impressive of these are settings of psalms (24, 54, 67, 90 and 150 – many more may be lost) written in 1894 for Center Church in New Haven. That any of them were performed at all is remarkable, for the directness of the texts inspired Ives to write some music of startling originality and aural challenge (see Example 41 for an excerpt from Psalm 90).

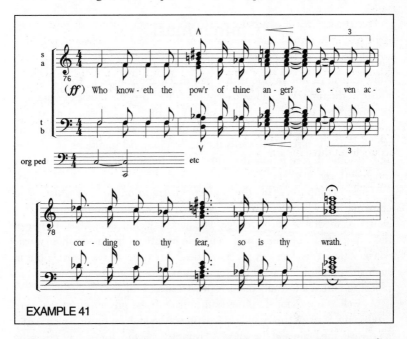

EXAMPLE 41

Ives drew out the spiritual implications of the psalm-texts as very few other composers have done before or since. It is a shame that such technical difficulties prevent the music from being sung by any but the most expert choirs. His settings are still rarely heard in the concert-hall, let alone in the Christian context for which he wrote them.

The yawning chasm between Horatio Parker's music and that of his pupil Charles Ives caused nothing but friction and unpleasantness. The problem was not only a difference of opinion, but a principled unwillingness of the teacher to understand the pupil. As Ives recalled: 'He would just look at a measure or so, and hand it back with a smile, or joke about "hogging all the keys at one meal" and then talk about something else.'[7]

Such a stifling desire on the part of learned composers to write music within an approved European style did not last far into this century. Between the wars a younger generation of American composers, stimulated by the startling and colourful developments in the new music of France, Germany and Austria, were encouraged to produce music of stimulus and challenge.

Church music

For a while the music of Tin Pan Alley and jazz came to be an archetype of American-ness, not an idiom that had much application in Christian art-music of the time. With a few exceptions, therefore, the music of American composers for the concert-hall is seldom heard in a Christian context, any more than the European or British. But there is a large group of composers whose music is directed towards the white Episcopal traditions of worship and to some degree follow the path of the 'Boston classicists' of the later nineteenth century.

These composers in the Episcopal tradition are organists and choirmasters who have lived and worked in the surroundings of a large church, cathedral or music college. The necessity of meeting at least some of the expectations of choirs and their congregations has made their music conservative. This does not preclude the ability to speak expressively, but in such surroundings there is the temptation to become complacent and to repeat too often a formula that has proved successful.

As well as music for the American cathedrals, far greater quantities were produced for parish choirs and choirmasters who look for music which is easy on the ear, the brain and the voice. A favourite structure for such pieces is the hymn-anthem, a choral fantasy woven around a well-known hymn. Some are well-written if predictable, but many others are thrown together (and still printed) by composers lacking technique and ideas. This was the kind of music which provoked the musicologist Paul Henry Lang to write in 1946:

> Only the artistically unfit continue to compose ritual music, and a more miserable, tawdry, tinsel-strewn collection than recent church music is hard to imagine.[8]

The demand for this music is immense and now beginning to be satisfied by the distribution potential of the Internet. Even on the local level, congregations are often very large and wealthy. They are often able to support a full-time music staff and several choirs drawn from their own resources.

Hymns

Hymnals and collections of Christian music in America have been numerous since the eighteenth century – in the last hundred years they have multiplied enormously. Such a diverse society has supporters of every possible Christian sect, each of whom has established its own series of hymn- or song-books, re-edited and revised every few years.

The Episcopal Church, for example, licensed an American edition of *Hymns Ancient and Modern* in 1862. It proved much less attractive and saleable than the English edition, but it influenced Episcopalian hymn-books produced later in the century, such as *The Hymnals* with editions in 1874, 1892 and 1916. These all lacked music and several music editions were produced for each one. Only in 1918 was an Episcopalian hymn-book published with music, the *New Hymnal*, encouraging the widespread association of tune with text.

Subsequent editions of the *New Hymnal* have not simply adapted the previous ones, but reflect some rapid changes in taste in Christian music this century. The 1940 edition, for instance, drew on far more diverse sources than previous hymn-books, from plainsong on the one hand to the music of contemporary American and English composers on the other (Vaughan Williams, Holst, Geoffrey and Martin Shaw among the latter). In these respects it resembles Vaughan Williams' *English Hymnal* of 1906. The 1982 edition once again shows a considerable change with the inclusion of much new music and through the influence of the English hymnologist and writer Erik Routley.

The Methodists, the Presbyterians, the Baptists, the Congregationalists, the Lutherans, the Roman Catholics and many others have produced hymn-books and supplements in similar quantity, while other editors and publishers have produced ecumenical collections for use in all circumstances. These, such as *Ecumenical Praise* or *Faith Looking Forward*, have contained the most challenging material for congregational worship.

A large number of new hymn-tunes have been written by many American organist/composers, relatively few of which stand the test of time or the scrutiny of conservative congregations. One superb tune which shows how the concept of 'hymn' is changing is *DeTar* by the composer Calvin Hampton (Example 42). Imaginative and noble though this tune is, it has not found its way into many hymn-books.

EXAMPLE 42

Notes

1. Quoted in J.S. Dwight, *Journal of Music*, 18 December 1852, pp. 83–84.

2. Critique of Paine's *1st Symphony* in *Atlantic Monthly*, June 1876, p. 764; quoted in B.L. Tischler, *An American Music*, New York, 1986, p. 32.

3. Quoted in H. and S. Cowell, *Charles Ives and His Music*, Oxford, 1955, p. 24.

4. See D. Wooldridge, *Charles Ives*, London, 1975, p. 109.

5. 'The most superficial trashy stuff that is in vogue: the negro melodies, the namby-pamby sentimental ballads, the flashy fantasias, polkas, waltzes, marches, etc., of native Americans…', *Dwight's Music Journal*, 1850s; quoted in E. Sanjek, *American Popular Music and its Business*, New York, 1988, vol. 2, p. 141.

6. A note at the foot of a short *Adeste Fidelis* for organ reads: 'Reverend J.B. Lee, others & Mrs Uhler said it was awful…', Wooldridge, p. 85.

7. J. Kirkpatrick, editor, *Charles E. Ives, Memos*, New York, 1972, p. 49.

8. P.H. Lang, 'Church Music — What's Left of It', in *Saturday Review of Literature*, 29 June 1946, p. 30.

PART 8
Latin America and Australasia

Chapter 38

Latin America

The invasion of Latin America by the West has had such dramatic and painful consequences over the last 500 years that a discussion of its effects on Christian music seems frivolous in comparison. The brutality with which the Spaniards subdued the natives is legendary. Among other things, human labour on an immense scale was required by the Spanish and Portuguese to create the infrastructure of roads and buildings. The indigenous Indians were put to work by the *conquistadores* and as the natives succumbed to ill-treatment and disease, slaves were imported from the west coast of Africa to supplement or replace them.

The missionaries were not happy to abet their masters in the exploitation of the Indians and some (Bartholomé de las Casas, 1474–1566, being the prime example) risked martyrdom in consequence. Their early attempts to teach the Christian faith – to replace coercion by conversion – involved music. Brazilian Indians, for example, were presented with miracle plays with native actors speaking their own language. The local Tupinambá music was syllabic and modal, allowing the missionaries to produce a workable parallel to Gregorian chant.[1]

However, the colonists were really only interested in enslavement and occupation and from the early years of colonial rule the enduring evidence of the new religion is in the magnificent churches and cathedrals built by the slave labour of the indigenous Indians. For not long after the arrival of missionaries, soldiers and politicians, came the European architects, artists and musicians. Their early efforts in the Americas are far too extensive for a thorough discussion, but even the briefest review of the centres established by the Roman Church in the sixteenth century tells an impressive musical story.

Peru was the administrative centre for the Americas in the early years of colonisation and the chief monuments to the church working alongside the colonial powers are its cathedrals of Lima and Cuzco, founded in 1535 and 1559. The musical provision in Lima was relatively modest until the appointment of the first *maestro de capilla* in 1612. From that point onwards, composers and professional musicians of high competence were employed there until the early nineteenth century. From the first, instrumentalists played alongside the choir, following a recommendation by the Third Lima Council of 1583. Andean culture already had a rich tradition of recorder-playing which transferred well to colonial church music. *Pinkillu*, recorder-like instruments still played today in the Andes, are evidence that flute-playing skills among the Indians were established long before the Spanish arrived.[2] The early relationship of Inca and Christian is recorded in a unique series of Inca drawings. By the late seventeenth century, Lima had a substantial orchestra of wind and strings and the cathedral's musical provision was said to match any in Europe.

From Cuzco, the celebrated city of the Incas, 11,000 feet above sea level in the Andes, comes further evidence of Indians being taught to play Western musical instruments for the liturgy of the cathedral. In spite of the assaults of earthquakes through the centuries, the building is much as it was when it was first built. The interior is breathtaking, full of images – pictures by fine Indian artists from the eighteenth century, the choir surmounted by a host of wooden carvings, the altars silver- or gold-plated. A huge lectern stands at the centre of the choir, one on which the Mass books of Morales and his contemporaries must once have been placed, with the choir and instrumentalists gathered round. It is typical that neither the architecture nor the music made concessions to the native traditions of the city's ancient culture. European models were the only ones felt suitable for Christian worship. The instruments played by the Indians were Western and their Spanish masters purchased them from Seville (the patriarchy of all Christian churches in the Americas).[3] In any case, early in the seventeenth century the Archbishop of Lima decreed that all indigenous instruments should be destroyed.

The cathedral in Mexico City is the oldest in New Spain, founded in 1528. Here again the musical provision was lavish. The indigenous Indians evidently understood Western music well, for within two years of the cathedral's founding it had a competent Indian choir singing the finest Renaissance polyphony, trained by a Franciscan missionary Pedro de Gante at a school founded by him. The texts of two surviving pieces from this early period are in Nahuatl, but such concessions to local culture were rare.

Instrumentalists retrained and drawn from the local population were involved in worship, their names appearing on the cathedral's payroll from 1543. Other cathedrals in South America soon followed the example of

Mexico and Lima. Some of those with lively musical traditions were Pueblo (Mexico) founded in 1531, Guatemala (1534), Caracas (Venezuela, 1567), Bogotá (Colombia, 1533), Quita (Ecuador, 1535) and La Plata (Bolivia, before 1564).

Artistic resources continued to pour into the cathedrals and churches across much of Central and South America, though not all appointments were successful. A certain Gonzalo Zorro (1548–1617), a *mestizo* (he was the son of a Spanish sea-captain who had married an Indian) was appointed cathedral organist at Bogotá. That he was not up to the job is clear from the tribunal that fired him in 1585:

> He does not know counterpoint nor understand the proper ways to make cadences. He is so unskilful that when a singer loses himself, he cannot immediately set him right nor help him find his place on the page… A person this ignorant deserves not even the name of a good student, much less the post of *maestro de capilla* in a metropolitan cathedral such as ours.[5]

But Zorro seems to have been an exception, and the cathedrals usually benefitted from fine composers able to equal the best musicians of Europe. Lima Cathedral, for example, enjoyed the excellent polychoral music of Torrejón y Velasco (1644–1728), followed by the more operatic music of his Peruvian successor, Orejón y Aparicio (1705–65).

Not far into the nineteenth century, the scene changed. Spain and Portugal gave up their colonial aspirations during a period of political turmoil. Vast tracts of Spanish territory were ceded to the United States or became independent. The close associations of the Roman Catholic Church with the former colonial powers now acted to its disadvantage – it suffered from strong anti-clerical feeling in some areas and financially fell into a decrepit state. The church remained strongest in Peru, Bolivia, Ecuador and Chile, but less so in Paraguay, Uruguay and Brazil. The new governments permitted a huge influx of immigrants from Europe. Thus, for example, a group of Scots settled near Buenos Aires in 1825, some Welsh moved to Patagonia the following year and Italian Protestants came to Uruguay in the 1850s. By the end of the century there were communities in South America representing virtually every Western European country. With them, borders were also open to Protestant missionaries – in many areas for the first time.

The extraordinary diversity of worship-music in Latin America springs from this cultural mixture. Africans brought their own powerful cultural traditions and mixed with the Indians and Europeans. Indigenous Indians have lived alongside people of European descent for just as long. Very slowly – perhaps over hundreds of years – the cultural mixture may settle and musical traditions merge. There are already signs of this in some areas of Christian music. Such a diverse and complex scenario can only be touched on here through one or two examples showing how the music of the cultures involved have exchanged and adapted their Christian music.

Syncretism

The Roman Catholic legacy is an extraordinary one. The Christianity forced on the natives was inevitably only partially absorbed: the names of the personalities were understood (Mary, Jesus, the saints), the liturgy was seen and enacted, but the essential tenets of the faith were not generally disseminated. In consequence pre-colonial religious practice is hidden under what is often a thin shell of Christian ritual. This syncretism is widespread in the countries where Roman Catholicism was weakest, applying equally to Indian, African and *mestizo*[6] cultures. Its most dramatic form can be seen in the eastern coastal areas of Brazil, most of all in Bahia, which has a high black population. Here the religious traditions of the African Bantu have created *macumbas*, the Yoruba parallels being *candomblé* in Bahia and *xangó* in the north east. In all these, African gods have become identified with Christian figures: Oxala parallels Jesus, Xangó Saint Jerome and Santa Barbara, Ogun Saint Anthony and Saint George... The music of the *candomblés* reflect the ecstatic elements of African tradition particularly strongly. As in some African indigenous churches, the aim is possession and trance, after the saint has been 'brought down':

> When all are properly arranged for the ceremony in the principal room of the *terreiro* – the *filhas* [sons/daughters] *de santo* in a circle, the *pai* [priest or father] and the *mae* [mother] *de santo* in the centre, the drummers on one side, and the spectators in the back of the room – the *pai de santo* begins the sacrifice to *Exú* [banishing evil]. After this *despacho* come the songs and dances dedicated to the various *orishas* [spirits]. These continue till late in the night, the rhythm marked by the beat of the drums. It is a choreography hallucinating to the *filhas de santo*, with the total participation of the body – arms, hands, legs

and head – in movements and contortions, rhythmic at first and progressively intensified and violent, unceasing until the onslaught of the spasmodic manifestations and the final phases of the *queda no santo* [falling into the saint, or trance]. The *filhas de santo* then seem to be dominated by a furious insanity, leaping about, giddily hallucinated by the monotonous and deafening noise of the drums and by the refrains of the magical songs. The most resistant sing and dance... the whole night through, unless they 'fall into a saint'.[7]

This *baixo espiritismo* – low spiritism, as it is locally known – is a powerful influence among the huge numbers of uneducated poor in the shanty-towns, but reflects a more general and fundamental recognition of a spirit world, further demonstrated by the success of spiritualist cults:

> We [Brazilians] still live under the full dominion of a magical world... impregnated by magic. The medicine man, the fetisheer, has... a prestige considerably greater than the director of our destinies... Any prophet with cabalistic formulas... attracts a large clientele. A spectre, the power of 'mana' dominates the festivals.[8]

Roman Catholic worship

Roman Catholic liturgical music earlier this century was not in a good position to edify its congregations. The people may have respected the church and its liturgy but they often did not understand it. The musical resources in most churches were exceedingly slender. Here is a description of a congregation at Good Friday mass held in a church in the small Andean town of Huaylas (in Peru, north of Lima), around 1960:

> Except for the most devout, an attitude of calm aloofness often prevails among the congregation... A good deal of the time, many were gazing at the floor or merely straight ahead... Some looked at the altar with occasional flashes of interest, but rarely... Old women came in dresses, generally ankle-length... they are treated with respect and... seem to participate in all the singing and responses, knowing the verses from memory. Most of the lower class people sat at the base of the side altars around the walls or else sat on the floor in the aisle... A large number of the people do not participate in the singing.[9]

Processions are always associated with the major feasts of the church year. These can be secular or sacred in tone, depending on the occasion and its tradition. The former, the *fiestas*, are extravagant excuses for general celebration, with dancing, singing in the streets and a great deal of drinking. The religious processions are more sober affairs, and in a small country town like Amusgos in Mexico, again on Good Friday, are strongly reminiscent of processions illustrated and recorded in medieval European documents:

> On arriving our way is blocked by a throng of people (most of the populace) in a religious procession, filling up the main... street. The sight is spectacular – the procession is depicting Jesus' walk to Calvary. There is a man dressed as Jesus, carrying a tall, heavy wooden cross, a 'centurion' colourfully costumed and riding a beautifully bedecked horse. There are four or five musicians – reeds, trumpet, trombone. They repeat a prayer-like intonation, the leader chanting/praying, and the murmur of the crowd behind them... Most of the women are barefoot, their hair dropping to their waist... We amble along with the procession towards the church. The musicians enter, and so do the characters in the dramatisation; the centurion and his horse, though, remaining outside.[10]

This description dates from 1980, by which time instrumentalists were welcome to enter the church, no doubt still playing (but not the horse). Vatican II was indirectly the cause of this and of further possibilities for renewal, eagerly grasped by the city churches. An early musical product of this liberation is the *Misa Criolla* (1964) by the Argentinian composer, Ariel Ramirez (b. 1921). This is a mass setting using an approved Castilian text, casting the various sections in the forms of traditional Argentinian dances. Thus the Gloria has the characteristic rhythms and melodic shape of the *carnavalito*, the Credo of the *chacarera* and the Agnus Dei of the slow and thoroughly sentimental *estilo*. The solo tenor is complemented by a chorus, the voices accompanied by a band of indigenous instruments such as the *quena* (flute), *sikus* (panpipes), *charango* (five-string guitar) and *bombo* (drum). The popularity of *Misa Criolla* is extraordinary. The recording sales have reached several million and every Latin American folk-group (Christian or not) plays or sings at least some of its numbers. Ramirez followed it with a delightful cycle of nativity pieces, *Navidad Nuestra*. In the remoter areas of Latin America, however, change is slow, and indigenous styles of music-making are only gradually making their way into formal worship.

Protestant worship

One of the phenomena of Latin America is the impressive growth of Protestant worship in the latter half of this century. churches supported by organisations based in the United States have become enormously successful. The Assemblies of God, the Pentecostal Evangelical Church and Brazil for Christ have been active in this area for a number of years and have experienced amazing expansion.

The Christian church has a huge task of evangelisation and teaching on its hands. The *candomblé* and other cults have been legitimised by the Brazilian state. Before 1976 any public ritual involving drum-beating or dancing had to be approved by the police *delegacia de Jogos e Costumes* (delegation of Games and Customs). Now they are seen as part of the traditions of the country and as an important tourist attraction.

Competing with hardened traditions on the one hand and ecstatic and wild rituals on the other, Christian music is now identifying more and more with the common stylistic currencies of popular music. The process began in the 1940s, when European missionaries began to question the wisdom of superimposing their own worship-music onto a different culture. It is surprising that this colonial attitude was still at work even in the remote country areas where the problem of assimilating alien music was most obviously acute.

Kenneth Case, a British missionary, illustrates the change of attitude that was long overdue. Among the Quechuan Indians of the Andean mountains traditions of music-making are linked closely with pre-colonial times. Some of their musical instruments date back to the Incas, as do the musical types associated with them. Up to the 1940s, Christians hoping to evangelise the Quechua had not looked to the indigenous music. The Quechuan pentatonic musical tradition was so secure that their singers were incapable of imagining or pitching a note lying between the minor thirds of the scale-system. European hymn-tunes caused insuperable difficulties. Furthermore, the missionaries brought with them English texts translated first into Spanish, then into a poor Quechua which the congregations hardly understood. From his arrival in Peru in 1940, Case was determined to improve the situation and studied the language, initially to make a better translation of the Bible. Then, with the help of a Quechua-speaking Christian, he composed hymns and choruses in Quechua. He immersed himself in the music too, writing dozens of melodies which were sufficiently stylish for the Indians to accept as additions to their folk-music.

The impact of these songs was profound, for through them the local people heard the essentials of the gospel for the first time. At first the music was accompanied by a small European harmonium and then by local musicians using the two most popular instruments, the *quena* (the long notched-flute of Inca tradition) and guitar-like *charango*. Two *quena* may present the melody in parallel fourths or fifths, rhythmically harmonised in simple triads by the *charango*. A fuller ensemble might include *sikus* and *bombo*. The hymns and choruses follow the simple metrical patterns of the folk-music, with clear cadences and structure. Case was lucky to be working with a style which could absorb Christian song so readily.

Example 43 shows one of Case's chorus melodies to a Quechuan translation of John 8:12.[11] This is similar to the musical idiom of *huayno*, a social Inca dance and now an emblem of Peru. More recently, Christian hymns and songs in the local dialects of Quechua have proliferated, encouraged by conferences which are held from time to time for bible-study, prayer and the exchange of songs now created by the Indians themselves.

In the coastal and city areas the Christian music is more cosmopolitan, disseminated by bands headed by a vocalist. Without doubt the best known of these at present is Marcos Witt, a Mexican evangelist and singer. His music is spreading to churches all over Latin America, but he is particularly well known in Mexico and Peru. His six-man group makes colourful music

EXAMPLE 43

with a driving beat (such as the song *Vencio*) provided by electric bass and keyboards, synthesising popular Latin-American dance-forms with plenty of indigenous percussion.

Dance music

Churches in Latin America have long agonised over secular society's enjoyment of music with strong erotic associations. Dance has long been at the centre of popular music on the continent and is now an icon of the huge *fiestas* held in every conurbation. At the beginning of the century the enthusiasm for dance was boosted by the extraordinary vogue for the *tango*, which spread like wildfire across to Europe in 1914. Church leaders, such as the Archbishop of Paris, did not hesitate to react:

> We condemn the dance of foreign origin known as the Tango, which by its lascivious nature offends morality. Christians ought not in conscience to take part in it. Confessors must in the administration of the sacrament of penance enforce these orders.[12]

The *bandonéon* was a type of accordion taken out to Latin America by nineteenth-century missionaries to accompany chant in the absence of an organ. The instrument was eagerly adopted as a folk instrument outside the church doors. The Archbishop of Paris was probably unaware that it was the *bandoneón* that epitomised the sound of the tango.

While there was no suggestion that the sound of the tango should be heard in churches in 1914, the present-day introduction of dance music to the liturgy by Christian bands is an issue for intense debate. It is seen as essential by some and inappropriate by others. During the ascendancy of the Protestant Pentecostal churches the trend is certain to continue, but it is an indication of the diversity of Christian music in Latin America that the Calvinist church in Lima continues to sing its unaccompanied psalms much like its denominational forebears did in sixteenth-century Switzerland.

Notes

1. J. de Léry, *Viagem à Terra do Brasil*, São Paolo, 1967.
2. See H. Stobart, 'The llama's flute', *Early Music*, vol. 24/3, August 1996, p. 471.
3. F. Guaman Poma de Ayala, *El primer corónica y buen gobierno*, J. Murra and R. Adorno, editors, Siglo Veintuno, Mexico, 1980.

4. See R. Stevenson, 'European Music in Sixteenth-century Guatemala', *Musical Quarterly*, vol. 50/3, July 1964 and R. Stevenson, *Music in Aztec and Inca Territory*, Cambridge, 1968, pp. 274–92.

5. Quoted in R. Stevenson, 'The First New World Composers', *Journal of the American Musicological Society*, vol. 23/1, Spring 1970, p. 99.

6. Combined Spanish and Indian descent.

7. T. Lynn Smith, *Brazilian Society*, Albuquerque, n.d., p. 140.

8. A. Ramos, *O Negro Brasileiro*, São Paulo, 1940, translated by T. Lynn Smith, Brazilian Society, Albuquerque, n.d., p. 126.

9. P.L. Doughty, *Huaylas*, Ithaca, NY, 1968, p. 224.

10. P. Garland, *Americas*, Santa Fe, 1982, p. 246.

11. Words from *Diospa Siminmanta Takikuna Huanta*, 4th edition, Peru, 1964; music from the 5th edition (n.d.).

12. Quoted in N. Slonimsky, *Music of Latin America*, New York, 1945, p. 61.

Chapter 39

Christian Music in Australasia

The Pacific islands

As a condition of support for his scientific expedition of 1765, the explorer James Cook (1728–79) was given secret instructions to search for *terra australia incognita*, the 'unknown southern land'. He landed in Tahiti in April 1769, a few months later rediscovering what turned out to be New Zealand. He then surveyed 2,000 miles of Australian coast before returning to Britain by the Indian Ocean and the Cape of Good Hope.

Thirty years later, in 1796, Tahiti was already known to be a likely spot for Christian missionary endeavour. Thomas Haweis persuaded several denominations to provide the funds for a mission:

> On frequent reflection upon all the circumstances of these islands, ever since their discovery, I have been persuaded that no other part of the heathen world affords so promising a field for a Christian mission: where the temper of the people, the climate, the abundance of food, and early collection of a number together for instruction, bespeak the fields ripe for harvest.[1]

Within a further thirty years Christians from all over Europe had caught the same vision and their presence was established all over the Pacific Islands – United States' missionaries arriving in Hawaii and Tierra del Fuego in the 1820s, Methodists in Tonga, the Solomon Islands and Fiji in the 1830s – and almost every other denomination was to follow.

The effect of this Christian invasion was profound. Along with the new religion came Western customs, a wide diversity of European languages, the destruction of the traditions of island life, the establishment of new political systems, literacy, a cash economy in place of barter, and 'cargo' – a word rapidly learnt by the indigenous populations and representing Western goods brought in the missionaries' supply ships. It included weapons, tobacco and alcohol. As the missionary James Chalmers wrote: 'Today's gospel with the natives is one of tomahawks and tobacco; we are received by them because of these. By that door we enter to preach the Gospel of Love...'.[2]

In some areas (New Guinea) the inhabitants welcomed their white guests; in others there was fierce resistance, from the Fijians in particular. However, the islanders in general proved surprisingly receptive to the Christian faith, which was brought to them in advance of the invasion of settlers. Churches became – and remain to this day – the focus for island social life as well as for worship and education.

By 1813 the missionary John Davies (d. 1856) was already introducing Christian music to the islanders of Tahiti:

> Mr Davies had by this time composed some Hymns in Tahitian, and introduced singing and prayers into the school which was a new thing and engaged the attention of the natives. Singing was also introduced to the native worship and catechising exercises, first by himself, and gradually adopted by the other brethren.[3]

As early as 1815 in Tahiti the gospels had been translated into the local language and a chapel was in use in which the worship included singing and prayer in Tahitian. By 1817 there were already '700 of the spelling books printed in London, catechism printed in Sydney 1,000, N Test[ament] history 400, Old ditto 400, hymns 100, spelling books 2,000 making in all 4600.'[4]

Clearly these hymnbooks were in English, for two years later a collection of John Davies' Tahitian hymns was published on the press recently set up on Huahine Island.[5]

At an early stage, too, it was evident that the Tahitians themselves, once converted to Christianity, often made excellent teachers and preachers:

> All the missions in Polynesia have availed themselves largely of native assistance. The Episcopalians in New Zealand, the Congregationalists in the Sandwich Islands [Hawaii], the Presbyterians in the New Hebrides, and the Missions of the London Society, early adopted this agency... The natives... have been styled Sunday-school teachers, schoolmasters, catechists, teachers, preachers, class-leaders, deacons and pastors.[6]

One of the first tasks of the missionaries was to wean the natives from their traditional cultic practices. This not only meant the destruction of the 'relics of idolatry', but the discouraging of 'native dances' and the music-making that went with them. However, the Tahitians were evidently interested in the praise-songs of the new God, and the *himeni* (songs) of the missionaries were quickly absorbed into a rapidly changing Tahitian culture.

While the loss of the music that the *himeni* replaced is seen to be a deep tragedy by many musicians nowadays, the legacy of the 200-year tradition of Christian music is a rich one. In churches all over the Pacific islands there is an amazing variety of music-making, the most interesting of which represents a symbiotic mixture of Western nineteenth-century hymnody and local traditional music.

In spite of the vast distances separating the hundreds of island communities (the extreme dimensions of the area exceed 8,000 kilometres) singing in harmony and often *a capella* is common practice. The choirs spring from the life of the churches, where they lead their congregations in generally unaccompanied singing. In return, the congregation support their choir in a spirit of friendly competition with neighbouring churches. On a small island there may be as many as four or five choirs, each eager to outdo each other in excellence. They may in consequence rehearse for long stretches two or three times a week. The music is learned by rote, either from a number notation (Example 44 from the Marshall Islands provides an example), orally from the conductor or perhaps off a blackboard.

EXAMPLE 44

358

There are a number of distinct musical types within this choral tradition, their styles varying widely between the islands. The generic term is *himeni*, *himeni tuki* (throat songs) being characteristic of the Protestant churches of the Cook Islands and *himeni nota* of the French Roman Catholic areas such as Samoa, Fiji and Tonga. The latter are the most clearly Western in origin (recognisably the songs of Sankey or Alexander) and are often accompanied by a chordal instrument of some kind. *Himeni tarava* (long-sounding songs) are perhaps the most extraordinary of this repertoire and are most highly developed on the Tahitian islands. The fundamental harmony is pentatonic, but (depending on the size and expertise of the choir) in a complex and dense web of as many as sixteen parts. A central homophonic core of singers, singing in dense chords and with words delivered rapidly and rhythmically, is surrounded below and above by other lines (several individual voices descanting) and underpinned by slower-paced men's voices. One of the independent voices will be the cantor, whose initial musical sentence sets a section of choral music in motion. The whole is quick, excitable, with a tight and syncopated ensemble, sung with full voice and an open throat. The brilliant wall of sound created by a large Tahitian choir with their superb intonation is electrifying.

A unique and possibly disorienting feature of *himeni tarava* is cultivated by some choirs: towards the end of each phrase (as the sustained final notes approach) the music slides flat – depending on the tradition, either imperceptibly or drastically – perhaps by a tone or more. To a Western listener it can cause the musical equivalent of vertigo, but for the Tahitians it is a device of beauty and clearly deliberate, as the cantor recovers the original (or an even higher) pitch level for the following phrase. No one knows how this extraordinary practice has arisen. While it may antedate the arrival of the missionaries, it may be that the islanders have turned to creative use one of the worst faults of western choral singing, providing another example of the renewal that can arise from cultural collision.

The complexity of the *himeni* differ – some are strophic and hymn-like, others are longer and formally more free, like anthems or short cantatas. While the traditional style of the music is highly prized, the words are usually recent, because many pieces are written in celebration of an event – the visit of a church dignitary, the name day or dedication of a church building – the music being commissioned by a local composer. Although these are Christian choirs, their music includes traditional songs about the history and ancestry of their society. 'Old' hymns are sung, but their words are unlikely to go back further than the lifetime of the singers. In this way, the musical tradition continues to evolve while new songs are being written.

The increasing average age of most choirs betrays the lack of interest the younger generations now show in island traditions. Those who have not left for a more hectic life in the big cities favour music from the United States. Younger Christians are singing worship songs with guitars in a style hardly different from their Western mentors. If their disinterest in their island traditions continues, the unique Christian music of Oceania will not last far into the next century.

New Zealand

Evidently the Maoris were not impressed with the Westerners who started visiting their islands after James Cook rediscovered them in 1769. They were perhaps aware of the threat that potential settlers posed – and their traditional settlement of disagreement by violence (*utu* – revenge) was a deterrent to settlement for some years. But Samuel Marsden, an Evangelical Christian with considerable missionary experience in Australia, had befriended some Maoris who had emigrated to New South Wales. With their help he was able to establish a mission to New Zealand and held what was probably the first Christian service there on Christmas Day 1814, in the Bay of Islands, beginning with the 'Old Hundredth'.

Progress in establishing Christianity was slow, but the party did not suffer a violent end, and by 1825 the first Maori baptisms began. From then expansion of the faith was rapid – within another dozen years there were fifty-one schools and thirty-five missionaries supervising congregations totalling about 2,000 people. Following the pattern in the Pacific islands the Maori language was given a written form, parts of the Bible translated, and catechisms, the liturgy and hymnbooks printed. At least one barrel organ had arrived by the late 1820s. Methodists characterised their missionary work by encouraging the Maori to retain their musical traditions, adapted to the new faith. Thus forms of worship characterised by the Maori language (and perhaps in part influenced by their traditional singing style) grew up before any white settlements were established.

The first permanent settlers arrived at Port Nicholson (Wellington) in 1840, then at Nelson and New Plymouth in 1841, but church activity was stronger in the settlements of the North Island, especially in Auckland, which was the colonial capital until 1865 and not far from the point Samuel Marsden first landed. It was at this time also that the French Roman Catholic missionaries began work among the Maori. The Treaty of Waitangi (1840) was an agreement between some of the North Island tribal chiefs to cede their lands to Queen Victoria in return for protection and security. It also proved a successful colonial move to prevent political domination by the French and the United States. Although Scottish Presbyterians arrived in Dunedin in 1848, where their Presbyterian Church continued the time-honoured practice of singing metrical psalms unaccompanied, the dominant Christian denomination has been, and still is, the Anglican Church.

There is some evidence of instruments being used to accompany singing among the Anglican settlers who arrived in Canterbury in 1850.[7] But George Selwyn, the first Bishop of New Zealand, was a high churchman with different musical ideals. Selwyn soon established a College (St John's) for the training of Maori clergy. Its wooden chapel outside Auckland, built in 1857, had no organ: 'We never had an organ or anything of the kind in the chapel: no need for it when the chants "Veni Creator", "Sanctus" etc could be rendered by the whole college for a choir.'[8] The chapel remained without an organ into the 1970s.

In the town itself, the band of the 58th Regiment was the potent musical resource, marching to church playing operatic airs, then, more controversially, entering and accompanying the hymns within. However, the Tractarian ideals of George Selwyn gradually gave Anglican worship in New Zealand a more decorous character, the early Maori influences turning quickly to an English pattern. The organist Robert Parker (1847–1937) contributed a great deal to the raising of musical standards in the Anglican choral tradition and by 1881 Christchurch Cathedral had a choir-school, and the elaborate services held there drew some local criticism. Its first organist and choirmaster was Henry Wells, who presided over a turbulent period of musical rivalry among a number of local choirs. Following a barren period, the musical standards at the Cathedral have been high since being raised from a low point by the organist J.C. Bradshaw (1876–1950).[9]

The high-art of the Anglican Church in New Zealand is thriving today. Five Anglican cathedrals (and the Roman Catholic cathedral in Christchurch) maintain a strong tradition in the traditional liturgy. The earlier pioneers of New Zealand feature little in their repertoire, but a number of living composers are making a strong contribution to sacred music: Douglas Mews (St Patrick's Roman Catholic Cathedral, Auckland), David Hamilton, Martin Setchell (Christchurch University), David Griffiths and John Wells are all writing significant choral music for worship. The choral conductor Peter Godfrey developed a choral tradition of world-class standing at Wellington Cathedral in the 1980s.

While it is right to expect that church music in New Zealand has generally followed a British pattern, represented by a similar denominational mixture, the Maori and immigrant Pacific islanders have a rich musical tradition which includes their own positive response to Christian music from an early point. As a missionary to the Maoris wrote in 1842:

> It is a most pleasant sight to see these people at church, and to hear them repeat the responses. Such perfect time do they keep, so completely in unison are their voices that the sound is as the measured tread of a large body of men.[10]

Since then the Maoris have responded creatively to European music and have continued to make Christian music their own, particularly through choral singing. Maori choirs were already strong early this century, such as the Waiati Maori Choir of the Methodist Maori Mission. Nowadays the Pacific island and Maori choral traditions can be heard in services in Auckland.

In 1990 the Anglican Church adopted a significant new constitution, dividing itself into three organisations, *Tikanga Maori, Tikanga Pakeha* and *Tikanga Pacifica*, representing the Maori, the European and Pacific Island peoples of New Zealand. They each have their own organisation and discipline, but are answerable to the General Synod and share a common Prayer Book (in the appropriate languages) and a common commitment which recognises different expressions of faith and worship.

The *Tikanga Pakeha* is experiencing many of the changes of priority that have affected churches in Britain, underpinned by a strengthening awareness and acceptance of the multiculture of New Zealand. Thus parish robed choirs have declined in number, sanctuaries have been redesigned, instrumental music and music groups flourish, Taizé music is widely used at prayer times and mid-week meetings and the worship song is to some extent replacing the traditional hymn. There is also some interest in singing *a capella*, perhaps influenced by the musical traditions of the other two *tikanga*. The publishing of music books *New Harvest* in the early 1970s and *Servant*

Songs (1987) reflected these changes, but the present situation is well represented by *Alleluia Aotearoa, Hymns and Songs for all Churches* (1993).

Other denominations are experiencing similar developments – the music of the Iona Community has been adopted by some Roman Catholic churches, which in turn are moving towards a renewed appreciation of their earlier musical heritage. In the Anglican *Tikanga Pakeha* there is a similar concern over the danger of a too-wholesale rejection of tradition. Across the denominations there is an interest in indigenous (as well as North American) Christian song-writers such as Geoff Bullock (Australia) and Colin Gibson (New Zealand). Along with the revised liturgy, John Wells has written settings of congregational texts, shortly to be published.

Australia

The early history of Australia is distinct from that of New Zealand, giving Christian music a different context in its earliest stages.

A British colony was first established in Australia in 1788, much earlier than in New Zealand. The development of new settlements was rapid, and within seventy-five years five states had been established and the interior explored. For the first years of this period Australia was a penal colony, the initial settlement in Port Jackson (later renamed Sydney) being for convicts. The population of local hunters and food-gatherers was too scattered to offer any resistance to the invading settlers; it simply moved further into the bush. Hence there was no advance guard of missionaries to the indigenous tribes of this vast continent. Christian missionary work and funds were directed mostly towards the settling population, who in the early years were almost all affiliated to the Church of England. It was some time before other denominations established an organised presence – the Methodists in 1815 (in the form of the itinerant preacher, Samuel Leigh), the Roman Catholics in 1820, Presbyterians in 1824, the Baptists in 1831. The development of non-conformist churches in Western and South Australia was delayed by many more years.

The Church of England in Sydney at this early point resembled the early years in New Zealand. With no organs in church (the first church building was put up in 1793) the military were asked to provide accompaniment for worship, as a letter from the Governor Macquarie makes clear:

> Sir – please pay to the bearer, M. Francis Dietrich, Master of the band of the 73rd Regiment, the sum of 2 pound, 11 shillings, 0 pence in lieu of six pairs of shoes due to him as remuneration for conducting the band in performing sacred music at church at Sydney from October 1, 1812 to March 31 inclusive, charging the same to the Police Fund.[11]

Macquarie was also instrumental in building a number of churches. By the time he retired, in 1821, there were six.

The Roman Catholic Church in Australia was created largely through Irish immigration, and when the first official priests arrived (Fathers Terry and Connolly were sent from Ireland in 1819) they were interested to find liturgical music in Sydney already in an orderly state. Catherine Fitzpatrick, an Irish schoolteacher, had been training the first congregation since her arrival in 1811 (she came to be near her convict husband). These early services were held in a hotel, which at other times would resonate to the sounds of the local regimental band playing polkas and quadrilles for dances. In 1830 the first chapel, St Mary's, was built, eventually becoming Sydney's Roman Catholic Cathedral.

What about Christian missions to the Aborigines? These proved far less successful than those among the Maori. After all, the Maoris' culture was not so different from the European that they were not able to understand and absorb the Christian faith with relative ease. The Aborigines had an utterly different lifestyle – possibly 40,000 to 60,000 years old and suffering little change in that immensely long time. Even the fundamental assumption of a settled life – living in fixed dwellings – could not be made. Consequently missionary activity among the Aborigines was particularly difficult and its history punctuated by projects abandoned after a few years.

One case, however, deserves attention, not only because music played a significant part, but because it illustrates the missionaries' methods and results in such an unlikely task. From the 1840s monastic orders were established in Australia, none now better known than the Benedictines of New Norcia, about 130 kilometres north of Perth. Bishop Rosendo Salvado, born in 1815, is still a well-known historical figure in his native Spain. He joined the Benedictine order of St Martin at Compostela when he was fifteen, where it was quickly evident that he had exceptional musical talents, especially as an organist. After moving to Cava in Italy on the suppression of Spanish monasteries, he offered his services as a missionary to Western

Australia, arriving in Perth in 1845 with twenty-seven companions. The group split into three, each being granted twenty acres of land from the Colonial Governer. Salvado was one of the four making up the central mission.

After a gruelling walk northwards for about 140 kilometres, it became clear that Salvado's party had miscalculated: they had insufficient resources to survive and Salvado had to return to Perth to raise desperately needed provisions:

> I decided to make the rounds of the richer Protestant families and ask them for contributions... when the idea occurred to me of offering the public a piano concert. The plan... seemed indeed to be blessed by God, because all the inhabitants of Perth vied with one another in making it possible... On the evening of May 21st I faced a distinguished and thickly packed audience.
>
> I wore my usual monastic habit, but was in a sorry shape indeed. My tunic reached only as far as my knees, and from there on was a thing of rags and tatters; my black trousers were patched with pieces of cloth and thread all of different colours... add to that a beard which had been growing for three months... and a deep tan on my face and hands.
>
> My heart was unable to share in the joyful congratulations and the excitement; I could only think of my four brethren dying of starvation in the bush.[12]

These inauspicious beginnings and the eventual establishment of a Benedictine community at New Norcia is told by Salvado in his memoirs. They reveal him to be an intelligent man, compassionate and respectful of the Aborigines whose welfare he put above all else. He detested the low esteem in which they were held:

> What can give a better idea of the attitude of many settlers towards the native than the plea put up by the barrister in Sydney at the trial of a settler accused of the wilful murder of a native... He had the audacity to claim that a cannibal savage stands under condemnation by the natural law, so that killing him cannot be regarded as a crime. How far can perverse philosophy go?[13]

Salvado was too busy in the early years of the development of his bush mission to turn his attention to music, but he was one of the few white colonists who won the respect of the Aborigines. He did this by learning their languages and studying their social customs, including their music and dance. In return, he gave them reading, writing (which they were exceedingly quick to grasp), Christian instruction and a host of practical skills which he hoped would allow them to hold their own in the culture that was overwhelming them:

> The first thing to do is to teach [the Aborigine] as quickly as possible how to fend for himself by means of agriculture or the basic trades, and after that one can improve his mind by forms of knowledge that belong to a civilised society.[14]

Eventually, music was to be one of those 'civilising' influences, particularly among the children. They were trained to sing the chants of the Roman Catholic liturgy, to play musical instruments and to give concerts. The *Daily News* gave a glimpse of the situation in 1892, albeit colonial, idealised and gently patronising:

> I am informed that the blacks for a hundred miles around have all been drawn within the humanising influence of the mission. Here is found a quiet, industrious, wage-earning, well-fed and happy lot of people. All their wants are attended to and well-supplied. And, in addition, they learn to read and write and have the ordinances of religion placed before them. To these they carefully conform, and more regular churchgoers and devout worshippers may not be found in Italy or Ireland. The Bishop, furthermore, has trained a band from among them for musical purposes, and there are string and band performances every evening of the week in the small millhouse. A Brother is in charge of them as director. Most of the village folk, including the white residents but not the Brothers, may be found here of an evening enjoying the performance and joining in the singing.[15]

The monastery and its community still thrive among Mediterranean architecture of surprising beauty. Its musical tradition continued in the work of the Spanish Benedictine Dom Stephen Moreno (1889–1953)[16] and more recently of Dom Eladio Ros. Moreno's numerous published Mass settings, motets and hymns were widely sung in Australia during the early years of the century.

After Salvado's death in 1900 the mission to the Aborigines and its unique musical outcome became less of a priority as attention was turned to

Christian education, mostly of white children. Recently, though, the identity of Aboriginal culture is being recognised and supported by the Roman Catholic Aboriginal Catholic Ministry in Melbourne. It was formed in 1986, a year marked by a meeting of Aborigines with Pope John Paul II.

Although the Roman Catholic population in Australia has always been numerous, it was the Anglican Church that put most energy into Christian music, as in New Zealand. In the nineteenth century the English traditions of Anglican worship provided a welcome psychological link to the Mother Country. English architects were commissioned to build cathedrals: Butterfield for St Peter's in Adelaide and St Paul's in Melbourne, J.L. Pearson for St John's in Brisbane (begun in 1901 and only now nearing completion). Symbolically, these cathedrals have material embedded in them from English counterparts: St John's has stone from Canterbury and altar marble from Iona Abbey; Grafton Cathedral has stone from Bristol, Adelaide from Canterbury and Westminster Abbey.[17] All these have contributed to the celebration of state occasions, holding parades and annual services for many organisations which have their close counterparts in Britain.

Naturally, the music conformed to the English Tractarian pattern – by the twentieth century the early days of instrumental accompaniment were long gone. The organists and choirmasters of the cathedrals and large parish churches created musical respectability both in and out of their buildings. As well as leading and teaching their choirs they established choral societies, offering music-making experience to large numbers of enthusiastic amateurs. After all, these were the days before the state funding of orchestras and opera, which only began with the Sydney Symphony Orchestra in 1946.

One of the Anglican composers directing energy into liturgical music today is June Nixon (b. 1942), who has been organist and master of the choristers at Melbourne Cathedral since 1973. Melbourne is the only Australian cathedral that sings seven services a week with their choir of men and boys, a tradition continued in the face of financial difficulties (the choir has no foundation). The scene is a lively one, centred musically round a fine organ by T.C. Lewis (1890, and recently restored).

The moment when the *Australian Prayer Book* was adopted (1978) was a moment of significant change for Melbourne Cathedral (some other cathedrals have chosen to remain with the 1662 Prayer Book). The Prayer Book's new texts in modern relaxed English (close to Rite B of the English

Alternative Service Book) created a need for new music which Nixon chose to compose herself rather than commission from outside. Over the next year or two she wrote three Eucharist settings which are still regularly used at the Cathedral, along with four settings of responses for evensong. These remain unpublished so far and form a modest contribution to musical individuality in the cathedral's worship. Nixon's music is in wider circulation in the form of organ works and hymn arrangements for choir.

June Nixon is among a number of composers who have responded to congregational opportunities in the revised Anglican liturgy, such as Paul Paviour (b. 1931) and Rosalie Bonighton (b. 1946).[18] The work of other Australian composers can be found in the *Australian Hymn Book* (1977, and soon to be revised), which is the product of a strong ecumenical movement among Anglicans, Methodists, Congregationalists, Presbyterians and Roman Catholics. Its indigenous music is well represented by some fine hymns by Robert Boughen (b. 1929, and organist of Brisbane Cathedral) and by the Roman Catholic, Russell Connelly (b. 1927), setting words by James McAuley. In most of the latter, hymn verses are interlaced with a refrain in the manner of a responsorial psalm. The hymn book is a remarkable compilation of the best of many English-language traditions, from metrical psalms and Lutheran hymnody to Welsh Methodist tunes, Vaughan Williams' transplanted English folk-songs, the best two hymns of the Twentieth Century Light Music Group, songs from the renewal movement of the 1970s and international songs from African and India. It is available outside Australia as *With One Voice* (1979).

As in Britain, the intensity of musical activity in the Roman Catholic community is less great than among the Anglican. Only two Roman cathedrals (Sydney and Melbourne) have choirs of men and boys, for instance. On the other hand, there is generally more new music being written for parish church worship. The best-known figure is the United States composer Marty Haugen (b. 1950), particularly through his *Mass of Creation*, but the psalm settings (*Psalms for Feasts and Seasons, Psalms for the Journey*) of the Australian composer Christopher Willcock are well known. Willcock has also written liturgical music for congregation and choir which attempts to give a creative role to each (*God Here Among Us*).

Evangelical worship-music in Australia has had strong ties with the United States for many years, but the last decade has seen an increasing number of Australian writers, composers and performers developing their own well-organised distribution. Two centres are influential, the Hills

Christian Life Centre and Christian City Church at Oxford Falls, both in New South Wales. The Hills Centre has a broad range of activities within the evangelical Christian world, including the *Hillsong* annual conference (established in 1988, and similar to *Greenbelt* in the UK) and a Leadership College (unusually) offering training in music as well as in ministry. Christian City Church (also known as CCC Brookvale) has been producing recordings since 1984 and its 'Seam of Gold' label is widely known. *Black Stump* and *Wonderfest* are two other lively Christian music festivals in Australia.

Perth is the centre for a number of Christian musical activities – it has a Christian orchestra (similar to the New English Orchestra) and a Christian radio station, *Sonshine fm*, which has been broadcasting since 1988. *Sonshine fm*'s manifesto suggests it is a church without walls: it offers a counselling service, is staffed by volunteers who must be committed Christians and is supported financially by a comprehensive variety of churches in the city. However, it divides its musical output between Christian and 'mainstream' music (in the idiom known in the trade as 'adult contemporary'), so it is debatable whether this can be said to bring worship into the home. Only a small proportion of its music is from Australian artists (most is North American), but the station will certainly be playing some songs which would find a place in the worship of evangelical churches. An offshoot of *Sonshine fm* is the Internet site *Australian Christian Music*, which co-ordinates information about musical events, personalities and recordings in contemporary Christian music.

Notes

1. T. Haweis, 'The very probable success of a proper Mission to the South Sea Islands', *The Evangelical Magazine*, 1795, vol. 1, pp. 261–70; quoted in C.W. Newbury, editor, *The History of the Tahitian Mission 1799–1830 Written by John Davies*, Cambridge, 1961, p. xxix.

2. Quoted in J. Pettifer and R. Bradley, *Missionaries*, London, 1990.

3. Newbury, p. 156.

4. Newbury, p. 209.

5. *E Parau Himeni, Oia Te Arue E Te Haamaitai I Te Atua*, Huahine, 1819.

6. *Missionary Magazine and Chronicle*, 1 November 1856, p. 227.

7. See J.M. Thomson, *The Oxford History of New Zealand Music*, Auckland, 1991, p. 33.

8. J.H. Evans, *Churchman Militant: George Augustus Selwyn, Bishop of New Zealand and Lichfield*, London, 1964, p. 110.

9. See Thomson, p. 95.

10. Quoted in Thomson, p. 194.

11. Quoted in J. Mansfield, 'Australian Church Music – then and now', *One Voice*, 1988, vol. 3, Part 1.

12. E.J. Storman, *The Salvado Memoirs*, Perth, 1977, p. 43.

13. Storman, p. 120.

14. Storman, p. 119.

15. *Daily News*, Perth, 13 February 1892, quoted in *The Story of New Norcia*, New Norcia, 1991, p. 24.

16. See Geoffrey Cox, 'Church Music', in *The Oxford Companion to Australian Music*, Oxford, 1997, p. 110.

17. D. Hilliard, 'Anglicanism', in S.L. Goldberg and F.B. Smith, editors, *Australian Cultural History*, Cambridge, 1988, p. 19.

18. A fuller picture is given in Cox, pp. 109–10.

PART 9
Music in Twentieth-Century Europe

Chapter 40

Roman Catholic Music
in Europe

In the twentieth century the Roman Catholic Church has made two of the most vigorous statements on music and its role in the liturgy – the *motu proprio* of 1903 and its culmination, the *Constitution on the Sacred Liturgy*, part of the Second Vatican Council (Vatican II) of 1962. The themes of the *motu proprio* – the revision of Gregorian chant, the restoration of unaccompanied polyphonic singing (following Palestrina's example) and the encouragement of the composition of modern liturgical music – were part of the reforming spirit of the times and have had far-reaching effects. The most dramatic of these was the widespread revival of Gregorian chant, in a form drastically revised by the monks of Solesmes and closer to its origins than at any time since the fifteenth century.

The author of the *motu proprio*, Pope Pius X, had this to say about the revival of Gregorian chant:

> Sacred music must… possess the qualities which belong to liturgical rites, especially holiness and beauty, from which… universality, will follow spontaneously… These qualities are found most perfectly in Gregorian chant… which… the Roman Church… insists on being used exclusively in some parts of her liturgy, and which, lastly, has been so happily restored to its original perfection and purity by recent study.[1]

He also proposed the chant as the ideal music for restoring congregational participation at parish level, so often neglected by the church in the past. Renewed interest in the chant provided an opportunity to redress this balance, for the chant contains a rich collection of melodies which, like the best folk-music, are tested by time and are simple and easy to learn. Although the *motu proprio* said nothing about chant accompaniment, it was quite explicit about banning the piano, along with all noisy or irreverent instruments such as drums, kettledrums, cymbals, triangles and so on... Bands are strictly forbidden to play in church...[2]

An unaccompanied choral repertoire was encouraged, as well as new music for the liturgy, though the restrictions were severe:

more modern music may also be allowed in churches... nevertheless, since modern music has become chiefly a secular art, greater care must be taken, when admitting it, that nothing profane be allowed, nothing that is reminiscent of theatrical pieces, nothing based as to its form on the style of secular compositions.[3]

Finally, Pius X recognised that none of these edicts would have the slightest effect without there being better provision and training for musicians and (the most desperate need) some education in Christian music among the priesthood. Theological students were therefore recommended to study the 'principles and laws of sacred music... with all diligence and love'.[4]

The French organist/composer tradition

The number of musicians in France who took advantage of the *motu proprio* formed part of a renaissance of Christian music in Europe as a whole, allowing French cathedral music to move away from the more dismal moments of the previous century.

At first the chief focus of activity was the *Schola Cantorum*, a school of liturgical chant and music founded in Paris in 1896 by Charles Bordes, Vincent d'Indy and Alexandre Guilmant. The talents of the most outstanding composers of the time, Debussy and Ravel, were lost to the cause of Christian music from the start – in spite of Debussy's appreciation of Palestrina – but the *Schola* did attract some fine artists in its early years, of whom Louis Vierne (1870–1937) is the best known among church musicians.

Vierne's world-wide reputation was acquired by his recital music for organ, virtuosic, highly coloured and sometimes aurally dramatic as in the finales to his organ symphonies. At the same time his *Pièces en Style Libre* for organ or harmonium significantly improved the music available to the parish church organist who did not know how to use his feet.

Vierne and Charles Marie Widor (1845–1937) were only two of a number of organist/composers working in France in the early part of this century. Between them they have provided organists with an exceptional variety and richness of music. Charles Tournemire (1870–1939) was one of the most industrious, writing a huge cycle of organ pieces, *L'Orgue Mystique*, based on Gregorian chant appropriate for every Sunday in the church year – a kind of parallel to the cycles of cantatas by Bach or Telemann. They demonstrate the continuing Roman Catholic tradition which allows the organ to substitute for as well to support voices. The practice has continued to give French organists important positions as improvisers and composers for the liturgy. Tournemire's music has the rhythmic flexibility and the modality of an inveterate improviser on plainsong, creating a heady and numinous atmosphere wholly in keeping with its Roman Catholic tradition.

A similar quality is to be found in the music of Jehan Alain (1911–40) but with memorable strokes of imaginative genius. His *Litanies* for organ (1937) takes only a few minutes in performance; it is wholly based on the chant but its obsessive repetition gives the piece a unique quality of excitable and desperate supplication.

In contrast to the small amount of music Alain was able to write before his untimely death in action, his teacher, Marcel Dupré (1886–1971) wrote copiously for the instrument and toured widely as a recitalist – especially playing his own music. But the interests of these composers, albeit fostered by the musical life of the great Parisian churches – Notre Dame, Ste Clotilde, St Sulpice or La Trinité – emphasise the organ at the expense of choral music.

Jean Langlais (1907–90), while working within this French organ-playing tradition and travelling widely as a concert organist and composer for the instrument, had broader interests. Apart from organ works of dramatic improvisatory gestures and colourful modal reworkings of the chant (the *Te Deum* from the *Trois Paraphrases Grégoriennes* of 1934 is a deservedly often-played and typical example), he also made a lasting contribution to Christian choral music, both for choir and congregation. Here he usually chose idioms which are simple and direct.

In his *Missa Salve Regina* (first sung at Notre Dame in 1954), for example, the intricacies of choral part-writing generally give way to massive blocks of sound from voices, brass and organ, shouts of praise derived from fragments of the medieval plainsong *Salve Regina*. In this and other Mass-settings he returned to the harmonic and melodic sound-world of the fourteenth century, dominated by fifths and fourths, a compromise with outright modernity well suited to the ancient building for which the music was conceived.

Langlais is also one of the few modern French composers whose congregational music has become well-known – even outside his native country. The breadth and grandeur of his hymn *Dieu, Nous Avons vu ta Gloire* (Example 45) has acted as a model for a number of other hymn-writers, especially in America, where Langlais developed an enthusiastic following.

EXAMPLE 45

Olivier Messiaen

Of all the composers in this French organist tradition, none has compelled more attention than Olivier Messiaen (1908–92). This is partly because he wrote more copiously and more broadly than the others, but it is also due to the content of the music and the ideas that brought it into being, which have ranged very widely – far beyond the usual confines of Christian music.

Messiaen's involvement with the church of his faith was intense, in spite of increasing demands on him as a teacher and celebrated composer. He was appointed organist at La Trinité in Paris in 1931 (at the early age of twenty-two), playing consistently for years for the three Sunday Masses; he also taught at the *Schola Cantorum* from 1936.

Chant, which Messiaen studied and endlessly accompanied, filled much of his perspective on music, but his inquisitive mind was remarkably inclusive – of the sounds of modern Western music, of the music of nature and of the East. Such a diversity of inspiration led him to imagine sounds of startling colour and variety, but with very clear, even obsessive, trains of thought binding them together and making his work instantly recognisable.

In common with other organist/composers in Widor's tradition he was a superb and striking improvisor. But again like them he wrote almost no vocal music for the liturgy:

> for example a traditional mass with Kyrie, Gloria, Sanctus, Agnus Dei, no, that I have never written. I have only composed long organ works… playable in whole or in part during a low mass, and which comment on the texts appropriate to each mystery, with the [prayer] that flows from them.[5]

The organ music he wrote even before his appointment to La Trinité demonstrates some extraordinary qualities. The most striking is its pace, which in terms of the conventions of Western music is painfully slow. *Le Banquet Céleste* (1928) is notated in 3/2 time but at a speed of fifty-two quavers to the minute. At this rate the first chord lasts almost seven seconds, every bar (whose contents are fairly sparse) takes almost a quarter of a minute to play and the whole piece (a mere twenty-five bars) at least six minutes.

It requires a special mental discipline from the player to slow his or her musical metabolism sufficiently to meet the needs of this music. Indeed, it can only be done peaceably by adopting a state of tranquil meditation and ceasing to expect anything of the music but an eternity of restful change. The player's technical difficulties at such a pace are slight, but unless one's expectations of music are profoundly rethought, such slow musical evolution can become tedious or frustrating. As in so many of his works, Messiaen is here contemplating a mystical truth, suggested both by the title and its sub-heading, which is based on the words of Jesus: 'He who eats my flesh and drinks my blood lives in me and I live in him.'

His choice of musical symbol is simplicity itself: a long melody, very gradually ascending in a series of arch-like contours to reach the upper limit of the organ keyboard, then slowly subsiding to extinction. It is a musical image to which he returned again and again, for instance in *Combat de la Mort et de la Vie* (no. 4 of *Les Corps Glorieux)* or in the motet *O Sacrum Convivium*. The underlying harmony of *Le Banquet* is based around the key of F sharp major, but the chord-changes are so infrequent that their dynamic sense of progression is very much dissipated.

Although *Le Banquet* was an early piece its composer already had a remarkably clear sense of purpose – to create music which is contemplative rather than dynamic, universal rather than personal, ecstatic and symbolic rather than rhetorical. To reinforce these characteristics, Messiaen soon moved away from using key signatures in his music and instead used scale systems of his own, which have little precedent in any music before the twentieth century.

Anyone who has struggled with the practising of scales knows that the distribution of their large and small intervals (the tones and semitones) is deliberately asymmetrical; it is this that allows the degrees of the scale to take on identifiable roles, such as 'tonic' (key-note) 'dominant' (the tonic's opposite pole) and so on. Because of Messiaen's choice of scales with a symmetrical plan of tones and semitones (he called them 'modes of limited transposition') such identities are no longer clear and any music written in these modes is bound to take a big step away from a conventional harmony that stresses progression through time, so-called 'functional' harmony.

In rhythm too, Messiaen soon moved away from tradition. The regular time signatures of *Le Banquet Céleste* gave way to an unpredictable and irregular barring – in which, as often as not, he will not trouble the player with time-signatures at all. Such a rethinking of tradition is commonplace among many Western composers since Stravinsky, the great renewer of rhythm, but Messiaen is spurred on as much by the text-governed rhythms of plainsong as by trends in modern classical music.

All these characteristics can be found in an organ piece entitled *L'Apparition de l'Eglise Eternelle* (1932). Its chord structures mostly conform to Messiaen's modes of limited transposition and begin the piece in a strange and exotic sound-world. Once again the arch-like melodic contours build culminatively to a high point, this time a long-sustained blaze of C major as the eternal church is sensed in its full glory before the vision fades to extinction. The rhythmic contour of the melody is an unpredictable weaving of long and short notes which refuse to fit to a regular pattern – a close parallel of the freely-flowing style of plainsong performance favoured at Solesmes. It must be remembered, too, that this music was first imagined in the huge spaces of La Trinité and is best heard in similar surroundings, the music rendered impersonal both by the cavernous acoustic and by the (probably) invisible performer.

During the 1930s Messiaen wrote much more for the organ, in carefully planned sets of pieces: *L'Ascension* (1934), *La Nativité du Seigneur* (1935) and *Les Corps Glorieux* (1939). In their complete form, these collections can have no place in liturgy, but the separate movements are heard as voluntaries and occasionally as meditations during worship. They are Christian music in the specific sense that their titles and their content draw the listeners' attention to spiritual and mystical dimensions of the faith. They do this not only by the specific images of their titles (such as 'God among us' or 'the mystery of the Holy Trinity') but also by quoting plainsong melodies which can provide associations with passages of scripture (even though the melodies are adapted to Messiaen's own special modes).

The most challenging and extraordinary developments in Messiaen's music began in about 1949. For some time he had been adorning and embellishing his basic principles of composition in a way that parallels the increasing complexity of medieval Christian music. He elaborated the melodic strands based on plainsong into streams of chords and superimposed modes on each other, sharply raising the level of dissonance. He heightened further the contemplative mystical and ritual qualities of the music by incorporating rhythmic patterns drawn from Hindu musical traditions and, most of all, by emphasising the independence of simultaneous events. Sometimes this conveys the impression that different strands of the music are evolving at differing speeds.

Then he wrote a series of keyboard pieces, some for piano, some for organ (*Livre d'Orgue, Messe de la Pentecôte*), in which his imaginative powers took a series of further leaps into unprecedented areas. Example 46 is the central

EXAMPLE 46

section of the 'Sortie' from *Messe de la Pentecôte* (1950). It is a compendium of Messiaen's favourite techniques, serving to symbolise God's creation in nature (through birdsong) and the universe (by number). The organist's left hand plays a stream of chords generated from Messiaen's fourth mode of limited transposition while the pedals play pitches from the sixth mode. In each case the durations of event either increase or decrease by one semiquaver (the numbers give the durations in semiquavers of each event). The right-hand stave is a freely chromatic transcription of the Song of the Lark.

The organ pieces are all the more remarkable for their new vocabulary of sounds, using combinations of stops and registers that had never before been considered musically viable. Messiaen seems here to revel in new possibilities of all kinds; and most startling of all, some of the music is intended for the liturgy.

Beyond his organ music, however, Messiaen was typical of many other French organists in showing less inclination to set texts for church use. Only his short (though beautiful) motet *O Sacrum Convivium* (1937) is really appropriate in the context of worship. His other settings of mystical texts have, on his own confession, another purpose:

> my two principal religious works played in the concert-hall are called *Trois Petites Liturgies de la Présence Divine* and *La Transfiguration de Notre Seigneur Jésus Christ.* These titles are not chosen at random: I intended to accomplish a liturgical act, in other words to carry a service or some kind of praise into the concert-hall. My chief gift is to have taken the essence of the Catholic liturgy intended for the faithful out of its stone edifices and to have placed it in other buildings apparently not made to accept this kind of music, but which in the end have strongly welcomed it.[6]

Notes

1. From the *motu proprio*, and quoted in R.F. Hayburn, *Papal Legislation on Sacred Music*, Minnesota, 1979, p. 224.

2. Quoted in Hayburn, p. 229.

3. Quoted in Hayburn, p. 225.

4. Hayburn, p. 230.

5. O. Messiaen, *Musique et Couleur (nouveaux entretiens avec Claude Samuel)*, Paris, 1986, p. 20.

6. Messiaen, p. 22.

Chapter 41

The Bible in the Concert Hall

Messiaen's achievement in bringing Christian meditation into the concert-hall is really nothing new – oratorios and Mass-settings still sustain a tradition, now more than 300 years old, of bringing such music into secular surroundings. Unfortunately, the church this century has shown little inclination to support composers of high art – especially where their style is challenging or uncompromising.

An era which has enmeshed millions in two world wars and which has seen some of the worst atrocities ever committed against humanity has extracted a powerful reaction from its artists. Many musical works, while not commissioned or even recognised by the church, have a spiritual depth virtually absent from the repertoire of the previous century which did receive ecclesiastical support. On the one hand, George Bernard Shaw, writing in England in the early 1890s, could remark with partial truth that

> with the exception of a few cantatas of Mendelssohn, all the Biblical music of this [nineteenth] century might be burnt without leaving the world any poorer.[1]

On the other hand, the church in the twentieth century has taken little part in what has turned out to be a renaissance in concert music of spiritual or Christian challenge. The composer John Joubert has written:

> It is a pitiful comment on the musical awareness of our church authorities that only in 1958 was Benjamin Britten invited to conduct a work of his own at a Three Choirs Festival. And William Walton's oratorio *Belshazzar's Feast* had to wait twenty-five years before being included in the same Festival programmes – long after it had been accepted everywhere else in the country.[2]

At the very beginning of the century in England, Edward Elgar (1857–1934) set to music an extended poem by the English Catholic and former Tractarian, Cardinal Newman. *The Dream of Gerontius* (1900) immediately put the artistic standards of the English oratorio onto a quite different plane from the 'religious' music that Shaw loved to hate. This was the work of which Elgar said: 'I have allowed my heart to open once'[3] and undoubtedly the emotional intensity which accompanies the spiritual journey of the poem is unprecedented in British music and has rarely been equalled since.

Soon after this, a younger generation of composers was acquiring new techniques and applying them to large-scale choral pieces. An early and vivid example is by the Swiss composer, Arthur Honegger (1892–1956). His *King David* (1921) is an oratorio drawing on the books of Samuel and presented by a narrator, with chorus, soloists and orchestra.[4] Honegger followed it with a number of other large-scale oratorios, some requiring staging, the most spectacular of which is *Joan of Arc at the Stake* (1935). In a few of his last works, such as the *Christmas Cantata* (1953) he turned from the epic and the stressful to the pastoral and quietly visionary.

The other outstanding Swiss composer of the century is Frank Martin (1890–1974). Like Honegger, his music is widely performed on the European mainland but seldom heard in Britain. He was the son of a Genevan Calvinist minister and became a convinced Christian himself. While believing that he had to express the individuality rather than the universality of his faith (which was certainly broader than Calvinism) he returned constantly to the central themes of Christianity in his work.

Martin's first and last important pieces (the *Mass for Four Voices* (1921–29) and the *Requiem* (1972)) draw on Roman Catholic liturgy, but perhaps his oratorios are the most compelling. The majority, apart from the war-torn *In Terra Pax* (1944), elaborate on central themes of the New Testament: *Golgotha* (1948), *The Mystery of the Nativity* (1959) and *Pilate* (1964).

For Igor Stravinsky (1882–1971), expatriate though he was for most of his life, it was Russian music that had the most enduring effect – not simply the classic and folk-music of his youth, but also that of his native Orthodox Church. In 1926 he reaffirmed his Orthodox faith, celebrating a new spiritual dimension to his life over the next few years by setting some liturgical texts in church Slavonic for unaccompanied chorus, *Otche nash'* (Our Father), *Simol' verî* (the Creed) and *Bogoroditse devo* (Hail Mary).

On a much larger scale Stravinsky designed a symphony around three psalms (39, 40 and 150). The serenity of the resulting *Symphony of Psalms* (1930), especially of its conclusion, partly stems from its reminiscences of Orthodox chant and from the pure sound of children's voices required for the upper parts of the chorus (though the latter request is seldom honoured in performance).

Stravinsky's desire to write music for the Ordinary of the Mass came some years later, in the form of the *Mass for Chorus and Ten Wind Instruments* (1948). Although Stravinsky intended this as Christian music – that is, for liturgical use – it was not commissioned by the church. Its manner is as distant as possible from the rhetoric and individualism of the Romantics, returning to the meditative universality of early Christian music, at one time so much desired by Roman Catholic reformers. Why therefore is it seldom heard in the context of the liturgy? The expense of engaging the musical expertise is doubtless one reason, but it is nevertheless another loss to the established church that it cannot find room for Western music that symbolises the faith so profoundly.

Since the composition of Elgar's *Dream of Gerontius* and the two large-scale oratorios that followed, *The Apostles* (1903) and *The Kingdom* (1906), British choral music has been as rich as the previous century's was poor. In particular, the threat of war or its reality has evoked some spiritually impassioned music, from Vaughan Williams' *Dona Nobis Pacem* (1936) – an uncannily prophetic piece – to Michael Tippett's *A Child of our Time* (1941) – the reaction of a courageous pacifist to war – and Benjamin Britten's *War Requiem* (1961).

More recently, Britten created further opportunities for biblical texts to be heard in concert as the result of experiencing the theatrical traditions of Japanese Noh. The result was *Curlew River* (1964), in which 'spiritual music theatre' is acted out in a setting of medieval Christendom. Britten wrote *Curlew River* as a concert piece designed for church performance and followed it by two more, *The Burning Fiery Furnace* (1966) and *The Prodigal Son* (1968).

In all these 'church parables', the influence of Noh-play and the spiritual dimension of the texts led Britten away from the emotional and expressive world of his earlier music. In doing so, he (and Stravinsky in the *Mass*) opened the way for a reassessment of the very nature of concert music, a move which has had an increasing effect on the way composers work and on the expectations of audiences.

New musical forms

In this century's music the grammar of 'functional' harmony, that is, the changes of harmony that are intended to convey a strong sense of journey through time, has been challenged. Generally the result has been an adaptation of this tradition rather than a complete rejection of it. Most twentieth-century music therefore expresses or evokes emotion through familiar means and by using familiar codes.

The Stravinsky Mass and the Britten 'church parables', however, suggest the possibility of music with new (or rather, much more ancient) priorities. Their music has been a cue for a number of more recent composers to distance themselves further from the rhetoric of the concert hall.

The keen interest in minimalism over the last few years – a movement which has strong connections with Eastern cultures – is a sign that composers and their audiences are rediscovering another function for music altogether, one which is contemplative and static. If there is a sense of journey in the music at all, the pace is very slow and travel is by foot rather than by air. There are strong resonances here with Messiaen.

The music of both Arvo Pärt and John Tavener, discussed in chapter 30, cannot often be called minimalist, but its evolution is leisurely and sometimes on an epic scale. Concert audiences have found some of this music difficult. John Tavener's large-scale musical canvasses, such as *Akhmatova: Rekviem* and *Prayer for the World* (both 1980) have conveyed to some 'a feeling of spiritual austerity rather inappropriate to the modern concert-hall'.[5]

But others have discovered a sense of renewal in concert music which explores once more the spiritual domain. The Hilliard Ensemble, a group of four singers specialising in both early and contemporary music, has established a special relationship with Arvo Pärt which came about in a significant way.

Up until 1987 his choral music was unknown in Britain and had received very few performances in Europe. Those few performances, given by choirs in tune with the Romantic classics (large numbers of voices, plenty of vibrato, a mass of individuals with little collective focus) dissatisfied critics and Pärt himself. The four voices of the Hilliard Ensemble concentrate on purity of sound, perfection of tuning and exquisite blend. Their voices revealed the true nature of Pärt's music for the first time: for them and for their audiences 'every performance is a spiritual experience'.[6] The Ensemble has since toured Pärt's *St John Passion*, a setting of Psalm 51 and other music springing from biblical texts in concert halls and cathedrals throughout Europe.

The British composer John Tavener has described concert music as a kind of outer courtyard to worship:

> Stockhausen has said that the concert hall will become the church of the future. I do not believe that this is the case, but I do think there is a kind of middle ground that deals with the sacred tradition bringing it back into the 'Temenos'. That is a Greek word that means 'the sacred area surrounding the temple'...[7]

The music of many Western composers today reflects both humanity's deep need for spiritual understanding and a tacit if not overt assumption of the existence of God. However, Tavener rightly regrets that the church seems so little prepared to support artists who have a Christian message. It is a tragedy that the vision of most Christians in positions of authority – at least in Britain – is still limited to a utilitarian function for music. Surely they should be alongside composers in their desire to stake out 'sacred areas', whichever temple they choose to surround.

Notes

1. Quoted in N. Tierney, *William Walton*, London, 1984, p. 64.

2. J. Joubert, 'Music and the Church' in F.J. Glendenning, editor, *The Church and the Arts*, London, 1960, p. 99. The Three Choirs Festival is an annual English musical week, dating from the early eighteenth century and originally solely of sacred works. It meets in turn at the cathedrals of Hereford, Worcester and Gloucester.

3. Elgar, letter to Jaeger, 9 October 1900.

4. *King David* is usually performed in the version for large orchestra with organ, but it can be even more effective in its original reduced version.

5. *Musical Times*, vol. 129, no. 1748, October 1988, p. 511. For the relationship of these works to the chant, see R. Taruskin, *Stravinsky and the Russian Traditions*, Oxford, 1996, vol. 2, pp. 1618–23.

6. *Music and Musicians*, vol. 38, no. 2, July 1990, p. 11.

7. *Music and Musicians*, vol. 38, no. 4, December 1989, p. 7.

Chapter 42

Vatican II and the Liturgy

After the long, too long stagnation of liturgical forms, the reform decided on by the Second Vatican Council was the signal to start moving. But waters held back too long and then released sometimes look more like a destructive flood than a necessary irrigation. The tide is the bringer of both life and death. It was high time the church made an effort to adapt, just as every other living body alters. But the change in the liturgy was so sudden and so radical, that it could truly be called a crisis.[1]

So wrote the French composer and priest Joseph Gelineau, on the radical reforms brought about in the Roman Catholic Church which started in 1963 with the publication of the *Constitution on the Sacred Liturgy*. Musicians involved in Roman Catholic worship were indeed impatient for that change long before it came about, particularly in the area of congregational participation.

The tenets of the *motu proprio* of 1903 had been emphasised and amplified by other documents (such as Pope Pius XII's *Apostolic Constitution, Mediator Dei* of 1947 and the *Instruction on Sacred Music and Sacred Liturgy* of 1958). All these urged that 'the faithful... should not be merely detached and silent spectators, but... should sing alternately with the clergy or the choir...'[2] But musicians such as Dom Gregory Murray (b. 1905) did not believe this could be achieved while the liturgy remained as it was. In the firm belief that even the simpler Gregorian chants were too involved for an average parish congregation to sing effectively, Murray wrote his *People's Mass* in 1950:

That it succeeded in achieving its aim was proved by the enormous sales the world over. Musically, as I am fully aware, it is undistinguished; but at last it made it possible for congregations to join in the singing of Mass with vigour and obvious enjoyment.[3]

Music for the people

The reforms put forward by the Second Vatican Council opened the door to drastic change. While stressing the timeless value of Gregorian chant in worship alongside other traditional aspects of Christian music, the *Constitution* emphasised the 'active participation of the people' again and again, permitting vernacular languages in worship instead of Latin. It noted:

> In certain countries, especially in mission lands, there are people who have their own musical tradition, and this plays a great part in their religious and social life. For this reason their music should be held in proper esteem and a suitable place given to it...[4]

To allow such a breadth of musical idiom in worship, the *Constitution* had to relax its attitude to the use of instruments, with the condition that instruments should 'truly contribute to the edification of the faithful'. Composers were encouraged to write under these new circumstances, allowing the congregation to participate actively.

The effect of this on music in the Roman Catholic Church was dramatic. In some areas the Council was only acknowledging what had already been tacitly accepted – for instance, that a great variety of styles of Christian music had developed across the world, from Africa to Latin America, and that the church should treasure and encourage it. But a selective adoption of this legislation, especially in Europe, led to rapid and sweeping changes. These, and the subjective interpretation of Vatican II, were viewed by traditionalists with alarm.

In an eagerness to bring Christian worship in closer touch with their congregations, churches abandoned Latin very quickly (a move permitted but not required by Vatican II) and as a consequence almost all the music associated with it was dropped. Inevitably, the incomparable heritage of chant and polyphony fell into immediate disuse.

The insistent demands that music was the property of the people generated strong anti-artistic feeling: singing in harmony by experts on behalf of the congregation was out, unison singing of simple music was in. Supporters and detractors of this trend were brought into sharp conflict. Lovers of the church's musical heritage were appalled at the erosion of valued tradition. In the initial wave of experiment, Roman Catholic churches throughout the West echoed to sounds never heard before within their walls. A flood of Christian music of the simplest kind was produced, taking its cue from all kinds of popular sources: dance music, modern folk idioms, pop ballads, and even from rock music. An extreme was reached in the late 1960s, when a few large liturgical events became difficult to distinguish from rock concerts.

In an attempt to clarify the dangers which they believed lay behind such musical permissiveness, a group of American Cecilians touched the heart of their problem: the reintroduction of the ecstatic and physical element of music in a tradition which had firmly resisted it since the times of the Church Fathers:

> Music which is directed predominantly toward the sensitive motor responses of man is not worthy of the liturgy. This music makes its appeal... only on the level of the purely sensual, even to the possible exclusion of the spiritual faculties... The rhythm of this music with its primitive and uniform impulse generates in the listener a sensual, driving excitement. This monotonous, continually repeated rhythm dulls consciousness... and dissipates into mere motor responses which serve to blot out all personal individuality. The prayer of a congregation, which ought to be vivified by the liturgy, is thus rendered impossible by music which evokes in men truly disorderly feelings and serves only to awaken essentially emotional drives...[5]

In reality, music with the overwhelming ecstatic qualities suggested here is the exception in Roman Catholic music of recent decades in the West. Quite apart from the continued resistance to it from some quarters, fairly few churches have the means or the expertise to produce it.

In among a great deal of ephemeral material which has been published in vast quantities for use among parish congregations, some music is of an order of excellence which amply justifies the turmoil that brought it into existence. The most enduring are the psalm-settings.

The renewal of psalmody

It was Joseph Gelineau who gave a new impetus to psalmody. In advance of Vatican II by ten years, he published a booklet entitled *Vingt-quatre Psaumes et un Cantique*, which proposed a way of singing the psalms in translations close to the original Hebrew and yet simple and tuneful enough for congregations. Unlike Gregorian or Anglican chant, it is based on the provision of regularly accented syllables (even though the number of syllables between them may vary). The provision of antiphons allowed for the psalms to be sung responsorially. These antiphons might be sung as a preface and conclusion to the psalm, or alternated with the verses, following the time-honoured practice of interlacing psalm-verses with a refrain. The music is of extreme simplicity, requiring only the most straightforward pitch-changes from one accented syllable to the next. Gelineau's psalms have proved immensely popular, well beyond their Roman Catholic origins. The gentle modality of his version of Psalm 23 (1952) has become a classic of its type (Example 47). Gelineau here closely follows the Hebrew verse patterns, with regular stresses but varying numbers of syllables. The unused notes of the chant formula come into play in subsequent verses. In time-honoured fashion an appropriate antiphon is sung at the beginning and end.

EXAMPLE 47

Gelineau's gift is not so much his settings as the method itself, for it encompasses so many possibilities for marrying biblical prose to music that many other composers have created their own versions of it.

In Britain, the composers Colin Mawby and Anthony Milner (among many others) have written some simple but tuneful responsorial psalm-settings for congregational use.[6] Milner's psalms alternate simple refrains for everyone with more involved settings of psalm-verses for choir; Mawby's are simple yet musically worthwhile. In Britain their example has been continued and extended by the St Thomas More Centre in London.

On another level, Joseph Gelineau has offered a valuable new perspective on the vexed disagreements over Roman Catholic liturgy. His deep spiritual awareness and firmly grounded love for God's people reads very differently from the indignation of the scholars concerning the effects of Vatican II. Writing in the late 1970s, he gave a positive view of the position in France:

> the assemblies do sing!... much more than they did a quarter of a century ago. Then nearly all the masses celebrated on Sundays, particularly in towns, were 'low masses', that is, without singing. The singing at high mass was generally mostly done by the choir. The Gregorian movement did succeed, with brave and persistent efforts, in getting some assemblies to join in the singing of the ordinary of the mass. But this never became general...
>
> Today the opposite is true. There is singing at most Sunday masses, especially in towns, where it is easier to find leaders of the congregation. And the singing is essentially by the congregation. The change was not brought about by a change in the general culture, but by the ideology of the liturgical renewal: 'The ideal form of community participation in the celebration is singing.' ... It is a product of the vitality of the assemblies or at least of their organisers.[7]

L'Abbaye de Silvanès

The need to foster Roman Catholic music of excellence has led to the founding of an important cultural centre at Silvanès in the Rouergue district of southern France. Its focus is a Cistercian abbey, abandoned and in ruins till about 1977. A number of artists then came together under the leadership of Père André Gouzes to re-establish it as a place of hospitality, of praise and of art.

The task of restoration is now complete and Silvanès offers a wide-ranging series of courses and spiritual activities associated with the liturgy. They include study of the history of the church and of chant, inter-faith colloquia, workshops on icon-painting, liturgical dance, calligraphy, bookbinding and even floral art, all within a Christian context.

But the main spiritual mission of Silvanès is its music, which is based on a respect for the church's liturgical heritage and can be seen as a reaction against the populist styles of worship permitted by Vatican II. Many of the courses are directed to helping choir-masters and clergy understand the nature and history of Christian music. Important feasts in the church's year are celebrated with large numbers of visitors, alongside opportunities to study voice-training, choral conducting and the theological context of chant. Père André Gouzes' *Liturgie Chorale du Peuple de Dieu*,[8] based on ancient chant from Western and Eastern Christendom, forms the musical basis of the centre's work and is being taken up in other parts of France.

Taizé

The ecumenical community at Taizé in France at present affects not only the musical taste but the worshipping patterns of congregations all over Europe – even world-wide. The community was founded in 1940 by Brother Roger, in an area where he had sheltered Jewish refugees during World War II. From the 1950s, small fraternities with the same commitment to celibacy and communal life were established throughout the world, particularly in places of poverty and need.

Although the first brothers were Protestants, Taizé has maintained close and warm contacts with the Roman Catholic Church and received constant encouragement from its popes. Indeed, in 1961 it arranged for a historic meeting of Protestant and Catholic clergy.[9] Today, the community of Taizé comprises almost 100 brothers of Catholic and Protestant origins. Since the 1960s the Taizé community has proved increasingly attractive to young people from all parts of Europe. The weekly meetings organised by the community of Taizé are for them a source of spiritual discovery and meditation. The numbers that pass through Taizé 'as one passes close to a spring of water'[10] is now very great and its style of worship has been carried back to Christian communities throughout the world.

EXAMPLE 48

The music of Taizé is characteristic, partly because it is closely bound up with the community's special dimension of peace and reconciliation, but also for the pragmatic reason that it has always had to be accessible to large numbers of people who speak many different languages. The community began by using psalmody from the sixteenth century and by Joseph Gelineau, but the composer Jacques Berthier was invited to create new music

> so that all could actively participate in the prayer of the Community...
> using simple elements... of real musical quality so that genuine prayer
> could be expressed through them... the brothers found a solution in
> the use of short musical phrases with singable melodic units that could
> be readily memorised by everybody.[11]

Latin is used quite extensively in these repeated refrains, not at all for traditional reasons, but because it is 'a foreign element for everyone, and hence neutral'. The verses sung by cantors or small groups may be in a number of languages in turn. Taizé provides evidence that the contention in the 1960s over the use or the abandonment of Latin in worship is no longer an issue for a new generation.

The excellence of the music of Taizé is not embodied in complexity or sophistication, but in orderliness. Some songs closely follow the strict balance of four parts required in the seventeenth or eighteenth century. Others use modal harmony with parallel movement more suggestive of the early twentieth. In every case, whatever the musical style, the link between the gentle stresses of the Latin and the rhythmic patterns of the music is very close.

Example 48 shows one of Taizé's best-known chants, in which the part-writing has been carefully balanced, even though the soprano and tenor are in unison for all except the final bars. The flexibility of Taizé music has brought it into use in all sorts of circumstances, from a small gathering with a guitar or keyboard to a large assembly accompanied by several instruments. In all cases, however, the music may appear empty unless it is used actively, for it is intended as a vehicle for prayer and meditation and is therefore only part of a greater Godward experience.

Notes

1. J. Gelineau, *The Liturgy Today and Tomorrow*, London, 1978, p. 9.

2. Pope Pius X, *Apostolic Constitution*, 1928.

3. Dom Gregory Murray, *Music and the Mass*, Leigh-on-Sea, Essex, 1977, p. 73.

4. A Flannery, editor, *Vatican Council II*, vol. 1, *The Conciliar and Postconciliar Documents*, New York, 1996, p. 33.

5. 'Resolution on the Use of Profane Music in Worship', quoted in J. Overath, *Sacred Music and Liturgy Reform after Vatican II*, Rome, 1969, p. 182.

6. Anthony Milner (b. 1925) is a fine composer of art-music – much of which is inspired by his Roman Catholic faith. He has made valuable contributions to congregational music, such as hymns and psalm-settings. Note also Colin Mawby's *Ten Psalms*, 1968.

7. Gelineau, p. 9.

8. Available from Atelier de Musique Liturgique, Abbaye de Silvanès, 12360 Camarès, France.

9. As Brother Roger has written: 'never resign yourself to the scandal of the separation of Christians, all so readily professing love for their neighbour, yet remaining divided'. *The Taizé Experience*, London, 1990, p. 57.

10. A comment by Pope Paul II on a visit to Taizé in 1986.

11. Music from Taizé (vocal edition), London, 1982, vol. I, p. vii.

Chapter 43

Lutheran Musical Revival

One beneficial effect of the Romantics' fascination for the past was the work that scholars did for Christian music. Quantities of early music were uncovered, for instance by the scholar J.A. Philipp Spitta (1841–94) who not only wrote a monumental study of J.S. Bach, but excited musicians' interests in the wider heritage of Lutheran music.

The heritage

Johannes Brahms (1833–97) was introduced to the music of Samuel Scheidt and Heinrich Schütz by Spitta. Brahms had a life-long interest in early music, but it is partially due to Spitta that he wrote so many unaccompanied motets under its influence. The *Two Motets*, opus 74 (1877), for instance, are reanimations of the spirit of the sixteenth and seventeenth centuries and dedicated to Spitta.

For a renowned composer of the time to turn his attention to this kind of music was most unusual. Compared with instrumental and solo vocal music (in the form of song or opera) there was little expertise or audience potential to draw on. Brahms' *Requiem* (1868) is in a form much more accessible to the music-loving and Christian public; it was reckoned in its day to be his greatest achievement.

Although the music of the *Requiem* adopts the accepted public manner of large chorus and symphony orchestra, its expert and pure polyphony still owes a great deal more to Christian music of the past than to the accepted conventions of the time. Brahms chose his own biblical texts for it, intending them to have a more universal application than those of the Roman Catholic liturgy. It is no coincidence that a number of them had already been set by Schütz (in the *Cantiones Sacrae* and *Geistliche Chormusik*).

Max Reger, in the next generation (1873–1916), was equally fascinated by early music. He too wrote a number of unaccompanied motets (*Geistliche Gesänge* opus 110, *Acht Geistliche Gesänge* opus 138) which are heavily indebted to Lutheran music of the seventeenth and eighteenth centuries. Their simplicity and emotional reserve contrasts starkly with Reger's turbulent *alter ego*, – for he also created music renowned for its intense emotionalism and uncompromising modernity. The dissimilarity within Reger's musical output is instructive, for it points up the vast gulf between what was then believed to be suitable for the rejuvenation of Christian music and the latest artistic developments of the Romantic movement. Some of Reger's many organ pieces provide striking examples of an intriguing but uneasy alliance of the old and the new. For in response to his view that J.S. Bach was 'the beginning and end of all music' Reger created organ pieces modelled on the typical structures of the early eighteenth century. Under these circumstances, the extreme emotionalism of their content is all the more shocking. Using techniques in common with Schönberg, he presents the listener with stormy and ambivalent music, chains of ambiguous chords changing so rapidly that a sense of key is all but suppressed.

Challenging and worthwhile though it is as music, this – the true voice of Reger – does not reconcile itself with the needs of the liturgy. Such intense rhetoric, typical of the way Romanticism was then developing, only serves to worsen the collision between the universal dimension of worship and the individuality of the music. To satisfy his heartfelt desire to renew Christian choral work Reger felt he had to lean heavily on ancient styles and techniques.

But after the First World War the unbridgeable gulf perceived to exist between the modern and the ancient became less of a problem. This was partly because a significant number of musicians found the self-conscious intensity of the Romantic movement cloying and jaded. Many of them were refreshed and much more inspired by the relative simplicity of Mozart or Pergolesi and through the prime example of Stravinsky found ways of renewing the past rather than merely of copying it.

New music

While these musical changes were taking place the Lutheran Church was beginning to reap the rewards of a long campaign to restore and revitalise its own music. By the 1920s organists and cantors were expected to be musically expert and were paid a reasonable wage in return. The state founded a number of schools where church musicians could be properly trained. First-class organs became more widely available in churches, many built following the traditions of Baroque times. Resources available for Christian music-making began once more to resemble those of the seventeenth century.

The reward of this injection of resources into Lutheran music was in the great number of composers writing for the church, many of them employed full-time. The list is a long one and includes such names as Arnold Mendelssohn (distantly related to Felix, 1855–1933), Johann David (1895–1977), Ernst Pepping (1901–81), Hugo Distler (1908–42) and Siegfried Reda (1916–68). Merely to mention these composers might imply their work to be of little interest. On the contrary it is truly excellent but simply too abundant to be discussed here. It includes music in the rich variety of forms characteristic of the seventeenth and eighteenth centuries: oratorios, passions, cantatas, motets, chorales and organ works.

Most important was the rediscovery of a way of setting words to music which heightens their intensity, rather than distracting attention from them by abstract musical invention. These composers allowed the natural rhythm and contour of dramatic speech to shape the musical lines, not the other way about. In this respect they share common ground with the most outstanding opera composers of their time such as Debussy, Janácek and Britten, but the inspiration still springs from Lutheran music of the past.

The wonderful dramatisations of the Passion story by Pepping and Distler for unaccompanied voices are good examples – both composers were inspired in a variety of ways by Schütz' *Passion* settings. In Ernst Pepping's *Passionbericht des Matthäus* (1950), the Passion story according to Matthew, the human drama is brought to life in the most compelling fashion.

The work of Hugo Distler, in particular, has added immeasurably to the stature of Christian music this century. It is a great loss that it is hardly known outside Germany. The music itself springs from a sincere faith, is inventive, skilled, accessible to its hearers and well written for choirs of all standards. Sensitive translation would certainly bring it a wider circle of admirers.

Distler (1908–42) felt his relationship to Schütz particularly strongly. He laid the foundations of his own music following Schütz' example, inspired by the knowledge that, like him, his motivations were a strong faith and the desire to make it known through music. The revitalising of word-setting was an essential part of that process of communication:

> [Distler] and other composers of his generation brought to an end the undisputed reign of instrumental music… through the rediscovery of the human voice, and of its marvellous, mysterious and plastic qualities… Because the voice is bound to the word, the burden of the words assumes paramount importance… For Hugo Distler this was, first and foremost, the message of the Gospel. He wished to spread it abroad through his music as a declaration, as sermon, song of praise, and as a proclamation… One can hardly fail to be affected by the forcefulness of his musical preaching.[1]

Distler worked at a number of churches, beginning in 1931 at the Jakobikirche in Lübeck. Here it was accepted that he should write the music for the church choirs:

> I have two choirs (a volunteer choir and a boys' choir) for which I compose everything myself. I already have a beautiful collection of this type of easy sacred music and hope that an entire year's repertoire will come into being from this. The children as well as the adults sing these polyphonic pieces with joy and ease.[2]

The result of this collaboration was, among much else, *Der Jahrkreis* (*The Year's Cycle*), easy three-part settings of Reformation chorales for each week of the year. This practical and edifying music sprang from the church's wholehearted encouragement of the creative gift of composition – rare outside the Lutheran community.

Distler's untimely and tragic death left much work unfinished – the nine motets which make up *Geistliche Chormusik* (1934–41) were intended eventually to number fifty-two – again, one appropriate for each Sunday of the year. Nevertheless, they are the most beautiful of all his work and include the remarkable *Totentanz*, a large-scale piece based on medieval texts from Lübeck's Marienkirche.

A more sinister parallel between Schütz and Distler is the political turbulence and oppression in which they lived. Where the Thirty Years War required Schütz to work with physical suffering and deprivation all around him, Distler was progressively caught up with the political oppression of the Third Reich. Soon after his move to Stuttgart in 1937, Distler was required to sit on a local examining board set up by the Reichsmusikkammer to 'protect the German people against the influence of undesirable and deleterious music, such as recordings by Jews and Negroes, or non-Aryan printed music'.[3] The tension of having to take part in such a flagrantly anti-Christian exercise may be imagined. Inexorably, too, the Lutheran Church was falling into disfavour with the Nazi government, who were alarmed by its continuing spirit of renewal. Hundreds of pastors who would not swear allegiance to the Nazi régime were removed to concentration camps; choirs were disbanded and calls to military service became more insistent. In spite of his appointment to the directorship of the Berlin Staat- und Dom-chor in 1942, the emotional strain was too great for Distler and he took his own life.

Example 49 shows Hugo Distler's manuscript of 'Wir danken dir, Herr Jesu Christ', a chorale for three children's voices which forms part of *Der Jahrkreis*.

After 1945

Since the Second World War, artistic creativity in Germany has continued at a high level. Perhaps in reaction to the suppression by the Third Reich of artistic modernity of any kind, a number of composers sought to renew Christian music with the techniques developed elsewhere by Bartók, Stravinsky, Hindemith and Schönberg.

In Siegfried Reda's music, for instance, the level of dissonance is noticeably higher than that of his teachers Pepping and Distler, with a consequent lessening of the numbers of choirs able or prepared to take it on. With Helmut Bornefeld he established the *Heideheimer Tage für Neue Kirchenmusik* which ran from 1946 to 1960 as a forum for new styles in Christian music.

This more exploratory attitude to Christian music had parallels with the startling developments in modern music in Germany, in which the *Internationale Ferienkurse für Neue Musik* (International Summer Courses for New Music) in Darmstadt, also established in 1946, played a large part.

It was here that young composers such as Karlheinz Stockhausen (b. 1928), Pierre Boulez (b. 1925) and Luciano Berio (b. 1925) came under the influence of Messiaen, taking aspects of their teacher's music (such as *Messe de la Pentecôte*) several stages further. Some of this music has Christian

EXAMPLE 49

resonances, such as Berio's orchestral *Nones* (1954) and *Allelujahs* (1954–58).

In 1956, Stockhausen wrote *Gesang der Jünglinge*, music of extraordinary originality and beauty based on the *Benedicite*, the canticle sung by Shadrach,

Meshach and Abednego when they were cast into the burning fiery furnace by Nebuchadnezzar. His resources were a recording of a boy's singing voice and electronic music, the resulting multi-track tape intended for five spacially separated groups of loudspeakers in the vast spaces of Cologne Cathedral. Church authorities could not cope with such sounds in such a context and the first performance was given by the radio station West Deutsche Rundfunk. A few years later Stockhausen severed his allegiance to the Roman Catholic Church because he 'could not abide by the rules'.[4]

Among composers for the liturgy, and hardly less controversially, Heinz Werner Zimmermann (b. 1930) has turned consistently to jazz as a renewing force in his Christian music. In a note to his setting of Psalm 113 he writes:

> Obviously unusual in this motet is the use of the double bass. Its even pizzicato must provide a strong rhythmic foundation for the five heavily syncopated choral voices above... I am conscious of the fact that this rhythm has parallels in the dance music of our day – as does the harmony. This is not necessarily unfortunate. I am hoping that a new vitality... may thus be injected into our church music.[5]

His congregational music follows the same pattern and has the same nervous energy. A great deal more hymnody and psalmody like this has been written in the last few decades.[6] Superficially it resembles the work of the Twentieth Century Light Music Group in Britain, but the music still stands on a foundation of Lutheran traditions and has a stronger intellectual basis.

Resources

The amount of activity in Christian music in Germany today is huge. It is symptomatic of the country's support for the arts in general: the city of Stuttgart spends more on the arts in a year than does the Arts Council on the whole of the United Kingdom. For Christian music a generous scale of funding is raised by a regional income tax.

This *Kirchensteuer* lies between eight per cent and nine per cent of the total tax paid depending on the region. The money raised is divided between the Lutheran (Evangelische), Roman Catholic and (interestingly) Jewish communities, according to the denominational representation of the particular region. Minority churches, such as the Anglicans, are not included in the scheme and therefore receive nothing. Opting out is possible: in the north it is easily and simply achieved by signing a form. In the south the regulations are tough: it might be necessary to go to court to avoid the tax. Even then there would be disadvantages in not paying, since the tax pays for a number of important facilities – such as funeral services.

The *Kirchensteuer* raises a large sum – well over 100 million DM every year – and is used for many purposes: to pay priests on the same level as civil servants (their salaries are perhaps four or five times those of Britain); to pay a living wage to full-time organists and choirmasters, even at parish level; to provide social welfare such as the intensive care of old people and to run many hospitals. As a result, churches remain important centres for parish life through the vital services they offer and have far-reaching opportunities for spiritual contact with the neighbourhood – which they may or may not take up.

However, in an increasingly multicultural world and during the necessary belt-tightening after German reunification, there is a growing chorus of complaint about the *Kirchensteuer*, with an increasing number of people refusing to pay because for them the activities it supports are irrelevant, or, they feel, should be supported in other ways.

In Lutheran Scandinavia church finances on a similarly generous scale come directly from the state, so for the moment the generous stipends for organists and choirmasters there is more secure.

In Britain the Lutheran Church of St Anne and St Agnes in London is the most active musically, following the German pattern, and spends nearly half of its budget on music, including the cantor's salary, fees for musicians and administration. Choral music accompanied by instruments is a regular feature of its services, including cantatas by Bach and Telemann. (Interestingly, new Lutheran music rarely features.) It also hosts an international programme of Lutheran Christian music played and sung by groups from all over the world, along with a regular series of lunchtime concerts of classical music each month.

Notes

1. Oskar Söhngen; quoted in L. Palmer, *Hugo Distler and His Church Music*, London, 1967, p. 104.

2. Letter from Distler to his former teacher Herrman Grabner, 17 April 1931; quoted in Palmer, p. 113.

3. For the musical ideology of the Nazi party, see N. Slonimsky, *Music Since 1900*, 4th edition, New York, 1971, p. 1393.

4. See R. Dufallo, *Trackings*, Oxford, 1989, p. 213.

5. Foreword to Zimmermann's *Lobet, ihr Knechte des Herrn*.

6. The hymn-book of the World Council of Churches, *Cantate Domino*, Oxford, 1980, contains Lutheran psalms and hymns by Zimmermann, Paul Rupperl (b. 1913), Rolf Schweizer (b. 1936) and Dieter Trautwein (b. 1928).

Chapter 44

Music in Britain

It must have been in 1904… when a cab drove up to the door and 'Mr Dearmer' was announced. I just knew his name vaguely as a parson who invited tramps to sleep in his drawing room… He went straight to the point and asked me to edit the music of a hymn book. I protested that I knew very little about hymns but… if I did not do the job it would be offered to a well-known church musician with whose musical views I was much out of sympathy… the new book was being sponsored by a committee… who were dissatisfied with the new *Hymns Ancient and Modern*…

I determined to do the work thoroughly, and that, besides being a compendium of all the tunes of worth that were already in use, the book should, in addition, be a thesaurus of all the finest hymn tunes in the world – at all events all such as were compatible with the metres of the words for which I had to find tunes. Sometimes I went further, and when I found a tune for which no English words were available I took it to Dearmer… and told him he must write or get somebody else to write suitable words. This was the origin of Athelstan Riley's fine hymn *Ye Watchers and Ye Holy Ones*…[1]

In this way the composer Ralph Vaughan Williams (1872–1958) helped to create the *English Hymnal*, one of the most influential hymn-books of the century. As Ursula Vaughan Williams pointed out

The eventual value of that uncomfortable job was his discovery that for many people the music the church gave them each week was the only music in their lives and that it was all too often unworthy both of their faith and of music itself.[2]

One of Vaughan Williams' most valuable contributions to the book was its new music, particularly the hymns by his lifelong friend Gustav Holst (1874–1934), such as *In the Bleak Midwinter*, and by himself. He made more excellent music available for use in worship through *The Oxford Book of Carols* (1928) and *Songs of Praise* (1925). In both these he collaborated with Martin Shaw (1875–1958), a composer with a similar vision for straightforward Christian music of the highest standard. Shaw's music for parish communion[3] and some of his hymns (for instance *Little Cornard*) are still sung.

The English musical renaissance

While the *English Hymnal* was setting new high standards in congregational hymnody and providing a welcome change from the sentimentalities of *Hymns Ancient and Modern*, Charles Villiers Stanford (1852–1924) was transforming Anglican service-music from its dismal and complacent state.

Stanford's Morning, Evening and Communion Services in G (1904) and in C (1909) are particularly fine, the first including a *Magnificat* of unusual serenity and beauty. With these settings and a number of anthems (less well-known), Stanford set standards for Christian music in Britain unknown since the days of Purcell and Handel. They have become so much the staple fare of cathedral and parish church choirs up and down the country that their continued use seems assured, in spite of recent changes to the Anglican liturgy.

Indeed, British music as a whole experienced a welcome renaissance at the beginning of the century, due not least to the inspiration and widespread influence of Stanford as a teacher. Much of the best and most enduring Christian music of this period came from composers whose careers lay outside the Anglican Church, where financial support of the kind enjoyed by the Lutheran musicians was not forthcoming.

An insecure Christian faith does not seem to have prevented a number of composers from writing very fine music for congregation or choir. Vaughan Williams himself, happy to be known as an agnostic, saw no reason why that should prevent him from writing liturgical music.[4] His celebratory settings of psalms and canticles, such as Psalm 47: *O Clap Your Hands* (1920), *Psalm 100* (1929) and *A Festival Te Deum* (1937) are all carefully designed to give amateur singers and players opportunities to worship through music of a high standard. As well as making dozens of traditional melodies more widely available (from the many seasonal carols to his arrangement for large forces of *The Old Hundredth Psalm Tune* (1953)), he composed some exquisite settings of words of Christian writers such as the *Five Mystical Songs* to poems by George Herbert (1911), and of scripture in the brief but unforgettable *O Taste and See* (1952).

In all this Vaughan Williams made no compromises with his creative personality in order to write Christian music. He experienced none of the problems of the Victorians as expressed by Barnby, nor did he turn, like Brahms or Reger, to a manner approved by its antiquity. The *Mass in G minor* (1921) might seem at first glance to be a loving reproduction of Tudor or Jacobean polyphony. It is certainly an expression of reverence for such music, which was then being heard for the first time since the seventeenth century, but the Mass is in the mainstream of Vaughan Williams' writing and does not copy anything. Its contemplative modality links it to his other outstanding art-works of the time – such as the *Pastoral Symphony* and *The Lark Ascending* – and in liturgical use has helped many cathedral choirs to escape from the faded sentimentality of their Victorian heritage.

Vaughan Williams was never employed by the church, and yet did more for Christian music than any of his contemporaries. John Ireland (1879–1962), however, was organist at St Luke's in Chelsea from 1904 to 1926, but this formal relationship with Christianity inspired little music from him.

As a pagan mystic and as a humanist, most of Ireland's energies went into other areas – his deserved reputation would never have been made on the strength of his service-settings and some very dull organ music. Just the same, his fine anthem *Greater Love* (1912) is firmly embedded in the cathedral repertoire and the excellent hymn-tune *Love Unknown* is known to millions.

Herbert Howells (1892–1983), like Vaughan Williams and Ireland, was a pupil of Stanford. Again, like them, he had doubts about the Christian faith but responded with profound respect to the people and places where the Anglican liturgy is sung:

> In all my music for the church, people and places have been a dual influence... Also a promise (mine) that if I made the setting of the Magnificat, the mighty should be put down from their seat without a brute force that would deny this canticle's feminine association. Equally, that in the *Nunc Dimittis*, the tenor's domination should characterise the gentle Simeon. Only the Gloria should raise its voice. The given promise dictated style, mood and scope.[5]

Thus Howells described his first set of Anglican canticles, called *Collegium Regale* and written for King's College Chapel Choir, Cambridge in 1944. In this and the five settings which followed[6] he adhered to these intentions sufficiently closely for them all to be instantly recognisable. Moreover, among cathedral musicians they are undoubtedly the most valued of the settings available. Howells' music, as he intended, seems the perfect response to the surroundings. Certainly the musicians can revel in the sensuous beauty of the opulent sounds required of them.

These canticles were written late on in Howells' career; like Vaughan Williams he made no concessions to the traditions of Christian music. They are also technically demanding. The melodies recall plainsong in their modality and rhythmic flexibility, but they are woven polyphonically around harmonies of a heady resonance that in other surroundings would delight the most hedonistic jazz enthusiast.[7]

The similarly high level of invention in Sir Michael Tippett's *Magnificat and Nunc Dimittis* (1961) unfortunately requires a level of ability which puts it beyond the reach of most choirs. Like Howells, he did not compromise his musical personality, which at the time was occupied with the new and astringent brilliance of the *Second Symphony* and the opera *King Priam*. Benjamin Britten (1913–76) wrote a great deal of choral music with a strongly Christian basis, but his choice of texts was broad and often influenced by his interest in drama and storytelling. The children's opera *Noye's Fludde* (1957) and the cantatas *Rejoice in the Lamb* (1943) and *St Nicolas* (1948) are in many senses music for worship, though they cannot often be used liturgically. Among a number of smaller choral pieces, it is the *Missa Brevis* (written in 1959 for Westminster Abbey) that has an assured place in cathedrals when the Eucharist is celebrated and a boys' choir only is available.

New music

All the above-mentioned composers are highly regarded in the world of British classical music and their contribution to liturgy is on a high artistic level. Today the standards may not be so impressive, but the quantity is as great as ever.

The Anglican tradition allows plenty of space for choral music in its sung services: anthems, two canticles, versicles and responses daily at evensong, with Communion settings and canticles for Sunday morning services in addition. Furthermore, changes to the Anglican liturgy and the two rites of the *Alternative Service Book* (1980) have created further challenges and opportunities. The quantity of music passing through a cathedral librarian's hands in a year is therefore enormous.

New pieces, however, are generally regarded (as they are in classical programming generally) as an occasional welcome diversion from the routine. With rehearsal time at a premium an unfamiliar piece must be 'user-friendly' if it is to have a chance of success. Most cathedrals and parish churches with expert choirs will commission pieces from time to time,[8] but under such pressured circumstances the music needs to conform to a house style to be successful at first use.

In this genre a convention for expressing celebration and joy consists of some modest syncopation (a distant echo of Stravinsky and Walton) to enliven the text, relatively easy part-writing achieved by doubling up sopranos with tenors, altos with basses, and a slightly tart harmonic language based on fourths rather than thirds and sevenths. William Mathias (1934–94), Bryan Kelly (b. 1934) and Kenneth Leighton (1929–88) show skills in this genre and between them have produced quantities of this type of Christian music. Leighton in particular offered greater depth. His settings of canticles are more challenging, but still widely sung and valued highly by good choirs.

There are, however, occasional pockets of enterprise and experiment. For example, every three years since 1980, Norwich Cathedral and the University of East Anglia nearby have presented a festival of Contemporary Church Music, a week of daily services in the cathedral interlaced with concerts. Alongside established canticles and anthems by living composers, the services give an opportunity to experience newly-commissioned music in the context of worship. The breadth of activity is wide-ranging: not only has the festival put music by composers of an advanced style into a liturgical setting (such as Harrison Birtwhistle, Peter Maxwell Davies, Paul Patterson, Philip Wilby and Giles Swayne) but at the opposite end of the spectrum it has provided a platform for the Christian orchestra of All Souls, Langham Place, and an evening of popular orchestral music and congregational song. Perhaps most significant of all is the organisers' willingness not only to ignore musical boundaries but denominational ones as well. The composers represent a wide spectrum of Christianity, not only Protestant and Roman Catholic: in 1989 a Vigil Service of the Orthodox Church was celebrated with music by John Tavener.

Winchester Cathedral is another centre which has established a fruitful relationship with new music, particularly through the work of Jonathan Harvey (b. 1939), a composer with a high and well-deserved reputation in the world of contemporary art-music. From about 1975, poetry, art, dance, drama and music have flourished at the cathedral. Harvey comments:

> The great building somehow both inspired and cautioned. It said: 'Do something fitting with my immensity, but woe betide anything vulgar or ordinary, because I will show it up with cruel clarity.'[9]

In music, the results were startling and remarkable. Jonathan Harvey was commissioned in 1978 to set the *Magnificat and Nunc Dimittis*. His musical vision for the *Nunc Dimittis* was vivid and unusual, a sharp contrast with Howells:

> I imagined the dark temple and blind old Simeon: I heard his hesitant step as he felt death approach. But as his joy increases to rapture, 'glory' grows to 'lighten': the whole inner world becomes illuminated by multiple repetitions – the light grows as more and more voices enter, repeating the bright vowel and final consonant 'light' until the full organ enters with a chord of universality (comprised of all twelve pitch-classes) in rich registration... In a large building this can fittingly symbolise an extreme spiritual experience.[10]

In the *Magnificat* Harvey asks the choir not only to sing, but to express the text in all manner of ways – speaking, whispering, shouting:

> We all know there's nothing difficult about speaking, but to get choirs to do it in a 'sung' *Magnificat* one had to ask them to make a very special effort – a change of attitude.[11]

Harvey suggests a parallel in religion:

> that is what religion often demands too – a change in attitude. As in religion, so in art... One is excited by one's religion if the familiar texts, rituals and dogmas are recreating the world and themselves. If one hears the Sermon on the Mount for the fiftieth time, it must still change one's perceptions... Jesus'... words are resonant, renewing themselves over the centuries ceaselessly... Religion and art both use familiar things as a platform to start out from... But then from that platform they both create the new from within the old and 'coalesce' the two into a higher synthesis...

It is because of this fundamental similarity between the functions of art and religion that religious art is such an appropriate art-form... Art and religion go together perfectly: both spiral out from the familiar, both aspire to the boundless.[12]

Such a stance requires an open mind and a willingness to take risks. Harvey believes that the art which is of profound importance to religion must be 'dangerously alive' and also that 'the clergy must live dangerously, that is what religion is all about, that is what art is all about – leaping into the dark.'[13]

In 1981, Harvey produced his largest Christian work to date, *Passion and Resurrection*. Although this does not suit itself to formal liturgy, it was conceived for church performance and makes dramatic use of the large open spaces of a cathedral setting. Most unusually for music with a strongly Christian theme, *Passion and Resurrection* was toured on the Contemporary Music Network throughout Britain during 1993. Some of Harvey's motets have been taken up by skilled cathedral choirs, notably *Come Holy Ghost*.

Clearly, cathedrals are well supplied with new music if they choose to sing it. A small proportion of it has been briefly described and is unequivocally superb. Most of the rest is technically assured but with a standard of creative thought which will not yield much excitement on close attention. For, as the composer Jonathan Harvey recently put it:

Many fine composers in Britain today have an aesthetic in sympathy with Christianity, even if they are not strictly practising. But they are hardly ever invited by the church. The church usually invites those it is very sure of, those it knows already, those who are totally predictable.[14]

Notes

1. Quoted in *The First Fifty Years, A Brief Account of the English Hymnal, 1906–1956*, Oxford, 1956.

2. U. Vaughan Williams, *R.V.W.*, London, 1964, p. 72. That discovery led to Vaughan Williams' lifelong fostering of amateur music-making.

3. Martin Shaw's views on Christian music and its renewal can be found in his book *The Principles of English Church Music Composition*, London, 1921.

4. 'There is no reason why an atheist could not write a good Mass' (quoted in Vaughan Williams, p. 138).

5. Quoted in C. Palmer, *Herbert Howells*, London, 1978, p. 78.

6. *Gloucester* (1946), *St Paul's* (1954), *Collegium Sancti Johannis Cantabrigiense* (1958), *Winchester* (1968) and *Sarum* (1968).

7. There was always a certain anticipation among the choir of York Minster in the early 1970s when Howells' music appeared on the schedule. Among much musical mediocrity, everyone knew that, for a change, they were going to face a tough technical challenge which offered the chance of making some first-rate music.

8. St Matthews Church, Northampton, has an honourable reputation in its support of new Christian music.

9. J. Harvey, *Musical Times*, January 1990, p. 53.

10. Harvey, p. 53. The 'chord of universality' contains all twelve notes of the chromatic scale, one each of all the note-names.

11. Harvey, p. 53.

12. Harvey, p. 52.

13. Harvey, p. 55.

14. Harvey, p. 52.

Chapter 45

The Popular Stream

For many people, living dangerously is a frightening experience. Christianity will be for them a defence against the unknown, a place of safety and familiarity that can be constantly revisited. In that case, where some composers respond to the Christian faith strongly and positively with music that questions and challenges, so those who seek safety in it will respond to music which is predictable and which constantly reworks familiar ground.

So in the vast majority of parish churches up and down the country, Christian music which is exploratory is given no space. Even what seems to be new turns out to be reliving the past. John Rutter (b. 1945) is a composer with a deep understanding of classical music whose original pieces and arrangements are widely sung in churches and schools throughout Britain. His considerable technical ability is turned to creating music of ease, music which is harmonious, tuneful, shapely, tasteful and enjoyable to sing. His contributions of original carols to *Carols for Choirs* brought his music to the attention of a very wide public. Where some years later there is still delight in *The Shepherd's Pipe Carol* and its companions, some of Rutter's more recent pieces conform closely to the idioms of commercial music – his new settings of *All Things Bright and Beautiful* and *For the Beauty of the Earth* are examples of this ephemeral trend.

With such pieces Rutter joins a type of Christian music which has run as a constant stream (even a flood-tide) for a century or more. Earlier in the twentieth century it was the song-books produced for Sunday School use that were in closest touch with popular music, for hymnals reflected the expectations of more formal worship. Even so, there has been a consistent time-lag between a musical fashion in the secular world and its adoption by Christian music. Thus the style of the three books of *Scripture Union Choruses* published between 1921 and 1939 is reminiscent of the heyday of the music-hall twenty years earlier.

In the 1950s the Twentieth Century Light Music Group initiated a significant change to Sunday worship. This group of priests, chaplains, musicians and schoolmasters suggested that:

> not only the great and lasting music of the past but also the ordinary and transient music of today – which is the background to the lives of so many – has a rightful place in our worship.[1]

Most of the music of the Twentieth Century Light Music Group indicates that, for them, waltzes, foxtrots and quicksteps were the 'transient music of today' just at the moment when Elvis Presley was turning popular taste in an entirely different direction. Just the same, though the best-known music of the group (by Geoffrey Beaumont and Patrick Appleford) is at best variable, it broke down a significant barrier in many churches which had always shunned music of secular styles. When finally the more relaxed worship of the Sunday School invaded the formality of Matins it was greeted with either relief or horror.

Youth Praise (1966) was the first of many song-books which attempted to reflect a balance of tastes, intending to appeal especially to the younger generation. Although the contents again betrayed the musical interests of its adult compilers and bore little relation to the secular youth music of the time (the Beatles, the Rolling Stones), it became widely used and was followed by *Youth Praise II* (1969) and *Psalm Praise* (1970).

The charismatic movement

In the early 1970s the traditional gospel songs of the turn of the century were suddenly ousted from some traditions of worship by a burst of creativity from Christians involved with the charismatic movement. This remarkable renewal of faith, particularly stressing the gifts of the Holy Spirit, swept through many churches in America and Britain. Unlike the Pentecostal churches, however, it grew from within the ranks of the established denominations and spoke strongly to intellectuals of the younger generation. The emphasis was on the gift of love, certainly not the free love of the 1960s, but nonetheless carrying a gentle resonance of the hippy movement.

The Episcopal Church of the Redeemer in Houston, Texas, was one of the first congregations to experience a period of liberating renewal from the late 1960s onwards. The musical consequences were considerable, with the habitual mould of formal Christian music being broken by the creative enthusiasm of a number of people from within the congregation. Their creative talents – in poetry, music and dance in particular – were valued as gifts of God's Holy Spirit. The atmosphere of freedom and love in which they were exercised was at once surprising and delighting:

> All aspects of parish life and ministry were [by 1967] under the guidance of community-trained leaders who brought a sense of communalism to everything the Church of the Redeemer did. But somehow that integrity was intensified into a deeper unity of praise at the Sunday parish Eucharists; a unique flavour of music was giving character to the gathering together of God's people... It was a 'people's music', a Gebrauchsmusik of high order; and there was an exciting new charism associated with it, one that clearly testified with prophetic comfort: 'This music is a gift for my praises upon this people.'[2]

While the new songs often had the same verse-and-refrain structure of the traditional white gospel music, the best of them possessed a new and refreshing quality of quietude and meditation. The musical invention was sometimes on a higher level than in the past, and best of all, there was (and still is) a renewed awareness of the value of biblical texts.

The persuasive sound of commercial music is more evident in the many musicals inspired by the renewal movement, which lack the innocence of its songs. These use the colourful and attractive surface of light orchestral rock-music to present a dozen or more songs in a loose structure which substitutes for traditional liturgy. 'Musical' is really a misnomer, for there is usually no staging, but simply spoken links provided by a minister. The audience is encouraged to join in through singing and prayer, and the invitation to sing 'in the Spirit'. *If My People* (1973) by Carol and Jimmy Owens is typical of this wave of musicals which has given a number of items to evangelical song-books.

Superficially this 'charismatic' music resembles the populist Christian styles of the previous decade, but there is a difference. Rather than a music imposed or recommended to a congregation by reformers from above or without, some (not all) of this music was created from within, as an expression of the intensity of the spiritual life of a Christian community. The idiom of songs created in this way has strong links with contemporary secular music, but there is a discernible move towards the contemplative, the symbolic and away from the easy rhetoric of earlier evangelical songs. The foreword to *Cry Hosanna* (1980) sets its face against 'the world's ways of romanticising, deadening, or making frivolous the songs of God. But we will sing his praises with a pure heart, fervently...'.

The Iona community

The musical influence of the charismatic movement of the 1970s can still be sensed today in the music of the Iona community, a group of Christians living on the island of Iona off the north-west coast of Scotland. The community was founded in 1938 by George MacLeod, an inner-city minister determined to establish a new way of training clergy. The task he set himself and six others – a uniting of worship and work, spiritual and material – was the rebuilding of the thousand-year-old abbey of Iona. In due course the clergy (and the many others who followed) returned to the challenge of ministry in large cities and to build housing there. Today the community's leadership (numbering about 200) is ecumenical and living in Britain and overseas. The rebuilding of Iona Abbey was completed in 1967 and thousands of visitors visit every year.

The musical impact of the community is due particularly to the talents of John Bell, its musical director and an ordained minister in the Church of Scotland. Not only is he an excellent communicator – particularly through singing – but he is also a hymn-writer and composer. The song-books of the Iona Community are his work. John Bell writes simply (sometimes very simply) but generally without triteness. He is a compiler as much as a writer, sensitive to the merits of folk-song (often recommending Scottish tunes) and drawing on material from across the world:

> I do think it's helpful to sing the songs of other cultures. By singing their songs, we can stand to some extent in deeper intercession with these people. And through that experience our understanding of mission and evangelism and the kingdom of God and the Trinity is enlarged.[3]

Another dimension of the Iona Community's songs is their breadth of subject. Like the biblical psalms, they address every human condition. Joy is matched by sadness, music for funerals by new songs for christenings and weddings. Unlike most hymn collections, negative emotions – frustration, uncertainty – are also faced (see *When Grief is Raw* or *Stumbling Blocks and Stepping Stones*).[4] When compared with most contemporary Christian song the music places an unusual and refreshing emphasis on part-singing:

> We are keen that people should learn to sing on their own and in harmony... For the past century religious music has relied so much on organ or piano or guitar that the beauty and potential of the human voice has been forgotten and the joy of singing in harmony has become, in many places, a long lost experience. We want to encourage people to redeem that loss. It can be done.[5]

The Roman Catholics in Britain, too, have musical strengths in the St Thomas More Centre in London, founded in 1969 as a result of the renewal of the 1960s. Besides being a bookshop and centre for courses and discussion, it publishes new music of a high standard. The Christian music of Paul Inwood, Christopher Walker, Bernadette Farrell and others is straightforward but cast in a variety of structures arising from liturgical need, such as acclamations, litanies and responsorial psalms. This music crosses denominational boundaries freely and is therefore becoming more widely known, especially in North America.

Music for all

Around Britain the speed and ease of modern music publishing has released an avalanche of spiral-bound music-books, *Mission Praise* (1983) and *Songs of Fellowship* (1985) being in wide circulation. The simplicity of their contents implies that the creation of Christian music is no longer only the province of the expert, but that it can be for all. A recent indication of this comes in the re-establishment of bands and orchestras to lead church worship.

The days of clamour against instruments in church have receded sufficiently for Bradford Cathedral to have its own music group (including electric guitars) and the Organist and Master of the Choristers to play electric keyboards for it. Increasing space is being given to the musical talents of the congregation, however diverse, heralding a return to the days of west-gallery players.

The singing tradition of men and boys in Anglican cathedral worship is also evolving. Both Bradford and Salisbury cathedral choirs have been able to call on either girl or boy trebles for some years now and York Minster intends to follow suit in late 1997. The ensuing debate has continued on and off at least since the early eighteenth century:

> If female quiristers were taken into quires instead of boys, it would be a vast improvement of choral musick, because they come to a judgment as well as voice, which the boys doe not arrive at before their voices perish. But both text and morality are against it.[6]

Graham Kendrick is a singing evangelist in the tradition of Sankey or Rodeheaver whose music has had a considerable impact on the contents of recent hymn-books. He is a self-taught musician, a guitar-playing product of the *Youth Praise* era. He toured extensively in 1978 with the organisation 'British Youth for Christ', an activity that developed the following year into Spring Harvest, a Christian festival of music and teaching. Spring Harvest has grown to cater for upwards of 80,000, in a series of eight week-long courses in two locations.

The hymns of Graham Kendrick have captured the imagination of many church-goers. They are finding their way into the worship of many denominations and, significantly, are better suited to instrumental accompaniment than to the organ. The light rock or ballad style keeps most of Kendrick's songs within the sound-world of commercial music (see Example 50), but there is a strong contact with earlier musical traditions through resonances with the past. *Make Way*, for example, is a truncated form of *Rule Britannia*, complete with eighteenth-century cadences. And as far as Victorian hymns go, Kendrick says 'I was brought up with them, I value and enjoy them... People try to cast me as an opponent of traditional hymns, but it is not true.'[7]

Amid much disposible music, some of Kendrick's songs have an intensity of character which may make them more than merely transitory. *Led Like a Lamb*, for instance, uses the men and women of the congregation in a simple but touching re-enactment of the dialogue between the risen Jesus and Mary Magdalene at the tomb on Easter Sunday. In verse two Mary's sudden and joyous realisation that Jesus is alive is the basis for the refrain that follows: 'He's alive, he's alive, he is risen...' The dramatic contrast of contemplation and jubilant rejoicing generates the structure of the song.

A recent project given its identity by Graham Kendrick is 'March for

Jesus', capturing the imagination of large numbers. It began in 1987 with 15,000 marching in the City of London and 'taking the walls off our churches to show what the church really is – people enjoying God's love in

Jesus'. Since then the occasion has become global, with an estimated 12 million participating across the world in 1994 and more since. Since Kendrick writes specially for the marches, his music is now reaching extraordinary numbers of people. In addition his music is distributed in as many forms as modern marketing can devise. Apart from the song-books and the recorded music, backing tracks are available to sing along with, karaoke-fashion; the songs have been recorded in lavish arrangements for symphony orchestra ('Kendrick Gold') and videos and handbooks help local churches to learn the songs.

New technology

The dissemination of contemporary Christian music is changing quickly. Where sheet music can still be bought at shops in the UK (usually specialist Christian retailers) the music is increasingly stored as computer files, to be printed off only when required. One or two shops have a computer terminal giving access to thousands of items, whose parameters (orchestration, key) can be chosen before requesting a copy. For those who do not read music well the songs are available as MIDI[8] files. These are computer floppy disks or CD-ROM[9] files which instruct digital electronic instruments to play the song. The most recent General MIDI system allows parts of the score to be assigned to the appropriate instrumental and vocal sounds, so that synthesisers can attempt an imitation of the music in its live form. Such scores and MIDI files can also be downloaded by computer users from the Internet.

Orchestras and musicals

An offshoot of the interest in instrumental accompaniment is the increasing number of orchestras made up of Christians, playing (with or without choirs) to large and festive gatherings. The London-based Prom Praise events are led by the orchestra of All Souls, Langham Place, itself the centre of an extensive programme of Christian arts. The New English Orchestra concentrates on classical concerts, the Christian membership of the group being a significant further dimension. The programmes of both are usually based on well-known pieces of classical music and popular Christian songs in orchestral guise, but new and exploratory music with a Christian basis is also encouraged by the New English Orchestra.

Many churches now venture into mixed media presentations at high points in the Christian year. A project may involve dance and drama as well as music, the results depending heavily on the resources available. The models are the musicals of Andrew Lloyd Webber, such as *Joseph and the Amazing Technicolor Dreamcoat* (1968) or his rock opera *Jesus Christ Superstar* (1970) and Christian musicals from America, such as those of Carol and Jimmy Owens.

Following these examples, hundreds of musicals are presented by churches all over the country. Roger Jones, a former music teacher in Birmingham, has devised dozens of such pieces for church use. They are not simply intended as entertainment but are often taken on as part of a ministry of spiritual encouragement and development. Such musicals are an important dimension to Christian music today: they are a clear indication of the desire of many fellowships to celebrate their faith in the most exciting way they know. The resources may be slim, the expertise to marshal them may be lacking, but the challenges involved are undoubtedly rewarding. Working on a large project of this kind can be a valuable spiritual challenge – a microcosm of life in the body of Christ, perhaps – though the artistic potential of the Christian musical has yet to be realised. Perhaps the most exciting and appropriate way of galvanising the peforming resources of a church is for a local composer (perhaps from within the church itself) to create a new work that matches the talents available.

Alternative worship

Alternative worship is a casual phrase, embracing the broadest span of attitudes, from liberal to fundamentalist. Indeed, the term may reveal as much about its user as the event. If alternative suggests anything in this context, it is a form of Christian worship which lies outside the mainstream, usually an attempt to suit the younger generation who appear alienated by most worship in the established church. Indeed, both from the charismatic and the liberal wing, there is often some overt dissatisfaction with traditional attitudes not only in forms of worship, but about the church's failure to meet the needs of many of its members – especially the young and the intellectual.

While such alternatives have always existed, they are at present gaining strength amid growing publicity. Greenbelt, an annual Christian arts festival (and its Irish counterpart, Summer Madness), is an important location for innovation and experiment and a number of groups have brought their characteristic styles of worship to it. Many of these fellowships spring from an ecumenical base, such as the Late Late Service in Glasgow, with its links to the World Council of Churches, and for almost all, music has a vital part to play in establishing the identity and character of the worship.[10]

Altogether there may be as many as forty locations in the United Kingdom where such services are held regularly, and while there is sufficient space here only to sketch the character of one or two, there are some common threads. The ambience of the events tends to move between extremes of quietude and meditation to noise and celebration, either dedicating specific occasions to one or the other (London's Epicentre Network provides examples of both) or combining them in an evening of extreme contrasts. Music inevitably features heavily, but most incorporate dance as a vital element. Dance can take the form of a visual spectacle (for instance symbolising a speaker's words or prayer) or be participatory. The latter is now commonplace, and along with the clichés of light show and stage smoke quite a few services are *visually* indistinguishable from rock concerts.

The contemplative element is often evocative of 'Celtic' forms of worship, although the connection may be based in some cases largely on fantasy. One community to which the Celtic dimension is important is the Revelation Church, based in West Sussex. Its founder is Roger Ellis, who emphasises the Celtic Christians' ability to enjoy a 'holistic expression of faith and spirituality' and whose approach 'enabled the tribes of Britain to keep their identity while worshipping Christ'. There is a message here, more commonly heard than in the past, of dissatisfaction and disillusion with the present establishment – which may include not only politicians, royalty and the state system but also the established church. In some places experimental worship is a sign that Christians are no longer interested in renewing the traditional churches from within, but are setting up alternatives to what they see as moribund.

The musical styles used in these events vary considerably and are not necessarily to be judged by the media's descriptions of them. The majority are Christian songs of the kind that might be heard at Spring Harvest, with a mildly aggressive beat, strongly tonal melodies and simple harmony. Amplified acoustic guitars, a keyboard synthesiser and an acoustic drumkit usually form the centre of the band, giving a folk-rock ambience. Quiet ballads will accompany the more meditative and prayerful moments.

What may be described as a 'rave' event is unlikely to bear much resemblance to the real thing. After all, rave music is associated with sex and drugs, the types of music being specifically designed to enhance the effects of the substances in circulation. This dimension of rave (which could be called essential) is happily and hopefully absent from alternative services; indeed, the Christian intention is to draw youngsters away from the drug culture. As the Late Late Service's Call to Worship begins:

> God is here. His Spirit is with us. This is not a performance. This is our worship. This is not a rave or a disco. This is our worship. This is not a special event for young people. This is our worship... [11]

Nonetheless some services do feature more recent musical styles – Epicentre uses house/garage club music, acid jazz or funk. Perhaps the most eclectic occasions were created by the Nine O'Clock Service, formerly led by Chris Brain. The Nine O'Clock Service unfortunately shot to prominence in August 1995 in a 'blaze of publicly revealed pain, anger and impropriety' and has been since wrestling with the hard process of rebuilding itself as the Nine O'Clock Community. In 1994 thirty-five members of the Nine O'Clock Service joined forces with the controversial American priest Matthew Fox to present what was carelessly called a 'rave mass' at Grace Cathedral in San Francisco. It included an indulgent mixture of 'techno music, Latin chants, a multi-media show, Tai-Chi, silent meditation and rave dancers wearing virtual reality goggles':

> At the centre of the room sat an oversized circular altar and a smaller crescent table... Surrounding the tables were a series of concentric circles, tracks marked off in tape, around which the Rave Mass team would walk and dance. Atop the eclipse altar sat a chalice, protected by a clear Plexiglass pyramid. Above the eclipse altar was the... screen – a large sphere of white cloth onto which the organisers projected images of revolving planets, decaying forests, human pulses and faces. Several young people emerged from the shadows carrying small flames... The music intensified. A few people, mostly Rave Mass organisers, danced... a woman in a white alb slowly walked the circle

making mournful... cries on her flute. [Later] the music cranked up to a pulsating beat. The thirty-five Brits... led the room in energetic dancing to: *Now we feel your lifeforce rising/ Raise the passion 10 by 10/ Now we breathe you, Christ, inside us/ Feel the freedom pushing on...* [12]

The event provoked passionate comment, both for and against, and revealed once again how polarised Christians are in matters of worshipping traditions. In this case the Internet became busy with a prolonged exchange of views (from many, it must be said, who were not at the service), a selection of which are worth reproducing here. They began with the remark that the 'Rave Mass' was 'a sad, sad day for the Episcopal Church and world-wide Anglicanism'. Others elaborated the point:

> Why do we come together: to worship, or to be entertained?... It seems to me that the message of Christ might be being ignored in favour of the message of glitz.

and

> Indeed, it is a sad day for the one holy catholic Church. When the mass becomes about us simply expressing ourselves before God, we have lost the plot. What does techno music, Tai-Chi and rave dancers wearing virtual reality goggles have to do with the death and resurrection of Jesus Christ? I'm sure it was all very entertaining, but then again so was Baal worship and we all know what Yahweh thought about that.

On the other hand:

> How is it that you have determined that rave music is 'entertainment' as opposed to 'worship'... I belong to a high church parish and know that among the congregation are many who come merely to worship the music and liturgy... Does this thereby invalidate the solemn eucharist itself as a vehicle for worship of the Most High? And are they worse off for having participated? One might conjecture that the music they idolise, wrongly, draws them ever so slowly closer to the true worship of God...
>
> Why is it that a variety of styles of worship cannot be authentic? Are jazz eucharists inauthentic? Folk masses? How would we determine which type of music would, intrinsically, be a vehicle for worship? [13]

But finally:

> The Rave Mass I attended on Hallowe'en weekend in San Francisco
> was the most oppressive spiritual experience I've known in more than
> ten years as a religion writer. The Rave Mass was not oppressive
> because it expressed Christian truth in a new liturgical form, but
> because it supplanted Christianity with a careless brew of paganism,
> manipulative imagery and an environmentalist hysteria... The Rave
> Mass is absolutely enthralled with the Spirit of the Age, uncritically
> incorporating popular trends in dance music, MTV-inspired videos
> and post-modernist theology.[14]

Not only do feelings evidently run high over such events, but the issues are
much the same as ever they were, in this case forming a strikingly close
parallel with the difficulties that the earliest Christians had with
instrumental music. For secular rave music has the specific function of
creating an aural ambience to the drugs circulating at the event, the effect of
particular drugs being complemented by specific musical types. Music and
drugs have been linked closely at many points in human history (the Be-Bop
era of the 1940s and 1950s is a recent Western example) but this recent
trend associates music with biblically-banned social behaviour more
intimately than ever. If the music is provided without the drugs, it is left
without its true function, and its use in worship is exposed as a failed
attempt to be fashionable.

Is rave music therefore finally irredeemable? Every argument raised in
favour of permitting a secular musical style in worship in the West, from
Ambrose to Luther to William Booth, has been based on the notion that
music has associations which can be redeemed. This has been true in the
experience of most Christians: in the course of time the melody to the love
song 'Innsbruck ich muss dich lassen' has acquired the Christian
associations of what many now call the Passion Chorale. The transformation
becomes complete as the memory of the tune's original associations
completely fades. The difficulties are most acute when the secular music in
question lives side by side with its counterpart in worship – for those who
know the film The Dam Busters (1955), singing a version of Psalm 96 to Eric
Coates' march provides an ephemeral example.

The problem exists as soon as a distinction is made between secular and
sacred. Musical style is perhaps the most concise indicator of the distance
between the two states and rave music exposes most starkly yet the distance

between them. The behaviour of the society which rave music represents is anathema to most Christians, just as was the decadence of Roman culture at the very beginnings of the faith. Early Christians set their faces emphatically against the music that came from the culture around them – does today's opposite reaction, wherever it occurs, indicate that 'we have lost the plot'?

There are still those who say (as they have said so many times before) that enough is enough. A small but vocal Calvinist tradition in North America and Canada still advocates the banning of all instrumental music in worship, even suggesting that 'the use of instruments in the public worship of God, in its final analysis, is to deny that Christ indeed came in the flesh'.[15] Truly this is an age of extremes.

Notes

1. Preface to *Thirty 20th Century Hymn Tunes*, London, 1960.

2. W.G. Pulkingham, *They Left Their Nets*, London, 1974, p. 125.

3. Quoted on the Internet at http://www.giamusic.com

4. J.L. Bell, *Love from Below*, Glasgow, 1992.

5. Bell, p. 7.

6. Roger North, *The Musical Grammarian*; see J.W. Wilson, *Roger North on Music*, London, 1959, p. 271.

7. *The Times*, 8 January 1993.

8. Musical Instrument Digital Interface.

9. Compact Disc Read-only Memory.

10. The Late Late Service is sufficiently well-established to have produced a number of recordings of their music – see Discography.

11. Words from the Late Late Service, Glasgow, n.d.

12. From a description of the service by Douglas LeBlanc, 'Stark Raving Mad', *United Voice*, January 1995, (Internet location http://206.1.24.2/EU/UV/1995/january/index.htm).

13. Excerpts from Anglican@american.edu, November 1994.

14. Douglas Le Blanc, 'Loud Style, Pagan Substance', *United Voice*, January 1995.

15. See L. Binger, Jr, *A Brotherly Testimony Against the Use of Instrumental Accompaniment in Public Worship*, Alberta, Canada, 1996.

Chapter 46

Good and Bad

Whereas the Orthodox churches of the East have to this day maintained a unity of purpose immediately recognisable in the greatest basilica or in the humblest country church, the church in the West has gradually become fragmented. The fundamental split created by the Reformers of the sixteenth century itself led to several factions, each with its own interpretation of the Christian faith and its own musical style. A continuing and increasing awareness of the injustices of a class-based society led to further divisions in the eighteenth century – the establishment of Methodism in England, or the rise of Pietism among Lutherans, for example.

It is easy for trained musicians to react to the musical diversity caused by such turmoil in terms of musical 'excellence'. After all, God deserves the best sacrifice of time and talent from his creatures. But in using this yardstick, it is possible to bypass entirely the way in which God himself responds to the worship offered. Enthusiastic congregational singing, which arises from positive spiritual commitment, may be a dimension far more important than the musical idiom. Similarly, the almost universal condemnation of the rough music of English west-gallery bands may be no indication of the pleasure that God received from that worship. And where artistic musical excellence was generally assured – in the seventeenth-century English Chapel Royal and the cathedrals and court chapels of Europe – a sincerity pleasing to God would often have required a specially large camel to squeeze through the needle's eye – perhaps not quite an impossibility, but certainly a great difficulty.

The judgment of Christian music by these two distinct criteria – musical excellence or spiritual sincerity – has created ever-widening chasms between the styles of music in churches of differing denominations. The contrast between the styles of twentieth-century Christian music so briefly described in Part 9 is immense. Not only is it a contrast of quality, of sophistication and of ability, but also of intention. It therefore possesses potential for explosive dissent, framed by the vexed questions of what is good and bad. For, as the composer and critic Hugo Cole observes, what is good for music may be bad for worship and vice versa:

> Go to King's Chapel [Cambridge] and listen to Lassus and Byrd, and the music does indeed soar aloft and is indeed glorious. Yet one understands the viewpoint of those who complain that evensong is no more than a concert in disguise. Music seems to be celebrating its own glory, which is fine for musicians. On the other hand, if we visit the church down the road where the whole congregation is singing, with genuine fervour and passion, our least favourite Dykes hymn, that is all right for the congregation but bad for musicians – and, the purist would add, 'bad for music'. In looking at church music, we are always subject to double vision: good is bad if it causes the congregation to fall apart in consternation – possibly if it is so good that (as in King's Chapel) it draws in an audience of connoisseurs and musical agnostics. Bad music is good if it fosters community spirit in the congregation and raises it collectively to higher spiritual levels.[1]

But is it really true that only bad music will satisfy a congregation's needs? Or that good music simply turns worship into a concert? Both scenarios are being acted out daily, it is true, and in their differing ways both are undesirable. But there is plenty of evidence from this last chapter that they are not inevitable.

The music of Taizé is good by a musician's standards of compositional grammar, yet thousands know it as a self-effacing servant of deepening spiritual awareness. Indeed, it is difficult to find a bad word said about it. Some of the music arising from the charismatic movement occupies a similar position, as does some from modern Lutheran and Catholic composers. A diligent search would reveal more from a host of national and denominational backgrounds.

The quality that distinguishes this deeply spiritual music from the rest has to do with the role that music plays in worship. A danger lies in the music becoming too insistent a voice, with the possibility that it invites too much attention. It is much more likely to do this if it is rooted in rhetorical traditions. It is highly significant that the nineteenth century, the age of the most passionate expression in classical music, found Christian music so poverty-stricken that societies had to be founded to try to rescue it. The assumption behind the Western Romantic movement – that art is a unique statement from an individual about his or her inner being – is fundamentally unhelpful to a diverse congregation. The 'all sorts and conditions' of humanity that visit Taizé are not asked to identify with music that conveys a strong emotional state through the traditions of rhetoric, but are offered music which is relatively unemotional and which allows people to sense the unity that it symbolises.

As far as Western culture is concerned, the late twentieth century is still part of the Romantic age. The emphasis in the creative arts is centred firmly on the individual's feelings and response to his or her surroundings. But some Christian artists (among the composers Arvo Pärt is one) are suggesting a new possibility, that art can express – no, not express, but perhaps inhabit or be part of – universal truths. In worship, this does not necessarily require a return to the ancient chant of the Christian church but it can only follow a rediscovery of the true nature of Christian music.

Perhaps such a reassessment will only be possible after profound changes in Western culture, which is at present so hectic, so concerned with the network of personal relationships that spiritual matters are given little space. For the present, Christians should not allow themselves simply to compromise their art with secular expectations, but through a leap of imagination (into the dark, perhaps) start once again to deal with 'the things of the spirit'.

Coats of many colours

Christian music today is as breathtaking in its variety as the natural world, and its traditions have evolved at equally varied rates. In the Eastern Orthodox Church, change has been almost imperceptibly slow, the Copts and Ethiopians moving at a glacier-like pace. Only in the Russian Orthodox Church have revisions to the liturgy been of sufficiently disturbing rapidity to generate sectarian division. That seventeenth-century scenario is now being revisited as the present resurgence of the Orthodox Church in Russia is complemented by the rise of countless other denominations and sects.

Western society has been turbulent far longer, with one of the many far-reaching effects of its cultural evolution being a fragmented perception of Christianity. Particularly since the Reformation, different elements in society have emphasised particular and limited aspects of the faith, splitting the white light of the gospel into a rainbow of colours. The diversity of hues has since become progressively greater, along with the segmentation of the culture that gives them expression.

A further pattern emerges from countries where Christianity has been implanted by Western Christians into a long-established culture. In Africa, for instance, European styles of worship (which include the music) are being questioned and progressively rejected in favour of patterns more in keeping with local and long-established cultural traditions. New African churches are multiplying as their indigenous presentation of the gospel captures the people's imagination. In the countryside the faith is expressed with music that is an offspring of African rather than European society; in the cities, African music has travelled full circle: across to North America with the slave trade, adopted and commercially exploited by white culture, and now returned to its homeland to be further transformed into a new gospel music.

It would be wrong to suggest that the variety of Christian music world-wide is a recent phenomenon; the picture of early Christianity was far from one of stylistic uniformity. But in spite of the early threat of schism between East and West, there was still a common understanding that music in its symbolic form was worship's most appropriate companion. Today, the archetypes of rhetoric, symbol and ecstacy can be discovered in countless interrelationships, for Christians across the world are prepared to consecrate every imaginable type of music to the worship of God.

Schism or reconciled diversity?

The separation of Christians is rightly understood as a scandal. It is true that the faith's hundreds of denominations were spawned by internal disagreements and have since sustained and encouraged mistrust and strife. There are now signs, however, that mutual tolerance and respect are holding sway against sectarian confrontation and this despite the collapse of a number of plans for unity.[2] Idealistic schemes which work towards some future monolithic church are being replaced by one which is more simple though no less ambitious: true love and acceptance of Christians in their colourful diversity.

There are clear signs from the Christian musical world that such reconciliation is in action. Disputes over style in worship no longer lead so quickly to the resignation of the organist; there is less news of churches whose singers of the older generation are at war with the instrumentalists of the next. A report on church music to the Archbishop of Canterbury has urged that

> Musical resources must be diversified: congregations, choirs, instruments, styles, cultural and denominational variety – all need to be exploited, with a combination of imagination and understanding of tradition...[3]

At the heart of such 'reconciled diversity' is Jesus himself and his new commandment:

> You must love the Lord your God with all your heart, with all your soul, and with all your mind. This is the greatest and the first commandment. The second resembles it: You must love your neighbour as yourself...[4]

Worship that is sincere and thus pleasing to God can only spring from love. The Bible records many instances of God rejecting worship which lacks love, from the story of Cain and Abel to the Christians of Laodicea.[5] By his own example Jesus gave a lifetime's demonstration of how love for God can be expressed, and sharing in communal worship was an essential component.[6] Indeed, he visited both temple and synagogue, never favouring a particular ritual and giving absolutely no indication that God might prefer one style of worship to another. Instead, Jesus' constant challenge, then as now, is that it is the state of the heart, mind and soul that matters.

Jesus' commands have a special significance for those musicians and composers who have the responsibility for aiding worship. A necessary part of his command to love is that we should live with integrity and seek the truth: love cannot develop without this. It follows that creative artists must have this goal not just for their life but also for their work. The idea that there is a truth to be sought in art was well known in earlier times when the musics of cosmos, human soul and voice were assumed to be in subtle synchrony. But truth in art is still a reality and has all the more importance for musicians on whom depends the quality of communal worship.

The Christian liturgies of the present day create so many different working conditions that it is impossible to suggest in every situation what a musician's search for truth might involve. But it will probably require a fight against artistic and intellectual laziness, against carelessness, against partial offerings of intellect or voice or body, against an unthinking contentment with gestures that have become meaningless through repetition, even against the easy and fatal hypocrisy which can make church music offensive: 'made so by the repulsive incongruity between its beauty and religious zeal and the state of things in the city slums.'[7]

In all this, nothing has been said about style itself, because nothing *needs* to be said. Good music, defined as such by its truthfulness, does not have to be abstruse or highly intellectual. Mozart once wrote to his father about some concertos he was working on:

> There are passages here and there from which connoisseurs alone can derive satisfaction; but these passages are written in such a way that the less learned cannot fail to be pleased, though without knowing why.[8]

Mozart recognised that good music need not alienate its audience. Even less does Christian music have to become the province of a few intellectuals in order to be profitable or edifying. But it must be honest and integral to its occasion. As Joseph Gelineau has pointed out:

> A very simple tune can be dismissed as worthless if taken in isolation but makes a marvellous contribution to the spirit and beauty of the celebration, whereas a great work which is too difficult or badly done can wreck it.[9]

Whatever the colour of their coats, the responsibilities carried by musicians working in Christian worship are heavy. But as in parenthood or in any other life-challenge that God may offer, if the task is embraced wholeheartedly and in his strength then there are rich rewards. The greatest delight of all is to know that the joy travels both ways, for God takes pleasure in us. As a well-known hymn expresses it:

> Lord, we know that thou rejoicest
> o'er each work of thine;
> thou didst ears and hands and voices
> for thy praise design:
> craftman's art and music's measure,
> for thy pleasure all combine.

> In thy house, great God, we offer
> of thine own to thee,

and for thine acceptance proffer
all unworthily
hearts and minds and hands and voices
in thy choicest psalmody.

Notes

1. H. Cole, *The Changing Face of Music*, Oxford, 1978, p. 91.

2. In Britain in 1991 the Anglican/Methodist reunion scheme was abandoned along with the Covenant for Unity and some long-held hopes for rapprochement between the Anglicans and Roman Catholics.

3. The Royal Academy of Music's Submission to the Archbishop's Commission on Church Music, February 1990, p. 23.

4. Matthew 22:36–38.

5. See for instance Genesis 4:4, Jeremiah 6:20, Revelation 3:15.

6. Luke 4:16, 6:6, John 7.

7. E. Routley, *Church Music and the Christian Faith*, Carol Stream, III, 1978, p. 9.

8. Letter from W.A. Mozart to his father dated 28 December 1782, in E. Blom, *Mozart's Letters*, Harmondsworth, 1956.

9. J. Gelineau, *The Liturgy: Today and Tomorrow*, New York, 1978, p. 90.

Appendix

Organ Music

No instrument seems to have had so much of its history invented for it as the organ. The common association of the instrument with Christian worship has led to all kinds of claims for its ancient use in church for which there now seems little evidence. On the contrary, it is worth reflecting that the organ has been generally absent from most of Christian history. After all, the Orthodox Church has always rejected it, along with the Copts and Ethiopians. The Roman Church seems to have shown little interest in it for the first millennium, and even after the Reformation many protestant voices (the Calvinists) continued to do so. Thus a small area of Christendom has been blessed (or cursed) by organ-playing over a relatively short period.

The absence of evidence for organs in worship in the first millennium in Europe does not mean that the instruments did not exist, but suggests rather that their uses were not usually liturgical. Pope John VIII (872–882) wrote of an instrument installed as a teaching aid in the science of musical proportions; other organs were used processionally (outdoors) and may even have served the purpose of summoning people to church as bells do now.

By what process then did they come to be in common use in large churches and cathedrals by the fifteenth century? One of the most powerful restraints on their acceptance in Christian worship is the same one that banned other instruments, as the organ was in Roman times an instrument used at gladiatorial contests, important political events and banquets. Christians may have shuddered to recall that Nero made it his favourite instrument. Over the course of time, however, the Church Fathers' indictments against instruments may have been balanced against the attractive idea of acquiring a visual and aurally impressive piece of church furniture. After all, Old Testament references could be cited to justify it.[1] Furthermore, occasional earlier references to the organ show it being used to acclaim the presence of royalty. In its need to impress the populace with its riches and power, it might not be surprising that the church took advantage of this particular rhetoric for its own use.

For whatever reason, from the eleventh century onwards an increasing number of references to organs in church may be found. The exact use to which they were put is unclear, often due to the many possible meanings of the word *organum*. A late thirteenth-century Spanish source puts the instrument in a familiar setting:

> This is the only musical instrument that the church employs in the various chants, prosae, sequences and hymns; because of the abuse by play-actors, the other instruments having all been banned together.[2]

By the fifteenth century there is not only documentary evidence of organs in worship, but a few of the instruments themselves still exist (Notre-Dame at Valère-sur-Sion in Switzerland and Saragossa Cathedral in Spain house two of the oldest) along with the music they played.

It is quite clear from this that the organ was used from these early times as a complement to or a substitute for singing, certainly not for accompaniment. The *Faenza Codex*, dating from about 1400, is the earliest known collection of liturgical organ music and its contents illustrate this well. Its most extensive item is an organ Mass, consisting of keyboard music to replace various sung items of the liturgy. The practice was for sections of sung plainchant to alternate with organ music. For example, in a sixfold *Kyrie* the first 'Kyrie eleison' would be sung, the second played and the third sung. The second phrase 'Christe eleison' would be treated in the same way.

Similarly, if a hymn was to be sung on a solemn occasion, then the *schola* might sing verses alternating with the organ, which would play its verses on the congregation's behalf. This concept of substitution extended to many different parts of the liturgy – antiphons, psalms and canticles. This gave the organ a central role in worship, on an equal footing with the voices. For this purpose an instrument was installed at Notre Dame in Paris at the beginning of the fourteenth century, where its use impressed a contemporary writer:

> We see many clerics who, owing to a certain miraculous prodigy of their innate musical talent, improvise and perform on the organ the most difficult musical melodies, which the human voice would scarcely have presumed to undertake.[3]

This substitution for and elaboration of the chant by the organ is yet another dimension to the medieval delight in beautifying the liturgy. It became a particularly strong feature in the Renaissance period and by 1600 the practice had been absorbed into ecclesiastical law:

At the solemn Mass the organ is played alternatim for the *Kyrie eleison* and the *Gloria in excelsis*... likewise at the end of the Epistle and at the Offertory; for the *Sanctus, alternatim*; then more gravely and softly during the Elevation of the Most Holy Sacrament; for the *Agnus Dei, alternatim*, and at the verse before the post-Communion prayer; also at the end of the Mass.[4]

Example 51 is the beginning of an organ verset of a *Kyrie de Sancta Maria* composed in Poland in the 1540s.[5]

At St Mark's Basilica in Venice, where in the sixteenth century the organists' posts were probably the most highly sought-after in Europe, the auditions were designed to test the player's ability to substitute for voices.

(chant in tenor - upper line LH)

EXAMPLE 51

The usual test for trying out the organists who competed for the post of organist at St Mark's in Venice was as follows:

1.   Opening a choirbook and finding at random the beginning of a *Kyrie* or a motet, one copies this and gives it to the competing organist. The latter must, at the organ… improvise a piece in a regular fashion, without mixing up the parts, just as if four singers were performing.

2.   Opening a book of plainchant equally at random, one copies a *cantus firmus* from an introit or another chant, and sends it to the said organist. He must improvise on it, deriving the other three parts [from it]; he must put the *cantus firmus* now in the bass, now in the tenor, now in the alto and soprano, deriving imitative counterpoint from it, not simple accompaniments.

3.   A group of singers is made to sing a rather unfamiliar verse of a composition, and he (the organist) should imitate and respond to them either in the same or in a contrasting mode. Improvisation of this kind will indicate the talent of the organist.[6]

In one case at least, the missing text of the versets played by the organ were restored by a bass voice, as a visitor to Rome noticed:

And at that verse which the Organs doth playe, one of the quyre in the meane time with a base voyce very leasurely, rather sayth than singeth which there is common, in other places I have not seene it.[7]

But generally the function of organ music as a substitute for singing persisted in the Roman Catholic tradition right through to the beginning of the twentieth century, when Pius X banned *alternatim* playing in his *motu proprio* of 1903. It is at this point that organists started in earnest to accompany chant, partly to encourage the singers, but also to restore a place for themselves in services where, with an increasing interest in plainsong and the discouragement of aria-like music, they were in danger of becoming noticeably silent.

Calvinist attitudes

The objections to organ music which led to the Calvinists stripping the Genevan churches of their organs were therefore little to do with the organ's secular associations (as was certainly the case with instruments associated with dancing – shawms, crumhorns, viols and the like). Rather it was its 'popish' habit of taking away from the congregation words which were rightly theirs to utter. Of course, the melody of a hymn can bring its associated words to mind, but for many reformers, this was not enough. They drove the organ out of the liturgy because it prevented the congregation from active participation in worship.

The consequences were far-reaching in areas where Calvinism was most strictly adopted. In Scotland, for example, a parish organ was not to be found until the latter half of the nineteenth century. Even J.S. Bach was affected, for in 1717 he gained the post of Kapellmeister at Prince Leopold's Calvinist court at Cöthen. Here, organ music, indeed, music for worship in general, was given little attention. The court did not require Bach to play for the chapel (though there was an organ) and only asked for the occasional ceremonial cantata. Instead, his efforts were concentrated largely on orchestral and instrumental music.

The Lutherans

The Lutherans were ambivalent about the organ. No hard and fast rules were drawn up and many large city churches had a fine instrument which they were happy to use in alternation with the congregation or choir in canticles and hymn-singing – primarily on the special feast-days of Easter and Christmas. The organ was for a time specifically excluded from some parts of the services, though by the end of the sixteenth century its use in providing continuity and moments of meditation was accepted. From then on the status of organists in the Lutheran Church rose; they were permitted to play preludes on hymn-tunes, either between the congregation's verses or elsewhere, and to play during Communion and maybe at the 'elevation of the host' (the moment before Communion where the priest held the bread up high for the congregation to see). There is plenty of evidence that Lutherans came to accept other instruments in worship as well.

Lutheran composers for the organ were inspired particularly by the Dutchman Jan Sweelinck (1562–1621). He lived and worked in a country riven with the tensions between Calvinism and Catholicism, but nevertheless acquired such a reputation as organist at the Oude Kirk in Amsterdam that his pupils came to him from all corners of Europe. Although the Calvinist traditions of the Netherlands did not allow accompanied congregational singing, the organ was too highly respected there to be eliminated entirely from worship (the reputation of Dutch organ-builders is still among the highest in the world). Thirteen of Sweelinck's organ pieces are devotional meditations on Calvinist and Lutheran hymn melodies. These would have found a place at the opening or close of a service, perhaps occasionally introducing or following the sermon. Their serene detachment and the precision and perfection of their invention convey a meditative intensity quite unlike the heady excitement of Frescobaldi's keyboard fantasies in Rome.

Sweelinck's influence was carried to Germany by his pupil Samuel Scheidt (1587–1654), chiefly known for his great collection of organ music called *Tablatura Nova*. Like Sweelinck, many of the pieces in this collection clothe Lutheran hymn-tunes with an intellectual music, a symbolic offering back to God of the composer's creative gift, reminiscent of the attitudes of medieval times. Later organist-composers such as Franz Tunder, Johann Pachelbel, Dietrich Buxtehude and Johann Kuhnau found a variety of ways to decorate and adorn melodies familiar to their congregations, such pieces being known as chorale preludes. J.S. Bach (who followed Kuhnau as organist at Leipzig) had the greatest talent of all for writing these devotional fantasies around congregational tunes.

The organ in Britain

In village churches the chances of hearing any organ music at all was remote, especially in Britain, where there was little tradition of church organ-building compared with that of the rest of Europe. Organ music was therefore confined to the larger and wealthier churches. It was excluded entirely from Scotland, which had won its way to a wholehearted Calvinism under John Knox in 1561.

The use of the organ in England was a continual source of controversy, but the manuscript called the Mulliner Book,[8] assembled between about 1550–75 and written at least partially for use in St Paul's Cathedral, well illustrates the role of the organ as a solo instrument in worship. The book contains music by several organists of the Chapel Royal (Redford, Blitheman, Tallis) and contains music dating from before and after the Reformation. It reflects in part the Roman tradition of the organ in alternation with voices, providing versets for plainsong hymns and substitutes for Mass chants.

In English country parishes organs were largely unknown, for the most part being installed for the first time in the nineteenth century on the expulsion of west-gallery choirs. Only at this point was the practice of accompanying voices on the organ firmly established. A few people still question this traditional scenario: some Calvinists (mostly in the United States) still see the organ as an unwelcome intruder, while others have doubts about the effectiveness of the organ as a means to improve congregational singing. An increasing interest in world music is reintroducing the delights of *a capella* singing to some congregations, and their musical directors are introducing brief opportunities for their congregations to sing unaccompanied.

Thus the chief contribution of the organ to Christian worship remains in the relatively narrow field of cathedral music, where its dynamic and tonal range can be exploited fully to complement an artistic choral repertoire.

Notes

1. For Psalm 150:4 the Vulgate reads 'laudate eum in cordis et organo'.

2. Gill of Zamora, quoted in P. Williams, *The Organ in Western Culture*, Cambridge, 1993, p. 2.

3. A. de St. Gilles (14th century) from M. Gerbet, *Scriptores Ecclesiastici de Musica*, San Blasianis, 1784, vol. 3, p. 316; quoted in C. Wright, *Music, and Ceremony at Notre Dame of Paris, 500–1550*, Cambridge, 1989, p. 160.

4. From Clement VIII, *Caeremoniale episcoporum*, Rome, 1600; quoted in S. Sadie, editor, *The New Grove Dictionary of Music and Musicians*, London, 1980, vol. 13, p. 780.

5. From the facsimile in *Monumenta Musica in Polonia*, Krakow, 1964.

6. Quoted in F. Caffi, *Storia della Musica Sacra*, Venice, 1854, vol. 1, p. 28.

7. G. Martin, *Roma Sancta*, 1581; quoted in T. Carter, *Music in Late Renaissance and Early Baroque Italy*, London, 1992, p. 102.

8. Published as vol. I of *Musica Britannica*, London, 1952.

Glossary

Alleluia

At Mass, the chant between the Gradual and the Gospel reading. It consists of a psalm verse preceded and followed by 'Alleluia'. The final syllable of the word 'Alleluia' is a long *melisma* called the *jubilus*, the rejoicing.

Anabaptist

A member of a sect that did not believe in infant baptism – common in Zwickau and Munster in Germany at the time of the Reformation.

Antiphon

A chant associated with psalm-singing, usually a prose text (often though not always biblical) which begins and ends the singing of a psalm or psalm verse. A few other free-standing chants are also called antiphons. To sing or play music antiphonally is to divide music between two groups of musicians.

Antiphonal, antiphoner

A compilation of antiphons and other chants, usually of the Divine Office.

Barrel organ

A mechanical organ operating by means of a horizontal barrel in which pins have been carefully positioned. The barrel slowly rotates and the pins push up triggers which let air into the pipes. Barrel organs became popular in the nineteenth century as replacements for church gallery players.

Basilica

Originally a palace (from the Greek *basilikos*, royal) but in Roman times a large building with aisles, nave and apse used for public meetings. Some were adapted for Christian worship; other churches were then built to the same pattern.

Breviary

Originally, any abridged or shortened book (from the Latin, *brevis*, short) but from the eleventh century, a liturgical book which contained a selection of items for the Divine Office.

Bull

An edict, from the Latin, *bulla,* seal.

Byzantine

From Byzantium, the centre of Eastern Christendom. The city of Byzantium was renamed Constantinople by Constantine in the fourth century and is now known as Istanbul. The traditions of Greek Orthodoxy are closely related to those of the Byzantine Church.

Canon

1. An ecclesiastical law. 2. A musical structure in which identical melodies are heard out of step with each other, but which still makes logical music. 3. A fixed form of prayer at Mass, running from the Sanctus to the Lord's Prayer. 4. A type of Byzantine chant – see *kanon*.

Cantata

A musical piece for one or more voices (from the Latin, *cantare*, to sing) with instrumental accompaniment. Church cantatas became a particular feature of Lutheran worship in the seventeenth and eighteenth centuries.

Canticle

The name given to hymns or other poetical texts in the Bible but outside the book of Psalms. They are often referred to by their first words in Latin translation; for example, the *Magnificat* is the song of Mary in the Gospel of Luke which begins 'My soul doth magnify the Lord.'

Cantillation

The chanting of sacred texts. The term is usually used in connection with Jewish and Christian traditions. The equivalent term in the Byzantine tradition is *ekphonesis*.

Cantor

Originally a solo or principal singer (from the Latin, *cantare*). Later (particularly in the seventeenth century) the term came to mean choral director or supervisor.

Cantoris

In cathedrals, the part of the choir on the cantor's side (the north). See also *decani*.

Cantus firmus (plural: *cantus firmi*)

A melody, usually borrowed from another source, used as the basis for a more complex composition. *Cantus firmus* is Latin for 'fixed melody', *canto firmo* being the Italian form.

Cecilian Movement

A group of societies created during the nineteenth century to restore Roman Catholic music to its former glories. They were particularly interested in re-establishing Gregorian chant and the polyphonic choral style of the later sixteenth century.

Centonisation

A phenomenon (from the Latin, *cento*, meaning patchwork) observed and analysed only this century, whereby melodies belonging to a particular mode tend to use the same or similar musical phrases. Centonisation has been observed in Christian chant (Gregorian, Byzantine and Slavonic) and in other music with an oral tradition, such as jazz and folk-music.

Charismatic

Concerning the *charismata*, the gifts of the Spirit discussed by Paul in his first letter to the Corinthians, chapters 12, 13 and 14.

Chromatic music

Music which exploits notes which lie outside the scale-system in use at the time. If chromaticism becomes intense, an underlying scale-system may become difficult or impossible to identify.

Cistercian

A monastic order formed in France at the beginning of the twelfth century to re-establish exact observance of the Rule of St Benedict.

Cithara

See *kithara*.

Clausula

In one of its many meanings, a technical term concerning early developments in Western polyphony, particularly those in the *Magnus liber organi* from Notre Dame. In this type of *organum*, sections of the original chant which are melismatic have a repetitive rhythm superimposed on them. These sections contrast strongly with their musical surroundings (where the chant is heard in very long notes) and are called *clausulas*. New *clausulas* came to be written to substitute for or to replace those already composed, giving them an independent musical identity. The addition of new text to the upper (organal) part(s) of *clausulas* created the medieval motet.

Concerto

A term which in its early use simply indicates a getting-together to make music. The Latin *concertare* means to dispute or to strive, but in the Italian concertare, a getting-together or an agreement is a more likely origin. Thus Schütz' *Kleine geistliche Konzerte* (Little Sacred Concertos, 1639) are not concertos in the much later sense of soloist-with-orchestra, but simply musical opportunities for singers and players.

Conductus

Originally a piece of vocal music sung as an accompaniment to the movement of celebrants in Roman liturgy of the Middle Ages. The Latin, *conducere*, means to guide or to escort. Some early references to conductus are in connection with the escorting of a reader to a lectern, but there are also examples in liturgical drama (for example the *Play of Daniel*). Later the term refers to a particular type of musical composition, mostly polyphonic.

Continuo

Short for *basso continuo*, meaning continuous bass. From about 1600 to 1760 almost all art-music was supported by a continuous presentation of the bass line and its associated harmonies. *Basso continuo* could be played on a wide variety of instruments, a working minimum being one bass instrument (cello, viola da gamba, bassoon) with an instrument capable of playing harmonies, for example keyboard, lute or harp.

Council of Trent

An ecclesiastical body of the Roman Catholic Church convened by Pope Paul III which met in Trento between 1542 and 1563 to pronounce on all aspects of church life.

Counterpoint

A term used first in the fourteenth century to describe the combination of musical lines according to certain rules. A 'point' was a short musical phrase. When such a phrase was heard successively in two or more musical lines, then 'point' was set 'counter [against] point'. Its most common use nowadays is in describing imitative music, such as *fugue*.

Decani

A term used in medieval monasteries and cathedrals referring to the 'dean's side' of the choir (the south side, where the dean traditionally sat). The word (together with its counterpart, *cantoris*) is still used in some Protestant churches where music is sung antiphonally.

Diatonic music

Music which is written according to scale-systems notated by conventional key-signatures.

Discant

A general term for polyphony, but also with specific meanings: 1. improvised polyphony, 2. a part added to the tenor, 3. the top line of a polyphonic piece (hence also 'descant').

Divine Liturgy

The Orthodox term for the service otherwise known as Eucharist, Holy Communion or Mass.

Divine Office

The daily services set out by the Rule of St Benedict.

Dumb organist

A mechanism attached to a pipe organ which played the instrument automatically with mechanical fingers. Dumb organists worked on the same principle as barrel organs and were used in some churches in the nineteenth century when the human variety could not be found.

Ekphonesis

A word often used over the last century to describe the cantillation of the Byzantine Church. *Ekphonetic* notation indicates the musical equivalents of grammatical signs, such as commas, full-stops and question-marks.

Friar

A member of one of the mendicant, or wandering, monastic orders, such as the Augustinians, Carmelites, Dominicans and Franciscans.

Fugue

A special case of counterpoint, whereby a succession of points is taken up in imitation between parts, such music alternating with passages in freer style.

Gradual

An item of the Proper in the Latin Mass, sung between the readings. From as early as the fifth century Graduals have been complex and demanding chants, intended for expert singers.

Graduale

A liturgical book containing Graduals and other chants applicable to skilled singers.

Gregorian chant

The generic name for the Latin chant of the Western church collated during the papacy of Gregory the Great.

Heterophony

The simultaneous singing or playing of different variations of the same melody.

Hirmos (plural: hirmoi)/heirmos

Part of a hymn of the Byzantine Church, the word meaning stanza in Greek. It is used to describe the first, or model, stanza of a *kontakion* or of one of the nine odes which make up a *kanon*.

Holler

Open vocal music made by African slaves in America, forming part of the complex web of music forming black spirituals.

Hoquetus/hocket

A device of medieval polyphony in which notes and rests alternate rapidly with each other in such a way that rests occur in one part at the same time as notes in another. As one fourteenth-century writer described it: 'one [part] overlaps the other in the manner of roof tiles, and thus they will cut each other off continually'.

Ikonostasis

The screen on which ikons are placed in an Orthodox church.

Introit

Part of the Proper at Mass. It is the first musical item of the service and usually consists of an antiphon appropriate to the theme of the service, a psalm verse, repeat of the antiphon (perhaps omitted), the doxology (Gloria Patri, 'Glory to the Father...') and the antiphon again.

Jacobite Church

A church formed from followers of Jacob Baradai (died in 578). It was based in Syria and Palestine and opposed the findings of the Council of Chalcedon on the nature of Christ.

Jesuit

A member of the Society of Jesus, founded by Ignatius Loyola (1491–1556). The Society was created in order to revive the spiritual life of the Roman Catholic Church.

Jubilus

See Alleluia.

Kanon (plural: kanones)

The most extensive and complex type of Byzantine hymn. A full *kanon* consists of nine odes, each based on a different biblical song.

Kapellmeister

The German term for precentor or chief church musician.

Kithara

The most common stringed instrument of Old Testament times, still widespread throughout the Near East and North Africa. It is shaped like a lyre but the sound chest is made from wood instead of tortoise-shell.

Kontakion (plural: kontakia)

An extended hymn of the Byzantine Church. It consists of many stanzas called *oikoi*. The word means scroll.

Kyriale

A book containing chants for the Ordinary of the Mass of the Western church.

Liber usualis

Literally (from the Latin), a practical or useful book. It is the name given to the Roman Catholic collection of chant in general use until the 1960s.

Liturgy

Originally a public office or duty, from the Greek, *leitourgos*, meaning public servant. The word has since come to mean a form of public worship.

Lyre

A plucked-string instrument whose strings are stretched between a soundbox and a wooden bar. The bar and soundbox are kept apart by two posts either side of the strings. The soundbox is usually made from the shell of a tortoise.

Maestro di capella

The Italian term for precentor or chief church musician.

Maronite Church

A church based in the Lebanon. It was founded at the time of the Crusades and is now uniate.

Mass

The name given by the Roman Catholic Church to the most important form of Christian liturgy, otherwise known as Communion, the Eucharist, the Lord's Supper or the Divine Liturgy. Low Mass indicates a liturgical celebration with little ceremony (it may be without music); High Mass is highly ceremonial and ornate.

Melisma

A word from the Greek for song. It means a group of several notes all sung to one syllable.

Melkites

The Christians in Egypt who did not choose to follow the Monophysites in the Chalcedonian Schism of 451. They were mostly state officials and were therefore nicknamed Melkites ('emperor's men') from the Syriac *malkoye*.

Mode

Literally, a manner or system of operation. In music this generates several meanings, some of which are archaic: 1. a scale-system to which the notes of a piece conform. 2. a rhythmic scheme to which a piece conforms. 3. a prevailing emotional quality to a piece (its mood). 4. the system by which long notes are divided into shorter in medieval and Renaissance times. The first meaning is the most common.

Monody/monophony

Music consisting of a single melody.

Monophysites

Christians who disagreed with the findings of the Council of Chalcedon in 451, believing that Jesus the Son of God has only one nature, which is both human and divine, instead of the orthodox formula of two natures. The Ethiopian and Coptic churches are Monophysite.

Motet

In medieval times, a sung musical item for two to four voices (most often three) built on a pre-existing melody, often a fragment of chant. See also *clausula*. Later on, the term came to mean choral music (probably unaccompanied) with a sacred text.

Motu proprio

A Latin phrase meaning 'of one's own accord'. It is applied to pronouncements from the pope made on his own initiative, independent of advice and signed by him alone.

Mutation stop

An organ stop whose pipes are tuned to reinforce a stop already drawn, thereby creating the illusion of a new timbre when both stops are heard together.

Neume

Originally a term from the Greek to denote a short musical gesture or fragment of a melody. Later (from the ninth century) the word was applied to written signs which stood for these fragments. Western neumes stood for between one and four notes and their Latin names suggest the melodic shape they represent; for example, *virga* – rod and *torculus* – twist.

Ngoma

Vocal sounds imitative of percussion instruments, a traditional part of African music.

Numerology

The study of numbers, in particular of their symbolic significance.

Obikhod

A chant-book for general use in the Russian Orthodox church.

Oktoechos

The system whereby the chants of the Byzantine church are organised into cycles of eight weeks, the chants for each week belonging to one of the eight modes.

Oratorio

An Italian word meaning 'prayer-hall'. Musical items sung in such buildings to illustrate or to comment on biblical stories became known as oratorios.

Ordinary

The term used to describe the items in traditional Christian liturgy whose texts never alter.

Organ Mass

A number of versets collected into book suitable for use by an organist at a particular type of service. François Couperin's *Messe pour les paroisses* (1690) is an example; its structure presumes that the singers alternate with the organ.

Organum

1. the Latin word for organ, the musical instrument. 2. a term which has no direct connection with the organ and whose derivation is obscure. From the ninth

century it was used to describe the addition of a second melody to a first. Over the next three centuries it refers to a type of music where additional 'organal' voices are added to an already existing chant.

Oxford Movement

See Tractarians.

Parody Mass

A setting of texts of the Ordinary of the Mass based on a pre-existing melody, popular in the later fifteenth and sixteenth centuries. The melody might be Gregorian chant, love-song or battle cry.

Polychoral

For many choirs.

Polyphonic

Literally 'many-sounding'; music made by combining melodies.

Precentor

Literally, 'chief singer'. The term is used in Protestant cathedrals for an important musical officer amongst the clergy, and in Scottish Presbyterian churches for a lay-person, perhaps the parish clerk, who begins the singing in the absence of any accompaniment.

Prokeimenon

The equivalent of the Roman Catholic Gradual in the Byzantine Divine Liturgy. Like Graduals, they consist of an elaborate psalm-verse with a refrain.

Proper

The term used to describe the items in traditional Christian liturgy whose texts change according to the subject of celebration. They are therefore 'proper', that is, appropriate to the occasion.

Prosaria

A liturgical book containing *prosae*, that is, sequences.

Psaltes

The Byzantine word for cantor. *Protopsaltes* is the equivalent word for precentor or chief singer. If a Byzantine choir is divided and positioned left and right, the *protopsaltes* leads the right-hand group.

Psalm metre

The system of versification applied to metrical translations of the psalms. In order that any number of tunes might be fitted to them, the metres of English metrical psalms were largely limited to three patterns whose syllable counts per line are as follows: Short Metre (SM) 6.6.8.6, Common Metre (CM) 8.6.8.6 and Long Metre (LM) 8.8.8.8.

Psalter

A book containing the biblical psalms, modified to make them suitable for liturgical use.

Requiem

The Mass for the dead. 'Requiem' is the first word of the service, beginning the introit: *Requiem aeternam dona eis, Domine* (Grant them Eternal Rest, O Lord).

Respond

Strictly, the response after a versicle, but nowadays synonymous with responsory.

Responsory

An elaborate chant of the Roman Catholic Church, sung after the lessons at Matins. As Isidore of Seville (c. 559–636) explained: 'Responsories are so called because a chorus responds... to a soloist.' As with the Gradual and other chants, a responsory consists of a choral refrain (the respond), an elaborate psalm-verse sung by a soloist, followed by a repeat of the last part of the respond. Originally the respond was congregational.

Responsorial

The word used to describe chant in which a choir or congregation responds to or answers a soloist.

Rhetoric

In classical antiquity, one of the *trivium*, the three essential skills in the spoken arts, along with grammar and dialectic. In 1416 *Quintilian's Institutio Oratoria* was rediscovered, providing a renaissance of ideas about possible connections between music and oratory, the art of persuasive speech. Since that time composers have sought rhetorical means to make music emotionally compelling. Connections between classical methods of rhetoric and musical structure were especially strong in the eighteenth century.

Schola cantorum

A school of singers, thus a choir in training and presumably expert.

Second Vatican Council

A reforming council of the Roman Catholic Church which met in 1962. It permitted some radical changes in the liturgy, notably the use of the vernacular (local languages) instead of Latin. The Council's views on music are contained in chapter 6 of the *Constitution on the Sacred Liturgy*, published in 1963.

Sequence

A type of Latin chant popular from about 850 to 1150. Though the style of sequences changed greatly over this period, earlier examples were composed in clearly-defined phrases, the music of each being repeated to different words. These lines of text did not rhyme, hence their common medieval name of *prosa* or prose.

Sequentia

A wordless melody added to *alleluias* to which words might be added to make a *prosa*, or sequence.

Shape notes

A type of notation popular in America in the eighteenth century to help church singers to learn to read music.

Shout

An informal and ecstatic assembly, with dancing, usually following a formal Black gospel service.

Solmisation

A method of indicating melodic intervals. The common Western methods in use today (tonic sol-fa, solfège) have their origins in the solmisation system of Guido.

Spiritual

Christian song, originating in eighteenth-century North America, sung at informal gatherings by both whites and blacks.

Sticheron (plural: stichera)

The Greek word for 'verse'. In Byzantine liturgy, it refers to verses for singing immediately after a psalm verse, like the Western antiphon.

Stile rappresentativo

Literally, 'theatrical style'. This solo vocal style developed rapidly in the early seventeenth century as composers sought to instill into music the persuasive qualities of ancient Greek theatre.

Talmud

A collection of moral precepts and traditions (the Mishnah) and further comments on it (the Gemera), from a Hebrew word meaning instruction. The most recent parts of the Talmud were completed in the fifth-century AD.

Tenebrae

The Matins and Lauds services of the Wednesday, Thursday and Friday before Easter. Following an ancient Roman Catholic tradition, candles are progressively extinguished during the psalms until finally Psalm 51 is sung in darkness, to symbolise Jesus' death.

Tenor

From the Latin, *tenere*, to hold. The voice singing the chant around which medieval polyphony was constructed was called the tenor. As late as the eighteenth century it was the tenor that was given the melody in harmonised hymn-tunes.

Thoroughbass/through bass

English terms for *continuo*.

Tract

A type of chant substituted for the Gradual at Mass in times of penitence and mourning.

Tractarians

Followers of the tenets of the Tracts for the Times, a series of pamphlets published in the 1830s by high-church reformers in the Church of England.

Tridentine

Of the Council of Trent.

Troparion (plural: troparia)

In the Byzantine tradition, originally a short prayer sung after each verse of a psalm, like a refrain. They now take the form of one-verse hymns.

Trope

An insertion of new music or words or both into an already existing chant (see chapter 7). Polyphonic elaborations of chant were also called tropes.

Troper

A liturgical book containing tropes. A well-known example, from the Old Benedictine Minster at Winchester in the tenth century, is the Winchester Troper, which contains *organum* as well as tropes for the Ordinary.

Uniate churches

Eastern churches in union with Roman Catholicism, though following their own liturgy.

Vatican II

See Second Vatican Council.

Verset

A piece of music for the organ, probably based on Gregorian chant, substituting for a sung part of Mass. They were widely used in the Roman Catholic Church from the fifteenth to nineteenth centuries. It was common practice to alternate organ versets with sections of chant from the choir. See Organ Mass.

Versicle

A short verse, answered by a response. The word is also used to describe the distinct phrases that make up sequences.

Villancico

Spanish popular song, popular from the sixteenth to eighteenth centuries, permitted in the liturgy with appropriately sacred words at certain times of the year. Nowadays the word means 'Christmas carol'.

Znamenny

Short for *znamenny raspev*, which means chanting by signs. It is the name given to the chief and most ancient chant of the Russian Orthodox Church, rarely sung nowadays.

Bibliography

This bibliography offers guidance for further general reading and in connection with each chapter. A substantial section (if not all) of each book should prove relevant to the topic in question.

General

Reference

Julian, J., editor, *A Dictionary of Hymnology: Setting Forth the Origin and History of Christian Hymns of all Ages and Nations*, 4 vols, London, 1907; reprinted New York, 1977.
Poultney, D., *Dictionary of Western Church Music*, Chicago, 1991.
Sadie, S., *The New Grove Dictionary of Music and Musicians*, London, 1980.

Historical surveys

Box, R., *Make Music to our God: How We Sing the Psalms*, London, 1996.
Gillen, G. and White, H., editors, *Music and the Church*, Dublin, 1992.
Long, K.R., *The Music of the English Parish Church*, London, 1972.
Routley, E., *The Church and Music*, London, 1967.
Routley, E., *Church Music and the Christian Faith*, Carol Stream, 1978.
Sadie, S. and Latham, A., editors, *The Cambridge Music Guide*, Cambridge, 1985.
Spink, I., editor, *The Blackwell History of Music in Britain*, 6 vols, Oxford, 1981.

Non-musical topics

Davies, H., *Worship and Theology in England*, Princeton NJ, 1961–75.
Every, G., *The Mass*, Dublin, 1978.
Gascoigne, B., *The Christians*, London, 1980.
Johnson, P.B., *A History of Christianity*, London, 1976.
Lane, T., *The Lion Book of Christian Thought*, Oxford, 1984.
Neill, S., *Anglicanism*, Oxford, 1977.

Collections of historical documents

Hayburn, R.F., *Papal Legislation on Sacred Music*, Collegeville MI, 1979.
Strunk, O., *Source Readings in Music History*, New York, 1996.
Weiss, P. and Taruskin, R., *Music in the Western World*, London, 1984.

World music resources of songs and hymns

Asian Institute for Liturgy and Music, *Sound the Bamboo*, Manila, 1990.
Bell, J., editor, *Many and Great* (World Church Songs vol. 1), Glasgow, 1990.
Bell, J., editor, *Sent by the Lord* (World Church Songs vol. 2), Glasgow, 1991.

Hamilton, M., *Sing Freedom! Songs of South African Life*, London, 1992.
Loh, I., editor, *African Songs of Worship* (cassette available), World Council of Churches, Geneva, 1986.
Marachin, J., *Brazilian Songs of Worship*, World Council of Churches, Geneva, 1986.
Martinez, R., editor, *Mil Voces para Celebrar: Himnario Metodista*, Nashville, 1996.
Murray, J., *Alleluia Aotearoa: Hymns and Songs for all Churches*, Christchurch, New Zealand, 1993.
Peacock, D. and Weaver, G., editors, *World Praise*, London, 1995.
Routley, E., editor, *Cantate Domino, An Ecumenical Hymnbook*, Oxford, 1980.
Vigil, J.M. and Torrellas, A., editors, *Misas Centro Americana* with cassette, Managua, 1988.
Wicker, V., editor, *The Hymnology Annual: An International Forum on the Hymn and Worship*, 3 vols, Buchanan MI, 1991–93.

By chapter

Introduction

Hamel, P.L., *Through Music to the Self*, Tisbury, Wilts, 1978.
Rouget, G., *Music and Trance: A Theory of the Relations Between Music and Possession*, Chicago, 1986.
Storr, A., *Music and the Mind*, London, 1992.

Chapter 1: Music in the Old Testament

Epstein, I., editor, *Hebrew-English Edition of the Babylonian Talmud*, 35 vols, London, 1936–48.
Langdon, S., *Babylonian Liturgies*, Paris, 1913.
Oesterley, W.O.E., *The Jews and Judaism During the Greek Period*, London, 1941.
Sachs, C., *The Rise of Music in the Ancient World*, New York, 1944.
Sendrey, H., *Music in Ancient Israel*, London, 1969.
Storr, A., *The Dynamics of Creation*, London, 1972.

Chapter 2: From Synagogue to Early Christian Church

Foley, E.B., *Foundations of Christian Music: The Music of Pre-Constantinian Christianity*, Nottingham, 1992.
McKinnon, J., *Music in Early Christian Literature*, Cambridge, 1987.
Pagels, E., *The Gnostic Gospels*, London, 1980.
Quasten, J., *Music and Worship in Pagan and Christian Antiquity*, Washington DC, 1983.
Seel, T.A., *A Theology of Music for Worship Derived from the Book of Revelation*, New Jersey, 1995.
Werner, E., *The Sacred Bridge*, London, 1959.

Chapter 3: The Western Middle Ages

Richards, J., *Consul of God: The Life and Times of Gregory the Great*, London, 1980.
Wilkinson, J., *Egeria's Travels*, London, 1971.

Chapter 4: The Monastic Tradition

Harper, J., *The Forms and Orders of Western Liturgy from the Tenth to the Eighteenth Century*, Oxford 1991.

Hiley, D., *Western Plainchant: An Introduction*, Oxford, 1993.
Knighton, T. and Fallows, D., editors, *Companion to Medieval and Renaissance Music*, London, 1992 (relevant for chs 4–8).

Chapter 5: Music of the Spheres – The Medieval World-View

James, J., *The Music of the Spheres*, London, 1995.
Meyer-Baer, K., *Music of the Spheres and the Dance of Death*, Princeton, 1970.
Page, C., editor, *Summa Musicae*, Cambridge, 1991.
Palisca, C.V., editor, *Fundamentals of Music: Anicius Manlius Severinus Boethius*, New Haven, 1989.
White, T.H., *The Book of Beasts*, London, 1969.

Chapter 6: Music for the Liturgy

Jungmann, J.A., *The Mass of the Roman Rite*, New York, 1959.
Marrocco, W.T. and Sandon, N., *Medieval Music*, Oxford, 1977.
Rankin, S. and Hiley, editors, *Music in the Mediaeval Liturgy*, Oxford, 1993.
Stevens, J.E., *Words and Music in the Middle Ages*, Cambridge, 1986.

Chapter 7: From the Ear to the Page

Bent, I., 'The English Chapel Royal before 1300', *Proceedings of the Royal Musical Association*, vol. 90, 1963/4.
Parrish, C., *The Notation of Medieval Music*, New York, 1978.
Rankin, S., *The Music of the Medieval Liturgical Drama in France and England*, 2 vols, London, 1989.

Chapter 8: From Gregorian Chant to Polyphony

Kelly, T.F., *Plainsong in the Age of Polyphony*, Cambridge, 1992.
Leech-Wilkinson, D., *Machaut's Mass: An Introduction*, Oxford, 1990.
Marrocco, W. and Sandon, N., editors, *Medieval Music*, Oxford, 1977.
Page, C., *The Owl and the Nightingale: Musical Life and Ideas in France, 1100–1300*, London, 1989.
Wright, C., *Music and Ceremony at Notre Dame, 500–1550*, Cambridge, 1989.

Chapter 9: Wycliffe's Challenge to the Church

Keen, M., *English Society in the Later Middle Ages*, Harmondsworth, 1990.

Chapter 10: Luther and the Reformation

Blume, F., *Protestant Church Music*, London, 1975.
Halter, C. and Schalk, C., *A Handbook of Church Music*, St Louis, 1978.
Leupold, U.S., *Luther's Works*, vol. 53: *Liturgy and Hymns*, Philadelphia, 1965.
Swihart, A.K., *Luther and the Lutheran Church*, London, 1961.

Chapter 11: The Swiss Reformers – The Calvinist Tradition

Labelle, N., *Les Differents Styles de la Musique en France*, vols 2 and 3, *Le Psaume*, Henryville PA, 1981.
Leaver, R.A., *'Goostly psalmes and spirituall songes', English and Dutch metrical psalms from Coverdale to Utenhove 1535–66*, Oxford, 1991.
Scholes, P., *The Puritans and Music*, London, 1934.

Chapter 12: The Reformation in England

Benham, H., *Latin Church Music c.1460–1575*, London, 1977.
Harrison, F., editor, *The Eton Choirbook in Musica Britannica*, vols 10–12, London, 1973.
Knowles, D., *Bare Ruined Choirs,* Cambridge, 1976.
Le Huray, P., *Music and the Reformation in England*, Cambridge, 1978.
Rivkah, Z., *English Metrical Psalms: Poetry as Praise and Prayer, 1535–1601*, Cambridge, 1987.
Stevens, D., *Tudor Church Music*, New York, 1973.
Wrightson, J., *The 'Wanley' Manuscripts: A Critical Commentary*, New York, 1989.

Chapter 13: The Chapel Royal and Cathedral Music

Ashbee, A., *Records of English Court Music*, 9 vols, Aldershot, Hants, 1986–96.
Boyd, M.C., *Elizabethan Music and Musical Criticism*, Pennsylvania, 1940; reprinted Westport CT, 1973.
Burden, M., *Purcell Remembered*, London, 1995.
Holman, P., *Henry Purcell*, London, 1994.
Payne, I., *The Provision and Practice of Sacred Music at Cambridge Colleges and Selected Cathedrals, 1547–1646*, London, 1993.
Phillips, P., *English Sacred Music, 1549–1649*, Oxford, 1991.

Chapter 14: Catholic Reform

Lockwood, L., *Palestrina, Pope Marcellus Mass*, New York, 1975.
Schroeder, H.J., *Canons and Decrees of the Council of Trent*, Rockford IL, 1978.
Stevenson, R., *Spanish Cathedral Music in the Golden Age*, Los Angeles, 1961; reprinted Westport CT, 1976.
Weber, E., *Le Concile de Trente et la Musique: De la réforme et la Contre-réforme*, Paris, 1982.

Chapter 15: Italian Splendour

Arnold, D., *The Oratorio in Venice*, Oxford, 1986.
Carter, T., *Music in Late Renaissance and Early Baroque Italy*, London, 1992.
Carver, A.F., *Cori Spezzati*, 2 vols, Cambridge, 1988.
Crowther, V., *The Oratorio in Modena*, Oxford, 1992.
Pahlen, K., *The World of the Oratorio*, Aldershot, Hants, 1991.
Smither, H.E., *A History of the Oratorio*, 3 vols, Oxford, 1977, 1987.

Chapter 16: The Music of the Lutheran Church

Irwin, J.L., *Neither Voice nor Heart Alone: German Lutheran Theology of Music in the Age of the Baroque*, New York, 1993.
Snyder, K.J. *Dieterich Buxtehude, Organist in Lübeck*, New York, 1987.
Walker, P., editor, *Church, Stage and Studio: Music and its Contexts in Seventeenth-century Germany*, Rochester NY, 1990.
Webber, G., *North German Church Music in the Age of Buxtehude*, Oxford, 1996.

Chapter 17: Heinrich Schütz

Rifkin, J. *et al.*, *The New Grove North European Baroque Masters: Schütz, Froberger, Buxtehude, Purcell, Telemann*, London, 1985.
Spagnoli, G., *Letters and Documents of Heinrich Schütz, 1656–72*, Ann Arbor MI, 1990.

Chapter 18: J.S. Bach

Boyd, M., *Bach*, Oxford, 1983.
David, H.T. and Mendel, A., editors, *The Bach Reader*, London, 1966.
Gerz, H., *Essays on J.S. Bach*, Ann Arbor MI, 1985.
Spitta, P., *Johann Sebastian Bach*, London, 1884.

Chapter 19: Turmoil in England – Commonwealth and Restoration

Fellowes, E.H., *English Cathedral Music*, London, 1969.
Mace, T., *Musick's Monument*, London, 1767; reprinted Paris, 1966.
Spink, I., editor, *The Blackwell History of Music in Britain: The Seventeenth Century*, Oxford, 1992.
Spink, I., *Restoration Cathedral Music 1660–1714*, Oxford, 1995.
Wilson, J.W., *Roger North on Music*, London, 1959.

Chapter 20: Congregational Music

Temperley, N., *Music of the English Parish Church*, 2 vols, Cambridge, 1979.
Davie, D. and Stevenson, R., *English Hymnology in the Eighteenth Century*, Los Angeles, 1980.
Hogwood, C. and Luckett, R., *Music in Eighteenth Century England*, Cambridge, 1983.
Burrows, D., *Handel: Messiah*, Cambridge, 1991.

Music and the Wesleys

Young, C.R., *Music of the Heart*, London, 1995.

West-gallery Music

Elbourne, R., *Music and Tradition in Early Industrial Lancashire*, Woodbridge, Suffolk, 1980.
MacDermott, K.H., *The Old Church Gallery Minstrels*, London, 1948.
Woods, R., *Good Singing Still*, Telford, 1995.

Chapter 21: Wales – Land of Song

Davies, L.W., *A History of Music in Wales from c. 1750 to 1996*, Aldershot, Hants, 1997.
Edwards, O.T., *Matins, Lauds and Vespers for St David's Day*, Cambridge, 1990.
Luff, A., *Welsh Hymns and their Tunes*, London, 1990.

Chapter 22: Music in the Courts of Europe

Anthony, J.R., *French Baroque Music from Beaujoyeulx to Rameau*, London, 1973.
Saunders, S., *Cross, Sword and Lyre: Sacred Music at the Imperial Court of Ferdinand II of Habsburg (1619–37)*, Oxford, 1995.

Chapter 23: The Romantic Movement

Harding, J., *Gounod*, London, 1973.
Merrick, P., *Revolution and Religion in the Music of Liszt*, Cambridge, 1987.
Redlich, H.F., *Bruckner and Mahler*, London, 1963.

Chapter 25: The Church of England and the Tractarians

Boston, N. and Langwill, L.G., *Church and Chamber Barrel Organs*, Edinburgh, 1967.
Curwen, J.S., *Studies in Worship-Music*, London, 1880, 2nd series, 1885.
Gatens, W.J., *Victorian Cathedral Music in Theory and Practice*, Cambridge, 1986.
Joyce, F.W., *Life of Sir F.A.G. Ouseley*, London, 1896.

Chapter 26: Revival in the Nineteenth Century

Boon, B., *Sing the Happy Song*, London, 1978.
Moody, W.R., *The Life of Dwight L. Moody*, New York, 1900.
Sankey, I.D., *My Life and Sacred Songs*, London, 1906.
Stevenson, R.M., *Patterns of Protestant Church Music*, Cambridge, 1953.

Chapter 27: The Orthodox Churches

Bryer, A., and Cunningham, M., editors, *Mount Athos and Byzantine Monasticism*, Aldershot, Hants, 1996.
Ware, T., *The Orthodox Church*, Harmondsworth, 1993.
Zernov, N., *Eastern Christendom*, London, 1961.

Chapter 28: The Greek Orthodox Church

Tillyard, H.J., *Byzantine Music and Hymnography*, London, 1923.
Wellesz, E., editor, *Studies in Eastern Chant*, Oxford, 1966.

Chapter 29: The Russian Orthodox Church

Gardner, J., *Liturgical Chant of the Russian Orthodox Church*, 2 vols, Jordanville NY, 1979.
Gardner, J., *Russian Church Singing*, New York, 1980.
Morosan, V., editor, *One Thousand Years of Russian Church Music, 988–1988*, Madison CT, 1991.
Roccasalvo, J.L., *The Plain Chant Tradition of the Southwestern Rus*, New York, 1986.
Swan, A.J., *Russian Music and its Sources in Chant and Folk-song*, London, 1973.

Chapter 30: The Coptic and Ethiopian Churches

Powne, M., *Ethiopian Music*, Oxford, 1968.

Chapter 32: Africa and the Influence of Western Music

Achinivu, A.K., *Ikoli Harcourt White: The Man and His Music*, no. 7, Beitrage zur Ethnomusikologie, Hamburg, 1979.
Kwabena Kyeta, J.H., *The Music of Africa*, London, 1982.

Chapter 33: The Independent Churches

Fashole-Luke, Gray, Hastings and Tasie, editors, *Christianity in Independent Africa*, London, 1978.
Jules-Rosette, B., 'Ecstatic Singing: Music and Social Integration in an African Church' in Jackson, I.E., editor, *More than Drumming*, London, 1985.

Chapter 34: Christianity Comes to the New World

Appel, R.G., *The Music of the Bay Psalm Book*, Brooklyn, 1975.
Billings, W., *Continental Harmony*, editor N. Nathan, Harvard, 1961.
Billings, W., *The Psalm-Singer's Amusement*, 1781; reprinted New York, 1974.
Drummond, R.R., *Early German Music in Pennsylvania*, 1910; reprinted New York, 1970.
Lowens, I., *Music and Musicians in Early America*, New York, 1964.
MacDougall, H.C., *Early New England Psalmody: An Historical Appreciation, 1620–1820*, New York, 1969.

Patterson, B.B., *The Sound of the Dove: Singing in Appalachian Primitive Baptist Churches*, Urbana and Chicago, 1995.
Patterson, D.W., *The Shaker Spiritual*, Princeton, 1979.
Pratt, W.S., *The Music of the Pilgrims*, Boston, 1921.

Chapter 35: Africans in America

Epstein, D.J., *Sinful Tunes and Spirituals: Black Folk Music to the Civil War*, Urbana IL, 1977.
Martin, S.V. and Keck, G.R., editors, *Feel the Spirit, Studies in Nineteenth-Century Afro-American Music*, Connecticut, 1988.
Southern, E., *The Music of Black Americans*, 2nd edition, New York, 1983.

Chapter 36: Gospel Music – White and Black

Broughton, V., *Black Gospel*, Poole, 1985.
Harris, M.W., *The Rise of the Gospel Blues: The Music of T.A. Dorsey in the Urban Church*, Oxford, 1994.
Heilbut, A. *The Gospel Sound*, New York, 1971.
Johnson, C.A., *The Frontier Camp Meeting*, Dallas, 1955.
Montell, W.L., *Singin the Glory Down: Amateur Gospel Music in South Central Kentucky 1900–90*, Kentucky, 1991.
Spencer, J.M., *Protest and Praise: Sacred Music of Black Religion*, Minneapolis, 1990.

Chapter 37: The United States and the European Classical Tradition

Ives, C., *Memos*, New York, 1972.
Pemberton, C.A., *Lowell Mason: His Life and Work*, Epping, Essex, 1985.
Wooldridge, D., *Charles Ives*, London, 1975.

Chapter 38: Latin America

Appleby, D., *Music of Brazil*, Texas, 1989.
Béhague, G., *Music in Latin America: An Introduction*, Englewood Cliffs NJ, 1979.

Chapter 39: Christian Music in Australasia

Cox, G., 'Church Music' in *The Oxford Companion to Australian Music*, Oxford, in press, 1997.
Thomson, J.M., *The Oxford History of New Zealand Music*, Auckland NZ, 1991.

Chapter 40: Roman Catholic Music in Europe

Overath, J., *Sacred Music and Liturgy Reform After Vatican II*, Rome, 1969.
Thomerson, K., *Jean Langlais: A Bio-Bibliography*, Westport CN, 1988.

Chapter 41: The Bible in the Concert Hall

Glendenning, F.J., *The Church and the Arts*, London, 1960.
Hell, H., *Francis Poulenc*, London, 1959.
Hillier, P., *Arvo Pärt*, Oxford, 1996.
Messiaen, O., *Musique et Couleur*, Paris, 1986.
Walsh, S., *The Music of Stravinsky*, Oxford, 1993.

Chapter 42: Vatican II and the Liturgy

Gelineau, J., editor, *Growing in Church Music: Report of 'Why Church Music?' Congress*, Washington DC, 1988.

Gelineau, J., *The Liturgy Today and Tomorrow*, London, 1978.
Jeffery, P., *Chant, Liturgy and Culture*, Washington DC, 1992.
Murray, Dom G., *Music and the Mass*, Leigh-on-Sea, Essex, 1977.
Music from Taizé, London 1982, 1986.
Roger, Brother, *The Taizé Experience*, London, 1990.

Chapter 43: Lutheran Musical Revival

Meyer, M., *The Politics of Music in the Third Reich*, New York, 1989.
Palmer, L., *Hugo Distler and His Church Music*, London, 1967.

Chapter 44: Music in Britain

Palmer, C., *Herbert Howells*, London, 1978.
Patten, J., *Eighty-eight Years of Cathedral Music 1898–1986*, London, 1993.
Shaw, M., *The Principles of English Church Music Composition*, London, 1921.

Chapter 45: The Popular Stream

Maries, A., *One Heart, One Voice*, London, 1986.
Marshall, M., *Renewal in Worship*, London, 1982.
Miller, S., *The Contemporary Christian Music Debate: Worldly Compromise or Agent of Renewal?*, Wheaton IL, 1993.
Peters, D., *What About Christian Rock?*, Minneapolis, 1986.
Pulkingham, B., *Sing God a Simple Song*, Basingstoke, 1986.
Pulkingham, W.G., *They Left Their Nets*, London, 1974.

Chapter 46: Good and Bad

Campling, C.R., *The Food of Love: Reflections on Music and Faith*, London, 1997.
Graham, Y.M., *The Church Hesitant*, London, 1993.
In Tune with Heaven: The Report of the Archbishop's Commission on Church Music, London, 1992.
Maries, A., *Church Music in the Mission of the Church*, Mildenhall, Suffolk, 1996.
Rees, R.L.D., *Weary and Ill at Ease: A Survey of Clergy and Organists*, Leominster, 1993.
Sheldon, R., editor, *In Spirit and in Truth: Exploring Directions in Music in Worship Today*, London, 1989.

Appendix – Organ Music

Bicknell, S., *The History of the English Organ*, Cambridge, 1996.
Williams, P., *The European Organ 1450–1850*, London, 1966.
Williams, P., *A New History of the Organ*, London, 1980.
Williams, P., *The Organ in Western Culture, 750–1250*, Cambridge, 1993.

Discography

Space demands that this guide to recordings is selective. Unless otherwise stated, the recordings are compact discs and the majority are commercially available as this book goes to the press. Identification is assisted by brief details of the performers, followed by the manufacturer's name and the recording number.

Introduction

The Gospel Ship, Baptist Hymns and White Spirituals, New World Records (LP) NW 294

Chapter 1: Music in the Old Testament

Babylonian Biblical Chants, Ezekiel Albeg, Smithsonian/Folkways cassette 8930
Bedouin Music of Southern Sinai, Smithsonian/Folkways cassette 4204

Chapter 2: From Synagogue to Early Christian Church

Ancient Greek Music (reconstructions of ancient Greek musical fragments), Madrid Atrium Musicae/Paniagua, Harmonia Mundi HMA190 1015

Chapter 3: The Western Middle Ages

12th-century Cistercian Chant, Organum Ens/Pérès, Harmonia Mundi HMC90 1392
Antiphons (Gregorian), Triors Notre Dame Abbey Monks/Lebon, Jade 74321-33326-2
Solesmes Abbey: Mass of Benedict (Gregorian chant), Solesmes Abbey Choir/Claire, Solesmes S820

Chapter 4: The Monastic Tradition

Hildegard: Ordo Virtutum, Sequentia, Deutsche Harmonia Mundi GD 77051
Hildegard of Bingen: Canticles of Ecstasy, Sequentia, Deutsche Harmonia Mundi, 05472 77320 2
Hildegard of Bingen: Symphony of the Harmony of Celestial Revelations, Symphonye/Stevie Wishart, Celestial Harmonies 13127-2

Chapter 6: Music for the Liturgy

The Italian Lauda c. 1400–1700, Huelgas Ensemble/van Nevel, Deutsche Harmonia Mundi 05472 77439 2

Chapter 7: From the Ear to the Page

Worcester Fragments, The Orlando Consort, Amon Ra CD-SAR59
Medieval English Music (includes Worcester Fragments and other liturgical polyphony), Hilliard Ensemble, Harmonia Mundi HMA 190 1106
Messe de le Nativité de la Vierge (Léonin and Pérotin), Organum Ens/Pérès, Harmonia Mundi HMC90 1538
The Age of Cathedrals (early medieval polyphony), Theatre of Voices/Hillier, Harmonia Mundi HMU90 7157

Chapter 8: From Gregorian Chant to Polyphony

Popes and Antipopes (sacred motets from 14th-century France and Italy), Orlando Consort, Metronome METCD1008
On Yoolis Night (includes medieval carols from the 15th century), Theatre of Voices/Hillier, Harmonia Mundi HMX290 825
Machaut: Messe de Notre Dame (in liturgical context), Taverner Consort/Parrott, EMI CDC7 47949-2

Chapter 12: The Reformation in England

Taverner: Missa Coronea Spinea, Sixteen/Christophers, Hyperion CDA 66360
New London Chamber Choir (includes masses by Pierre de la Rue and Josquin), Amon Ra CD-SAR24
A Tudor Collection (boxed set includes sacred music by Cornysh, Taverner, Tallis, Byrd's three masses), Tallis Scholars/Phillips, Gimell CDGIMB450
Thomas Tallis: Nine Psalm Tunes from Archbishop Parker's Psalter, Tallis Scholars/Phillips, Gimell CDGIM999
Music from the Eton Choirbook, Sixteen/Christophers, Meridian CDE 84175

Chapter 13: The Chapel Royal and Cathedral Music

Elizabethan Christmas Anthems (includes devotional consort songs), Red Byrd/Rose Consort of Viols, Amon Ra CD-SAR46
Tomkins: Cathedral Music, St George's Chapel Choir/Robinson, Hyperion CDA 66345
The English Anthem, vols 1–6, St Paul's Cathedral/Scott, Hyperion CDA 66374, 66519, 66618, 66678, 66758, 66826
Purcell: Complete Anthems and Services, vols 1–11, King's Consort/New College Choir/King, Hyperion CDA 66585, 66609, 66623, 66644, 66656, 66663, 66677, 66686, 66693, 66707, 66716
Music of the Chapels Royal (includes Purcell, Humfrey, Blow, Locke), Monteverdi Choir/Gardiner, Erato 2292-45987-2
John Blow: Anthems, Parley of Instruments/Holman, Hyperion CDA 67031/2

Chapter 14: Catholic Reform

Dufay: Missa L'Homme Armé, Oxford Camerata/Summerly, Naxos 8 553087
The Brightest Heaven of Invention (includes motets by Regis, Obrecht, Josquin, Brumel, Dufay, Busnois), New London Chamber Choir/Wood, Amon Ra CDSAR 56
A Palestrina Collection (boxed set includes Missa Papae Marcelli and other masses), Tallis Scholars/Phillips, Gimell CDGIMB400
Palestrina: Missa Papae Marcelli (in the context of Tridentine Pontifical High Mass of 1613), William Byrd Choir/Turner BBC CD 572
Spanish and Portuguese Harpsichord Music (includes Cabezón), Sophie Yates, Chandos CHAN0560
Victoria: Sacred Choral Works, Westminster Cathedral Choir/Hill, Hyperion
Juan de Araujo – L'Or et L'Argent du Haut-Pérou (17th-century villancicos), Jos Records K617049 CDA 66129
Masterpieces of Mexican Polyphony (de Padilla, Franco, Capillas, de Salazar), Westminster Cathedral Choir/O'Donnell, Hyperion CDA 66330

Chapter 15: Italian Splendour

Monteverdi: Sacred Choral Works, Sixteen/Christophers, Hyperion CDA 66214
Venetian Music for Double Choir (includes Willaert and G. Gabrieli), Currende Vocal
Ensemble/van Nevel, Accent ACC 93101D
Frescobaldi: Primo libri di Capricci, Leonhardt, Philips 432 128-2PH
Venice Preserved (includes music by Bassano, A. and G. Gabrieli, Monteverdi), Gentlemen of
the Chappell/Bassano, ASV CD GAU 122
Stradella: San Giovanni Battista, Musiciens du Louvre/Minkowski, Erato 2292-45739-2
Carissimi: Jephte, Monteverdi Choir/Gardiner, Erato 2292-45466-2
Venetian Vespers (as celebrated in 1643, includes music by Monteverdi, Rigatti, Grandi,
Cavalli), Gabrieli Consort/McCreesh, Archiv 437552-2
Monteverdi: Vespers, New London Consort/Pickett, l'Oiseau-Lyre 425 823-2OH2

Chapter 16: The Music of the Lutheran Church

German Church Cantatas and Arias (Buxtehude, J. Christoph Bach, Telemann), Kuijken
Consort, Accent ACC7912

Chapter 17: Heinrich Schütz

Schütz: Kleine Geistliche Concerten etc, Paris Chapelle Royale/Herreweghe, Harmonia Mundi
HMC90 1261, see also Janequin Ensemble/Saqueboutiers de Toulouse, Harmonia Mundi
HMC90 1255
Schütz: Christmas Oratorio (includes SWV 435, 398–418, 493) Schütz Ens/Kelber, Calig
CAL50941

Chapter 18: J.S. Bach

J.S. Bach: Cantatas in 10 vols, various artists/Harnoncourt/Leonhardt, Teldec 4509-91755-2
to 4509-91764-2
J.S. Bach: Mass in B Minor, Amsterdam Baroque/Koopman, Erato 4509-98478-2
J.S. Bach: Complete Motets, Sixteen/Christophers, Hyperion CDA66369
J.S. Bach: St John Passion, Monteverdi Choir/Gardiner, Archiv 419 324-2AH2
J.S. Bach: St Matthew Passion (complete), Amsterdam Baroque Orchestra/Koopman, Erato
2292-45814-2
J.S. Bach: St Matthew Passion (arranged by Mendelssohn for performance in 1829), Chorus
Musicus/Spering, Opus 111 OPS30-72/3
J.S. Bach: Complete Organ Works, Peter Hurford, London 444 410-2LC17

Chapter 20: Congregational Music

Under the Greenwood Tree (the carols and dances of Hardy's Wessex), Mellstock Band and
Choir, Saydisc CD-SDL360
Sing Lustily and with Good Courage (English west-gallery hymns and carols), Maddy
Prior/Carnival Band, Saydisc CD-SDL383
Georgian Anthem (18th-century English anthems), New College Choir/Higginbottom,
Meridian CDE84151
Handel: Messiah, Taverner Choir/Parrott, Virgin VMD5 61330-2

Chapter 22: Music in the Courts of Europe

Mozart: Sacred Works (includes Mass K317, Epistle Sonatas, Vesper K339), Academy of

Ancient Music/Hogwood, L'Oiseau-Lyre 436 585-2OH
J. Michael Haydn: Masses and Vespers, Trinity College Choir/Marlow, Conifer CDCF220
Lully: Motets, Paris Chapelle Royale/Herreweghe, Harmonia Mundi HMC90 1167
Henri Du Mont: Sacred Choral Works, Paris Chapelle Royale Choir/Herreweghe, Harmonia Mundi HMA 190 1077
Marc-Antoine Charpentier: Advent Anthems, Arts Florissants/Christie, Harmonia Mundi HMA 190 5124
Marc-Antoine Charpentier: Tenebrae, Musica Polyphonica/Davos, Erato 4509-96376-2
Delalande: Regina Coeli (motets for Louis XIV) Ex Cathedra/Skidmore, ASV CDGAU141
François Couperin: Leçons de Ténèbres, Nelson/Kirkby/Ryan/Hogwood, L'Oiseau-Lyre 444 169-2OM

Chapter 23: The Romantic Movement

Romantic Choral Music (includes motets by Liszt, Brahms, Bruckner, Schubert), Stuttgart Südrundfunkchor/Huber Hänssler CD98 933
Liszt: Hungarian Coronation Mass, Budapest Symphony Orchestra/Lehel, Hungaroton HCD12148
Gounod: Mors et Vita, Toulouse Capitole Orchestra/Plasson, EMI CDS7 54459-2
Gounod: Harmonies Célestes (various sacred songs), Gleusteen/Vernet etc, Ligia Digital LIDI202011
Fauré: Requiem (includes other sacred works), Corydon Singers/Scott, Hyperion CDA 66292
Bruckner: Mass no 2 in E minor, CBSO Choir/Halsey, Conifer CDCF 192

Chapter 25: The Church of England and the Tractarians

My Soul doth Magnify the Lord – Anglican Evening Service, St Paul's Cathedral Choir/Scott, Hyperion CDA 66249
My Spirit hath Rejoiced – Anglican Evening Service, St Paul's Cathedral Choir/Scott, Hyperion CDA 66305
Psalms from St Paul's, vols 1–4 (Anglican chant), St Paul's Cathedral Choir/Scott, Hyperion CDP 11001 to 11004
John Maunder: Olivet to Calvary, Guildford Cathedral Choir/Rose, CFP CD-CFP4619
John Stainer: The Crucifixion (recorded 1930), CLAR CDGE78-50-50
Stanford: Cathedral Music, Worcester Cathedral Choir/Hunt, Hyperion CDA 66030

Chapter 26: Revival in the Nineteenth Century

The Hymns of Ira Sankey, Daybreak Gospel Singers, Ambassador Productions DCD 180
Just as I Am (Ira Sankey hymns), Kingsway KMCD 987
All Things Bright and Beautiful (Havergal and Alexander hymns), Kingsway KMCD 851
Melodies from the Heart, Portsmouth Songsters, Salvationist Promotions and Supplies BHSS 0304
Let the Morning Bring, Music Leaders' Conference 1997, Salvationist Promotions and Supplies CSP&S 112
Partita, Salvation Army Staff Bands SP&S 111
Fully Persuaded, Beverley Shea, Alliance Music SSD 0101

Chapter 28: The Greek Orthodox Church

Many recordings on the IKON label

Chapter 29: The Russian Orthodox Church

Ancient and Monastic Orthodox Chants (from Russia), Rospev Ensemble/Grindenko, CdM
Russian Season LDC288 003
The Feasts of the Russian Orthodox Liturgical Year, vols 1 and 2, Ural Choir/Novik, CdM Russian
Season LDC288 076/077
Russian Church Music (18th- and 19th-century composers), Slavyanka, Harmonia Mundi
HMU90 7098
Tchaikovsky: Liturgy of St John Chrysostom opus 41, Moscow Choral Academy/Popov, CDM
RUS288 096
Rachmaninoff: Vespers opus 37, Robert Shaw Festival Singers/Shaw, Telarc CD-8017

Chapter 30: The Coptic and Ethiopian Churches

Coptic Music (St Mark, Cairo), Smithonian/Folkways cassette 8960

Chapter 31: Christianity, East and West – Worlds Apart?

John Tavener (born 1944): Orthodox Vigil Service, Christ Church Cathedral Choir/Grier, Ikon
IKO16/7
John Tavener: We Shall See Him As He Is, BBC Welsh Symphony Orchestra/Hickox, Chandos
CHAN9128
Arvo Pärt: Passio Nostri Jesu Christi Domini secundum Johannem, Western Wind/Hillier, ECM 837
109-2

Chapter 32: Africa and the Influence of Western Music

God Is Working His Purpose Out – Namirembe Cathedral Evensong Choir, Uganda (music by
Wassanyi-Sserukenya and others, LP 1974), Afromarket, London, Ekitala Kyomoyo OOX 100
Psalms of the Cameroons, Smithonian/Folkways cassette 8910
Loh, I., editor, *African Songs of Worship* (with cassette), World Council of Churches, Geneva
1986

Chapter 34: Christianity Comes to the New World

Billings: Anthems and Fuguing Tunes, His Majestie's Clerks/Hillier, Harmonia Mundi HMU90
7048
Goostly Psalms – Anglo-American Psalmody (includes Tans'ur, Billings and others), His Majestie's
Clerks/Hillier, Harmonia Mundi HMU90 7128
Music of the Americas (choral survey, includes Billings and Moravian anthems), Gloria Dei
Cantores/Patterson, Gloria Dei Cantores GDC010
Music of the Shakers – Glee Clubs of Smith and Amherst Colleges, Smithonian/Folkways cassette
5378

Chapter 35: Africans in America

Wade in the Water vol. 1: *African American Spirituals, the Concert Tradition*, Fisk Jubilee Singers
etc, Smithonian/Folkways SF 40072
Wade in the Water vol. 2: *African American Congregational Singing: 19th Century Roots*, McIntosh
County Shouters/Rev C.J. Johnson etc, SF 40073
Wade in the Water, vol. 3: *African American Gospel: The Pioneering Composers*, Sweet Honey in
the Rock etc, SF 40074

Chapter 36: Gospel Music – White and Black

The Gospel Ship (Baptist Hymns and White Spirituals), New World Records (LP) NW 294
Wade in the Water, vol. 4: *African American Community Gospel*, Gospel Harmonettes etc, SF 40075
Urban Holiness Service (Elder Charles D. Beck), Smithonian/Folkways cassette 8901
I Sing because I'm Happy (gospel songs from and interviews with Mahalia Jackson), Smithonian/Folkways cassette SFSP 90002
If Ever We Needed the Lord Before (Marion Williams), Columbia 471545 2
Get Right with God – Hot Gospel (1950s/60s, various historic recordings), Heritage HTCD 01
Friends in High Places (contemporary gospel and soul, various artists), Expansion CDEXP 10

Chapter 37: The United States and the European Classical Tradition

Leo Sowerby: American Master of Sacred Song (anthems, psalms, organ works), Gloriae Dei Cantores/Patterson, Gloriae Dei Cantores GDCD016
Alleluia! – Sacred Choral Music in New England (includes Bay Psalm Book, music by Chadwick, Parker, Paine, Ives), Northeastern NR247-CD
Charles Ives: Choral Works (includes psalms), BBC Singers/Cleobury, Collins Classics COLL1479-2

Chapter 38: Latin America

Nueva España (includes music by many colonial composers of South America with instrumental accompaniment), Boston Schola Cantorum etc/Cohen, Erato 2292-45977-2
The Historic Organ of San Jeronimo Tlacochahuaya, Mexico (16th- and 17th-century music), Ferran, Jos Records K617049
Juan de Araujo – L'Or et L'Argent du Haut-Pérou (17th-century villancicos from Peru), Jos Records K617049
Masterpieces of Mexican Polyphony (de Padilla, Franco, Capillas, de Salazar), Westminster Cathedral Choir/O'Donnell, Hyperion CDA 66330
Gospel Songs from the Bahamas, Smithonian/Folkways cassette 6824
Spiritual Baptist Music of Trinidad, Smithonian/Folkways cassette 4234
He Aqui Estoy Contigo (Peruvian Christian songs by Kerygma Canta), Decamen Productions, P.O. Box 5342 Lima 100, Peru (cassette)
Ariel Ramirez: Misa Criolla (includes other works), Lagun Onak Choir/Ramirez, Milan, CDCH805
Vigil, J.M. and Torrellas, A., editors, *Misas Centro Americana* (with cassette), Managua 1988

Chapter 39: Christian Music in Australasia

Spirit of Polynesia (includes *himeni tuki, humeni nota, himeni tarava*), The David Fanshawe recordings 1978–88, Saydisc CD-SDL403
Spirit of Micronesia (recordings by David Fanshawe 1978–88), Saydisc CD-SD414
Tubuai Choir (recordings by Pascal Nabet-Meyer), Sanachie 64049
The Tahitian Choir, 2 vols (recordings by Pascal Nabet-Meyer), Sanachie 64054, 64055
A Sound Came from Heaven (Leighton: Mass opus 66, Douglas Mews: A Sound Came from Heaven etc), Wellington Cathedral Choir/Walsh, Herald HAVPCD191
Christopher Willcock – recordings available from GIA Publications Inc.

Chapter 40: Roman Catholic Music in Europe

Laetabunda – Gregorian chant and chant-inspired choral and organ music by Langlais and Duruflé, Farnborough Abbey Choir/Noble, Herald HAVPCD 179
Charles Tournemire – Organ Music (includes part of L'Orgue Mystique), Dufourcet, Priory PRCD328
La Jeune France (Jolivet, Messaien, Daniel-Lesur), Sixteen/Christophers Collins Classics COLL1480-2
Messiaen: Trois Petites Liturgies etc, London Sinfonietta/Edwards,Virgin Classics VC 7 91472-2
Messiaen: Organ Works (includes Messe de la Pentecôte), Weir, Collins Classics COLL7031-2

Chapter 41: The Bible in the Concert Hall

Stravinsky: Choral Works, New London Chamber Choir/Wood, Hyperion CDA 66410
Elgar: The Dream of Gerontius, Royal Liverpool Philharmonic Orchestra/Handley, EMI CD-EMXD2500
Britten: The Burning Fiery Furnace, English Opera Group Choir and Orchestra/Britten, Decca 414 663-2LM
Vaughan Williams: Dona Nobis Pacem/Sancta Civitas, London Symphony Orchestra/Hickox, EMI CDC7 54788-2
Walton: Belshazzar's Feast, BBC Symphony Orchestra/Mackerras, Carlton Classics CD 15656 91612
Honegger: Le Roi David, Lille National Orchetra/Casadesus, EMI CDC7 54793-2
Honegger: Une Cantate de Noël, Poulenc: Mass in G and motets, Winchester Cathedral Choir/Neary EMI CD-EMX2275
Poulenc: Gloria (includes motets), Cambridge Singers/Rutter, Collegium COLCD 108
Evocation of the Spirit (includes sacred music by Gorecki, Pärt, Barber, Schönberg, Martin: Mass (1922)), Robert Shaw Festival Singers/Shaw,Telarc CD80406

Chapter 42: Vatican II and the Liturgy

Cantate! (music from Taizé), Taizé T505
Resurrexit (music from Taizé), Taizé T508

Chapter 43: Lutheran Musical Revival

Cantate Domino (includes Schütz, J.S. Bach, Distler and Pepping: Deutsche Messe), St Lorenz Bach Choir/Harrassowitz, Motette CD50261
Ernst Pepping: Passionsbericht de Matthäus, Danish National Radio Choir/Parkman, Chandos CHAN8854

Chapter 44: Music in Britain

Praise to the Lord (includes hymns from the *English Hymnal* 1906 and late 19th-century anthems), St Pauls Cathedral
British Choral Works (includes Vaughan Williams G minor Mass, Howells Requiem), Corydon Singers/Best, Hyperion CDA 66076
A Sound Came from Heaven (Leighton: Mass opus 66, Douglas Mews: A Sound Came from Heaven etc), Wellington Cathedral Choir/Walsh, Herald HAVPCD191
Herbert Howells: Church Music (2 vols), New College Choir/Higginbottom, CRD 3454/5
Britten: Choral Music, Westminster Cathedral Choir/Hill, Hyperion CDA 6622
Michael Tippett: Choral Works, Finzi Singers/Spicer, Chandos CHAN 9265
William Mathias Church and Choral Music (Christ Church Cathedral Choir/Darlington), Nimbus NI 5243

The English Anthem, vol. 5 (includes anthems by Jonathan Harvey, Kenneth Leighton, Lennox Berkeley, Herbert Howells, Richard Rodney Bennett), Magdalen College Choir/Harper, Abbey CDCA915

Chapter 45: The Popular Stream

Gloria (the sacred music of John Rutter), Cambridge Singers/Rutter, Collegium COLCD 100
John Bell – *Heaven Shall Not Wait*, The Iona Community, Wild Goose Publications, WP 0267
John Bell – *Love From Below*, The Iona Community, Wild Goose Publications, WP 0270
Shine, Jesus, Shine, Graham Kendrick ALD 093
Only by Grace, Graham Kendrick, HOS CD 01
Spring Harvest Live 1997, ICC D 21030 and ICC D 21130

Alternative Worship

God in the Flesh – the Late Late Service, Sticky Music, PO Box 176, Glasgow G4 9ER

Christian Rock

No Doubt, Petra, Word 701962460X
Jesus Freak, DC Talk, FFD 5140

Dance

Jumping in the House of God, Worldwide Message Tribe, Alliance (2 vols) MOVED 801 and 803

Celtic

Treasures – Best of Iona, Iona, Word WHAD 1303
Celtic Praise, vol. 3, ICC D21530

Appendix – Organ Music

Early English Organ Music (includes Tomkins, Purcell, Blow, Handel), Koopman/Mathot, Capriccio 10 254
Sweelinck – Organ Works, Leonhardt, Deutsche Harmonia Mundi GD77148
Early French Organ Music (2 vols, includes de Grigny, Titelouze, Du Mont, Couperin, d'Anglebert etc), Payne, Naxos 8553214/5

Index

ACKNOWLEDGMENTS

We would like to thank all those who have given us permission to include quotations in this book, as indicated in the list below. Every effort has been made to trace and acknowledge copyright holders of all the quotations included in this book. We apologise for any errors or omissions that may remain, and would ask those concerned to contact the publishers, who will ensure that full acknowledgment is made in the future.

Example 33: 'And One of the Pharisees', by Arvo Pärt, reproduced by kind permission of Universal Edition Ltd.

Example 40: *Precious Lord, Take my Hand,* by Thomas A. Dorsey, Carlin Music Corporation, London.

Example 41: Extract from 'Psalm 90', by Charles Ives © Merion Music, c/o Theodore Presser Co., Presser Place, Bryn Mawr, PA 19010.

Example 42: Hymn tune 'De Tar' by Calvin Hampton.

Example 45: *Dieu, Nous Avons vu ta Gloire,* by Jean Langlais, Secrétariat des Editeurs des Fiches Musicales, France.

Example 46: Excerpt from *La Messe de la Pentecôte* by Olivier Messiaen reproduced with the kind permission of Alphonse Leduc, Paris, publisher owner of the work worldwide.

Example 47: Extract from Psalm 22 (23) *Dominus Regit Me* in English from *Twenty-four Psalms and a Canticle* by Joseph Gelineau, Grail Press, London.

Example 48: *O Lord, hear my Prayer* by Jacques Berthier, © Ateliers et Presses de Taizé.

Example 50: *We Shall Stand* by Graham Kendrick, copyright ©1988 Make Way Music, P.O. Box 263, Croydon, Surrey CR9 5AP, UK. All rights reserved. International copyright secured. Used by permission.